OR REFERENCE

Do not take from this room

D1201109

The Law of Libraries and Archives

The Law of Libraries and Archives

Bryan M. Carson

The Scarecrow Press, Inc.
Lanham, Maryland • Toronto • Plymouth, UK
2007

O FC
REF
KF
4315
. C37
2007

SCARECROW PRESS, INC.

Published in the United States of America
by Scarecrow Press, Inc.
A wholly owned subsidiary of
The Rowman & Littlefield Publishing Group, Inc.
4501 Forbes Boulevard, Suite 200, Lanham, Maryland 20706
www.scarecrowpress.com

Estover Road
Plymouth PL6 7PY
United Kingdom

Copyright © 2007 by Bryan M. Carson

All rights reserved. No part of this publication may be reproduced,
stored in a retrieval system, or transmitted in any form or by any
means, electronic, mechanical, photocopying, recording, or otherwise,
without the prior permission of the publisher.

British Library Cataloguing in Publication Information Available

Library of Congress Cataloging-in-Publication Data
Carson, Bryan M., 1965–
   The law of libraries and archives / Bryan M. Carson.
      p. cm.
   Includes bibliographical references and index.
   ISBN-13: 978-0-8108-5189-4 (hardcover : alk. paper)
   ISBN-10: 0-8108-5189-X (hardcover : alk. paper)
   1. Library legislation–United States. 2. Archives–Law and legislation–United
States. 3. Fair use (Copyright)–United States. I. Title.
KF4315.C37 2007
344.73'092–dc22   2006020318

♾™ The paper used in this publication meets the minimum requirements of
American National Standard for Information Sciences — Permanence of
Paper for Printed Library Materials, ANSI/NISO Z39.48-1992.
Manufactured in the United States of America.

To my parents,
Ada Lou Carson and Herbert L. Carson,
who taught me how to write

and

to my wife, Gayle Novick,
who has provided my inspiration for the past six years

Contents

Expanded Table of Contents

The Process of Getting Permission   174

Conclusion   176

Chapter 8   Information Malpractice, Professionalism, and   177
             the Unauthorized Practice of Law and
             Medicine

             Avoiding the Unauthorized Practice of Law   178
             and Medicine

             A What Kinds of Assistance May   179
                Librarians Provide?

             B The Virginia Bar Association Weighs In   181

             C How to Keep Out of Trouble   183

             D The Library Profession's Ethical Code   186

             Does Information Malpractice Exist?   188

             A What Is a Professional?   189

             B Defining the Information Professional's   194
                Duty of Care to Patrons

             Conclusion   198

Chapter 9   Search Warrants, Investigations, Library   201
             Records, and Privacy

             The Basics of Search Warrants for Libraries 202
             and Archives

             A The FBI Library Awareness Program   202

             B The Fourth Amendment and Search   203
                Warrants

             C Probable Cause   204

             D Particularity   205

             E Due Process in the Library Setting   207

             State Privacy Laws for Libraries and   209
             Archives

             A What Type of Library Is Covered?   210

Acknowledgments

I would like to thank the following people, without whom this book would not be possible:

Michael Binder, Dean of the Western Kentucky University Libraries, and Brian Coutts, Head of the Department of Library Public Services. Dr. Binder and Dr. Coutts encouraged me to pursue this project and supported me throughout in many ways, including granting me leave to work on my writing. Phil Myers, the chair of the Intellectual Property Committee at WKU, and Laura Hagan, WKU's intellectual property attorney, both contributed information and suggestions. Sally Kuhlenschmidt and the Teaching Resource Faculty grant committee provided financial support so that I could attend the conference *Intellectual Property in the Digital Age*.

Terri Baker, Debra Day, Selina Langford, and Jan Gao in the Interlibrary Loan office helped to facilitate my research by finding materials the university didn't own. Without their assistance, my work would have been much more difficult. My colleague Haiwang Yuan provided emotional support and advice, and helped me find sources for some quotes.

It was my colleague Jack Montgomery who first suggested that I apply my law background to an analysis of legal issues in libraries. Jack introduced me to Katina Strauch, the editor of *Against the Grain*. Many of the concepts discussed in this book began life as columns in *Against the Grain*. Katina's assistance and support were instrumental to the completion of this project.

My colleague Robin McGinnis assisted me with proofreading. Even more importantly, it was Robin who suggested that I write about the legal aspects of lobbying and marketing campaigns, and she became my co-author for an article on that topic in *Against the Grain*. Wendy Drake helped me by providing information on the Jet Librarians at Northwest Airlines.

Laura "Lolly" Gassaway, director of the law library at the University of North Carolina, Chapel Hill, gave me permission to include a table from her Website with information on the duration of copyright. I also received permission to use material the from Website of Georgia Harper, the intellectual property expert for the General Counsel's Office at the University of Texas System.

I would be remiss if I didn't thank my staff for all the assistance and understanding that they have given me during the time I was writing this book. They have helped me in ways too numerous to mention. I really could not have completed this work without the assistance of (in alphabetical order) Paula Bowles, Philip Edwards, Alan Logsdon, Nancy Marshall, Christina Muia, Renee Reader, and Carubie Rodgers.

Sally Craley and the proofreaders at Scarecrow worked hard to help eliminate errors. If you find any mistakes in the text, it is my fault, not theirs. My indexing team, Colleen Dunham Indexing, Inc., and Chris Banta in particular, took extra steps to ensure that readers will be able to find information in the book.

I need to thank my editor, Martin Dillon, for providing assistance, answering my questions, and generally guiding me towards a better book. Martin, I couldn't have done this without you. Thank you for everything!

Last but not least, I need to thank my parents, Ada Lou Carson and Herbert L. Carson, who taught me how to write; and my wife, Gayle Novick, for putting up with me and providing as much assistance as possible while I finished the book.

1

Libraries and the U.S. Legal System

Law is often considered to be a specialized area, inaccessible to the ordinary person, a subject you have to go to law school to understand. Yet at the same time, laws impact us on a daily basis. The law binds everyone; after all, society lives by the old maxim that "ignorance of the law is no excuse."

The philosophy behind this book is that the law should be accessible to everyone. My goal is to explain legal concepts in plain English so that librarians and archivists will be able to understand the principles that affect them on a daily basis. This book will provide its readers with answers, or at least it will raise issues for the readers to think about. Although this work is a basic overview, it contains enough details to allow readers to make informed choices and to talk intelligently with legal counsel.

I believe that librarians and archivists should learn the basic legal principles that apply to our daily lives. Librarians and archivists who know the law are not just operating in the dark; they have an understanding of the legal forces that impact their profession. It is my belief that, as professionals, librarians and archivists need to have a much deeper understanding of the principles of library law than most of us currently have.

Many people know a few rules that seem to provide quick answers. However, most people don't understand why the law is the way it is. There is a large amount of legal information in this book. My goal is not to make you into a lawyer, but to help you understand the law so that you can stay within the law.

Alexander Pope once said, "A little learning is a dangerous thing."[1] Just knowing a few rules can be dangerous; understanding the law is not like applying a cataloging rule. When you apply a cataloging rule, "The rule is the rule is the rule." There are no exceptions, no "applications" to the situation. In the law, on the other hand, it is the policy and the history behind the rule that is more important than the rule itself. In

1

the law, rules are flexible enough to apply to each particular set of facts. For that reason, librarians need to know the policy and history behind the rules in order to stay within the law.

Sometimes this book may read more like a law book than a library science book; however, that is deliberate. The idea is that, after you have read this book, you will not only understand the rules, but you will also understand why the law is fashioned the way it is. Being able to understand the reasons for the law will help libraries and archives to run in a more efficient way, and will also allow information professionals to work with attorneys at a much higher level. This will, in turn, allow legal counsel to do a better job of representing libraries and archives. Of course, the main goal of understanding the law is to enable us to better assist our patrons.

In this book, I will occasionally offer advice based upon my education and experience in law and librarianship. In some cases, I will advocate principles not specifically relating to librarians or archivists, nor specifically addressed by professional ethical codes. The advice I offer represents only my views and does not represent the view of my employer, my publisher, or my editors.

The medieval philosopher Maimonides once said that the highest form of charity is to teach a person to help himself. My goal is to educate readers so that they understand the fundamental concepts, keeping themselves within the law and avoiding problems.

The following pages contain brief summaries of the book's remaining chapters.

Chapter 2. Contracts: A Meeting of the Minds

The basic glue of our lives is the contract, which will be discussed in Chapter 2. *Contract law* is the underpinning for everything else we do. We sign contracts on a daily basis, for everything from buying books to licensing databases, and from hiring new employees to ordering new computers. Chapter 2 will tell you how contracts are formed, and will explain the law behind contract formation—including offers, acceptance, rejection, and counteroffers. This chapter will also discuss which contracts need to be put into writing so as to be enforceable.

Since many libraries are governmental entities, Chapter 2 will also discuss the process for forming governmental contracts, including an overview of the Request for Proposal (RFP) process and the Federal

Acquisition Regulation System.[2] This chapter will also discuss legal and equitable remedies for breach of contract. Chapter 2 will conclude with a discussion of illegal contracts and contracts against public policy.

Chapter 3. Copyright and Patent Law

Chapter 3 will discuss *copyright law* and *patent law.* Copyrights and patents are basic forms of intellectual property guaranteed by the U.S. Constitution. Intellectual property protects the creations of the mind, such as the work of authors, artists, and inventors. The reason we have copyright law and patent law is to encourage authors, artists, inventors, and other creative individuals, while also allowing the public to have access to written materials and to new inventions.

Chapter 3 will begin with the basics of *copyright law,* a discussion of what types of materials can be copyrighted, and an indication of how international copyright protection works. Copyright infringement is an important topic in any discussion of intellectual property. This section of Chapter 3 will also discuss remedies for copyright infringement. The section will also discuss the Sony Betamax[3] case and the recent *file-sharing* cases involving Napster,[4] Grokster,[5] and StreamCast.[6] These cases have great significance for the free exchange of information and for the ability of library patrons to access copyrighted materials.

One very important concept in all areas of intellectual property is the *Work for Hire* doctrine.[7] This section of Chapter 3 will help to answer questions about what kind of employment is included in the *Work for Hire* doctrine. There will also be a discussion of *Work for Hire* on college campuses. In addition, Chapter 3 will discuss the duration of copyright, including the Sonny Bono Copyright Term Extension Act.[8]

Next, Chapter 3 will discuss *patent law.* Librarians and archivists are a very important part of the patent system because inventors, lawyers, and patent agents must search scientific and popular literature. Information professionals can assist in determining whether the invention was the result of "prior art" (published materials and widely circulated unpublished materials). Finally, this section gives details on the U.S. patent requirement of "First to Invent," and discusses current proposals to change this patent requirement to "First to File."

Chapter 4. Fair Use and Intellectual Property Rights: The Basics of Using Information Legally

The *fair use doctrine*[9] is the basic principle that keeps copyright law from creating an absolute monopoly. Because of fair use, we are free to quote and comment on published and unpublished materials. Fair use is the principle that helps to reconcile the Freedom of Speech guarantees of the First Amendment with the intellectual property restrictions of copyright. The fair use doctrine is the subject of Chapter 4, which discusses how much of a writer's product can be borrowed, copied, or quoted by another writer.

In order to determine whether a specific situation constitutes fair use, researchers need to ask basic questions about the nature of the utilization, the nature of the copyrighted material, the amount of the material that is used, and the effect of that use on the potential market for the copyrighted item. Another question involves the difference between the style of an artist versus plagiarism of that artist's materials. This issue is illustrated by the case of singer/songwriter John Fogerty.

Fair use may also apply to common law copyright, although there is some controversy about this issue. Common law copyright applies to materials that don't qualify for Federal copyright protection. Unfixed works such as lectures are covered by state common law. Chapter 4 will discuss the question of fair use in common law copyright.

Chapter 5. Copyright and Education

How does copyright law affect the library and classroom? How does copyright law affect library e-reserves? What kinds of uses are legal for distance education? These questions about *copyright and education* will be discussed in Chapter 5.

This chapter will discuss issues relating to copyright law both on campus and in distance education. Chapter 5 will include the basic rules for classroom use. There will also be an extensive discussion of the TEACH Act,[10] which allows for transmission of some performances in a distance education class.

Chapter 6. Trademark and Trade Secret Law

Trademark law and *trade secret law* are often thought of as only pertaining to large companies. Nothing could be further from the truth, as you will see in Chapter 6.

Trademarks consist of "[w]ords, names, symbols, or devices used by manufacturers of goods and providers of services to identify their goods and services, and to distinguish their goods and services from goods manufactured and sold by others."[11] The trademark must be "famous" and "distinctive."[12] Libraries and archives not only use trademarked material on a daily basis, but they also create material that could be trademarked. There are also issues that involve libraries and concern the relationship between copyright law and trademark law.

One issue of great importance to the library and archival world involves the use of trademarks on the World Wide Web. This topic begins with domain names and cybersquatting, but also involves the legality of linking and framing. Library and archival workers need to be especially aware of these legal concerns when creating web pages.

Trade secret law involves, among other matters, efforts to maintain secrecy about business materials, secret formulas, and inventions that have not yet been patented. In these cases, the information has independent economic value, and a competitor who learns a trade secret could bring economic ruin for the person or organization that is trying to maintain the trade secret. Trade secret law has important implications for librarians and archivists, particularly in terms of patron confidentiality.

Chapter 7. Licensing of Intellectual Property

Most intellectual property is licensed rather than sold. This statement is particularly true in the library world for online databases and e-journals. Chapter 7 discusses the laws pertaining to *licensing of intellectual property*.

The rules pertaining to licensing of intellectual property are created by state law, which varies from one state to the next. The Uniform Computer Information Transactions Act (UCITA) is an attempt to standardize these laws. Unfortunately, UCITA is very controversial, and many people (and professional associations) disagree with some of the provisions of this proposed law. Chapter 7 will discuss UCITA and will explain the controversial provisions.

Another issue relating to licensing involves the inclusion in databases of articles written by freelance writers. This topic was the basis of the case of *Tasini v. New York Times*.[13] Chapter 7 will discuss the *Tasini* case in detail.

In order to stay within the law, you need to get permission to use intellectual property. Luckily this doesn't mean that you have to write to each property holder individually. There are a number of agencies that exist solely to assist users in getting the necessary permissions.

Chapter 7 contains a list of these agencies, along with their contact information. By using these agencies, permissions and licensing issues can be handled in an effective way, so that intellectual property can be used legally.

Chapter 8. Information Malpractice, Professionalism, and the Unauthorized Practice of Law and Medicine

What happens if librarians or archivists provide incorrect information? Are we then subject to lawsuits for malpractice? This issue provides the framework for Chapter 8.

Nowhere are librarians and archivists more vulnerable than when answering questions that involve law or medicine. Nowhere is there more potential for damage from incorrect information. As a result, it is vital for information professionals to avoid *the unauthorized practice of law and medicine*.

When serving patrons with legal or medical questions, the amount of help that can legally be provided depends on who the patron is and what kind of question he or she is asking. Since the unauthorized practice of law or medicine is a crime, it is vital that information professionals handle these questions appropriately.

The Virginia Bar Association has written several opinions on how libraries should deal with patrons who have legal questions. These principles can be applied by analogy to patrons with health-related questions. Library associations have also created guidelines for answering legal and medical questions without straying across the line.

In addition to the potential of legal liability for giving incorrect information in law and medicine, there are also problems relating to *information malpractice* in other areas. Malpractice occurs when a professional has breached his or her duty of care towards a client or patron. A professional is not liable for ordinary negligence as long as the professional's standard of care has been met. This is why it is important for librarians and archivists to be considered professionals.

This issue raises the question: What is a professional? Does the law define librarians and archivists as being professionals? This issue will be discussed in Chapter 8. The chapter will also define the duty of care that information professionals owe to our patrons. I will also discuss some of the cases in which incorrect information has led to lawsuits.

Chapter 9. Search Warrants, Investigations, Library Records, and Privacy

Search warrants are an important part of any investigation. Library and archival patron records have always been subject to requests by law enforcement officials *if they have a search warrant*. However, libraries do not have to turn over records without a search warrant. Chapter 9 discusses the basics of *search warrants, investigations*, and *state library privacy laws*.

In order to balance the individual's rights of privacy with law enforcement's need to keep us secure, information professionals should learn the basics of search warrants. Librarians and archivists also need to understand how search warrants relate to investigations of library crime. Chapter 9 discusses the Fourth Amendment requirement for search warrants and explains the concepts of *probable cause* and *particularity*. This chapter also discusses how the Due Process clauses of the Fifth and Fourteenth Amendments relate to the library or archival setting, and how Due Process applies to investigations, including stopping a patron who is suspected of stealing materials.

The laws relating to library privacy vary from state to state. Chapter 9 will explain the similarities and differences among these laws. Some of the issues that will be discussed in this chapter include (A) what type of library is covered, (B) what type of information is private, and (C) what type of information can or can't be disclosed. The statutes from each jurisdiction are available at the Scarecrow Press support Website for this book.

Two states—Kentucky and Hawaii—do not have library privacy statutes. Instead, these states protect library patrons with opinions from the state Attorney General's office. (The Kentucky and Hawaii opinions are also available at the Scarecrow Press support Website for this book.) Chapter 9 will discuss these opinions on library privacy. The chapter will also discuss the controversial USA PATRIOT Act, and will explain how this statute affects the library world.

Sometimes patron confidentiality is not entirely supreme. Under certain circumstances, librarians and archivists may have an ethical duty to society *not* to keep patron information confidential. The most common scenarios involve a suicidal patron or a patron who poses an immediate threat of physical violence to an identifiable target.

Chapter 9 will discuss this ethical quandary, and will use analogies with other professions in order to help librarians and archivists determine what to do when faced with a suicidal or homicidal patron. Although this book can't tell you what to do in such a situation, reading Chapter 9 will help you work through the ethical questions and potential responses in order to come to your own conclusion.

Chapter 10. Internet Use Policies and the Filtering Debate

The debate over *filtering of Websites* in libraries and archives has been raging almost since the beginning of the World Wide Web. The Children's Internet Protection Act (CIPA)[14] mandates that schools and libraries that receive Federal funding must use filtering software for juveniles. This issue is the basis for Chapter 10.

The chapter will discuss the CIPA District Court decision,[15] which was eventually overturned by the U.S. Supreme Court.[16] Unfortunately, the Supreme Court decision was one of the most complicated opinions in recent history. This opinion was a plurality decision. While five Justices were able to agree that filtering was legal in some circumstances, they were not able to agree on the legal reasons for this ruling. There are, however, several principles that can be ascertained from this decision. As a result, the Supreme Court opinion requires close reading in order to determine just what the rules are for libraries and archives.

The decision in the CIPA case requires a number of changes in library policies. Chapter 10 will interpret this opinion, and will also provide some guidance for the creation of Internet use policies in libraries and archives. The chapter will also include some articles and Websites with information to help write policies and procedures for Internet use, both among adults and by minors.

Chapter 11. Employment and Workplace Law

Libraries and archives are employers, and in order to avoid problems these organizations must know what is legal and what is not legal. Chapter 11 will discuss *employment and workplace law*. Library and archival workers need to know the basics of workplace law in order to remain legal.

Employment law is based on the law of agency. Agency law is also important for determining when an individual is acting on his or her own behalf or on behalf of an organization. It is also important to determine whether the individual is an employee or an independent contractor.

Many workers don't have employment contracts. These people are subject to the *employment-at-will* doctrine. However, some organizations do have personnel policies or employment handbooks that operate as an employment contract. It is very important for both organizations and employees to understand how these policies work and what they mean for the employment relationship. Labor unions and collective bargaining add another layer to this relationship.

All employees and organizations should understand some of the legal provisions relating to the Fair Labor Standards Act[17] and to child labor laws. Chapter 11 also discusses drug testing, discrimination and harassment, the Americans with Disabilities Act,[18] and the Family and Medical Leave Act.[19] The chapter will also explain how to hire and fire employees without being sued.

Chapter 12. Forming a Nonprofit Organization

Because many libraries and archives are nonprofit organizations, it is imperative for information professionals to understand the basics of *forming a nonprofit organization*. This is the topic of Chapter 12. Knowledge about nonprofits will also be valuable for creating Friends of the Library groups and for forming private foundations to handle donations.

Some of the issues that will be discussed in Chapter 12 include creating a mission statement and selecting a board, writing the organizational articles of incorporation and the bylaws, and creating ethical policies for board members. The chapter will also discuss the Sarbanes-Oxley Act[20] and its relevance to the nonprofit world. Last but not least, Chapter 12 will provide information on obtaining and maintaining a tax-exempt status.

Supplemental Materials on Website

Scarecrow Press provides a supplemental Website for this book. The Website includes the text of library privacy laws from every state, along with the Attorney General opinions on library privacy from Kentucky and Hawaii. The site also includes opinions and guidelines on the unauthorized practice of law in the library context. There are also valuable sources that discuss serving library patrons with disabilities. In addition, the Website lists articles about Website accessibility under Section 508, as well as articles about the ADA and employees with disabilities. To access this Website, go to the bibliographic record for this book at http://www.scarecrowpress.com/ISBN/081085189X.

The remainder of Chapter 1 will cover the very important topic of how to read legal citations.

How to Read a Legal Citation

Like any other subject area, the ability to conduct legal research is dependent upon good references and good citations. The basic building block of legal citation is *A Uniform System of Citation*, also known as the *Harvard Bluebook*.[21] The *Bluebook*—compiled by the editors of the *Columbia Law Review*, *Harvard Law Review*, *University of Pennsylvania Law Review*, and *Yale Law Review*—has been published since 1926.

Many of the main style formats, such as the *American Psychological Association* (APA) and *Modern Language Association* (MLA) handbooks, refer users to the *Bluebook* for legal citations. The *Chicago Manual of Style* also suggests that writers consult the *Bluebook* when citing legal materials. The *Bluebook* style, however, is vastly different from any of the other style guides.

In this book, I will be using *Bluebook* format (17th ed.) for all citations. There are several reasons for this use of the *Bluebook*. First of all, since the purpose of this book is to introduce librarians and archivists to the laws that affect their professional lives, I have included many legal citations. It makes sense to keep to a single style instead of switching styles back and forth. Secondly, using *Bluebook* style in the book will help readers to become familiar with this citation format. Finally, using legal citation formats will not only help library and archival workers to research legal issues for their work, but will also help them in answering patron's questions, working on collection development, and cataloging legal materials.

The basic foundation of the legal citation is the abbreviation. Each of the standard legal research sets has a standardized abbreviation. For example, the *United States Reports* (the official publication which contains cases from the U.S. Supreme Court) is always designated as *U.S.*

Often the same case or statute is published in more than one location. When that happens, the official publication put out by the government is always listed first. Privately published sets are then listed *after* the official publication information.

It is not considered improper to give a citation to the official set, even if you have used an unofficial version. In fact, it is recommended. Since the text of the case, statute, or regulation is always the same in each version, you should provide the citation to the official source. Citing the unofficial sources is optional.

Whenever you see a legal citation, the number before the abbreviation is the volume number, and the number after the abbreviation is the page number. A legal citation may look like the following:

United States v. American Library Association, 539 U.S. 194; 123 S. Ct. 2297; 156 L. Ed. 2d 221; 2003 U.S. LEXIS 4799; 71 U.S.L.W. 4465 (2003), *available at* http://laws.findlaw.com/us/000/02-361.html.

This citation breaks down as follows:

After the case name (*United States v. American Library Association*), the first citation is to the official publication. In volume 539 of the *United States Reports*, the case will begin on page 194. The official citation should always be used, even if the case has been retrieved from another source. The other citations that follow are privately published sets that also include this case:

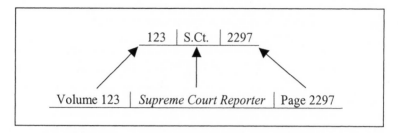

The *Supreme Court Reporter* is published by West Group and contains the full text of all Supreme Court opinions. This set also contains a number of editorial enhancements, including a classification system (similar to the Library of Congress Classification System) for legal principles found in each case. The *Supreme Court Reporter* also includes helpful summaries of the cases.

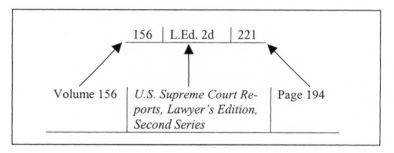

The *United States Supreme Court Reports, Lawyer's Edition* is published by LexisNexis. Like the *Supreme Court Reporter*, the *Lawyer's Edition* contains the full text of the Supreme Court opinion, along with editorial enhancements. The *Lawyer's Edition* began renumbering the volumes again in a second series, hence the 2d in the citation.

Many researchers find the *Lawyer's Edition* to be useful because it provides cross-references to other research tools—such as the American Law Reports (ALRs)—which are also published by LexisNexis. These cross-references are very helpful. In addition, the *Lawyer's Edition* and the *Supreme Court Reporter* both contain references to articles in law review journals that discuss the case. Using the annotations in the *Supreme Court Reporter* or the *Lawyer's Edition* is a helpful way to perform research.

The next citation is for the publication *United States Law Week*:

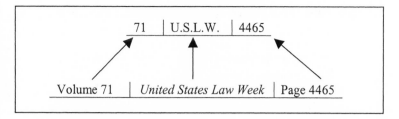

Published weekly, the *U.S. Law Week* contains the full text of cases from Federal courts, state courts, and administrative agencies. The editors publish all U.S. Supreme Court cases, as well as cases from other courts that "establish new precedents, address new statutes, contribute to emerging legal doctrines, tackle current controversies, or [cause] splits in the Circuits."[22]

The citation example of *United States v. American Library Association* also contains some references to fee-based electronic products. The premier databases for legal research are LexisNexis and Westlaw, although other fee-based services (such as LoisLaw and VersusLaw) can be used. In the citation for *United States v. American Library Association* used earlier, *2003 U.S. LEXIS 4799* refers to the LexisNexis database. The listed Website, which is part of a comprehensive free legal research site called Findlaw, also contains the full text of this case.

Like LexisNexis, Westlaw has a unique identifier number for cases. The Westlaw citation for the *United States v. American Library Association* case is *2003 WL 21433656*. Westlaw's current policy is to remove the WL number once the official citation (to the *U.S. Reports*) is available. However, if you find an item that still has the WL number, you can enter that number into the database and retrieve the case.

Statute citations are also very important. Statute information is generally written using either a public law number, a citation from the *U.S. Statutes at Large*, or a citation from the *United States Code*. When a statute is first passed, it is officially published in the U.S. Statutes at Large. The West Group also publishes the statutes in the *United States Code Congressional and Administrative News (U.S.C.C.A.N.)*. The statutes are published in the order that they were passed. Once this has occurred, the statutes are collected by subject arrangement in the *United States Code*.

To illustrate how a statute citation is created, I will use the Library Services and Technology Act as an example. The entire statute as it was passed by Congress is cited as:

The Library Services and Technology Act, P.L. 104-208

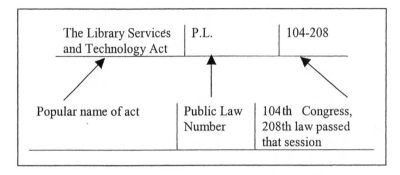

The next example contains the same statute after it has been codi-fied. (Codification puts the sections of the law together with other laws on the same subject.) The citation contains the symbol § (like a double letter S). In legal citations, the symbol § means "section number." When a citation contains multiple section numbers, this is often shown by using §§. In addition, if a statute includes multiple code sections in a row, legal citations often use the phrase *et seq.* after the initial section number (*et seq.* may or may not be italicized, but it is always written in lowercase letters). Finally, the volume numbers for codes are often called "Titles." For example, copyright law is contained in Title 17 of the *U.S. Code*. Here is an illustration of the proper citation for a codi-fied statute:

The Library Services and Technology Act, 20 U.S.C. § 9121 *et seq.*

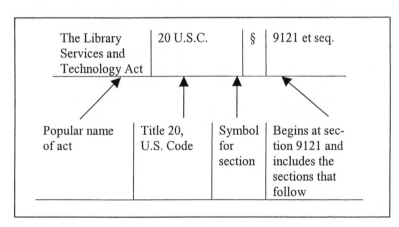

With this information, you should be able to read legal citations. The ability to interpret legal citations will help librarians and archivists find statutes and judicial rulings. Even more important, this skill will translate into better service for our patrons.

Table 1.1 shows the official citations of major reporters that contain judicial cases from each state. Table 1.2 shows the citation abbreviations for reporters which include Federal court cases. Table 1.3 gives the citations for sets that contain Federal statutes and regulations. Table 1.4 gives information on legal encyclopedias, digests, and annotations. For more information on legal citations and abbreviations, please consult *A Uniform System of Citation* (the *Bluebook*).

Table 1.1. Reporters Containing State Court Cases

Reporter Title	Citation Abbreviation	Description
Atlantic Reporter	A.	Cases from CT, DE, DC, ME, MD, NH, NJ, PA, RI, and VT.
California Reporter	Cal. Rptr.	California cases (unofficial).
Northeastern Reporter	N.E.	Cases from IL, IN, MA, NY, and OH.
Northwestern Reporter	N.W.	Cases from IA, MI, MN, NE, ND, SD, and WI.
New York Supplement	N.Y.S.	New York cases (unofficial).
Pacific Reporter	P.	AK, AZ, CA, CO, Guam, HI, ID, KS, MT, NV, Northern Marianas, NM, OK, OR, UT, WA, and WY.
Southeastern Reporter	S.E.	Cases from GA, NC, SC, VA, and WV.
Southern Reporter	So.	Cases from AL, FL, LA, and MS.
Southwestern Reporter	S.W.	Cases from AR, KY, MO, TN, and TX.

Table 1.2. Reporters Containing Federal Court Cases

Reporter Title	Citation Abbreviation	Description
United States Reports	U.S.	Cases from the United States Supreme Court (official).
Supreme Court Reporter	S.Ct.	Cases from the United States Supreme Court. Unofficial version of United States Reports. Contains headnotes and other editorial enhancements.
United States Supreme Court Reports, Lawyer's Edition	L.Ed.	Cases from the United States Supreme Court. Unofficial version of United States Reports. Contains cross-references and other editorial enhancements.
Federal Reporter	F.	Cases from the U.S. Circuit Courts of Appeal. Also contained cases from the United States District Courts before 1932.
Federal Appendix	Fed. Appx.	Unpublished cases from the U.S. Circuit Courts of Appeal. Does not include the 5th or 11th Circuits. Cases can't be cited to courts as precedent.
Federal Supplement	F. Supp.	Cases from the United States District Courts since 1932. Before 1930, use the Federal Reporter.
Federal Rules Decisions	F.R.D.	Federal cases that discuss or interpret Federal Court Rules.
United States Law Week	U.S.L.W.	Weekly summary of cases from state and Federal courts.

Table 1.3. Sets Containing Federal Statutes and Regulations

Title of Set	Citation Abbreviation	Description
United States Code	U.S.C.	Federal statutes passed by Congress, arranged by topic (official).
United States Code Annotated	U.S.C.A.	Unofficial version of the *United States Code*. Each statute contains references to cases that discuss them. Published by West Group.
United States Code Service	U.S.C.S.	Unofficial version of the *United States Code*. Each statute contains references to cases that discuss them. Published by LexisNexis.
United States Statutes at Large	Stat.	Official text of statutes passed by Congress, in the order the statutes were passed.
U.S. Code Congressional and Administrative News	U.S.C.C.A.N.	Unofficial version of *Statutes at Large*. Also contains Legislative History documents for each statute. Published by West Group.
Code of Federal Regulations	C.F.R.	Administrative regulations promulgated by Federal administrative agencies, arranged by topic. Official publication by the U.S. Government Printing Office (GPO).
Federal Register	Fed. Reg.	Official source of new and proposed Federal administrative regulations, standards, programs, etc. Published daily by GPO.

Table 1.4. Encyclopedias, Digests, and Annotations

Reporter Title	Citation Abbreviation	Description
American Jurisprudence	Am. Jur.	Legal encyclopedia.
Corpus Juris Secundum	C.J.S.	Legal encyclopedia. Often referred to as C.J.S.
American Digest (includes Century Digest, Decennial Digest, and General Digest)	Am. Dig.	References to cases from the courts of all 50 states and the Federal system. Arranged by topic, using the West Key Number system.
Federal Practice Digest	Fed. Dig.	References to Federal cases by topic, using the West Key Number system.
American Law Reports	A.L.R.	Contains extremely detailed articles (annotations) about legal topics.

Conclusion

If you work in the information profession, you need to know about the law. Laws affect our daily lives, underlying every commercial transaction and every employment relationship, every article copied and every database licensed. My purpose in this book is to explain the principles behind our laws so that librarians and archivists will understand the law rather than just blindly following a few rules.

In this book, I sometimes use the term "libraries" to mean both libraries and archives. Similarly, when I use the term "librarian," I also include archivists. As information professionals, librarians and archivists have much more in common than they have differences. Most of the laws that relate to libraries and librarians also relate to archives and archivists. Unless otherwise designated, all of the concepts covered in the book are equally applicable to both professions.

Librarians and archivists often become involved in issues relating to intellectual property, even if these issues have no immediate implications for traditional library and archival services. This happens because copyright restrictions can be a form of censorship, and our profession has traditionally helped to guard society against limitations on expression as well as restrictions on the dissemination of information. A free and open marketplace of ideas requires that ideas may be expressed, challenged, and discussed. Information professionals work to maintain this open marketplace so that ideas are available to everyone.

By doing more than merely learning rules, information professionals will be better able to assist patrons, remain within the law, and communicate with legal counsel about matters relating to the library or archive. Reading this book won't make you a lawyer. However, reading this book will help you to think about and understand the legal foundations of your daily work and to make better decisions about legal and ethical issues.

My goal is to help information professionals deal with the issues we all encounter. Now, fasten your seat belts, and I will take you on a journey through the law of libraries and archives.

2

Contracts: A Meeting of the Minds

Contracts are one of the fundamental building blocks of our society, constituting basic agreements that allow us to function.[1] Everyone encounters contracts daily; even the library card is a contract! Forming a "meeting of the minds," contracts are important to many day-to-day aspects of librarianship, publishing, and book distribution. Some of the areas that are affected by contracts include employment, collection development, licensing agreements, and intellectual property. Before learning about other topics, it is important for us to begin with a strong base of contract law.

The law of contracts is a function of state law; the Federal government does not have anything to do with contract law. Contract law evolved in the Common Law tradition. However, in recent years, most states have passed the *Uniform Commercial Code*, known as the UCC, which in Article II contains extensive language about sales.

The UCC was created in an attempt to bring uniformity to the rules of contracts in each state.[2] This uniform law has been passed in every state except Louisiana. The UCC has also been passed in every U.S. Commonwealth and Territory, although Puerto Rico has only passed some of the articles (and has not passed Article II, which covers sales).[3]

The *Uniform Commercial Code* does not include materials relating to licensing agreements. Although there was a proposal to create a UCC section 2B, this provision became controversial and was never adopted. For more information on the proposals for UCC section 2B, see **Chapter 7, Licensing of Intellectual Property**.

This chapter will discuss the elements of contract law in a straightforward, easy-to-understand format. I will begin by explaining what a contract is and what constitutes an agreement, followed by a discussion of some of the issues that we need to understand in order to do our jobs as information professionals. Some of the concepts that I will discuss include offer, acceptance and rejection, counter-offer, and consideration.

Chapter 2

Definition of a Contract

The basic definition of a contract is a promise to do something (or *not* to do something). However, there are some important distinctions between a promise and a contract.[4] Unlike a promise, a contract has a specific set of rules for its formation. Also, the law provides for legal consequences in the event that a contract is not fulfilled.[5]

Lawyers refer to contracts as being "a meeting of the minds," since both parties agree on what is to be done. "In both popular and legal usage, a promise is an assurance, in whatever form of expression given, that a thing [an action] will or will not be done.[6] The parties concerned undertake a legal obligation when a contract is formed, and there are legal ramifications if the contract is not fulfilled."[7]

Here is an example of the difference between a promise and a contract: If I promised to come over to my friend's house on Monday to paint his living room, but I didn't do it, my friend would not be able to sue me in court. However, if my friend had paid a decorator to paint his living room and the decorator didn't do the work, my friend could sue in court. The contract is more than just a promise because of the legal obligations that a contract creates.

A. Offers

Contracts are formed when two or more interested parties agree. One party makes an offer, and the other party accepts or rejects the offer. Let us assume that we have two libraries in adjacent communities, the Greentown Public Library and the Largetown Public Library. The Largetown Public Library has recently obtained a grant for new computers, even though the existing computers are only a year old. As a result, Largetown Public Library offers to sell the old computers to the Greentown Public Library for $200 each. At this point, Largetown has made an offer. Greentown may accept the offer, reject or decline the offer, or make a counter-offer.

An offer is a legal willingness to enter into a contract. At the time that a person makes an offer, he or she is willing to enter into the contract if both parties agree. However, making an offer is different from an invitation to enter negotiations. "An invitation to enter into negotiations is not an 'offer' which, together with acceptance thereof, forms a 'contract.'"[8] Being willing to receive proposals does not rise to the level of an offer. Just because I indicate a willingness to receive proposals does not mean that I have to accept them. I can reject any of the proposals for any reason, or for no reason.[9]

Many governmental entities and large businesses use a system known as a "Request for Proposal," or RFP. These documents are not considered to be offers. The RFP contains specific information as to the mission of the agency (or business). The RFP contains specific requirements, standards, and deadlines. Sometimes an RFP is published in a legal newspaper, and sometimes it is circulated to a prequalified list of vendors. One drawback of using an RFP is that writing and responding to proposals takes a lot of time. In the last 30 years, some agencies and businesses have moved to a system called a "Request for Information," or RFI. The RFI is basically a shorter version of the RFP, and takes less time to process.[10] Remember, however, that neither the RFP nor the RFI is a contract; they simply show a willingness to enter into negotiations.

B. Acceptance, Rejection, and Counter-Offers

Before a contract can be formed, the offer must be accepted and the parties must agree to enter into the contract. If the offer is rejected, no contract is formed. Once an offer has been rejected, it cannot be accepted later. An attempt to accept an offer once it has been rejected constitutes a new offer.

For example, suppose that Largetown Public Library wanted to sell a valuable first edition from their collection. They offer the book to the local college, Metro University, for $100,000. Metro University rejects the offer. The following week, Metro University realizes that the book is actually worth $1.5 million. Since the offer has already been rejected, Metro University can't go back and accept the offer from Largetown Public Library. However, if Metro University tells Largetown that Metro would now like to buy the book for $100,000, the university has made a new offer that Largetown can either accept or reject. Once the Largetown offer was rejected, Metro is now offering to purchase the book for $100,000. Largetown can either accept or reject this new offer.

Another possible scenario involves a counter-offer. A counter-offer is actually a rejection of the original offer, along with a new offer. Suppose that Largetown offers Metro University the rare book for $100,000. Metro University replies that they would like to take the book for $85,000. Largetown has the choice of either accepting Metro's offer, rejecting the offer, or giving Metro another counter-offer. Until

Largetown and Metro University *both* agree on the price and the terms, no contract has been formed.

To illustrate the difference between entering negotiations and forming a contract, we can use the Greentown Public Library and the Largetown Public Library as an example. Both libraries decide to build new branches. Let us assume that the two towns have different bidding rules, so that Greentown is required to use an RFP and must award contracts to the lowest bidder. Largetown, however, is allowed to enter into direct negotiations with any vendor on its prequalified list. (I am assuming that both libraries complied with all applicable rules and regulations, and that everything was done correctly.)

Greentown uses a Request for Proposal that specifies what type of work the library wants to have done and that details the requirements the library has for its new building. The lowest bidder is the XYZ Construction Corporation. One of the provisions in the XYZ bid specifies that even if the project is canceled for any reason whatsoever, Greentown will still have to pay 10 percent of the contract price. The director of the Greentown Public Library tells XYZ that the board will take 10 days to consider the document.

Largetown also wants to build a new branch, but it selects the contractor differently. Since Largetown has worked with XYZ Construction Corporation in the past, the library's leaders go directly to XYZ. They know exactly what they want done and how much they want to spend, and so they create a document specifying that XYZ will build the branch within certain specifications and for a particular price. The document specifies that even if the project is canceled for any reason whatsoever, Largetown will still have to pay 10 percent of the contract price. Largetown signs the document, and so does XYZ Corporation.

Five days later, the state decides to cut the budget for local libraries. Both Greentown and Largetown are affected by the cuts and are forced to cancel their branch-building projects. XYZ sues both Greentown and Largetown for 10 percent of the contract price, despite the fact that no work has been done and that the contractor has spent no money. Who wins?

Because the two libraries used very different bidding procedures, the results would be very different. A "Request for Proposal" is exactly that—a request that the contractor enter into negotiations with the library. As such, the RFP does not constitute an offer that XYZ can accept. Instead, the proposal by XYZ was an offer that Greentown had not yet accepted. Therefore, there was no contract. Greentown would win, and XYZ would not be successful in its lawsuit. Although there may be other factors that could change this outcome, the court would still find that Greentown did not have a valid contract.

Largetown, on the other hand, proposed that XYZ build a specific building for a specific price. There were details given as to the way in which the branch was to be constructed. Both the library and XYZ signed the document after it was presented to the contractor. The library made an offer to XYZ, and XYZ accepted its offer. As a result, a contract was formed. Therefore, XYZ will win its lawsuit, and the library will have to pay 10 perent of the construction fee as a penalty for not fulfilling the contract. Needless to say, this problem could have been avoided by being more careful while drafting documents.

C. The Concepts of Consideration and Reliance

According to *American Jurisprudence 2d*, the definition of the term "consideration" is "[s]ome right, interest, profit, or benefit [owed] to one party or some forbearance, detriment, loss, or responsibility given, suffered, or undertaken by the other."[11] Consideration consists of both parties giving up something that they are not required to give up, or doing something that they do not otherwise need to do. Since a contract is a legally enforceable promise, consideration is the price each party pays to the other for the promise. Therefore, consideration is a large part of the difference between promises that are legally enforceable and promises that are not legally enforceable.

In order for a contract to be formed, there must be consideration on the part of both parties. This is why a mere promise is not enforceable as a contract. For example, suppose that Bob told Sally he would give her a stereo for her birthday. He does not ask for money from Sally. Since there is consideration on only one side, no contract has been formed. If Bob doesn't give Sally the stereo, she can't take him to court to obtain it.

The legal system provides for two situations in which a promise can be enforced in court: either the contract was formed with consideration, or else one of the parties has relied upon the promise in some fashion to that party's detriment.[12] If one of the parties gives up something of legal value[13] that he or she is not legally obligated to give up in exchange for a contract, that party has given consideration. This item of legal value can be any of the following:

◆ A physical item or object (cash, check);

◆ A benefit or a detriment;[14]

◆ Something the party will do;

◆ Something the party will refrain from doing.[15]

Likewise, in order for consideration to be sufficient to create a contract, the consideration must be the result of bargaining between the parties. The promisor (the party who makes the promise) must receive a benefit or the promisee (the party to whom the promise was made) must suffer a detriment. As an example, suppose the Greentown Public Library wants to purchase two computers from the North American Computer Company. Greentown makes an offer that North American accepts. North American promises they will send the computers to Greentown in exchange for $2,000. In this instance, North American is the promisor and Greentown is the promisee. Greentown's consideration consists of giving up $2,000, a benefit to the computer company (the *promisor*) and a detriment to the library (the *promisee*).

However, consideration does not have to be limited to the physical payment of money. Consideration could mean refraining from doing something the promisee is entitled to do, such as an act of forbearance. For example, there was a famous 19th-century case in which a man promised to pay his nephew $500 (the equivalent of $11,020 in current dollars[16]) if the nephew agreed not to smoke or drink until he turned 21.[17] The legal drinking age was lower in those days, so the nephew had the legal right to smoke and drink. Because he gave up his legal right to smoke or drink, he had satisfied the requirements for consideration.[18] Since the nephew had a legal right to use alcohol and tobacco, not using them in exchange for $500 was considered a legal detriment. Therefore, when the uncle did not keep his promise, the nephew sued in court and won.

Contracts can be formed with consideration, even when the benefit or the detriment is very slight. For example, consideration may be formed by as simple an act as naming a child after a relative in exchange for being included in the relative's will.[19] The only requirement is that the consideration must be something of actual value in the eyes of the law. "Any real consideration, however small, will support a promise. So long as a man gets what he has bargained for, and it is of some value in the eye of the law, the courts will not ask what its value may be to him, or whether its value is in any way proportionate to his act or promise . . . ."[20]

A promise to do something in the future may also be used as consideration. In this case, the future promise serves as consideration for the other party's promise. "[A]s a rule, a promise to do a thing is just as valuable a consideration as the actual doing of it would be."[21] On the other hand, the individual must actually have the legal right to do what he or she is promising. There is no consideration if the party doesn't have a legal interest in the item, or if the promise is for something that is illegal.[22] For example, suppose that a farmer agrees to allow one acre of his farm to remain fallow in exchange for $400. It is an enforceable promise for a farmer to agree not to grow corn in his field in exchange for $400 per acre. However, a promise by the farmer not to grow marijuana in exchange for $400 is not enforceable, since growing marijuana is illegal. By the same token, an agreement by the farmer to sell marijuana to his neighbor for $400 an ounce is not enforceable, due to the illegality of the proposed act.[23] The subject matter of the contract is illegal, and the consideration is illegal, so a court could not enforce this "agreement."

In order for a contract to be valid, both parties must provide consideration. A publisher agrees to sell books to a library in exchange for money, and the library agrees to give up money in exchange for books. This "mutuality of consideration" is the basis of the bargain and is a part of why contracts are sometimes called a "bargain for exchange." After all, each party in a contract gives up something.

Consideration is also necessary in employment contracts. In an employment situation, the library agrees to pay money, and the information professional agrees to perform work. These actions on both sides constitute consideration. "Any labor promised by the employee will be adequate consideration for the employer's promises of compensation, and the employer's promise of any remuneration will be adequate consideration for the employee's labor or promise to provide labor."[24] Together, the money and the work constitute mutual consideration.

D. The Statute of Frauds

One important question that must be answered for every contract is *whether the contract needs to be in writing in order to be enforceable.* Unless state law specifies otherwise, contracts need *not* be in writing. Nonetheless, a written contract is much easier to enforce, since it eliminates the potential for mistakes or miscommunication. In 1677, England began requiring certain types of contracts to be in writing in order to be enforced. Since the primary purpose of this statute at the time it was enacted was to prevent fraud in the formation of contracts, the law became known as the "Statute of Frauds."[25]

The Statute of Frauds was passed by Parliament in 1677.[26] According to Parliament, "some agreements are deemed of so important a nature, that they ought not to rest in verbal promise only, which cannot be proved but by the memory (which sometimes will induce the perjury) of witnesses."[27] The Statute of Frauds was one of the most important laws ever passed by the British Parliament and has been adopted by most of the former British colonies (including the United States). In general, the kinds of contracts that are subject to the Statute of Frauds include:

- ◆ Contracts for the sale of land.[28]
- ◆ A contract that can't be performed within one year or a contract that is greater than one year in duration. This includes contracts for employment and contracts for personal services.[29] However, a contract for at-will employment, where either party can terminate the relationship at any time, is not subject to the Statute of Frauds because it has the potential of being completed in less than one year.[30]
- ◆ Contracts for the sale of goods or securities worth more than a specific amount. In 1677, this amount was 10 pounds sterling. The *Uniform Commercial Code* and many states are currently requiring written contracts for the sale of goods over $500.[31]
- ◆ Contracts in which one of the parties is agreeing to be responsible for someone else's debt, both when the party is acting as a surety (a person who guarantees a debt) and when the promise is made by an executor to pay a debt from an estate.[32]

Technically speaking, the Statute of Frauds is not a requirement for the formation of a contract; rather, it is a requirement for certain contracts to be enforced. "There are certain situations in which a promise that is not in writing can be denied enforcement. In such situations, an otherwise valid contract can be unenforceable if it does not comply with the formalities required by the Statute of Frauds."[33] If you want to enforce your contract, you will need to comply with the provisions of this law.

The two ways in which publishers, book distributors, libraries, and archives are most affected by the Statute of Frauds are employment contracts and contracts for the sale of goods. This means that if you sell books that total over $500, you need to put the agreement in writing.

The *Uniform Commercial Code* specifies that: "[A] contract for the sale of goods for the price of $500 or more is not enforceable . . . unless there is some writing sufficient to indicate that a contract for sale has been made between the parties and signed by the party against whom enforcement is sought or by his authorized agent or broker. A writing is not insufficient because it omits or incorrectly states a term agreed upon but the contract is not enforceable under this paragraph beyond the quantity of goods shown in such writing."[34]

When writing a contract for the sale of land or of goods or securities over $500, always put it in writing. Similarly, if the contract is not capable of being performed within one year (including employment contracts), put it in writing. Finally, any agreement to assume the debt of another person must always be put in writing. Although other kinds of contracts don't need to be written, you should always remember, "Prudence is the better part of valor." I *always* recommend that contracts be placed in writing.

Governmental Contracts

Many libraries are governmental units, and as such are subject to special procedures. The general principles of contract law remain the same, however. Governmental procedures are generally more for the purposes of making sure that people who have the proper authority enter into the contracts in a competitive environment. Although the principle of sovereign immunity says that the government cannot be sued, this immunity is waived once the government enters into a contract. As a result of entering a contract, the general laws of contract formation apply to the government. When the government "comes down from its position of sovereignty and enters the domain of commerce, it submits itself to the same laws that govern individuals there."[35] Thus, a library or archive is subject to ordinary contract law, regardless of whether it is public or private.

Governmental contract procedures vary from one entity to another, but the Federal Acquisition Regulation System (known as FAR)[36] provides a good example of the process. Contracts must be let in a competitive environment, both to obtain the lowest possible price and to prevent corruption (or the appearance of corruption, which can be almost as bad). Before a contract is let, the government produces a *Request for Proposal*, known as an RFP. The RFP lets potential bidders know what the government is attempting to acquire and what conditions the government is looking for. Some entities use a Request for

Information (RFI) instead. The RFI is considered to be easier to create and more flexible to the needs of the individual governmental unit.

In addition to the Federal Acquisition Regulation System (which is an administrative regulation), there are a number of statutes which govern the Federal contractual process. The most important statutes include the Small Business Act[37] and the Office of Federal Procurement Policy Act.[38] Under FAR and the major acquisitions acts, the government must publish a pre-solicitation notice in the *Commerce Business Daily*, which is the official newspaper of the Federal government. Here is a summary of the way that the system works:

> When a CBD notice announces a proposed acquisition, interested firms ordinarily respond by requesting a copy of the solicitation. As required by FAR (sec) 5.102, the contracting officer must maintain a reasonable number of solicitations and provide copies on a first-come-first-served basis. (Some agency regulations state that solicitations will be provided to any person upon request.) The contracting officer also may require payment of a fee (not exceeding the actual costs of duplication) for a copy of the solicitation documents. Furthermore, under FAR (sec) 5.102(a)(4), the contracting officer must give special assistance to small business concerns responding to the CBD announcement.[39]

Most state and local governments specify that agencies use either an RFP or RFI so that competition will result in the lowest possible bid. Although private businesses are not required to request bids, they usually circulate RFPs or RFIs in order to obtain the best price or the most favorable terms. Many state and local governments create a legal template for their RFPs and RFIs. This standardized language, which is known as *boilerplate language*, is found in every RFP or RFI. For example, some of the terms may include which jurisdiction and venue lawsuits can be brought in, penalties for breach of the contract, etc. The part known as the *Technical Specifications* contains the portion of the document which is unique and which indicates what the organization is really looking for in a contract.

An RFP or an RFI is not an offer. The response of the bidder is the offer. An RFP or RFI simply indicates a willingness to enter into negotiations. In effect, the RFP or RFI is *asking* the vendor to make an offer. The proposal of the vendor created in response to an RFP or RFI is the actual offer.

For example, suppose that the Greentown Public Library wants to buy furniture for a reading room. The library administration creates an RFP requesting bids on five 72-inch walnut reading tables with attached glass lamps. The RFP also states that the tables must be delivered within 10 weeks of signing the contract. Companies that sell furniture can respond to the RFP by creating a proposal that includes specifications and price. The Greentown Public Library can then choose the proposal with the lowest price.

The basic process of formation for government contracts is similar to the rules that apply to private entities. However, it is important for libraries to learn the legal requirements of their own governmental entities. These requirements can generally be found in the state codes, as well as in state administrative regulations and Attorney General opinions. Before proceeding with an acquisition for the first time, check with your local governmental purchasing office; they should be able to provide some advice about the rules and regulations of your particular jurisdiction.

Legal Damages for Breach of Contract

Suppose that you enter into a contract, but the other party breaches the contract. You want to go to court and sue, but you need to choose what kind of remedy you want. The two basic types of remedies available for contractual disputes are *legal damages* and *equitable damages*.

Legal damages are the most common remedy that courts provide and are often also called "monetary damages." Most of the time, when a party says "I'll sue," he or she is looking for legal damages. There are four kinds of legal damages: compensatory damages, punitive damages (also sometimes called exemplary damages), consequential damages, and liquidated damages.

A. Compensatory Damages

The point of compensatory damages is to "make the party whole again." Basically, compensatory damages "put the injured party in the same position he would have been in had the contract been completed as originally planned."[40] In order to compute compensatory damages, the courts will look at the plain language of the contract to find the market value of the items or services for which the parties bargained. The courts will also look at what the non-breaching party (the innocent party) had to spend or was deprived of as a result of the breach of contract.

For example, suppose that the Largetown Public Library signs a contract with the SAS Company for the purchase and installation of a new security gate. SAS agrees to give the library a 10 percent discount if Largetown agrees to pay for the gate in advance. The library prepays $12,000. SAS stops carrying library security gates and is unable to complete the contract. The compensatory damages would be the $12,000 that the library paid.

B. Punitive Damages

Punitive damages are given not to compensate the innocent party, but to punish the party that breached the contract. Generally speaking, punitive damages are very difficult to obtain for breach of contract. Usually, there is some other type of underlying conduct—such as breach of trust, antitrust violations, or fraud—that accompany the contractual breach. State statutes usually govern the granting of punitive damages for contracts cases.

For example, suppose that Metro University finds out that the FFG Gallery is selling a Picasso painting. The description of the painting reads: "This is a wonderful Picasso painting, and an excellent example of his unique style." The signature on the painting simply says "Picasso." Experts from Metro University examine the painting, which is hung on the wall of FFG Gallery, and agree to purchase it for $1.5 million. However, when the painting arrives, it turns out that the dealer had lied; instead of being by Pablo Picasso, the painting was by an unknown artist named Diablo Picasso. The painting clearly has Diablo Picasso's signature on the back of the canvas. The gallery owner knew that this painting was by Diablo Picasso, but he advertised it as a "Picasso painting," hoping that prospective purchasers would think that the painting was by Pablo Picasso. In addition, the gallery owner kept the painting hung on the wall while it was being examined so that the experts would not see the artist's signature. In addition to receiving compensatory damages for the $1.5 million that the university spent, the university may also be entitled to receive punitive damages due to fraud and misrepresentation on the part of the gallery owner.

C. Consequential Damages

Consequential damages are awarded when the innocent party incurs special expenses or consequences as a result of the breach of contract. For example, suppose that the Greentown Public Library has a leaky roof. The roof needs to be repaired before winter in order to avoid having serious water damage. On September 1, the library signs a contract with Rapid Roofing Inc. for work to begin no later than November 15 and to be completed no later than December 1. These dates are important because the winter weather would seriously strain the existing roof and the library would run the risk of losing some of its collection to water damage. Greentown prepaid $10,000 to Rapid Roofing for the job.

On November 15, the day that work was supposed to begin, Rapid Roofing breached the contract, telling the library that they did not have enough time to do the work. The library then had to find another contractor. The Quality Roofing Company said that they could do the work, but it would be February before they were able to do it. In January, water leaked into the library, causing the loss of the entire science fiction collection. Replacement of this collection cost the library $5,000. Here is a summary of the damages for the Greentown Public Library:

Money paid to Rapid Roofing (Compensatory damages)	$10,000
Replacement of damaged collections (Consequential damages)	$5,000
Total Damages	$15,000

The library is out $10,000 to Rapid Roofing for the work. However, because the breaching party did not do the work on time, the library is also out $5,000 for the replacement of the damaged collections. After all, the collections would not have been damaged if Rapid Roofing had not breached their contract. The library's total financial loss would be $15,000: the amount paid ($10,000) plus the extra amount spent for replacing the damaged books ($5,000). This is the amount that a court would award the library in a lawsuit against Rapid Roofing.

D. Liquidated Damages

Liquidated damages come from the contract itself. In some cases, contracts contain a clause that the parties have negotiated specifying what the damages will be if there is a breach of the contract. "When liquidated damages are specified, the court will usually award those damages, and the parties are generally precluded from arguing that the amount is too high or too low."[41] After all, the parties agreed on the damages, so why would the court second-guess those negotiations?

WELSHIMER MEMORIAL LIBRARY

For example, suppose that the Greentown Library had a contract for roof repair. The contract specified that the repair should begin on November 15, and would be finished no later than 5 p.m. on December 1. The contract specified that the roofing company would incur a $500 penalty for every day the project was overdue. This penalty constitutes the liquidated damages.

Another example of liquidated damages involves overdue books. When a borrower with a library card takes out a book, he or she is promising to return the material. The borrower's agreement (which the patron signed when the library card was issued) allows patrons to check out books; in return, the borrower promises to return the books on time, take care of their condition, etc. The agreement also states that the borrower will be charged five cents for every day that the book is overdue. The overdue fine constitutes a liquidated damages clause.

The key thing to remember with liquidated damages is that, like all other clauses in a contract, the judge will assume that you negotiated with the other party. Therefore, if you see terms that you don't like, make sure you question them before the contract is signed.

E. Promissory Estoppel

The rules for contract formation may seem harsh, and they are. There is a saying that "Hard cases make hard law." This means that most of the rules came about because of what someone did or didn't do in a contract situation. Remember that contract rules exist to protect everyone involved.

One problem is that you might enter into a contract and begin performance only to find out that something isn't right. Perhaps, for example, you relied on an oral promise when the agreement needed to be in writing, or perhaps there was a promise but you didn't receive consideration. What can you do?

In order to handle situations like this, there is a doctrine in contract law called *promissory estoppel*. *Black's Law Dictionary* defines "estoppel" as being "a bar or impediment which precludes allegation or denial of a certain fact or state of facts . . . in a court of law."[42] In other words, because of his or her prior actions, one of the parties cannot make certain claims in court.

In his work *Farnsworth on Contracts*, Professor E. Allen Farnsworth uses the following example: "Suppose that an employer promises to pay an employee a pension of $500 a month upon retirement. Relying on the promise, the employee retires at an age when other employment is unavailable. If the employer then refuses to pay the pension, is the employee without recourse because the promise lacked consideration? Today, most courts would allow the employee to enforce the promise on the grounds of reliance."[43] Reliance is one of the categories of promissory estoppel. Farnsworth's list of promissory estoppel categories includes the following:

♦ Gratuitous promises to convey land.[44]

♦ Failure to obtain insurance when goods are subsequently destroyed.[45]

♦ Gifts to charities (charitable subscriptions).[46] [This type of promissory estoppel would include pledges to fund-raising drives and estate gifts for libraries and archives.] Some cases have held that the work of the charity was part of the consideration.[47] Other courts have held that the consideration consisted of the promise to use funds as specified by the subscriber.[48] "Sometimes [courts have] found that the subscriber had bargained with other subscribers for their similar promises, a finding that was encouraged if the first subscriber had appeared as the 'bellwether' of the flock and promised a large sum if others would pledge a stated amount."[49]

♦ Promises made within a family that were not negotiated at arm's-length market conditions.[50]

♦ Reliance: "[A] representation of fact made by one party and relied on by the other."[51]

Reliance is the most common form of promissory estoppel. The law of reliance is found in section 90 of the *Restatement of Contracts 2d*. The *Restatement* says: "A party whose duty of performance does not arise or is discharged as a result of . . . frustration of purpose . . . is entitled to restitution for any benefit that he has conferred on the other party by way of part performance or reliance."[52]

Basically, if one of the parties performs actions because he or she believes there is a valid contract, the courts have the ability to enforce, even though the "contract" isn't valid because of lack of consideration. Reliance has taken the place of consideration because the party performed under the contract. Reliance and promissory estoppel have been described as the "moral aspects of contract law."[53]

One important point to remember is that promissory estoppel is limited to the scope of the promise itself, just as it would be if there had been consideration:[54]

According to this notion, the reason for the enforcement of a promise is the justifiable reliance upon the promise. Reliance makes it wrongful for the promisor to withdraw from the promise because he has aroused an expectation in the promisee and induced him to act. Most courts today, following the lead of the Restatement (Second), would probably view reliance as an independent ground upon which to enforce promises. Most courts suggest that reliance alone would not serve as consideration in the absence of a bargain, but that the promisee's reliance may make the promise enforceable even in the absence of consideration. [55]

For example, suppose that the Largetown Public Library held a fund drive to build a new branch. Joe Generous agreed to donate $2 million to the cause. Based on this promise, the library engaged a contractor and began construction. Joe Generous subsequently withdrew his promise, leaving the library without enough money to complete the branch. Based on the principles of promissory estoppel and reliance, the library would be able to sue Joe Generous and compel him to fulfill his promise.

Equitable Damages

In the English legal system, the courts of law were only permitted to award monetary damages. However, the established legal principles didn't always help the innocent party. In certain circumstances, "the prescribed or customary forms of ordinary law seem to be inadequate."[56] In those cases, either the law did not do justice to both parties, or the award of monetary damages was not sufficient in order to ensure that justice was done. Since the king always had the sovereign power to ensure that justice was done, subjects could apply directly to the mercy of the king by sending him a petition for relief. Because the king was too busy to hear all of these petitions, the Courts of Chancery were created so that judges could hear equitable petitions on behalf of the king. "In time the custom of sending [the petitions] to the chancellor led to the addressing of such petitions to that official directly, and in this way chancery became a recognized forum for the relief of litigants and the correction of legal abuses."[57]

In the English legal system, the Court of Chancery became an entire court system that was separate from the law courts. The Courts of Chancery granted petitions for justice in situations where the legal system was not able to adequately serve the innocent parties. The Courts of Chancery dispensed a type of justice known as *Equity*. (The terms

"Chancery" and "Equity" are often used interchangeably because they mean the same thing.)[58] The general rule is that equitable remedies are only available so that justice will be done to the innocent party when the legal remedies have been exhausted.

When the English legal system was adopted in the United States, the equity system and the legal system were combined, so that one court could do it all. As a result, there are no special courts of equity in the United States; all general courts have equity jurisdiction as well as legal jurisdiction. Therefore, equitable remedies and legal remedies can be available from the same judge in the same case. As with the English system, equitable remedies are only available once the party has exhausted all of the legal remedies.

There are four types of equitable damages that are used for breach of contracts. These types of damages consist of *injunctions, specific performance, reformation* of a contract, and *quasi-contractual remedies*.

A. Injunctions and Specific Performance

Injunctions and specific performance are related but separate issues. Both are orders of the court. An injunction is a negative order that requires a party *not to do* (or to stop doing) something. Specific performance is an affirmative order requiring the party *to do* something. For example, if an employee who knows the secret recipe of a soft drink gets a new job with a competitor, the court might order the former employee not to reveal the secret recipe.

Specific performance, on the other hand, is basically a court order for the breaching party to perform his or her duties under the contract. "Specific performance means 'performance specifically as agreed.' The purpose of the remedy is to give the one who seeks it the benefit of the contract . . . by compelling the other party to the contract to do what he or she has agreed to do—perform the contract on the precise terms agreed upon by the parties—and, hence, a decree for specific performance is . . . a means of compelling a party to do precisely what he or she ought to have done without being coerced by a court."[59]

To help illustrate the difference, let's use a sale of land as an example. Suppose that the Largetown Public Library enters into a contract with John Smith to purchase land for a new branch. On the day of closing, the director of the library arrives with the money, only to find out that John Smith has decided instead to sell the land to Metro University for a higher price. If the Largetown Library asks the court to block John

Smith from selling the land to Metro University, this would be an injunction. If, however, the Largetown Library asks the court to force John Smith to sell the land to the Largetown Library, this would be an order of specific performance.

B. Reformation of Contracts

Reformation of a contract occurs when the underlying contract does not actually represent the agreement of the parties, whether through "misrepresentation, duress, misunderstanding or mistake."[60] Reformation of a contract is not meant to correct mistakes that the parties make in bargains; rather, the remedy is meant to fix errors in the contract itself because the document does not represent the bargain that was agreed to by the parties. For example, reformation of a contract is often used to fix typographical errors. "Courts give effect to the expressed wills of the parties; they will not second-guess what the parties would have agreed to if they had known all the facts."[61]

In order to have a contract reformed by the court, there first must be an agreement between the parties. The parties must have arranged to put their agreement in writing, and there must be a difference between the written contract and the previously agreed-upon bargain. The correction of a mistake in the writing must be mutual; i.e., both parties must have the same concept of the underlying bargain and of the erroneous terms within the writing.

Sometimes the mistake is only in one part of a contract. For example, the parties may have agreed that a particular term would be included when the bargain was put into writing. If this term is left out, the contract may then be subject to reformation in order to correct this error.

For example, suppose that, during a telephone conversation, the director of the library at Metro University agrees to purchase a first edition of *Huckleberry Finn* from the Greentown Public Library. In exchange for the rare book, Metro University will pay Greentown $19,000, along with transferring to Greentown a facsimile edition that Metro University had purchased a few years earlier. The first edition has been appraised at $20,000, while the facsimile is valued at $1,000.

The agreement between the two libraries is written up into a contract and signed by both parties. However, due to a mistake, the cash amount in the contract is listed as being $18,000 rather than $19,000. This mistake could be fixed by reformation of the contract. Similarly, if the contract has the correct cash amount, but the contractual term relating to the facsimile edition has been mistakenly left out, reformation would be the equitable remedy taken to fix the contract so that it reflects the intentions of the parties. However, if the facsimile turns out to be worth only $200, reformation is not the proper remedy. A contract can only be reformed if the written agreement itself does not reflect the original bargain.

C. Quasi-Contractual Remedies

Sometimes the courts will try to give justice by using what are known as "quasi-contractual" remedies. *Quasi contracts* are also known as *implied contracts*. These terms refer to situations in which there is no actual contract between the parties, but the court will infer a contract in order to give justice to the parties.[62]

Some common examples of implied contracts include preservation of another's life or health, protection of another's property, performance of another's duty to protect public health or safety, performance of another's duty to supply necessities to a third person, and presumption of an intent to charge for business or professional services.[63]

Most instances of implied contracts are really judicial enforcement of social policies. For example, suppose that a hurricane rips the roof off the Greentown Public Library. The phone lines are down, and no one can reach the director or the employees. A roofing contractor whose business is located next door fixes the roof in order to protect the books. The courts would probably find an implied contract, since the roofer spent money to make the repairs and the library received the benefit of a new roof.[64]

Another instance of implied contracts involves the presumption that professionals, such as doctors, lawyers, and accountants, intend to charge for their services. This presumption occurs when dealing with someone who usually provides goods or services as his or her business. For example, suppose that the director of the library at Metro University consults an architect about a new building. The director asks the architect for drawings. Since providing architectural drawings is the way in which the architect makes a living, there is a presumption that the architect intended to charge for the drawings, even if the director never discussed a fee.

The two types of remedies for implied contracts are called *quantum merruit* and *quantum valebant*. *Quantum merruit* is a remedy in which the court awards the value of the services rendered; i.e., the cost of roofing the Greentown Public Library or the cost of the architectural drawings for Metro University. *Quantum valebant* consists of the value of the property received. An example of *quantum valebant* would be if the director of the Largetown Public Library asked a bookseller for a copy of a novel to evaluate for purchase. Instead of returning the novel, the library placed it in the collection and began to circulate the book. The bookseller could request *quantum valebant* for the value of the property received; i.e., for the cost of the book.

Illegal Contracts and Agreements
Against Public Policy

Although the general rule is that contracts are enforceable when they are made, there is an exception to this rule. Illegal acts can't constitute proper consideration to form a contract, as indicated earlier in this chapter in the example of the farmer who offered to sell marijuana to his neighbor. If the contract is for the performance of an illegal act, or an act that is against public policy or is opposed to public or social welfare, the contract is considered to be invalid and will not be enforced by the courts.[65] "It has been said that bargains are illegal if they violate an express provision of positive law or the purpose of positive law, although not expressly prohibited, or if they are otherwise inimical to public policy."[66]

For example, suppose that X hires Y to murder Z for a fee of $50,000. After the murder, Y is caught and put on trial. He implicates X in the process. The person who hired the hit man refuses to pay the $50,000. There is no court in the land that would enforce this contract, even though it meets the requirements for contract formation. The hit man (Y) can't collect the murder fee from X because the contract is for the performance of an illegal action.

Another type of contract that is not enforceable is an IOU for gambling debts in a state where gambling is illegal. For example, suppose that Jim, Beth, and Rob get together every Friday night to play poker. In that state, poker is illegal except in licensed casinos. Jim runs out of money, and Rob covers him at the table in exchange for an IOU. That night Beth is the big winner. Jim defaults on his note to Rob. Rob can't sue for the gambling debt, because the underlying agreement involves an illegal act. The entire bargain is considered to be void *ab initio* (a Latin phrase meaning that the contract is void from the very beginning). Because the contract is void, the courts will not enforce it. Even

if a void contract has satisfied all the requirements of contract formation (offer, acceptance, consideration, and Statute of Frauds), the fact
that the contract is void *ab initio* will prevent it from being enforced in
a court of law.

The other reason that a contract would be considered void *ab initio*
involves agreements that, while not requiring the commission of an
illegal act, are in some manner against public policy. Sometimes these
agreements stem from misrepresentation, fraud, or other types of unethical behavior by one of the parties. At other times, one (or more) of
the terms in the contract is merely something that the legislature or the
judiciary has determined to be against public policy. For example, section 434.100(1) of the Missouri Revised Statutes states:

> Except as provided in subsection 2 of this section, in any con-
> tract or agreement for public or private construction work, a party's
> covenant, promise or agreement to indemnify or hold harmless an-
> other person from that person's own negligence or wrongdoing is
> void as against public policy and wholly unenforceable.[67]

Suppose that a contractor in Missouri is renovating part of a library
building. If the workers damage some books and computers, the contractor can be held liable for the damage. This is true even if the contract has language that waives all responsibility for harm. The idea is
that, whether or not the specifics of contract formation have been satisfied, contractors and construction workers should not be able to avoid
responsibility for their own negligence. In addition, they should not be
able to shift that responsibility to another person. (This point has nothing to do with principles of agency; the employer can still be held responsible for his or her employee's negligent actions performed within
the scope of employment.)

In the past, the general rule was that if there was no fraud, duress,
or misrepresentation, the parties were assumed to have been equal bargaining partners who came upon the terms of their agreement through
mutual negotiation. Recently, however, "there has been a growing recognition . . . that agreements which are unconscionable as the result of
inequity of bargaining power or sharp practices are to be recognized as
offensive to public policy and subject to being declared unenforceable
or to other equitable adjustment or rescission."[68]

There are difficulties with the area of contracts that are void as being against public policy. Sometimes the legislature has determined that
a particular type of provision is void; at other times, the judiciary refuses to enforce certain provisions because they feel that justice is not

being done. The kinds of provisions that are void vary from state to state. In most cases, the provisions within normal contracts are perfectly acceptable, and most libraries, archives, and other cultural institutions don't have to worry too much about contracts that are against public policy.

Conclusion

The formation of contracts is one of the most basic elements of our legal system. In our society, contract formation is relevant to every entity and every person. Yet we don't always think about the way we enter into or write a contract. In order to have a contract, there must be a "meeting of the minds." There must be an offer, followed by an acceptance. Once an offer is rejected, it can't be accepted later. A counter-offer constitutes both a rejection and a new offer. It is also important to pay attention to the Statute of Frauds in order to determine whether the contract needs to be in writing.

Consideration involves the promisee (the person receiving the promise) giving up something of legal value to provide a benefit to the promisor (the person who has given the promise). Consideration can involve paying money, providing goods or services, providing a future benefit, or even agreeing *not* to do something. The consideration is the bargain that has been negotiated. Each party must provide consideration in order for the contract to be valid.

Although not all contracts must be in writing in order to be valid, the Statute of Frauds requires many agreements to be in writing for the protection of both parties. The Statute of Frauds applies to contracts for the sale of land, for the sale of goods (or securities) over $500, contracts that can't be performed within one year, and agreements to assume the debt of another person.

My recommendation is that, whenever possible, contracts should be placed in writing. The basic rule to remember about contracts is the old truism: "An oral contract is only worth the paper it is written on." Contracts are the glue that holds society together. The "meeting of the minds" creates the tie that binds.

3

Copyright and Patent Law

> Jody is a librarian at a medium-sized midwestern university. Her du-
> ties include writing instruction sheets for the library catalog. As part
> of her employment, Jody also creates pathfinders and research guides
> for library patrons. In addition—of her own volition—Jody has cre-
> ated for publication a bibliography of reference sources. Who owns
> the copyright on these works?

Intellectual property is one of the most important areas where the law
affects information professionals.[1] "Intellectual property describes a
wide variety of property created by musicians, authors, artists, and inventors. . . . It is designed to encourage the development of art, science,
and information by granting certain . . . rights which allow artists to
protect themselves from infringement."[2] These intellectual property
rights are protected by copyright law for literary works, by patent law
for inventions, and by trademark law for commerce. All of these protected areas affect libraries, archives, museums, and other cultural organizations.

Intellectual property protection gives creators the exclusive right to
use the products of their imaginations for a limited period of time. The
basic framework for copyright and patent law comes from Article 1,
Section 8, Clause 8 of the U.S. Constitution, which reads: "The Congress shall have Power . . . To promote the Progress of Science and
useful Arts, by securing for limited Times to Authors and Inventors the
exclusive Right to their respective Writings and Discoveries." The
Constitutional provision has been implemented by a variety of statutes,
administrative regulations, international treaties, and judicial decisions.
This patchwork of laws has shaped our system of intellectual property
rights.

Although copyrights and patents are the only categories of intellectual property mentioned in the Constitution, there are other types of

intellectual property. These other forms of intellectual property will be discussed in ***Chapter 6***, *Trademark and Trade Secret Law.*

Creating a work and registering it with the Copyright Office are initial steps. However, information professionals need to go beyond the basics in order to really understand what copyright is all about. Librarians and archivists need to understand copyright law in all of its complexities. This important need will be explained in this chapter, particularly in the section on exceptions to copyright law for libraries and archives. It is also important for information professionals to understand how the patent law system works so that they can assist patrons with patent searches. This chapter will give librarians and archivists knowledge that will enable them to be useful and helpful to their patrons.

Copyright Law

We have all seen the symbol © followed by a year and a name, such as *©2001 Bryan Carson.* The © symbol is so familiar that we don't even think about the laws behind it. Yet copyright is at the heart of the laws that libraries, archives, museums, and other cultural institutions need to understand in order to avoid legal problems.

Copyright is the basis of our system of publishing. There have been several copyright acts over the years, but the current one is the Copyright Act of 1976 (which took effect on January 1, 1978).[3] Copyright not only protects the written word but also protects several other categories, including:

- ♦ Literary works.
- ♦ Musical works, including any accompanying words.
- ♦ Dramatic works, including any accompanying music.
- ♦ Pantomimes and choreographic works.
- ♦ Pictorial, graphic, and sculptural works.
- ♦ Motion pictures and other audiovisual works.
- ♦ Sound recordings.
- ♦ Architectural works,[4] including "[b]uilding designs, whether in the form of architectural plans, drawings, or the constructed building itself."[5]

The copyright laws state that in order "to receive copyright protection, a work must be 'original' and must be 'fixed in a tangible medium of expression'. . . . The originality requirement is not stringent: A work is original in the copyright sense if it owes its origin to the author and was not copied from some preexisting work. A work can be original without being novel or unique. Only minimal creativity is required to meet the originality requirement. No artistic merit or beauty is required."[6] (I will discuss the "tangible medium of expression" in more detail in *Chapter 4, Fair Use and Intellectual Property Rights.*) Since computer programs contain written codes, they can be protected by either copyright or patent.[7]

Several types of materials are not eligible for copyright. Items created by the Federal government may not be copyrighted, although most state governmental materials do use copyright.[8] Also, news reports may not be copyrighted, although there are exceptions to this rule. However, most written works (and building designs) are eligible for copyright.

Unlike patents or trademarks, copyright is granted automatically upon creation (at least since the passage of the 1976 Copyright Act). You don't need a lawyer to get a copyright. You own the copyright in something you create at the exact instant that you create it.

You do also have the option of registering your copyright with the U.S. Copyright Office. If you go through the process of registering with the Copyright Office and someone later infringes your copyright, you will be able to sue in Federal court rather than in state court. Also, you will be able to use your copyright registration to help show that you created your item first. These two benefits are why Federal copyright registration is beneficial.

To register a copyright, you need to pay a fee ($30, as of Fall 2005) and send a copy or copies of the item to the U.S. Copyright Office. (In some cases, such as buildings or hull designs, you would send photographs or architectural drawings instead.) In order to register copyright for a computer program, you would need to print out the first 100 pages. The copyright office has a form for each type of item that can be copyrighted. These forms are located online at the Website of the U.S. Copyright Office (www.copyright.gov/).

The owner of a copyright has certain exclusive rights. These rights are laid out in section 106 of the Copyright Act and include the following:

(1) to reproduce the copyrighted work in copies or phonorecords;
(2) to prepare derivative works based upon the copyrighted work;
(3) to distribute copies or phonorecords of the copyrighted work to the public by sale or other transfer of ownership, or by rental, lease, or lending;
(4) in the case of literary, musical, dramatic, and choreographic works, pantomimes, and motion pictures and other audiovisual works, to perform the copyrighted work publicly;

(5) in the case of literary, musical, dramatic, and choreographic works, pantomimes, and pictorial, graphic, or sculptural works, including the individual images of a motion picture or other audiovisual work, to display the copyrighted work publicly; and
(6) in the case of sound recordings, to perform the copyrighted work publicly by means of a digital audio transmission.[9]

The exclusive rights of a copyright owner can be sold or licensed, but they belong to whoever owns the copyright. Of course, these rights are subject to some exceptions, which are listed below and in *Chapter 4*, *Fair Use and Intellectual Property Rights*. However, the general rule is that the owner of a copyright has the right to control his or her property.

A. Derivative Works

Sometimes one work becomes the basis upon which another work is built. For example, the novel *Gone with the Wind* became the movie *Gone with the Wind*. Who owns the copyright? According to the statute, "A 'derivative work' is a work based upon one or more preexisting works, such as a translation, musical arrangement, dramatization, fictionalization, motion picture version, sound recording, art reproduction, abridgment, condensation, or any other form in which a work may be recast, transformed, or adapted. A work consisting of editorial revisions, annotations, elaborations, or other modifications that, as a whole, represent an original work of authorship, is a 'derivative work.'"[10] Section 103 of the Copyright Act goes on to explain:

> The copyright in a compilation or derivative work extends only to the material contributed by the author of such work, as distinguished from the preexisting material employed in the work, and does not imply any exclusive right in the preexisting material. The copyright in such work is independent of, and does not affect or enlarge the scope, duration, ownership, or subsistence of, any copyright protection in the preexisting material.[11]

In other words, the copyright for the movie *Gone with the Wind* is separate from the copyright for the book. The rights to the movie have nothing whatever to do with the rights to the book. In *Chapter 6*, *Trademark and Trade Secret Law*, we will explore the case of *Dastar Corporation v. 20th Century Fox Film Corporation*,[12] in which a TV series was in the public domain but the book it was based on was still covered by copyright.

A good example of the relationship between original works and derivative works can be found in the song "Roots of Oak," originally composed by the noted Scottish folk and rock musician Donovan and released on his legendary 1970 album *Open Road*.[13] In 2004, progressive Celtic folk musician Jack Montgomery[14] recorded an album called *Everywhere I Look*.[15] This album contains a rockin' version of "Roots of Oak" with additional lyrics that Montgomery wrote himself. Montgomery obtained a license to record this song legally. Donovan still owns the original lyrics; Montgomery owns the portion of the lyrics that he wrote. If Donovan wished to re-record the song with Montgomery's additional lyrics, he would need to obtain a license.

Suppose that another singer wishes to record "Roots of Oak." He or she would need to get permission from Donovan for *his* lyrics, and from Jack Montgomery for *his* lyrics. If the person only wanted to record Donovan's original lyrics, there would be no need to ask Montgomery for permission. Another scenario arises if the singer wishes to use a different tune and only wants to use Montgomery's lyrics. In this situation, he or she would only need to ask Montgomery for permission, since the artist is not using Donovan's words or music.

B. International Protection for Copyright Law

In 1886, the Convention for the Protection of Literary and Artistic Works was signed in Berne, Switzerland.[16] Commonly referred to as the Berne Convention, this international treaty provides for reciprocity among member nations. Although the United States was not originally a member, the United States ratified the treaty in 1988 and became a member of the Berne Convention on March 1, 1989.[17]

Another treaty for international protection of copyright is called the Universal Copyright Convention. The United States is also a member of this group. The Universal Copyright Convention was signed in Geneva on September 6, 1952, and revised in Paris in 1974. The United States joined the *Geneva Round* of the Universal Copyright Convention on September 16, 1955, and the *Paris Round* on July 10, 1974.[18]

Most countries belong to at least one of these conventions. Several countries, including the United States, belong to both. Members of the two international copyright conventions have agreed to give nationals of member countries the same level of copyright protection that they give to their own nationals.

Under the terms of the two treaties, U.S. authors automatically receive copyright protection in all Berne or Universal Copyright Conven-

tion member countries. Works of foreign authors who are nationals of
countries that have signed either pact receive copyright protection in
the United States. Works which are first published in a country that has
signed the Berne Convention or the Universal Copyright Convention
are also protected in the United States. Under both treaties, unpublished
works are subject to copyright protection in the United States without
regard to the nationality or domicile of the author.[19]

The signing of the Universal Copyright Convention and the Berne
Convention treaties by the United States caused a significant change in
the way publishers conducted their business. Prior to that time, books
that were first published in a Berne country did not receive copyright
protection in the United States, even if they were subsequently published in the U.S. Books that were first published in the United States
did not receive protection in Berne countries, even when they were
subsequently published in a member country. The protection depended
on where the book was first published.

In order to avoid the copyright problems created by the U.S. not
being part of the Berne Convention, many publishers set up offices in
both the United States and Canada (which was a member of the Berne
Convention). By publishing books "simultaneously" in the United
States and Canada, publishers were able to make use of both forms of
protection. The entry of the United States into the ranks of the Berne
countries made that legal fiction unnecessary.

The newest international convention is the World Intellectual
Property Organization (WIPO). A specialized agency of the United
Nations, WIPO deals with intellectual property.[20] Prior to the creation
of WIPO, many international intellectual property issues had been dealt
with under the umbrella of the General Agreement on Tariffs and Trade
(GATT). The WIPO Copyright Treaty has now succeeded GATT.[21]

The creation of the WIPO Copyright Treaty had been one of the
basic goals of the Clinton administration, and on October 21, 1998, the
United States became the first nation to ratify the treaty. As of June 12,
2005, 182 countries had signed the WIPO treaty.[22] With a staff of 938,
the goals of WIPO include:

◆ Harmonizing national intellectual property legislation and procedures.

◆ Providing services for international applications for industrial
property rights.

◆ Exchanging intellectual property information.

◆ Providing legal and technical assistance to developing and other
countries.

◆ Facilitating the resolution of private intellectual property disputes.

◆ Marshalling information technology as a tool for storing, accessing, and using valuable intellectual property information.[23]

In addition to copyright laws, WIPO helps to administer a number
of trademark and patent treaties.[24] The World Intellectual Property Organization provides a wide and much-needed range of protections for
those who create literary, scientific, or technical works.

C. Fair Use

Although the copyright laws prohibit the duplication of copyrighted works, there is a provision in the law for making limited copies.
This provision is known as "fair use." The provisions of the fair use
doctrine allows users of copyrighted materials to make copies for purposes such as criticism, comment, news reporting, teaching (including
multiple copies for classroom use), scholarship, or research. The principles of fair use apply to both published and unpublished works, although there are some differences in the range of use for unpublished
materials.[25] The factors that are used to determine fair use include:

◆ The purpose and character of the use, including whether such
use is of a commercial nature or is for nonprofit educational
purposes;

◆ the nature of the copyrighted work;

◆ the amount and substantiality of the portion used in relation to
the copyrighted work as a whole; and

◆ the effect of the use upon the potential market for or value of the
copyrighted work.[26]

The fair use doctrine is the bedrock of copyright use. Without fair
use, the owner of the copyright would have an absolute monopoly on

his or her work, and no one would be able to use it. There are also some First Amendment freedom of speech issues relating to copyright. Fair use helps to provide breathing space between the First Amendment and the protections of copyright. For more information on the fair use doctrine, see **Chapter 4**, *Fair Use and Intellectual Property Rights.*

Infringement of Copyright

To paraphrase Shakespeare, "He who steals my purse steals trash, but he who steals my good words makes me poor indeed."[27] The rationale behind copyright is to protect the use of an individual's words. What happens if copyright is violated? This section will explain what to do about copyright infringement.

A. Remedies for Copyright Infringement

When copyright has been infringed, there are a number of possible remedies. Sections 501 to 513 of the Copyright Act lay out the procedures and remedies. The possible options include:

♦   Obtaining an injunction.[28]
♦   Having the infringing item impounded and destroyed[29] or seized and forfeited to the government.[30]
♦   Pressing criminal charges.[31]
♦   Obtaining damages and profits from the infringing item.[32]
♦   Obtaining costs and attorney's fees.[33]

One option that is frequently used is to request an injunction that will block the infringement. Sometimes this is done before the infringement actually occurs, and sometimes it is done afterwards. An example of an injunction issued *before* infringement was the case of *Harry Potter and the Half-Blood Prince*. The Harry Potter novel was scheduled to be released at 12:01 a.m. on July 16, 2005. The books were delivered beforehand to the retailers. On July 7, 2005, an employee at the Great Canadian Superstore location in Vancouver, British Columbia, accidentally sold 14 copies of the book. Later, a Calgary, Alberta, bookstore also sold 6 copies, but was able to retrieve them. The publisher of the book obtained an injunction from the British Columbia Supreme Court "that forbids copying or disclosing any part of the book before 12:01 a.m. on July 16, the day of the book's formal release."[34]

The reasoning behind the injunction had to do with the copyright owner's rights of distribution and copying, which are similar in Canadian law to those in the United States. Micheal Vonn of the British Columbia Civil Liberties Association wasn't worried about the prior restraint, saying that this was a "very small, small issue. It's such a limited scope for such a limited time. . . . The point is moot so soon that our concern about major harm coming from this injunction is very small. This is not like a publication ban on court proceedings where the public has a right to know. It's not like banning a book. Civil libertarians are not tied up in knots about it."[35] Once the book was actually released, the injunction expired.

Another example of the use of an injunction as a prior restraint against copyright infringement was the *Wind Done Gone* case. For more information about this case, see **Chapter 4**, *Fair Use and Intellectual Property Rights.*

A more substantial example of an injunction came in the case of the file-sharing Website Napster.[36] Users would download Napster's software, which created a list of songs that were located on the computers of each user. Participants could then use the Napster software to send the computer files to each other. Napster maintained the central file of songs and provided technical support to members in helping them to share files.[37]

Led by A&M Records, a coalition of record companies and studios filed suit against Napster for copyright infringement. These companies were able to obtain an injunction against Napster. Since Napster maintained the centralized directory of infringing materials and helped its users to share infringing files, this was a fairly easy case. The courts were able to find infringement without too much difficulty and granted an injunction against the infringement.[38]

After the decision, Napster was briefly shut down. Then it reopened as a legal music download site. Users can now go to Napster and pay for legal music. The company also has been promoting itself to college administrators.[39] The Napster subscription service allows colleges to pay a fee in order to give their students access to legally downloaded music and video files. Whether this new operating model will be profitable remains to be seen; however, there is anecdotal evidence of students and administrators requesting that libraries purchase a Napster subscription.

In certain circumstances, such as a bootleg copy of a movie, obtaining an injunction does not work. For example, suppose that Jim

buys tickets to the opening showing of a *Star Wars* movie. He takes
along a video camera and makes a copy of the film. Jim then sells the
copy on the corner in Times Square. What recourse does the copyright
owner have?

Certainly the copyright holder would be able to obtain a ruling for
damages and lost profits (although the holder may have difficulty getting a corner bootleg merchant to pay up). However, the illegal items
are still in circulation. An injunction ordering Jim not to sell the tapes
probably would not work, since he already knows that he is violating
the law by selling them. A much better remedy would be for the courts
to order the illegal copies to be seized and forfeited to the government;
even better would be if the bootleg copies were destroyed. (The copyright law does provide this remedy; *see* 17 U.S.C. § 503 and 17 U.S.C.
§ 509.)

Incidentally, it was just this bootleg type of infringement that led
Congress to pass a new amendment to the copyright law in the spring
of 2005. The Artists' Rights and Theft Prevention Act of 2005, or
"ART Act," made it illegal to make an audiovisual recording in a
movie theater.[40] The ART Act provides for the forfeiture and destruction of illegal copies. The ART Act also provides immunity for movie
theaters to detain and question—in a reasonable manner and for a reasonable time—any person who is suspected of violating this law.[41]

B. Actual Damages and Statutory Damages

There are two kinds of monetary damages available to copyright
owners whose rights have been infringed. These two types are *actual
damages* and *statutory damages*.

Actual damages consist of the amount that the copyright owner has
lost because of the infringing behavior. In the previous example, Jim
was selling bootleg copies on the corner. Suppose, however, that ABC
Computer Company obtained one copy of a word processing program
created by XYZ Software and then gave out unauthorized copies with
all the ABC computers that were purchased. A computer without the
bootleg software cost $500; a computer with the illegal software was
sold for $600. A computer user purchasing a legal copy of the software
alone from XYZ would pay $250.

In this case, the best remedy for XYZ Software would be a combination of a lawsuit for actual damages and for profits (which punishes
the past illegal actions), along with an injunction prohibiting the company from violating the law in the future. Section 504 of the Copyright

Act allows the copyright owner to sue for actual damages and lost profits.[42]

Thus, XYZ Software could obtain actual damages and lost profits
from ABC Computer Company. The amount of the damages would be
$250 in damages (the cost of the legal software) for each illegal copy,
along with the $100 that ABC Computer made in profits. The total
would be $350 per bootleg copy.

However, the law also provides for an award of *statutory damages*.
Statutory damages are an amount set by the law. In order to win an
award of statutory damages, the copyright must be filed with the U.S.
Copyright Office within three months of publication or before the infringement occurred. Copyright owners choose either to receive their
actual damages and profits, or to ask the court for statutory damages.

Section 504 of the Copyright Act allows statutory damages of not
less than $750 and not more than $30,000 per act of copyright infringement. If the court finds that the copyright infringer acted willfully, the court may increase the statutory damages up to $150,000 per
act of infringement. On the other hand, if the infringer proves that his
or her act was unintentional, that he or she was not aware of infringement, and that he or she had no reason to be aware of infringement, the
court may decrease the award to as low as $200 per act.[43]

In the case of the bootleg software delivered by ABC Computer
Company, the XYZ Software Company might want to request statutory
damages instead of actual damages and profits. The minimum statutory
damages would be $750 per bootlegged copy, while the actual damages
and profits would only be $350 per copy.

Most copyright cases involve a combination of remedies. For example, a case may ask for damages, destruction of infringing items, an
injunction prohibiting infringement in the future, and attorney's fees.
This situation is relevant to libraries because copyright owners can always ask for statutory damages, even if there is no commercial loss.

C. The *Sony* Case

In the early 1980s, when VCRs became popular, the U.S. Supreme
Court was asked to decide whether using a VCR to record a television
program was a violation of copyright.[44] This opinion, popularly called
the *"Betamax* case" or the *"Sony* case," came in the case of *Sony Corporation of America et al. v. Universal City Studios, Inc.* The *Sony* case
involved the question of whether VCRs were legal. This case is relevant for libraries because it sets the background for *Napster*, *Grokster*,

and other cases that came after, helping to define the principles of fair use and keeping libraries from liability for copyright infringement. Libraries (particularly academic and public libraries) were very involved in these cases, because they involved users' access to information. As a result, the American Library Association filed briefs in the *Sony*, *Napster*, and *Grokster* cases.

In the *Sony* case, the U.S. Supreme Court decided that VCRs are indeed legal, and that viewers—without violating copyright—may legally record TV programs on a VCR in their own homes for their own use. Using fair use and the First Amendment as its basis, the Supreme Court ruled that this act of recording was merely a form of "time-shifting."[45] According to the *Sony* opinion, "the purpose of this use served the public interest in increasing access to television programming, an interest that 'is consistent with the First Amendment policy of providing the fullest possible access to information through the public airwaves.'"[46] [Citations omitted.]

The most important copyright principle that came out of the *Sony* decision was the issue of copyright infringement. Universal Studios urged the Supreme Court to find that the VCR was an illegal device because it was used to infringe copyright. Sony claimed that there were substantial noninfringing uses for its Betamax VCR. Some of the programs that could be copied without objection included sports, religious programs, and educational television. Sony also discussed a survey showing that "75.4% of the [VCR] owners use their machines to record for time-shifting purposes half or most of the time. Defendants' survey showed that 96% of the Betamax owners had used the machine to record programs they otherwise would have missed."[47]

Sony was therefore able to show both infringing and noninfringing uses of their device. Although the users of the device were the ones infringing copyright, it was Sony that was being sued for providing the means to make these illegal copies. In order to decide this case, the Supreme Court looked at patent law for guidance in what to do in this situation. Patent law contains a provision for contributory infringement. According to the Court's opinion:

> If vicarious liability is to be imposed on Sony in this case, it must rest on the fact that it has sold equipment with constructive knowledge of the fact that its customers may use that equipment to make unauthorized copies of copyrighted material. There is no precedent in the law of copyright for the imposition of vicarious liability on such a theory. The closest analogy is provided by the patent law

cases to which it is appropriate to refer because of the historic kinship between patent law and copyright law.[48]

The Supreme Court came to the conclusion that:

> [C]ourts [must] look beyond actual duplication of a device or publication to the products or activities that make such duplication possible. . . . Accordingly, the sale of copying equipment, like the sale of other articles of commerce, does not constitute contributory infringement if the product is widely used for legitimate, unobjectionable purposes. Indeed, it need merely be capable of substantial noninfringing uses.[49]

The *Sony* case was important for libraries because it helped to allow the legal use of copying technology. Many of our digital library initiatives would not have occurred if this technology were not available. Once the *Sony* court ruled on the legal standard, the only question was whether the Betamax was able to show substantial noninfringing uses. Since the trial court had found these uses as a matter of law, the Supreme Court ruled in favor of Sony.

D. The *File-Sharing* Cases

The *file-sharing* cases involve a type of software that allows users to exchange their files, which often include copyrighted music and videos. As was mentioned earlier, the first major company to popularize this type of software was Napster. (The *Napster* case is discussed above in *Section A*, in the context of injunctions.) The case was fairly easy, since the Napster Corporation maintained a central directory of files and gave users assistance in sharing copyrighted files. The major significance of the *Napster* decision was to pave the way for the *Grokster* case.

In the wake of the *Napster* case, other companies rose to fill the file-sharing void. Grokster and StreamCast are two of these companies. The two competitors each created a decentralized peer-to-peer file-sharing product. Members could use the software product to exchange files. Unlike Napster, neither Grokster nor StreamCast maintained a central list of users. Once the software was distributed, the users had to find each other and agree to exchange files. Because many of the shared files were music and videos that had been illegally downloaded, a coalition of movie and record producers sued Grokster and Stream-Cast for contributory copyright infringement.[50] MGM claimed that nearly 90 percent of the files available for download were copyrighted works. According to the Supreme Court's opinion:

> The question is under what circumstances the distributor of a product capable of both lawful and unlawful use is liable for acts of copyright infringement by third parties using the product. We hold that one who distributes a device with the object of promoting its use to infringe copyright, as shown by clear expression or other affirmative steps taken to foster infringement, is liable for the resulting acts of infringement by third parties.[51]

The significance of this decision for libraries applies to our patrons' use of the materials. Although libraries don't "distribute" such devices, they *do* make photocopiers, tape players, and computers available to the public. As a result, the *file-sharing* cases are very significant, and many librarians were concerned that the *Sony* decision would be overruled, as the record companies requested.

In a unanimous opinion written by Justice Souter, the Supreme Court followed the *Sony* rule, but found that there was substantial evidence that the entire business models of Grokster and StreamCast were designed to encourage infringement of copyright. The Court's opinion stated that:

> Grokster and StreamCast are not, however, merely passive recipients of information about infringing use. The record is replete with evidence that from the moment Grokster and StreamCast began to distribute their free software, each one clearly voiced the objective that recipients use it to download copyrighted works, and each took active steps to encourage infringement. . . .[52] An internal e-mail from a company executive stated: "We have put this network in place so that when Napster pulls the plug on their free service . . . or if the Court orders them shut down prior to that . . . we will be positioned to capture the flood of their 32 million users that will be actively looking for an alternative."[53]

The 9th Circuit Court of Appeals had ruled in favor of Grokster and StreamCast. The Court of Appeals opinion read the *Sony* case as meaning that if there were any instances in which the software could be used to copy materials that did not infringe copyright, there should be no legal liability for Grokster and StreamCast.[54] The record companies urged the Supreme Court either to overrule the *Sony* decision or to adopt a rule that interpreted the amount of noninfringing use necessary to be deemed "substantial." The Court declined to do either one. Instead, the Supreme Court found that the 9th Circuit's understanding of the *Sony* decision was flawed, since:

> [N]othing in *Sony* requires courts to ignore evidence of intent if there is such evidence, and the case was never meant to foreclose rules of fault-based liability derived from the common law. . . .[55] Thus, where evidence goes beyond a product's characteristics or the knowledge that it may be put to infringing uses, and shows statements or actions directed to promoting infringement, [*Sony*] will not preclude liability.[56]

The real problem with the Grokster and StreamCast companies involved their knowledge that the product was going to be used to infringe copyright. In fact, as mentioned above, this infringement was an integral part of the two companies' plans.

As with the *Sony* case, the Supreme Court applied patent law principles in the *Grokster* case to the analysis of copyright. Patent law allows a finding of "inducement of infringement" when a device is advertised in such a way as to promote an infringing use.[57] An advertisement may also infringe patent law when the device can only be used in conjunction with the patented invention. (For example, if I invented and advertised a device that only worked with a patented invention, I would be violating patent law.)

The Supreme Court ruled that it did not matter whether these proposed advertisements were actually published or distributed. The ads showed the business model of the company and, therefore, revealed what the company and its executives were thinking.[58]

The evidence showed that Grokster and StreamCast intended that their software be used for infringing purposes and that they did not develop any filtering software to remove the infringing uses. The evidence also showed that, since both companies made their profits by selling advertising that was based on the volume of business the networks did, the companies had an incentive to get as much business as possible regardless of whether or not the downloads were legal.[59] According to the Supreme Court's opinion, "The unlawful objective is unmistakable."[60]

Because of Grokster's and StreamCast's statements, the Supreme Court did not need to rule on the issue of how much noninfringing use was necessary in order to be protected under *Sony*. This issue, however, was the subject of debate in the two concurring opinions. Justice Ginsburg, joined by Chief Justice Rehnquist and Justice Kennedy, urged the adoption of a strict rule as to what constitutes "substantial" noninfringing use under *Sony*. Justice Breyer, joined by Justices Stevens and O'Connor, disagreed and stated that the *Sony* test was sufficiently clear. Justice Breyer, however, believed that Grokster and StreamCast were indeed "capable of substantial or commercially significant noninfringing uses."[61]

The Breyer opinion proposes that the *Sony* test is the best possible way of interpreting the law. Justice Breyer indicates that the rule is clear and that it strongly protects new technology. "Thus *Sony*'s rule shelters VCRs, typewriters, tape recorders, photocopiers, computers, cassette players, compact disc burners, digital video recorders, MP3 players, Internet search engines, and peer-to-peer software. But *Sony*'s rule does not shelter descramblers, even if one could *theoretically* use a descrambler in a noninfringing way."[62]

Justice Breyer also believes that the test proposed by Justice Ginsburg will have a substantially chilling effect on the development of technology. He states that "Justice Ginsburg's approach would require defendants to produce considerably more concrete evidence—more than was presented here—to earn *Sony*'s shelter. That heavier evidentiary demand, and especially the more dramatic (case-by-case balancing) modifications that MGM and the Government seek, would, I believe, undercut the protection that *Sony* now offers."[63]

Neither Justice Ginsburg's analysis nor Justice Breyer's opinion is the law of the land. Each interpretation received three votes, with three justices (Souter, Scalia, and Thomas) deciding not to join in the debate at all. A future case might raise this issue again. We may not have heard the last of the issue of contributory infringement.

The *Work for Hire* Doctrine

One concept that is very important for understanding both copyright and patent law is the idea of *Work for Hire*. What we write on our own time belongs to us. What we write for our employer belongs to our employer. The copyright law states that "[i]n the case of a work made for hire, the employer or other person for whom the work was prepared is considered the author for purposes of this title, and, unless the parties have expressly agreed otherwise in a written instrument signed by them, owns all of the rights comprised in the copyright."[64] This provision is based on well-settled laws of agency and principal, which state that the work of the employee is always supposed to be done for the employer.

The basic concept of *Work for Hire* is fairly clear, although there have been many lawsuits about what was and what was not within the scope of an employee's duties. However, it is much more difficult to decide whether an item is a Work for Hire if the person who created the work is an independent contractor. (For more information on agency law, employment law, and independent contractors, see *Chapter 11, Employment and Workplace Law.*)

Because independent contractors are not employees, an independent contractor may be able to retain the rights to his or her own work. Frequently, this is not what the hiring person or organization intended. For example, suppose that the X Corporation is planning a direct-mail campaign with advertising flyers. There is no doubt whatsoever that the flyers would belong to the company if an in-house graphics department developed them. However, if an outside design agency prepares the flyers, there is a question about who owns the copyright for the design.

In order to get around these issues, many independent contractor agreements include sections relating to *Work for Hire*. However, these provisions are not always valid. There are only nine statutorily defined categories where the *Work for Hire* doctrine applies to contractors. Even if the situation falls within one of these categories, there must be a *written* agreement (oral agreements are only worth the paper they are written on); otherwise the doctrine of *Work for Hire* will not apply. According to section 101 of the Copyright Act, a *Work for Hire* agreement with an independent contractor is only valid if it involves one of the following types of material:

♦   Works specially ordered or commissioned for use as a contribution to a collective work.

♦   Works that are part of a motion picture or other audiovisual work.

♦   A translation.

♦   A supplementary work.

♦   A compilation.

♦   An instructional text.

♦   A test.

♦   Answer materials for a test.

♦   An atlas.[65]

Unless the work created by an independent contractor fits into one of these categories and the agreement is in writing, the product won't be a Work for Hire. The independent contractor would own the work. Of course, creators can always assign their rights to others. However, this is a separate transaction and must be done by means of a valid contract with sufficient consideration.

A. Employees versus Independent Contractors: The *Reid* Case

In trying to determine whether the *Work for Hire* doctrine applies, the first thing that needs to be considered is whether the creator was an employee or an independent contractor (the term in the Copyright Act is "consultant"). The major Supreme Court case on this topic is *Community for Creative Non-Violence et al. v. Reid.*[66] In this case, a nonprofit group called the Community for Creative Non-Violence (CCNV) hired sculptor James Earl Reid to create a statue. Neither party discussed copyright in their agreement, and once the statue was completed both parties attempted to file copyright registrations. Besides emphasizing the point that parties should negotiate copyright beforehand, this case also takes a good, hard look at the meaning of the term "employee" as used in the Copyright Act.

A large part of the decision of the Supreme Court involved the meanings of the terms "employee" and "scope of employment." According to the Supreme Court's decision:

> The starting point for our interpretation of a statute is always its language. . . .[67] It is, however, well established that "[w]here Congress uses terms that have accumulated settled meaning under . . . the common law, a court must infer, unless the statute otherwise dictates, that Congress means to incorporate the established meaning of these terms."[68] In the past, when Congress has used the term "employee" without defining it, we have concluded that Congress intended to describe the conventional master-servant relationship as understood by common-law agency doctrine.[69] [Internal citations contained in endnotes]

According to the facts of the case, CCNV paid Reid for only that one statue. CCNV did make suggestions as to the aesthetic design of the statue, and they supervised the process while the statue was created. However, the members of CCNV did not themselves design the statue; most of the design was Reid's artistic product. The Court held that "a Work for Hire can arise through one of two mutually exclusive means, one for employees and one for independent contractors, and ordinary canons of statutory interpretation indicate that the classification of a particular hired party should be made with reference to agency law."[70] (For more information on agency law, see **Chapter 11**, *Employment and Workplace Law*.) The Court went on to say:

> Reid was not an employee of CCNV but an independent contractor. True, CCNV members directed enough of Reid's work to ensure that he produced a sculpture that met their specifications. But the extent of control the hiring party exercises over the details of the product is not dispositive. Indeed, all the other circumstances weigh heavily against finding an employment relationship. Reid is a sculptor . . . [and] supplied his own tools. He worked in his own studio in Baltimore, making daily supervision of his activities from Washington practicably impossible. Reid was retained for less than two months, a relatively short period of time. . . . CCNV had no right to assign additional projects to Reid. Apart from the deadline for completing the sculpture, Reid had absolute freedom to decide when and how long to work. CCNV paid Reid $15,000, a sum dependent on "completion of a specific job, a method by which independent contractors are often compensated."[71] Reid had total discretion in hiring and paying assistants. "Creating sculptures was hardly 'regular business' for CCNV."[72] Indeed, CCNV [was] not a business at all. Finally, CCNV did not pay payroll or Social Security taxes, provide any employee benefits, or contribute to unemployment insurance or workers' compensation funds. . . .
>
> However . . . CCNV nevertheless may be a joint author of the sculpture if . . . CCNV and Reid prepared the work "with the intention that their contributions be merged into inseparable or interdependent parts of a unitary whole."[73] In that case, CCNV and Reid would be co-owners of the copyright in the work.[74]

The final decision in the *Reid* case is that the words of the Copyright Act mean exactly what they say. If the person is an employee of an organization and creates the work within the scope of his or her employment, the *Work for Hire* doctrine applies. If the person is an independent contractor or consultant, the *Work for Hire* doctrine only applies if there is a signed agreement (with proper consideration) and the work falls into one of the nine statutorily defined categories. If both of those factors are not present, it is not a Work for Hire, and the creator retains all rights to the work.

One important issue in the *Reid* case was whether CCNV might be a joint author because of the design suggestions that it gave and the control that it exercised. As a result of this question, the Supreme Court remanded the case back to the District Court with instructions to determine whether CCNV was a co-author. However, the parties settled before this issue could be decided, agreeing that Reid was to be the sole owner for three-dimensional reproductions, while CCNV had co-ownership of the rights for two-dimensional reproductions.[75]

Most of the problems in the *Reid* case could have been averted had the parties agreed on copyright when they signed their agreement. Although the statue does not fit into any of the categories enumerated in the Copyright Act, the parties could have agreed in their contract that Reid would assign his copyright to CCNV. Naturally, if copyright assignment is included in a contract, there must be sufficient consideration. There is no reason why the parties could not have provided for copyright assignment. In fact, it is routine for such clauses to be included in contracts. For example, publishers regularly require the assignment of copyright from an author. (My contract with Scarecrow Press for this book includes an assignment of copyright.) Buying the copyright rights is different from using a *Work for Hire* agreement and requires specific wording in the contract.

B. Statutory Categories and *Work for Hire* Agreements

The only time that a *Work for Hire* agreement can be valid is when the work fits within one of the categories listed in the Copyright Act. Several of these categories are clear, i.e., translations, tests and test answers, and atlases. (The statute does not mention maps, but by analogy maps might be covered by these provisions.) However, other provisions contain nuances within their definitions. These categories include (1) contributions to collective works and compilations, (2) supplementary works, and (3) instructional texts.

The Copyright Act defines collective works and compilations as follows:

> A "collective work" is a work, such as a periodical issue, anthology, or encyclopedia, in which a number of contributions, constituting separate and independent works in themselves, are assembled into a collective whole. A "compilation" is a work formed by the collection and assembling of preexisting materials or of data that are selected, coordinated, or arranged in such a way that the resulting work as a whole constitutes an original work of authorship. The term "compilation" includes collective works.[76]

It is not always possible to distinguish ownership of collective works. For example, in the *Reid* case, it would not have been possible for a court to determine that one part of the statue belonged to Reid and one part belonged to CCNV. This is why the Supreme Court remanded the case to the District Court for a determination as to whether CCNV was a co-creator.

The difference between a collective work and other types of compilations is that each individual item within a compilation itself constitutes a "separate and independent" work that qualifies for copyright protection. "[T]here is a basic distinction between a 'joint work,' where the separate elements merge into a unified whole, and a 'collective work,' where they remain unintegrated [sic] and disparate."[77]

For example, suppose that two authors work together to write a novel. Their contributions creatively merge into a unified whole, leaving no way to assign copyright to particular sections. The two co-authors have joint copyright.

On the other hand, a book of short stories by several different authors would allow a relatively easy apportionment of copyright. Each story is an individual work that can stand on its own, so the author of each story retains his or her copyright.[78]

According to the Copyright Act, "a 'supplementary work' is a work prepared for publication as a secondary adjunct to a work by another author for the purpose of introducing, concluding, illustrating, explaining, revising, commenting upon, or assisting in the use of the other work, such as forewords, after words, pictorial illustrations, maps, charts, tables, editorial notes, musical arrangements, answer material for tests, bibliographies, appendixes, and indexes."[79] For example, if I am commissioned to write an introductory essay for a new critical edition of *Huckleberry Finn*, the essay would fall into the category of supplementary work, meaning that a *Work for Hire* agreement could be included in my contract with the publisher.

Another category that qualifies for *Work for Hire* agreements is an "instructional text." The Copyright Act defines an instructional text as being "a literary, pictorial, or graphic work prepared for publication and with the purpose of use in systematic instructional activities."[80] (Of course, many works are created that are subsequently used as textbooks; the statute is not talking about these kinds of materials.) Works that are specifically created to be used in the classroom fall within the category of instructional texts and can be the subject of a *Work for Hire* agreement. (Instructional texts are also treated differently for purposes of the education exceptions to copyright; for more information, see **Chapter 5**, *Copyright and Education*.)

Even if the work falls within one of the statutory categories, there must be a signed agreement in order for the material to be considered a

Work for Hire. For example, if a publisher commissions a collective work, the issue of *Work for Hire* must be specifically addressed within the contract—*in writing*—at the time that the agreement is entered into. The contract must include all of the normal formalities of contract formation, including adequate consideration, and the parties must truly have a meeting of the minds in order to have a valid *Work for Hire* agreement.

When the work of an independent contractor does not fall into one of the categories listed in the Copyright Act, you still may be able to include a valid transfer of ownership provision in a contract. The Copyright Act says that "ownership of a copyright may be transferred in whole or in part by any means of conveyance."[81] For example, suppose that the contract between CCNV and Reid had included the language in figure 3.1.

> James Earl Reid (hereinafter, "Seller"), a sculptor with principal place of business in Baltimore, Maryland, for valuable consideration, the receipt and sufficiency of which is hereby acknowledged, hereby sells, transfers, assigns, conveys, and delivers to Community for Creative Non-Violence (hereinafter, "Purchaser") all of Seller's right, title, and interest in and for the work of visual art described in this agreement, including its frame, mounting, base, or support, and including Seller's copyright interest therein (hereinafter, the "Property"), to have and to hold the Property unto Purchaser, its successors and assigns, forever.

Figure 3.1. Copyright Assignment Clause (based on Nimmer).[82]

Had the contract between CCNV and Reid included such a clause, there would have been no need whatsoever for litigation. This clause was omitted from the contract between CCNV and Reid because the issue was never discussed. Certainly a lot of problems would have been solved, and the rights of the parties would have been clear from the beginning. It is important to remember that the copyright of an object and the physical ownership of the object are two different things, and that the physical object and the copyright "may be transferred . . . and owned separately."[83]

Agreements with independent contractors should always specify which party receives the copyright. This helps to avoid trouble later. Although it may cost more to receive both the object and the intellectual property rights, in the end it will be worth the effort. After all, the best way to win a lawsuit is to avoid it entirely.

C. *Work for Hire* on the College Campus

The *Work for Hire* doctrine is an important issue in the academic world. The basis of academic freedom is that faculty members (within normal limits) can say whatever they want, write whatever they want, and publish whatever they want. This principle has been applied by extension to many information professionals working in public libraries, schools, archives, museums, and other cultural institutions. What faculty members publish is supposed to belong to them, and college professors supposedly can't be fired for their theories. This is the premise upon which most academic scholarship is based. Yet the scholar is an employee of a larger institution. How can the two principles be reconciled?

Let us examine this issue from a library standpoint, using the example at the beginning of the chapter. In this example, a librarian named Jody has created instruction sheets for the library catalog, pathfinders and research guides for the library patrons, and a bibliography of reference sources for publication. Using the principles of the *Work for Hire* doctrine, we can determine which works the library owns copyright on and which works Jody owns the copyright on.

The instruction sheet, the pathfinders, and the research guides are "works for hire." Therefore, the copyright resides with the university. The bibliography Jody prepared for publication is her own work, so she owns the copyright, regardless of whether it was created during working hours. A problem arises if Jody wishes to expand the pathfinder and create a bibliography for publication. The copyright situation is somewhat unclear, since the pathfinder might be a part of Jody's job and therefore a "Work for Hire." Or the pathfinder may be a work she has created on her own, and therefore she owns it.

To some extent, ownership depends on the job description of the librarian. If Jody was expected to produce pathfinders as part of her job, then the university owns the work. If Jody voluntarily created a pathfinder that she was not required to write, then the situation is akin to the bibliography for publication.

Even the fact that Jody wrote the pathfinder while she was at work does not make a difference. "If a work would not otherwise be regarded as falling within the employment relationship, the fact that a portion of the work was done during working hours, and that the assistance of the employer's facilities and personnel was obtained in some degree in preparing the work, will not necessarily render the work the property of the employer. Conversely, a work within the scope of an employee's duties, but prepared at home during non-working hours, is not *ipso facto* outside the [scope of] work for hire. . . ."[84]

The courts have borrowed legal principles from the field of agency law (for more information, see **Chapter 11**, *Employment and Workplace Law*) and have articulated "three standards as to when an employee's conduct falls within the scope of employment: 1. It is the kind of work (s)he is employed to perform; 2. It occurs substantially within authorized work hours and space; 3. It is actuated, at least in part, by a purpose to serve the employer."[85] Once ownership by the institution is established, the next step is to find out whether the institution has an intellectual property policy.

Some schools, libraries, and research institutions grant rights that are not found in standard copyright law. If the institution has a policy that grants additional rights to creators, then the general copyright law does not apply. In that case, Jody and her publisher need to make certain that they have read the institution's intellectual property policy. For example, Indiana University's intellectual property policy reserves to the university the rights to everything written by faculty and staff members except "traditional works of scholarship and creativity."[86] Western Kentucky University has a similar policy.[87]

Many universities have intellectual property policies that differentiate between the "traditional scholarly work generally expected of faculty," and "University assigned efforts."[88] Western Kentucky University is no exception.

Under general copyright law principles, the university would own student work, including papers written for a class. For the purposes of copyright law, student assignments are a Work for Hire. However, at Western Kentucky University, works produced by students are considered to be exempt from the *Work for Hire* doctrine as long as they fall within the definition of "traditional products."[89] The university's Intellectual Property Policy defines "traditional products" as including:

- ◆ Books, monographs, articles, reviews, and works of art (including paintings, sculptures, plays, choreography, musical compositions).
- ◆ Individual course materials such as syllabi, exams, transparencies, study guides, workbooks, and manuals.

♦ Instructional software, Webpages, and Internet-based instructional materials developed by faculty members in the course of their usual scholarly, pedagogical, and service activities.[90]

In our example of Jody the librarian, let's assume that her bibliography is a Work for Hire. Jody still has the right to copy, display, modify, and prepare derivative works as long as she does so on behalf of the library. "The university is not a house divided,"[91] i.e., university-owned intellectual property can be used for university business without obtaining copyright clearance.

Anyone publishing a work should make sure that he or she knows who owns the copyright, whether the work was prepared within the scope of employment, and whether the institution has an intellectual property policy. Each one of us needs to be aware of copyright law and of our employer's intellectual property policies. Knowing these policies is very important; it always pays to be safe.

Exceptions to Copyright Law
for Libraries and Archives

U.S. copyright law recognizes that libraries and archives have a special place in our society, and that some of the work that information professionals do on a daily basis might constitute technical violations of copyright. As a result, section 108 of the Copyright Act contains several exceptions for libraries and archives. These exceptions allow librarians and archivists to make copies for patrons and give libraries and archives the right to make copies of published or unpublished works for preservation or for replacement. Section 108 also discusses copying materials for interlibrary loan and duplicating works in their last 20 years of copyright if the works are no longer readily available.

Section 108 allows employees working within the scope of their employment to reproduce *one copy* for patrons of a work, provided that (1) there is no direct or indirect commercial advantage (to the patron), (2) the collection is open to the public or researchers in the field, and (3) the copy either includes the copyright notice or "a legend stating that the work may be protected by copyright."[92]

Section 108 also allows up to three copies of an unpublished work to be made for preservation purposes or for deposit in another library or archives for scholarly use, if (1) the copy or phonorecord reproduced is currently in the collections of the library or archives; and (2) any such copy or phonorecord that is reproduced in digital format is not otherwise distributed in that format and is not made available to the public in that format outside the premises of the library or archives.[93]

Section 108 also allows libraries or archives to make up to three copies or phonorecords of a published work for the purposes of preservation or for "replacement of a copy or phonorecord that is damaged, deteriorating, lost, or stolen, or if the existing format in which the work is stored has become obsolete. . . ."[94] Before using this exception, the library or archives must first make a reasonable effort to find a replacement at a fair price. This requirement is usually interpreted to mean that if the only copy available is a first edition, it is legal for the library to make a duplicate, but if there are other copies available that cost more than the library would like to pay, the library must still purchase the replacement copy. In other words, "fair price" doesn't mean the price the library thinks is fair; it means the price the market thinks is fair.

Copyright regulations allow the copyright owner or agent to file with the copyright office a "Notice to Libraries and Archives of Normal Commercial Exploitation or Availability at Reasonable Price."[95] If this notice has been provided, the exception in section 108(h) does not apply. The required notice is found in Appendix A to 37 C.F.R. § 201.39.[96] The notice is available at the Scarecrow Press support Website for this book.

Section 108 has the following guidance to offer in deciding whether a format has become obsolete: "For purposes of this subsection, a format shall be considered obsolete if the machine or device necessary to render perceptible a work stored in that format is no longer manufactured or is no longer reasonably available in the commercial marketplace."[97] For example, if the library owns a sound recording on 8-track, it is permissible to copy the recording into another format. The copy could be in an analog format such as a cassette or in a digital format such as a CD.

The only restriction is that if the library makes a digital copy (such as a CD), it can't be loaned out to the public. The digital copy must only be used on the premises of the library or archives.[98] The statute contains this restriction because a digital copy can be itself copied so easily and with such great clarity that copyright infringers can use the digital copy to get around the usual restrictions.

One of the most important exceptions to copyright law contained in section 108 deals with interlibrary loan. Libraries and archives are allowed to make one copy of an article from a periodical or collection, as long as (1) the copy becomes the property of the patron, (2) the library has no notice or reason to believe that the patron intends to use the copy for any purposes other than private study or research, and (3) "the library or archives displays prominently, at the place where orders are accepted, and includes on its order form, a warning of copyright in accordance with requirements that the Register of Copyrights shall prescribe by regulation."[99]

Section 108 also allows libraries to reproduce an entire work for interlibrary loan if a copy cannot be obtained at a fair price. (See the discussion of fair price above.) As with other interlibrary loans, the copy becomes the property of the user, and the library must provide a copyright notice to the patron.[100]

Under the library exception, libraries and archives are not liable for infringements made by their patrons, as long as the workers don't have knowledge that the items are going to be used in an infringing manner.[101] However, there is no exception if the library workers have actual knowledge of copyright infringement or are deliberately reproducing an item in order to avoid purchasing it.[102] The library or archives must also post a notice of copyright—using the wording found in 37 C.F.R. § 201.14—near the photocopiers and on the copy order form.[103] The current wording of the display notice is contained in figure 3.2.

**NOTICE: WARNING CONCERNING
COPYRIGHT RESTRICTIONS**

The copyright law of the United States (title 17, United States Code) governs the making of photocopies or other reproductions of copyrighted material.

Figure 3.2. Copyright Notice for Libraries.[104]

The copyright exceptions for libraries and archives are very important. Without these exceptions, information professionals would not be able to provide as wide a range of services to patrons. Information professionals need to understand the provisions contained in section 108 of the Copyright Act. By understanding these principles, we can better assist library and archival users.

Duration of Copyright

The duration of copyright depends on when the work was created or when it was published. The length of copyright also depends on whether a personal author created the work or whether it was created as a Work for Hire by a corporate author. Personal authors have a different term than corporate authors.

The first Copyright Act (1790)[105] allowed works to be protected for 14 years, with the option of extending the term for another 14 years.[106] The 1909 Copyright Act protected authors for 28 years. Since 1960, the copyright term has been extended 11 times.[107] When the 1976 Copyright Act was passed, new copyrights were granted for the life of the author plus 50 years, while works that were registered before 1978 (when the 1976 Copyright Act became effective) would be protected for 75 years from the date of creation.[108]

By 1993, however, the music and entertainment industry began to press for longer terms and more copyright protection. This intense lobbying resulted in the 1998 passage of the Digital Millennium Copyright Act and the ratification of the World Intellectual Property Organization (WIPO) Treaty.[109] The lobbying effort also resulted in the extension of the term of copyright.

On October 7, 1998, the Sonny Bono Copyright Term Extension Act (also known as the Copyright Term Extension Act, or CTEA) was passed by the U.S. House and Senate, and then signed into law by President Clinton.[110] This statute extends by 20 years the term of copyright protection for all materials. The statute was subsequently challenged in the U.S. Supreme Court, but was found to be constitutional.[111] The passage of the Sonny Bono Copyright Extension Act and the Digital Millennium Copyright Act made possible the complete implementation of the WIPO treaties.[112]

The Copyright Term Extension Act added an extra 20 years to the life of all copyrights, including those that were created before the Act was passed.[113] After the new law was passed, copyrights created before 1978 were given a life of 95 years. Works created after 1978 were protected for the life of the author plus 70 years. In addition, works for hire would be covered by copyright for 95 years.[114]

One reason Congress passed the copyright term extension was that, "as a result of increases in human longevity and in parents' average age when their children are born, the pre-CTEA term did not adequately secure 'the right to profit from licensing one's work during one's lifetime and to take pride and comfort in knowing that one's children—and perhaps their children—might also benefit from one's posthumous popularity.'"[115]

Almost immediately after the Copyright Term Extension Act was passed, Eric Eldred, the publisher of Eldritch Press, challenged the new law in the courts. Eldritch Press is a nonprofit publisher of Internet books. Most of the materials that Eldred publishes are in the public domain.[116] As a result of the copyright term extension, many works that were scheduled to be published by Eldritch Press were unavailable.

Eldred claimed that "the new law is unconstitutional because . . . the U.S. Constitution . . . clearly states that the term for copyright [must] be of 'limited times'. . . . [T]he practice of continually extending copyright retroactively means that Congress, in effect, is granting copyright holders more than a 'limited term'. . . . [This extension] limits access and therefore harms the public good. . . . [The copyright term is] beyond any reasonable expectation of the life expectancy of an author, since few authors begin creating works until they are at least adolescents and since there are few, if any, authors who have lived to an age of 110 years."[117] In addition, Eldred claimed that the copyright extension was a restriction on his rights of freedom of speech.

The District Court dismissed the Eldred case with a summary judgment,[118] and the Court of Appeals affirmed this decision.[119] Eldred then appealed the case to the U.S. Supreme Court. In an opinion written by Justice Ginsburg, the Supreme Court affirmed the lower court 7-2. Justices Breyer and Stevens each filed separate dissents.[120]

The Supreme Court found that a term of life of the author plus 70 years was still a limited term, and it was within the power of Congress to fix this term. The opinion stated that: "The CTEA reflects judgments of a kind Congress typically makes, judgments we cannot dismiss as outside the Legislature's domain."[121]

Eldred did no better with the Supreme Court on his First Amendment claim that the copyright monopoly was a violation of freedom of speech. The Court rejected this argument, noting that since the Copyright Clause and the First Amendment were adopted almost simultaneously, the framers of the Constitution did not find the two concepts to be incompatible. In addition, since fair use rights and other types of exceptions are available, the copyright monopoly has been mitigated for free speech purposes. According to the opinion:

> Indeed, copyright's purpose is to *promote* the creation and publication of free expression. . . . "The Framers intended copyright itself to be the engine of free expression. By establishing a marketable right to the use of one's expression, copyright supplies the economic incentive to create and disseminate ideas."[122]

As a result of this decision, the Sonny Bono Copyright Term Extension Act is constitutional, and the additional 20-year period for copyright is currently in effect. Table 3.1 illustrates how long a copyright will last.[123]

Table 3.1. Duration of Copyright

DATE OF WORK	WHEN COPYRIGHT PROTECTION BEGINS	TERM OF COPYRIGHT FOR PERSONAL AUTHOR	TERM OF COPYRIGHT FOR WORKS FOR HIRE (CORPORATE AUTHORS)
Published before 1/1/1923	In public domain	In public domain	In public domain
Published between 1/1/1923 and 12/31/1963	When published with notice of copyright	28 years; can be renewed for 67 years; if not renewed, now in public domain	95 years
Published between 1/1/1964 and 12/31/1977	When published with notice of copyright	95 years	95 years
Created on or after 1/1/1978	When work is fixed in tangible medium of expression	Life of the author plus 70 years	The shorter of: 95 years from publication or 120 years from creation
Created before 1/1/1978 but not published before 12/31/2002	1/1/1978, the effective date of the 1976 Act which eliminated common law copyright	Life of the author plus 70 years or 12/31/2002, whichever is greater	95 years
Created before 1/1/1978 but published before 12/31/2002	1/1/1978 (the 1976 Act includes un-published items)	Life of the author plus 70 years or 2/31/2047, whichever is greater	95 years

Based on Laura "Lolly" Gassaway, *When U.S. Works Pass into the Public Domain*, University of North Carolina Task Force on Intellectual Property (updated November 4, 2003). *Available at* http://www.unc.edu/~unclng/ public-d.htm. Used by permission.

The U.S. Patent System

Just as the United States Constitution guarantees copyright, so too does it protect patents.[124] Librarians, in assisting patrons, must understand some patent law—not to advise but rather to assist in researching the complexities of patent law. Information professionals are also called upon occasionally to help with literature searches in preparation for filing a patent application.

Patents protect inventors, giving them an exclusive monopoly on the use of their product so that the expenses of development can be regained. At the same time, however, patents give knowledge back to the community and encourage the continuance of research and invention by making the patent holder give a detailed description of the invention so that the public can find out how it works.

There are two kinds of patents. *Utility patents* are granted for inventions, while *design patents* are granted for ornamental designs for articles of manufacture. Utility patents are valid for 20 years from the date of issue or 20 years from the application filing date, while design patents are valid for 14 years.

A utility patent covers "[a]ny new and useful process, machine, manufacture, or composition of matter. . . . Inventions can be electrical, mechanical, or chemical in nature."[125] Some examples of utility patents include the microwave oven, genetically engineered bacteria for cleaning up oil spills, a computerized method of running cash-management accounts, and a method for curing rubber.[126] In the computer realm, utility patents can include networking and communication protocols, interfaces, encryption techniques, data compression, etc.[127]

In addition to utility patents, there are design patents. Design patents are granted for devices that are new, original, and ornamental. Some examples of design patents include a design for the sole of running shoes, a design for sterling silver tableware, or a design for a water fountain.[128] The creator of a design will usually apply for trademark protection instead of using a design patent, since trademarks have the potential to continue indefinitely. (For more information on trademarks, see **Chapter 6**, *Trademark and Trade Secret Law*.) Design patents are generally not suitable for protecting elements of Internet-related software processes and are very rarely used as such.

The United States allows the inventor to file a provisional patent application. This application gives the inventor protection for one year. During that time, the inventor can do more research, get his or her paperwork in order, and work with the patent agent to perfect the application for a regular (non-provisional) patent. If the application for the non-provisional patent is filed within one year of the provisional application, the item will be protected from the date of the provisional application. If the non-provisional application is not filed within one year of the provisional application, the U.S. Patent and Trademark Office considers the provisional patent to be "abandoned."

According to the U.S. Code, "Whoever invents or discovers any new and useful process, machine, manufacture, or composition of matter, or any new and useful improvement thereof, may obtain a patent . . . ."[129] In order for the invention to qualify for a patent, the subject matter must be unique and "useful," and must not be obvious from the "prior art" ("prior art" refers to inventions that already exist or have been described).[130] The item must have *some* beneficial use in society; it does not need to have commercial potential.

For example, in the 1890s a patent was issued for a device that allows the user to take a shower while riding a bicycle. Although not "useful" by commercial standards (i.e., not practical), this device met the guidelines for protection by patent, since the item worked and had a use. This is an example of an item that is not practical, although in the area of patent law it is considered "useful."

To qualify for patent protection, the item must be new and nonobvious from the "prior art." The invention must not have been known or used by others, or described in print prior to the time it was created by the applicant. Nor can the inventor get a patent if the item was logically obvious from previously published works or from previous inventions. "The invention must be sufficiently different from existing technology and knowledge so that, at the time the invention was made, the invention as a whole would not have been obvious to a person having ordinary skill in that field. This requirement makes sure patents are only granted for real advances, not for mere technical tinkering or modifications of existing inventions by skilled technicians."[131]

The inventor must file a patent application (either provisional or non-provisional) within one year of the time that he or she publicly describes the item. Otherwise it will be considered to be prior art. This is different from the rule in other countries. In most countries, an invention will lose its patentability once the item has been described or disclosed in public.

In some circumstances, the invention may be new, useful, and nonobvious from the prior art, but it may be based upon another device that is still protected by a patent. In this circumstance, the USPTO will grant a patent for the item, but the patent holder is precluded from marketing the device without obtaining a license from the owner of the underlying device. As one patent agent has said, "There is no right to practice your patent once you receive it."[132]

The waterbed is a good example of an invention that was described first in print and therefore did not qualify for patent protection. In 1961, the noted science fiction writer Robert Heinlein published his most famous work, *Stranger in a Strange Land*.[133] In the novel, Heinlein's protagonist, Michael Valentine Smith, rested on a waterbed while in the hospital. At the time the book was published, there was no such device.

Heinlein, who was trained as an engineer, described the workings of a waterbed in great detail. He had already thought through many issues such as the pump mechanism, floor load factors, thermostat controls, and even safety interfaces to prevent electrical shock. Heinlein thought of this device as being a hospital bed, and was surprised when it became a hot-selling consumer item.[134]

Soon after *Stranger in a Strange Land* was published, an inventor filed a patent application for a waterbed. As a result of Heinlein's description, however, the patent was denied as being obvious from the prior art. In most cases, description in a fictional work would not have mattered. Fictional works generally don't give enough information about inventions to qualify as prior art. In this case, however, the significant details that Heinlein provided were enough to cause the patent application to be denied.[135]

At the time that the waterbed was created, a patent searcher probably would not have found Heinlein's description in a fictional work, unless he or she happened to be a science fiction fan. The description of a waterbed was not included in the type of professional or popular science journals that would have been searched. However, now that library databases and Internet searches are available, patent searchers should be able to find fictional depictions of inventions. This experience with the waterbed patent application emphasizes the necessity of checking all sources of information and not just limiting a patent search to professional literature.

Since the original Patent Act was passed in 1790, the United States has always given priority to the first person to invent something, rather than to the first person to file for a patent. The "first-to-invent" rule has led to a large number of legal challenges. The United States is the only country to use the "first-to-invent" rule; every other country uses the "first-to-file" rule. The development of the telephone provides an excellent example of the "first-to-invent" rule:

There's a well known tale that [Alexander Graham] Bell beat another inventor, Elisha Gray, to the patent office by a few hours. While true, it's not the whole story. Bell filed a patent application, a claim that "I have invented." Gray, on the other hand, filed a caveat, a document used at the time to claim "I am working on inventing." Priority in American patent law follows date of invention, not date of filing. Still, filing first helped Bell avoid a possible costly and time-consuming dispute. The U.S. Patent Office issued patent #174,465 to Bell on March 7, 1876.[136]

One important piece of legislation that is currently pending before Congress (Fall 2005) is a new patent act which would be the first complete overhaul of the system in many years. This bill is H.R. 2795, the Patent Reform Act of 2005. Although the patent bill makes a variety of revisions in the patent laws, the most important changes involve who obtains priority in a patent challenge, and a tighter definition of prior art.

The patent reform bill changes the legal standards for issuing a patent to make them more in accord with the rules in other jurisdictions which use the "first-to-file" rule instead of the "first-to-invent" rule as their standard. The new patent bill would change the United States standard to "first-to-file." Had the United States used the "first-to-file" standard in the 19th century, and had Alexander Graham Bell waited two hours to file for a patent, the telecommunications industry would be singing the praises of Elisha Gray instead of Bell (and BellSouth would be GraySouth!).

The change to the "first-to-file" rule will help to harmonize the United States patent system with patent laws in other countries, and will also help to eliminate costly challenges to patents. In addition, the change will help the United States uphold its guarantees under international treaties.

The new patent bill also contains a good working definition of the term "prior art." Prior art includes situations where:

(1) the claimed invention was patented, described in a printed publication, or otherwise publicly known–
  (A) more than one year before the effective filing date of the claimed invention; or
  (B) before the effective filing date of the claimed invention, other than through disclosures made by the inventor or a joint inventor or . . .

(2) the claimed invention was described in a patent issued . . . or in an application for patent published or deemed published . . . in which the patent or application . . . names another inventor and was effectively filed before the effective filing date of the claimed invention.[137]

Although the new patent bill contains a number of changes dealing with procedures and remedies, the main changes in the law are the "first-to-file" rule and the stricter definition of prior art. This definition will put patent searchers on notice that they will need to conduct a thorough search, not only of scientific literature but also of all types of publications. (A search of this type would have picked up the waterbed description by Robert Heinlein.) In addition, the "first-to-file" rule will help small businesses, since studies suggest that "first-to-invent" challenges "are more often used by large entities to challenge the priority of *small entities*, not the reverse."[138] [Emphasis added.]

Conclusion

There are many issues relating to intellectual property, issues about which information professionals need to be aware. Copyright laws protect books and literary works—and many other types of materials as well. Every employee needs to be aware of the *Work for Hire* doctrine and should always check the policies of his or her employer. Patent laws protect "useful" and "nonobvious" inventions, as long as they have not been previously described and are not logical continuations of previous devices.

In order to obtain a utility patent or a design patent, you must file an application with the U.S. Patent and Trademark Office. The application must include the complete design plans and specifications for the invention, along with a working model. The patent goes to the first person to invent, not the first person to apply, so proving that your device was invented first can cause a competitor's patent application to be denied. If passed by Congress, the Patent Reform Act of 2005 (H.R. 2795) would change the "first-to-invent" rule to a "first-to-file" rule.

The American system of intellectual property is complicated, but libraries and archives must know the law in order to stay within the law. Remember that ignorance of the law is no excuse. In order to stay legal in our day-to-day lives, information professionals need to be aware of the rules of intellectual property. Only then can we properly advise our patrons and only then can libraries and archives stay within the law.

4

Fair Use and Intellectual Property Rights: The Basics of Using Information Legally[1]

> Jim is writing an article about a famous author. As part of his research, Jim has found unpublished letters and manuscripts. He would like to quote some of this material in his article. How much material can Jim quote, and what restrictions does he need to be aware of?

Although the copyright laws prohibit duplication of copyrighted works, there is a provision for making limited copies. This provision is known as "fair use." Fair use allows users of copyrighted materials to make copies "for purposes such as criticism, comment, news reporting, teaching (including multiple copies for classroom use), scholarship, or research."[2] Under the Federal copyright statute, fair use applies to both published and unpublished works.[3] The fair use doctrine allows us to quote copyrighted material, and fair use helps to preserve our Freedom of Speech rights when using copyrighted works.

One important point to remember is that fair use is a defense that can be employed when an individual has already been found to have infringed a copyright. Fair use is *not* an exception to copyright. Rather, it is an argument that is presented in order to avoid liability for violating copyright. This is a very important distinction, since the fair use argument can only be employed if in the first place the person admits to violating copyright restrictions (or has been judged in violation by a court). In effect, the defendant is saying, "Yes, I violated copyright, but I was entitled to do it."

Fair use "allows copying of protectible expression to such a quantitative or qualitative degree that absent a valid fair use claim, judgment for the plaintiff is mandated."[4] In other words, without the fair use doctrine, the copyright owner would win a lawsuit. The concept of fair use is very different from the copyright exceptions for libraries, class-rooms, etc. Under those circumstances, the defendant is saying that he or she did not violate copyright law at all.

Because fair use is a defense rather than an exception, the judicial interpretations of the doctrine are more closely related to the facts of the cases themselves, meaning that there are still many questions as to what constitutes a fair use of an item. However, there are certain principles that have become generally accepted over time.

What Is Fair Use?

Although originally a matter of common law, the fair use doctrine was included in the 1976 Copyright Act. Section 107 deals with the factors that are used to determine fair use. The section reads:

> Notwithstanding the provisions of sections 106 and 106A, the fair use of a copyrighted work, including such use by reproduction in copies or phonorecords or by any other means specified by that section, for purposes such as criticism, comment, news reporting, teaching (including multiple copies for classroom use), scholarship, or research, is not an infringement of copyright. In determining whether the use made of a work in any particular case is a fair use the factors to be considered shall include–
>
> 1) the purpose and character of the use, including whether such use is of a commercial nature or is for nonprofit educational purposes;
>
> 2) the nature of the copyrighted work;
>
> 3) the amount and substantiality of the portion used in relation to the copyrighted work as a whole; and
>
> 4) the effect of the use upon the potential market for or value of the copyrighted work.
>
> The fact that a work is unpublished shall not itself bar a finding of fair use if such finding is made upon consideration of all the above factors.[5]

The four factors above work together to determine whether or not a particular situation constitutes fair use. For example, reproducing a factual or noncommercial work is more likely to be fair use than reproducing a literary or commercial work. A brief quote in a review is more likely to be acceptable than publishing longer excerpts. Also, if you are setting yourself up in competition with the original, or if your actions will cause the market for the original to diminish or disappear, you are probably not going to be making fair use of the material. If you cannot establish fair use, you could be held liable for copyright infringement.

A. The Nature of the Use

One important question involves the "commercial" nature of the use. This point is a little more complicated than it sounds. For example, suppose that the library at Generic State University, a nonprofit state-assisted educational institution, makes copies of articles for faculty members. This practice is allowed under the fair use doctrine.

Once a for-profit business is involved, however, the results are different. For example, in the case of *American Geophysical Union et al. v. Texaco, Inc.*,[6] the Texaco corporate library copied articles and sent them to scientists. The American Geophysical Union, a publisher of journals, sued Texaco for copyright violation. The District Court found that there was no fair use of the materials,[7] and the Court of Appeals affirmed this decision. Although the case was supposed to go to the U.S. Supreme Court, the parties eventually settled out of court.[8] As a result, the Court of Appeals decision is currently the most authoritative statement governing fair use in a for-profit setting. According to the opinion, "courts will not sustain a claimed defense of fair use when the secondary use can fairly be characterized as a form of 'commercial exploitation,' i.e., when the copier directly and exclusively acquires conspicuous financial rewards from its use of the copyrighted material."[9]

Other cases have involved the manufacturing of course packs by such copy shops as *Kinko's Copies*[10] and *Michigan Document Services*.[11] As with the *Texaco* opinion, these cases held that the commercial nature of the businesses, and the fact that these copies were subsequently sold, meant that the copy shops needed permission to duplicate in order to avoid copyright infringement. It did not matter that the materials were being put to an educational use.

The cases on course packs have a number of implications for libraries. As a result of the *Texaco* case, a proprietary (private for-profit) educational institution such as the University of Phoenix would have to obtain copyright permission in order to make copies, even though a nonprofit educational institution such as the University of Arizona could do the same thing, and the duplication would be considered fair use.

B. The Nature of the Copyrighted Work

The second factor in determining fair use, the nature of the copyrighted work, involves an analysis of whether the work is something that is fictional or literary in nature as compared to a work that is nonfiction or factual. The courts are going to be more disposed to finding fair use if the item in question is an academic or scholarly work rather than fictional or literary, particularly if proper attribution is given. Similarly, copying or quoting factual materials is more likely to be deemed fair use by a court than copying or quoting fictional or literary works.

Facts and news reports are not protected by copyright, although compilations of facts (and compilations of news reports) may be protected. It all depends on whether there was creativity in the selection and arrangement of the compilation, a question that was investigated in the case of *Feist Publications, Inc. v. Rural Telephone Service Co., Inc.*[12]

In the *Feist* case, Rural Telephone Service Company was exactly what its name implies, i.e., a rural telephone company service. The company is located in Kansas. As a telephone provider, Rural is required by Kansas law to publish a phone book annually, including both white and yellow pages. As with most phone companies, Rural gives away the books free to subscribers, but makes money by selling ads in the yellow pages.

Feist Publications, Inc., is a company whose business is publishing area-wide telephone books. Its books cover multiple communities, some of which are served by different telephone utilities; in fact, the case before the U.S. Supreme Court involved a phone book that covered the area of 11 phone companies.

As with Rural, Feist makes its money by selling ads in its yellow pages. Rural obtained information for the phone books by using its subscriber lists, while Feist licensed the rights to the numbers from local phone providers. Of the 11 phone companies, only Rural refused to license its information to Feist:

> Unable to license Rural's white pages listings, Feist used them without Rural's consent. Feist began by removing several thousand listings that fell outside the geographic range of its area-wide directory, then hired personnel to investigate the 4,935 that remained. These employees verified the data reported by Rural and sought to obtain additional information. As a result, a typical Feist listing includes the individual's street address; most of Rural's listings do not.

Notwithstanding these additions, however, 1,309 of the 46,878 listings in Feist's 1983 directory were identical to listings in Rural's 1982-1983 white pages. Four of these were fictitious listings that Rural had inserted into its directory to detect copying.[13]

Because Feist used the listings in Rural's area without permission, Rural sued Feist for copyright infringement. The District Court found in favor of Rural, stating that telephone directories were copyrightable material and that there was no fair use in this situation. The 10th Circuit Court of Appeals affirmed the decision. However, the U.S. Supreme Court was not inclined to rubber-stamp these results, stating that the lower courts had missed the point and had asked the wrong questions. According to the Supreme Court, the case involved the interplay between factual compilations and the originality requirement for copyrighted materials. Facts can't be copyrighted because they are not original. On the other hand, compilations of facts may be copyrighted. The U.S. Supreme Court ruled that:

> This case concerns the interaction of two well-established propositions. The first is that facts are not copyrightable; the other, that compilations of facts generally are. Each of these propositions possesses an impeccable pedigree. That there can be no valid copyright in facts is universally understood. The most fundamental axiom of copyright law is that "no author may copyright his ideas or the facts he narrates."[14] Rural wisely concedes this point, noting in its brief that "facts and discoveries, of course, are not themselves subject to copyright protection."[15] At the same time, however, it is beyond dispute that compilations of facts are within the subject matter of copyright. Compilations were expressly mentioned in the Copyright Act of 1909, and again in the Copyright Act of 1976.
>
> There is an undeniable tension between these two propositions. Many compilations consist of nothing but raw data—i.e., wholly factual information not accompanied by any original written expression. On what basis may one claim a copyright in such a work? Common sense tells us that 100 uncopyrightable facts do not magically change their status when gathered together in one place. Yet copyright law seems to contemplate that compilations that consist exclusively of facts are potentially within its scope.[16]

The reason why facts are not copyrightable involves the originality requirement in copyright. In order for an author to obtain a copyright, the material must be original. The Supreme Court stated that: "The vast majority of works make the grade quite easily, as they possess some creative spark, 'no matter how crude, humble or obvious' it might be."[17] However, the Court also reminded us that: "The originality requirement is *constitutionally mandated* for all works."[18] [Emphasis in original.] The opinion continues, saying: "The distinction is one between creation and discovery: The first person to find and report a particular fact has not created the fact; he or she has merely discovered its existence."[19]

Compilations usually are protected because the editor has selected and arranged them. "These choices as to selection and arrangement, so long as they are made independently by the compiler and entail a minimal degree of creativity, are sufficiently original that Congress may protect such compilations through the copyright laws. Thus, even a directory that contains absolutely no protectible written expression, only facts, meets the constitutional minimum for copyright protection if it features an original selection or arrangement."[20] [Citations omitted.]

In the *Feist* case, however, the Supreme Court found that the subscriber's names and phone numbers were facts, and therefore were not copyrightable. The *Feist* opinion stated:

> This is a straight-forward application of the originality requirement. Facts are never original, so the compilation author can claim originality, if at all, *only in the way the facts are presented.* [Emphasis added.] To that end, the statute dictates that the principal focus should be on whether the selection, coordination, and arrangement are sufficiently original to merit protection. . . . Certainly, the raw data does not satisfy the originality requirement. Rural may have been the first to discover and report the names, towns, and telephone numbers of its subscribers, but this data does not "owe its origin" to Rural. Rather, these bits of information are uncopyrightable facts; they existed before Rural reported them and would have continued to exist if Rural had never published a telephone directory. . . . [B]y no stretch of the imagination could [Rural] be called the author."[21] [Citations omitted.]

The Court ruled that the arrangement of facts did not meet the originality requirement. The opinion contained two reasons why the telephone directories were non-original. The arrangement was not picked by Rural, but rather was required by Kansas law. Also, the Court held that:

> The white pages do nothing more than list Rural's subscribers in alphabetical order. . . . But there is nothing remotely creative about arranging names alphabetically in a white pages directory. It is an age-old practice, firmly rooted in tradition and so commonplace that it has come to be expected as a matter of course. It is not only un-

original, it is practically inevitable. This time-honored tradition does not possess the minimal creative spark required by the Copyright Act and the Constitution.[22]

The ruling in the *Feist* case settled the question of what constitutes originality for a compilation of facts, and helped to foster competition in the marketplace for telephone directories. However, this case has also been very significant in terms of copyright law, having been cited in the *2 Live Crew* and *Tasini* cases, as well as many other recent copyright decisions. The *Feist* case helped to define what constitutes originality, and so contributed to an understanding of what constitutes fair use.

C. Amount Used, Substantiality, and Effect on Potential Market

As we have seen elsewhere in discussions of fair use, the amount of material copied is an important factor. This is one question, however, that really doesn't have an easy answer. What might be considered a reasonable and limited portion of the work in some cases may be considered excessive in others.

One myth that people often believe is that copying a single chapter of a book is fair use. While it may be permissible for a library to lend a chapter under the library copyright exception in section 108, this provision has nothing to do with fair use. (For more information, see the section on exceptions to copyright law for libraries and archives in *Chapter 3, Copyright and Patent Law*.) On the contrary, the *Kinko's Copies*[23] and *Michigan Document Services*[24] cases found copyright infringement to exist even in the copying of a single chapter.[25]

Certainly when larger amounts of material are used, a finding of infringement becomes more likely and a finding of fair use becomes less likely.[26] "The larger the volume (or the greater the importance) of what is taken, the greater the affront to the interests of the copyright owner, and the less likely that a taking will qualify as a fair use."[27] As one court put it:

> There are no absolute rules as to how much of a copyrighted work may be copied and still be considered a fair use. In some instances, copying a work wholesale has been held to be fair use,[28] while in other cases taking only a tiny portion of the original work has been

held unfair. Questions of fair use may turn on qualitative assess-
ments. "One writer might take all the vital part of another's book,
though it might be but a small proportion of the book in quantity."[29]

As courts have struggled with this issue, so have academics writing in
law review articles. In many cases, amount and substantiality work
together, along with the impact on the original's market. Frequently,
the issue comes down to whether the heart of the original work was
reproduced. One article has stated:

> Just as the percentage of the original copyrighted work used is
> important, consideration of whether the portion of the material
> used—large or small—constitutes a central or critical part of the
> copyright owner's work is required by substantiality analysis. . . .
> Hence, if the "essence" of the copyright holder's work is not used
> and there is no adverse market impact, use of a rather extensive por-
> tion of copyrighted material may still qualify as a fair use.[30]

An important case that discussed whether a use was substantial was
Harper & Row, Publishers, Inc. v. Nation Enterprises.[31] This case involved the autobiography of former president Gerald Ford.[32] When
President Ford wrote his autobiography, *The Nation* magazine published an article about the book and included an excerpt of about 300
words.[33] Under normal circumstances, this short excerpt would not be
considered to be substantial. However, in this case, the part that was
quoted was the part that dealt with Ford's decision to pardon ex-
President Richard Nixon. This portion of the book was described as
being among "the most interesting and moving parts of the entire
manuscript."[34] The Supreme Court stated that:

> In absolute terms, the words actually quoted were an insubstan-
> tial portion of "A Time to Heal." The District Court, however, found
> that "[The] Nation took what was essentially the heart of the book."[35]
> We believe the Court of Appeals erred in overruling the District
> Judge's evaluation of the qualitative nature of the taking. . . .[36] The
> portions actually quoted were . . . among the most powerful passages
> in those chapters. [The publisher of The Nation] testified that he used
> verbatim excerpts . . . precisely because they qualitatively embodied
> Ford's distinctive expression.
>
> As the statutory language indicates, a taking may not be excused
> merely because it is insubstantial with respect to the *infringing* work.
> As Judge Learned Hand cogently remarked, "no plagiarist can excuse
> the wrong by showing how much of his work he did not pirate."[37]
> Conversely, the fact that a substantial portion of the infringing work

was copied verbatim is evidence of the qualitative value of the copied material, both to the originator and to the plagiarist who seeks to profit from marketing someone else's copyrighted expression.[38] [Internal citations contained in endnotes.]

Since President Ford's decision to pardon ex-President Nixon was the "heart of the book," the excerpt was found to be substantial. In fact, the excerpt had a definite impact on the market for the work. *Time Magazine* had previously agreed to publish a section of the book. A portion of *Time*'s fee was for the copyright permission. After *The Nation* published its article, *Time* canceled the planned excerpt and refused to pay the remaining amount of the fee. The decision to pardon Nixon was considered the main reason most people would read the book, and so the unauthorized excerpt had a significant effect on the book's market.

Unfortunately, there is no standard test for what constitutes a legal amount of borrowed material as opposed to a substantial amount. However, when the amount used is combined with the effect on the market for the original, it does become clear on a case-by-case basis whether or not a fair use is being made. The best advice I can give is to use as little borrowed material as possible, while making sure that you are not using the "heart" of the work or reproducing something so substantial that you would have an impact on the market for the original work.

D. Can an Artist Plagiarize Himself? The Case of John Fogerty

One fair use issue from the 1980s sounds like the punch line to a bad joke. The question is whether an artist can plagiarize himself or herself. It turns out that the answer is "No Way!"

In 1969, the band Creedence Clearwater Revival (also known as CCR) recorded the song "Run Through the Jungle" on one of the greatest albums of the classic rock era. The album, released by Fantasy Records, was called *Cosmo's Factory*.[39] The same year, CCR recorded "Bad Moon Rising" on the album *Green River*.[40] Lead singer John Fogerty wrote both of these songs, as well as most of the other music recorded by CCR. In order to obtain their recording contract, Fogerty and CCR had signed away their rights in all of their music.

CCR broke up in 1972. Once the band was no longer recording for Fantasy Records, the record company began putting pressure on Fogerty. For nearly 15 years, Fogerty did not perform any of his songs due to the record company's demands for the payment of royalties. Fogerty finally began performing his work again in 1986, starting with a concert in Aleppo, Syria.

Meanwhile, the singer-songwriter had released new material. His 1985 album, *Centerfield*, is considered to be the masterful reappearance of an old friend. One of the biggest hits on the album was a song called "The Old Man Down the Road."[41] The return of John Fogerty thrilled many of his fans, but not the people at Fantasy Records. Claiming that there was a similarity between "Run Through the Jungle" and "The Old Man Down the Road," Fantasy sued Fogerty for plagiarism and copyright infringement.[42]

When the case came to trial, Fogerty was forced to admit that there were substantial similarities between the songs, and that he had been exposed to "Run Through the Jungle" before he wrote "The Old Man Down the Road." (Naturally, since Fogerty wrote the first song!) These admissions seemed to fulfill the elements of a copyright infringement case.

Fogerty's only defense was that he had simply written both songs in his own style, and that it was impossible for an artist to plagiarize himself. When the case came to trial, the jury ruled in favor of Fogerty, finding (as a ruling of fact) that using one's own style does not constitute plagiarism, and that it is not possible for an artist to plagiarize himself or herself. It is fair use for us to use our own style, no matter to whom we sell the rights.

With this case, Fogerty struck a blow for artists everywhere, showing that his work was more important than the label on which he recorded. Thanks to John Fogerty, we know that artists can't be sued for using their own style. You can't plagiarize yourself, and an artist's style doesn't constitute copyright infringement.

Fair Use and the Constitution: A First Amendment Right?

Recently there have been some suggestions that fair use is actually a constitutional principle, and therefore applies to common law state copyright as well as to the Federal copyright statute. One case which considered the fair use doctrine in terms of Freedom of Speech rights was *Hemingway v. Random House, Inc.*[43] (The *Hemingway* case will be discussed again later in this chapter in the context of fair use for unpublished materials.)

In the *Hemingway* case, author A. E. Hotchner wrote a book entitled *Papa Hemingway: A Personal Memoir*. The book included the text
of many conversations between Hotchner and Hemingway, as well as
quotations from some of Hemingway's writings. Hemingway's widow
and his estate sued Hotchner and the publisher, Random House. The
suit contended that the book violated Hemingway's common law copyright and constituted unfair competition with the works of Ernest
Hemingway.[44]

In the *Hemingway* case, the court considered the constitutional
status of fair use in the context of unpublished and unprepared conversations. One of the plaintiff's claims was that Ernest Hemingway's
conversations were subject to common law copyright. According to the
court's opinion:

> Were anyone to have common-law copyright in his mere con-
> versations (as opposed to prepared lectures or speeches), then the
> same right would have to extend to everyone. The effect on the free-
> dom of speech and press would be revolutionary. It is a basic tradi-
> tion of our society that . . . what any man says or does may be re-
> ported, quoted or written about in the interest of maintaining the free-
> dom of access to all kinds of information which may be of legitimate
> interest. It is generally left to writers and publishers to determine
> what is of such interest. Only in rare cases does the law interfere with
> the freedom, and then only to protect some paramount interest, such
> as the national security, or the individual's right to be free from mali-
> cious falsehood or invasion of privacy. The limitation drawn to pro-
> tect such interests have [sic] generally been as narrow as the courts
> could make them.[45]

According to Professor David Lange of Duke Law School, "Fair
use gives the Constitution breathing space between the limits on expression inherent in copyright, and the freedom of expression guaranteed by the First Amendment."[46] This quotation itself is actually an
application of Professor Lange's thesis, since it came from a lecture
covered by state common law copyright. One of the main points of
Professor Lange's presentation was that there is a constitutional problem with a view of copyright so strict that reasonable quotations are not
allowed. Under the *Hemingway* case, the protections of fair use still
exist even though the copyright is common law rather than statutory
law.

In addition to common law copyright, there have been several
cases which have dealt with constitutional arguments in favor of fair
use in terms of the Copyright Act. One decision that discussed the

constitutional background of fair use was the Betamax case, *Sony Corporation of America et al. v. Universal City Studios, Inc*,[47] which was discussed in **Chapter 3**, *Copyright and Patent Law.* According to the *Sony* case, "the purpose of this use [VCR recordings] served the public interest in increasing access to television programming, an interest that 'is consistent with the First Amendment policy of providing the fullest possible access to information through the public airwaves.'"[48] [Citation omitted.]

The Supreme Court has also found that parody, which is protected by the First Amendment, is allowed by the fair use doctrine. In the past 20 years, there have been three significant cases involving constitutional protection for parody under the First Amendment. These cases were *Hustler Magazine and Larry C. Flynt v. Jerry Falwell*,[49] *Luther R. Campbell aka luke skyywalker, et al. v. Acuff-Rose Music, Inc.*,[50] and *SunTrust Bank v. Houghton Mifflin Company*.[51] While *Flynt v. Falwell* was not about intellectual property, it laid the foundation for the other two cases.

Why are librarians and archivists interested in parody? Because the information profession views anything that deals with information as being within their purview. Therefore, even though parody as such doesn't have much to do with traditional library services, these cases are often discussed in library publications, and the American Library Association filed briefs in the *2 Live Crew* and *Wind Done Gone* cases. In addition, when someone sues to stop the publication of an item, it is a form of censorship. Therefore, librarians and archivists are always interested in copyright issues as they pertain to access to information.

Larry Flynt is the publisher of *Hustler Magazine*, and Jerry Falwell is a minister and an important public figure. In the November 1983 issue of *Hustler*, there was a cartoon with a picture of Falwell. The cartoon was entitled "Jerry Falwell talks about his first time."[52] At this time, Campari Liqueur had been running a set of ads in which various celebrities talked about their first times, meaning the first time that they tried Campari Liqueur.[53] "[T]he ads clearly played on the sexual double entendre of the general subject of 'first times.'"[54]

The *Hustler* cartoon was a parody of the Campari ads, and consisted of a fictional interview of Jerry Falwell. In the cartoon, Falwell "states that his 'first time' was during a drunken incestuous rendezvous with his mother in an outhouse. The *Hustler* parody portrays respondent and his mother as drunk and immoral, and suggests that respondent is a hypocrite who preaches only when he is drunk. In small print at the bottom of the page, the ad contains the disclaimer, 'ad parody—

not to be taken seriously.' The magazine's table of contents also lists the ad as 'Fiction; Ad and Personality Parody.'"[55]

Soon after the cartoon appeared, Falwell sued *Hustler Magazine* and Larry Flynt for invasion of privacy, libel, and intentional infliction of emotional distress.[56] The District Court found in favor of Flynt on the invasion of privacy and libel claims, stating that "the ad parody could not 'reasonably be understood as describing actual facts. . . .'" However, the District Court awarded damages to Falwell for intentional infliction of emotional distress.[57] The Court of Appeals affirmed this decision.[58]

Upon appeal, the U.S. Supreme Court found unanimously for Larry Flynt.[59] The basis of this decision was that parody is protected speech under the First Amendment. According to the Court's opinion:

> This case presents us with a novel question involving First Amendment limitations upon a State's authority to protect its citizens from the intentional infliction of emotional distress. We must decide whether a public figure may recover damages for emotional harm caused by the publication of an ad parody offensive to him. . . . Respondent would have us find that a State's interest in protecting public figures from emotional distress is sufficient to deny First Amendment protection to speech that is patently offensive . . . even when that speech could not reasonably have been interpreted as stating actual facts. . . . This we decline to do. . . .[60]

The Supreme Court stated that "[w]ere we to hold otherwise, there can be little doubt that political cartoonists and satirists would be subjected to damages awards without any showing that their work falsely defamed its subject." The Court ruled:

> We conclude that public figures and public officials may not recover for the tort of intentional infliction of emotional distress by reason of publications such as the one here at issue without showing in addition that the publication contains a false statement of fact which was made with "actual malice. . . ."[61]

The next case to examine the role of parody was *Campbell v. Acuff-Rose Music, Inc.*,[62] also known as the *2 Live Crew* case. Luther Campbell was the leader of the hip-hop group 2 Live Crew and wrote a parody of the Roy Orbison song "Oh, Pretty Woman."[63] 2 Live Crew felt that the pretty woman in Orbison's song was really being exploited as a woman because of her body. The purpose of the song was to point out our society's double standards with respect to women and sexuality, and to show that Orbison's song, rather than being a sweet rendition of a young man looking for a woman, was in fact both a product of and a perpetuating factor in our social fabric.

The Supreme Court pointed out that: "Judge Nelson, dissenting below, came to the same conclusion, that the 2 Live Crew song 'was clearly intended to ridicule the white-bread original' and 'reminds us that sexual congress with nameless streetwalkers is not necessarily the stuff of romance and is not necessarily without its consequences. The singers . . . have the same thing on their minds as did the lonely man with the nasal voice, but here there is no hint of wine and roses.'"[64]

Although the District Court found in favor of 2 Live Crew, the Court of Appeals reversed. However, the U.S. Supreme Court found in favor of 2 Live Crew, ruling that parody was clearly within the scope of fair use. The Court said:

> While we might not assign a high rank to the parodic element here, we think it fair to say that 2 Live Crew's song reasonably could be perceived as commenting on the original or criticizing it, to some degree. . . . [The] words can be taken as a comment on the naivete of the original of an earlier day, as a rejection of its sentiment that ignores the ugliness of street life and the debasement that it signifies. It is this joinder of reference and ridicule that marks off the author's choice of parody from the other types of comment and criticism that traditionally have had a claim to fair use protection as transformative works.[65]

After *Flynt* and *2 Live Crew*, the concept of parody seemed to be generally established; however, there was still additional room for fine-tuning. The case which provided that enhancement was *The Wind Done Gone*. SunTrust Bank is the trustee for the Margaret Mitchell Trust, which owns the copyright to the classic Southern novel *Gone with the Wind*. In 2000, the Mitchell Trust sued for copyright infringement after finding out that Houghton Mifflin Company was planning to publish a work by first-time novelist Alice Randall entitled *The Wind Done Gone*. The work took Mitchell's novel and turned it on its head, re-telling the story from the perspective of a black slave who was Scarlett O'Hara's half-sister. Randall's book used Mitchell's situations and characters to show the historic problems of slavery and racism, as well as how Mitchell's book glamorized the slave owners and glossed over the problem of slavery.

The Mitchell Trust filed suit against Houghton Mifflin alleging copyright infringement, violation of trademark under the Lanham Act, and deceptive trade practices. The District Court granted a preliminary injunction banning the publication, sale, or distribution of Randall's novel.[66] Upon appeal, the 11th Circuit Court examined "to what extent a critic may use a work to communicate her criticism of the work without infringing the copyright in that work," and reviewed the relationship between copyright and the First Amendment.[67]

According to the opinion:

> The case before us calls for an analysis of whether a preliminary injunction was properly granted against an alleged infringer who, relying largely on the doctrine of fair use, made use of another's copyright for comment and criticism. As discussed herein, *copyright does not immunize a work from comment and criticism.* . . . As we turn to the analysis required in this case, we must remain cognizant of the First Amendment protections interwoven into copyright law.[68]

The court analyzed the history of the fair use defense, and the previous parody cases, and then stated:

> Before considering a claimed fair-use defense based on parody, however, the Supreme Court has required that we ensure that "a parodic character may reasonably be perceived" in the allegedly infringing work. . . .[69] For purposes of our fair-use analysis, we will treat a work as a parody if its aim is to comment upon or criticize a prior work by appropriating elements of the original in creating a new artistic, as opposed to scholarly or journalistic, work. Under this definition, the parodic character of TWDG is clear. TWDG is not a general commentary upon the Civil-War-era American South, but a specific criticism of and rejoinder to the depiction of slavery and the relationships between blacks and whites in GWTW. The fact that Randall chose to convey her criticisms of GWTW through a work of fiction, which she contends is a more powerful vehicle for her message than a scholarly article, does not, in and of itself, deprive TWDG of fair-use protection.[70] [Citations omitted.]

The court went on to say:

> TWDG is more than an abstract, pure fictional work. It is principally and purposefully a critical statement that seeks to rebut and destroy the perspective, judgments, and mythology of GWTW. Randall's literary goal is to explode the romantic, idealized portrait of the antebellum South during and after the Civil War.[71]

One argument that the trust made against Randall's novel was that it was not a "funny" book. Their premise was that parody meant that the book had to be "funny," or it wasn't a parody. The Court of Appeals considered that argument, but did not agree. Looking to the decision in the *2 Live Crew* case, the court found that the purpose of parody was social criticism. While this criticism often takes the form of humor, a work doesn't always have to be humorous in order to be a parody.

The court also considered the amount of material that *The Wind Done Gone* took from *Gone with the Wind*. After all, this was an entire novel, rather than a fleeting reference. Again, the court looked to *2 Live Crew* for guidance, stating that:

> The Supreme Court in [*2 Live Crew*] did not require that parodists take the bare minimum amount of copyright material necessary to conjure up the original work. . . . "Parody frequently needs to be more than a fleeting evocation of an original in order to make its humorous point. . . . [Parody uses] the original as a known element of modern culture and [thus is] contributing something new for humorous effect or commentary."[72]

The Court of Appeals opinion went on to say:

> A use does not necessarily become infringing the moment it does more than simply conjure up another work. Rather, "once enough has been taken to assure identification, how much more is reasonable will depend, say, [1] on the extent to which the [work's] *overriding purpose and character is to parody* the original or, in contrast, [2] the likelihood that the parody may serve as *a market substitute* for the original."[73] As to the first point, it is manifest that TWDG's *raison d'etre* is to parody GWTW. The second point indicates that any material we suspect is "extraneous" to the parody is unlawful only if it negatively effects [sic] the potential market for or value of the original copyright.[74] [Citations omitted.]

The Court of Appeals found that *The Wind Done Gone* was a commentary on the social situations described in Margaret Mitchell's book, and therefore was protected as parody under the First Amendment. It is important to remember that before the preliminary injunction granted in this case, no book in the history of the United States (not counting allegedly "obscene" works or books containing libelous or classified information) had ever been banned from publication by the government. Thanks to the relationship between parody and the First Amendment, *The Wind Done Gone* was able to be published, and its publication was not considered a violation of copyright.

Parody is much more than just humor. Parody uses humor to criticize and critique society. As the playwright Thornton Wilder said, "The comic spirit is given to us in order that we may analyze, weigh, and clarify things in us which nettle us, or which we are outgrowing or trying to reshape."[75] It is for this reason that parody is a First Amendment issue.

The Supreme Court decisions in the parody cases upheld the First Amendment as an important check on the monopoly powers of copyright. Fair use allows us to comment, criticize, and critique, without running afoul of the copyright laws. The parody cases all help to establish some balance in the laws, so that content providers and content users both have their rights protected.

As champions of content users, we information professionals are naturally interested in making sure that our patrons' rights to access information are protected. Fair use provides the foundation upon which our information society rests. It is the ability to quote or comment upon the work of others that makes libraries and archives necessary stops on the road to research.

Fair Use and the Common Law of Copyrights

Unpublished lectures, letters, and manuscripts are the staples of historical and archival work. The current Copyright Act provides that all of the materials covered by this statute will automatically become copyrighted *upon creation*, regardless of whether the work is published or whether it includes a formal notice of copyright.[76] This rule is a change from the previous law, which required the notice of copyright to be included in the work if the material was to be protected, and which applied mainly to works that were published.[77] The Federal Copyright Statute, however, is not the only source of copyright law. In addition to Federal law, state statutes and the common law protect the use of an individual's words.

There are some significant differences between the Federal copyright statute and the common law of copyrights. State law copyright and common law copyright often protect materials that do not qualify for protection under the Federal statute—including conversations, letters, unpublished manuscripts prepared before 1978, lectures and lecture notes, etc. There is no Federal common law of copyrights; instead, common law copyright is a function of state laws and can therefore vary from state to state.

The following discussion of common law copyright will cover some basic principles in a general way rather than dealing with the laws of specific states. However, most of the principles that will be discussed exist in the majority of jurisdictions.

A. State Common Law, Federal Copyright, and the Question of Pre-Emption

The first copyright issue of significance is the relationship between Federal statutory law and the common law. Sometimes when a Federal statute is passed, the Federal laws "occupy the field" so completely that the states lose the ability to create any law in that area. This situation is called *Federal pre-emption*. A recent example of an area in which the Federal law has pre-empted the states is the area of security for passenger airports and passenger airlines. The states no longer have the ability to create security laws for airports; the Federal government now enacts all airport security laws.

Most scholars do not believe that the Federal Copyright Act has totally pre-empted state copyright law.[78] According to section 103(b) of the Copyright Act: "Nothing in this title annuls or limits any rights or remedies under the common law or statutes of any State with respect to subject matter that does not come within the subject matter of copyright . . . including works of authorship not fixed in any tangible medium of statement."[79] The prevailing interpretation has been that Congress did not totally pre-empt common law copyrights, and that the rights granted by the common law can coexist with the rights granted by the Copyright Act.[80]

B. Common Law Copyright and the Fair Use Doctrine

Because the fair use doctrine is based on the Federal copyright statute rather than on common law,[81] there have been several cases which indicate that there is no such thing as fair use under the common law. These cases suggest that the fair use doctrine only applies to the Federal copyright statute. The question of whether fair use applies in common law copyright is not just of academic interest to librarians and archivists. Since libraries and archives are filled with materials that fall under the common law, information professionals need to be aware of this issue.

In the debate over common law fair use, the case that is most often cited is the California case of *Stanley v. CBS*.[82] The *Stanley* case involved the idea for a radio show that was submitted to the network by the plaintiff. Although Stanley's idea did not fall under the protection of the Federal copyright statute, the idea was covered by state common law copyright. The plaintiff had created an original work of authorship, had fixed the work in a tangible medium, and had shown his idea (in the tangible medium) to the broadcasting company.[83] The company claimed that the abstract idea was not worthy of protection.[84]

Although the California Supreme Court did not mention the term "fair use," the ability to apply abstract ideas is one of the basic principles of the fair use doctrine. In effect, the California Supreme Court made a fair use ruling without using the term "fair use." The majority opinion found in favor of Stanley, rejecting the concept that abstract ideas are available for anyone. According to the majority opinion:

> [Stanley] did not write a story or a play. He does not claim originality in the handling of any dramatic plot. He does claim to have originated a plan for a radio program, and to have written and recorded the formal script for the proposed program. Such a plan, together with its script, if truly original, may constitute a protectible [sic] "product of the mind."[85]

The dissenting opinion in the *Stanley* case suggested that the majority had gotten it wrong, and that abstract ideas could not be protected under common law copyright. The dissenting opinion stated:

> Abstract ideas are common property freely available to all. What men forge out of these ideas with skill, industry, and imagination, into concrete forms uniquely their own, the law protects as private property. It gives the special form the stamp of recognition; it does so to stimulate creative activity. It does something more to stimulate creative activity: it assures all men free utilization of abstract ideas in the process of crystallizing them in fresh forms. For creativeness thrives on freedom; men find new implications in old ideas when they range with open minds through open fields.[86]

In effect, the court stated that the "abstract idea" itself was protected by the common law. Under the statute, using such an "abstract idea" would constitute fair use.[87] As a result of the *Stanley* decision, there are many questions about the status of the fair use doctrine in common law. The treatise *Nimmer on Copyright* states that: "[A] minimal amount of copying falling short of *substantial* similarity does not constitute an infringement of common law copyright."[88]

There is one case cited which maintains that there is a right of fair use for common law copyrights. This case is *Hemingway v. Random House, Inc,*[89] which we have already explored earlier in this chapter in the context of fair use as a constitutional right.

In the *Hemingway* case, the trial court was specifically concerned with the common law copyright given to unpublished works. The plaintiffs claimed that "65% of the contents of 'Papa Hemingway' consists of 'literary matter created and expressed by Ernest Hemingway.'"[90] The plaintiffs were talking about both the published words of Hemingway from his books and the unpublished conversations that the author had engaged in with Hemingway. (In effect, the plaintiffs were claiming that every time Hotchner quoted Hemingway saying "good morning," the author was using Hemingway's words without permission.)

The court was not persuaded by the plaintiff's argument and stated in the opinion that: "In works of this nature, authors and publishers are not prohibited from making some use of quotations from the creations of others. Before an action may be maintained, there must be a showing of a significant appropriation of plaintiffs' property—significant both in volume and impact. In this regard, the Federal law of copyright and the State law of common-law copyright are in accord." [Citations omitted.][91]

The decision in the *Hemingway* case went on to discuss the concept of fair use. According to the opinion, "Where there is a mere minor use of fragments of another's work, especially in historical, biographical, or scholarly works, such appropriation is characterized as a 'fair use,' and is permitted."[92] Thus, Hotchner's fair use rights were upheld, even though the material was subject to common law copyright.

The *Hemingway* opinion also quoted the case of *Rosemont Enterprises v. Random House.*[93] In the *Rosemont* case, the 2nd Circuit Court of Appeals stated that "[b]iographies, of course, are fundamentally personal histories and it is both reasonable and customary for biographers to refer to and utilize earlier works dealing with the subject of the work and occasionally to quote directly from such works. This practice is permitted because of the public benefit in encouraging the development of historical and biographical works and their public distribution."[94] [Citations omitted.]

The general conclusion that emerges out of the *Stanley*, *Hemingway*, and *Rosemont Enterprises* cases is that fair use probably applies to works that are subject to common law copyright. However, the amount of material that can be used is probably less than if the item is subject to the Federal Copyright Act. Remember that the 1976 Copyright Act has dramatically reduced the scope of materials that are subject to common law copyright, but the Federal act still does not cover everything. Librarians and archivists need to be aware of the differences between types of materials in order to advise our patrons and to stay within the law ourselves.

C. Copyright Law and Unfixed Works

One use that is sometimes made of common law copyright is to protect items which are "unfixed." The Federal copyright statute applies only to fixed works, which are: "Original works of authorship fixed in any tangible medium of expression, now known or later developed, from which they can be perceived, reproduced, or otherwise communicated, either directly or with the aid of a machine. . . ."[95] In other words, a work is "fixed" as long as it is somehow in a permanent form, such as being written or recorded.

Because of the requirement for the material to be fixed, many types of works are not protected under the Federal copyright statute. Some of these types of works include: "choreography that has never been filed or notated, an extemporaneous speech, original works of authorship communicated solely through conversations or live broadcasts, and a dramatic sketch or musical composition improvised or developed from memory and without being recorded or written down."[96] Yet these same materials would be eligible for protection if they were fixed. Therefore, if the item "otherwise constitutes a 'work of authorship,'" which would be copyrightable if fixed, these materials are subject to protection by state common law.[97]

One type of work that is protected under the common law copyrights in many states is the unpublished lecture. The topic of unpublished lectures is important to librarians and archivists both as information creators (we often give lectures) and as information users (we often help patrons by finding lecture materials).

The issue of copyright for lectures has received more attention recently because commercial note-taking services on the Internet have become very popular among students. If the speaker gives a lecture from a prepared text, that text is considered to be an unpublished manuscript and is protected under common law.[98] Similarly if the speaker gives a lecture from notes, the notes are protected under the Federal copyright statute. The problem arises when a lecture is not based on notes, or when a full lecture is given but only cursory notes are used. These lectures are not "fixed in any tangible medium of expression."[99]

Since these lectures do not meet the "fixed" test, they are not eligible for protection under the Federal copyright statute.[100]

Luckily for the lecturer, however, unfixed copyrights are protected by common law in most states. Prior to the 1976 Copyright Act, common law copyright protected all works until they were published. Once items were published, they were subject to Federal copyright protection. This situation changed when the 1976 Copyright Act was passed. "Today, however, works are protected from the moment of their fixation, rather than from the date of publication, so there's very little left for common law copyright to protect. Thus, 'unfixed' works are one of the few remaining categories of works protected by state law. So long as the [person giving the lecture] can clearly establish that she is the author, most states will fully protect her lecture, calling upon concepts similar to those found in federal law to determine whether the common law copyright has been infringed."[101]

D. Unpublished Manuscripts

One of the most important parts of the 1976 Copyright Act (which took effect in 1978) was that it made unpublished manuscripts subject to the Federal statute.[102] It is important to remember that the rules were different for unpublished manuscripts created before 1978. "Early law granted 'common-law' copyright for works that remained unpublished. A manuscript left in the desk drawer had common-law privileges, and the statutory privileges began only upon publication and registration."[103] Basically, manuscripts received protection under the common law, while the Federal copyright statute protected published materials. The general rule was that the common law copyright protection ended upon publication; once the item was published, it was covered by the Federal copyright.[104]

The first question involves asking what constitutes a publication. The definition of "publishing" now includes not only traditional publication, but also placing material on a web page.[105] "Although the posting of material on a Website does not technically result in the distribution of tangible copies, the Copyright Office has taken the position that works made generally accessible through the World Wide Web may be considered published."[106] This statement is based on Copyright Office Circular 66, which says: "For works transmitted online, the copyrightable authorship may consist of text, artwork, music, audiovisual material (including any sounds), sound recordings, etc."[107] The idea that materials placed on Websites have been "published" makes sense, since these items are available to the public just as much as are printed books.

A second method for publishing a work is "making works available for 'unrestricted access' in a public library."[108] This method is based on *Copyright Office Compendium II.*[109] This issue was discussed in two cases, *Salinger v. Random House*,[110] and *Wright v. Warner Books.*[111] Interestingly, the courts in these two cases came to different conclusions about this issue.

J. D. Salinger is the author of *Catcher in the Rye*. He sued Ian Hamilton, who had written an unauthorized biography entitled *J. D. Salinger: A Writing Life.*[112] Hamilton used excerpts from letters written by Salinger which were available at "the libraries of Harvard, Princeton, and the University of Texas, to which they had been donated by the recipients or their representatives."[113]

One of Salinger's claims was that because the letters were unpublished and were subject to state copyright law, the use of these letters fell outside of the scope of fair use. As discussed above, the fair use doctrine is narrower in common law.[114] The fair use doctrine, however, is still a valid defense against infringement of a common law copyright.[115] The 2nd Circuit Court of Appeals recognized the availability of the fair use doctrine in the *Salinger* case, but stated that the privileges were narrower because the letters were unpublished. Hamilton argued that the letters were in fact published and available for use by scholars because they had been donated to libraries.

The court's opinion in the *Salinger* case states: "The author of letters is entitled to a copyright in the letters, as with any other work of literary authorship . . .[116] [and] the recipient . . . [of the letter] is entitled to deposit it with a library." [117] The person who donates the letters may also specify the conditions under which the materials may be accessed and used. The basic rule is: "The copyright owner owns the literary property rights, including the right to complain of infringing copying, while the recipient of the letter retains ownership of 'the tangible physical property of the letter itself.'"[118] The court decided that "Salinger's letters are unpublished, and they have not lost that attribute by their placement in libraries where access has been explicitly made subject to observance of at least the protections of copyright law."[119]

Because the court found that the letters were not published, Salinger still owned the copyright under common law. The court also ruled that fair use was subject to greater restrictions under state common law copyright than under the Federal copyright statute, and found in favor of Salinger because the excerpts Hamilton used were larger than the amount allowed by common law fair use principles.[120]

One important case in which the conclusion differs from the *Salinger* case is *Wright v. Warner Books*.[121] Richard Wright was the author of *Native Son* and *Black Boy*. Wright's widow sued Warner Books over the creation of a biography by Margaret Walker entitled *Richard Wright: Daemonic Genius*.[122] The case involved several letters written by Richard Wright which Mrs. Wright claimed were unpublished and therefore subject to common law copyright.[123] One of the plaintiff's claims was that the fair use doctrine was more restrictive for unpublished materials which are subject to common law copyright than for published (or unpublished) materials which are protected by the Federal copyright statute. Thus, something that might be fair use under the Federal copyright statute would not be allowed under common law copyright. Mrs. Wright claimed that Walker's book had used more material than was allowable under state common law copyright.

The District Court did not rule on the issue of how much use constitutes fair use. Instead, the judge ruled that a large part of the materials had been published and were therefore subject to the fair use doctrine under the Federal copyright statute.[124] The judge decided this point based upon the sale "for a considerable sum" of Wright's letters to the Beinecke Library at Yale University, stating that "[t]he sales contract specifically states that Yale purchased the right to 'use the Wright Archive,' and the University agreed to restrict access to only one manuscript not at issue here. It seems reasonable to conclude that for the purchase price, and pursuant to the sales contract, the University became free to share Wright's work with interested scholars."[125]

The trial judge went on to analyze Walker's book according to the fair use doctrine under the Federal copyright statute. According to the opinion:

> [T]he works' status as published or unpublished is just one—albeit a "critical"—aspect for the court to consider. . . . Additional circumstances present here suggest that Walker's use of the works in question is fair. First, she has paraphrased, rather than directly quoted, Wright's work. And second, the paraphrasing by and large involves straightforward factual reportage. While Salinger, too, concerned paraphrasing but nonetheless concluded with a finding of infringement, there the Second Circuit confronted attempts not merely to paraphrase factual data but also—and significantly—to adopt creative expression that was distinctly personal. . . .[126] [Citations omitted.]

When the Court of Appeals heard the case, it found that, although some manuscripts were indeed published, others were not.[127] (Because

Mrs. Wright did not challenge the decision that the sale to a library constituted publication, the Court of Appeals did not examine this issue.) The court focused on whether there was a fair use of the materials, regardless of whether they were subject to the Federal statute or to the common law. According to the Court of Appeals opinion:

> Weighing the amalgam of relevant factors, we are convinced that defendants' [sic] use of Wright's works is fair. Dr. Walker's biography of Richard Wright is a scholarly work, one that surely will contribute to the public's understanding of this important Twentieth Century novelist. The book does not exploit the literary value of Wright's letters or journals. Nor does it diminish the marketability of Wright's letters or journals for future publication. While the biography draws on works that we have characterized as unpublished for the purposes of this appeal, it takes only seven protected segments from Wright's letters and journals. These portions are short and insignificant, with the possible exception of a fifty-five word description of the art of writing. This use is de minimis and beyond the protection of the Copyright Act. . . . In short, this is not a reprise of *Salinger*. . . . The biography's use of Wright's expressive works is modest and serves either to illustrate factual points or to establish Dr. Walker's relationship with the author, not to "enliven" her prose.[128]

The *Wright* decision is a contrast to the decision in the *Salinger* case. In *Salinger*, donating the letters to a university library did not constitute publication. In the *Wright* case, however, the letters were *sold* to the library for a fee. Also, the sales contract with Mrs. Wright did not specify restrictions on the use of the materials. The trial court in the *Wright* case felt that this distinguishing fact made all the difference. In addition, since Salinger was alive, there were privacy concerns with his materials that did not exist in the *Wright* case.[129] Regardless of these other factors, and regardless of whether or not the materials were published, the Court of Appeals found that Dr. Walker's use of Wright's materials was exactly the type contemplated by the fair use doctrine.

If the works have been sold to the library by the copyright owner and are available to the public with no restrictions, then according to the *Wright* case the items have been published.[130] *Nimmer on Copyright* also provides some support for this position by discussing situations in which copies of the work (such as architectural plans) are placed in public files where the public has the authority to make unlimited copies of the work.[131] The case which *Nimmer* cited is *Certified Engineering, Inc., v. First Fidelity Bank.*[132] This case was about "deposit of engineering plans for a real estate subdivision. Although prior cases had held no general publication to have occurred from deposit of architectural plans for approval of constructing a single building, the court distinguished those cases from the circumstances . . . of securing approval for an entire subdivision, which purportedly made the plans available to the public for general copying."[133]

The third method of publication involves making copies freely available to the public without restriction. The *Copyright Office Compendium II*[134] notes that making an unrestricted gift of copies, giving them away on the street, or leaving them in a public place to be picked up are all sufficient to effect publication. "As with any form of publication, the key element is that the works be available to the general public, without restriction as to who may have access or what use may be made of the published material."[135]

Publishing an item by making copies available to the public has many similarities to publication by library deposit. In both situations, the materials must be made available to the public without restrictions, and the materials must be available to be copied without restrictions.[136] However, it is important to avoid the problems involved with limited publication, since a limited publication does not fall within the statutory definition of "publication." According to *Nimmer*, "A limited publication has been held to be a publication 'which communicates the contents of a manuscript to a definitely selected group and for a limited purpose, without the right of diffusion, reproduction, distribution, or sale.'"[137] The right to make reproductions is the most important distinction between publishing by deposit in a library on the one hand, or distribution to the public on the other hand, and thereby creating a limited publication.

The 1976 Copyright Act provides for copyright of all items, published or unpublished, that are created after January 1, 1978. Some items that were written earlier but were unpublished have now entered the public domain, while others may have subsequently been published and are therefore still under copyright.[138]

Duration is the biggest difference between Federal copyrights and common law copyrights. Common law copyright does not expire; it lasts forever.[139] "As long as the manuscript, letter, or other work remained unpublished, the common-law rights never expired. The author may be dead for centuries, but the copyright lived on."[140]

As a result of this change in the law, many items in libraries and archives that had formerly been subject to common law copyright are now in the public domain. As a result, this material may now be used without restriction, subject to the normal rules of citation and plagiarism.

The new law also applies to unpublished works that were created before 1978, bringing them into the Federal system for the first time.[141] In order to ensure an orderly transition to the new rules, unpublished works created before 1978 remained protected until December 31, 2002,[142] because "Congress was of the view that such a peremptory divestiture of copyright . . . might [violate] constitutional requirements of due process."[143]

As attorney Robert Clarida pointed out, after December 31, 2002, "Untold billions of works . . . subject to [common law] copyright protection will go into the public domain simultaneously. . . . Thus Congress ensured that every letter Jack Kerouac ever wrote to his mother, every notebook sketch by Matisse, every Mozart counterpoint exercise, would eventually, someday, lose its copyright protection."[144]

Since January 1, 2003, unpublished manuscripts are no longer protected by common law copyright. Those unpublished manuscripts will become part of the public domain 70 years after the death of their author.[145] However, the Copyright Act also contained provisions for the works to be published before the end of 2002.[146] According to the Federal copyright statute, "if the work is published on or before December 31, 2002, the term of copyright shall not expire before December 31, 2047."[147] The Federal copyright statute designated the date of December 31, 2047, as the expiration date for copyright because that will be 70 years after the statute took effect in 1978.

Conclusion

The fair use doctrine provides breathing space between the monopoly restrictions of copyright law and the Freedom of Speech requirements of the First Amendment. Because of the principles of fair use, scholars and information professionals are free to make limited copies of copyrighted works and to quote them. Satirists are also free to create parodies in order to point out flaws in society or in the way in which the original work depicts the world.

What do these differences and complications mean to library and archival professionals? In our assistance to patrons, we must ensure that we temper our advice according to the laws of fair use. Of course, in materials we prepare for distribution, we must also conform to fair use principles. And fair use must be our goal when we engage in writing down our ideas for publication. Our advice, our library and archival materials, and our writings are all subject to the laws of fair use.

5

Copyright and Education

Once upon a time, librarians confronted the complexities of sharing printed materials with patrons. However, new media have made the librarian's task even more challenging. A vast array of information is available through recordings, films, and cyberspace. Librarians must assist clients as they navigate through the thickets of information restrictions and copyright laws. The list of clients also includes a growing number of educators trying to figure out what they can or cannot use in their classes.

It is vital for educators, and the information professionals who assist them in their research, to understand the basics of copyright. Fortunately, copyright laws provide a number of exceptions for educators. The fair use doctrine establishes important rights for educators. There are also well-defined rules for classroom use and for placing materials on reserve. E-reserves are somewhat more problematic, but there are some guidelines to help libraries stay within the law.

Distance education, however, is subject to different rules than traditional classroom classes. There is a whole host of legal issues that are raised by Internet-based distance education. These issues have implications not only for academic librarians but also for professionals in other types of libraries.

What Can You Do in a Classroom or Library?

There are several parts of the Copyright Act that help educators stay within the law in traditional on-campus education. If you are teaching a class on campus, copyright law allows you to make copies of articles for your students. You can show movies in class. You can play music. This is all perfectly legal because of the fair use provisions contained in section 107 of the Copyright Act,[1] and because of the educational performance exceptions listed in section 110.[2]

Section 110(1) allows "performance or display of a work by instructors or pupils in the course of face-to-face teaching activities of a nonprofit educational institution, in a classroom or similar place devoted to instruction. . . ."[3] Because of section 110, a professor may show a movie or play a recording in class. The concept of a "similar place devoted to instruction" includes the library, auditoriums, etc., provided that the performance comes from a legal copy and that any copies are legally made. The purpose of this copyright exception is for education, so the school may not charge admission. Also, the performance should be accompanied by a lecture that explains the educational significance of the performance. Remember, however, that this instruction must be "face-to-face." In other words, section 110(1) does not provide an exception for distance education. That exception is contained in the TEACH Act, which amended section 110(2) of the Copyright Act.[4] The TEACH Act will be discussed later in this chapter.

As has been pointed out in previous chapters, section 107 of the Copyright Act states that: "[T]he fair use of a copyrighted work, including such use by reproduction in copies or phonorecords or by any other means specified by that section, for purposes such as criticism, comment, news reporting, teaching (including multiple copies for classroom use), scholarship, or research, is not an infringement of copyright."[5]

If a professor wants to create a course pack or anthology for sale in the bookstore, he or she will need to obtain permission from the copyright owner for each item. (See *Chapter 4*, *Fair Use and Intellectual Property Rights*.) Section 107 allows the duplication of multiple copies for in-classroom use only, but this exception is also subject to a few rules. During the creation of the 1976 Copyright Act, publishers agreed on a set of guidelines for the fair use of materials in the classroom. This agreement was included in the House of Representatives' report accompanying the Copyright Act.[6]

According to the agreement, a teacher can make multiple copies for classroom use as long as each student only receives one copy. The copy must be brief and must contain a notice of copyright. The agreement on classroom use defines brevity as follows:

i. Poetry: (a) A complete poem if less than 250 words and if printed on not more than two pages or, (b) from a longer poem, an excerpt of not more than 250 words.
ii. Prose: (a) Either a complete article, story or essay of less than 2,500 words, or (b) an excerpt from any prose work of not more than

1,000 words or 10% of the work, whichever is less, but in any event a minimum of 500 words.

iii. Illustration: One chart, graph, diagram, drawing, cartoon or picture per book or per periodical issue.

iv. "Special" works: Certain work in poetry, prose or in "poetic prose" which often combine language with illustrations and which . . . fall short of 2,500 words in their entirety. Paragraph "ii" above notwithstanding such "special works" may not be reproduced in their entirety; however, an excerpt comprising not more than two of the published pages of such special work and containing not more than 10% of the words found in the text thereof, may be reproduced.

(Each of the numerical limits stated in "i" and "ii" above may be expanded to permit the completion of an unfinished line of a poem or of an unfinished prose paragraph.)[7]

The first time that the teacher uses the material, he or she may do so without permission. However, if the material is reused in another term, the teacher will need to obtain copyright permission. There are also restrictions on the number of items that may be copied. These restrictions are as follows:

i. The copying of the material is for only one course in the school in which the copies are made.

ii. Not more than one short poem, article, story, essay or two excerpts may be copied from the same author, nor more than three from the same collective work or periodical volume during one class term.

iii. There shall not be more than nine instances of such multiple copying for one course during one class term.

(The limitations stated in "ii" and "iii" above shall not apply to current news periodicals and newspapers and current news sections of other periodicals.)[8]

The instructor is not allowed to charge the students for copying costs, and the materials should not be used as a substitute for anthologies or collections or for book purchases. There are also certain types of copyrighted materials that are intended to be "consumable" (the word used in the statute) during the course, such as "workbooks, exercises, standardized tests and test booklets and answer sheets and like consumable material."[9] These "consumables" are not covered by the fair use guidelines. If the instructor wants to use more material than is allowed under fair use, or if the instructor wants to reuse material in another term, he or she must obtain permission from the copyright owner.

Similar restrictions apply to items placed on reserve at the library. Traditional paper reserves (photocopies from books, journals, manuscripts, etc.) rely on the provisions of section 108(b), which permits libraries or archives to create a copy for purposes of preservation and security, as long as the item is currently in the collection. All students must have access to these copied materials. The basic method has been to make a photocopy and place it in a filing cabinet or on a shelf. This copy is seen as being a surrogate for the actual journal issue. Since patrons are permitted by section 108 to make a copy for themselves, there is no violation of copyright law if the student makes a copy of the article that is on reserve.

Remember that copyright permission must still be obtained if the library keeps reusing the material from term to term, or if the item on reserve constitutes too large a portion of the work under consideration. If the item is an entire book, libraries should simply place the book itself on reserve. Similarly, if several articles are being used from the same journal issue, the journal itself should be placed on reserve.[10] Always remove the item after the end of the semester, and be sure to obtain copyright permission if the professor wants to use the item again.

Electronic reserve systems (e-reserves) have become very popular in recent years. The Association of American Publishers (AAP) has taken the position that there is no difference between an e-reserve system and a course pack. According to the AAP, all articles need copyright licenses every time they are used in an e-reserve system.[11] The AAP's position is that "[u]nlike traditional paper reserves, posting readings in e-reserves always requires making copies of the original materials, and e-reserve systems typically make the readings available simultaneously to all students in the class, anywhere or anytime they choose."[12] The AAP feels that an e-reserve is more like a course pack than like a paper reserve in the library.

A. Copyright and E-Reserves

Between 1994 and 1996, the Conference on Fair Use (CONFU) met monthly in an attempt to create guidelines for libraries.[13] These guidelines were not agreed to by all of the conference members, and so they are not the law of the land. However, many libraries voluntarily follow the guidelines, which provide much valuable direction.

The CONFU guidelines support the application of traditional reserve policies to the electronic world by allowing works to be placed online as long as they are protected behind a password wall. Some systems allow any student to obtain the item, while others restrict the material to students in a specific class. Items on e-reserve should not be left online longer than necessary and should not include too much material. (See the fair use limitations discussed earlier.) Many libraries believe that these restrictions protect them from copyright infringement. However, the AAP has taken the position that this type of authentication does not relieve libraries of the need to obtain copyright permission for the materials.

In 2005, the AAP sent a letter to the University of California, San Diego, demanding that the library cease and desist using e-reserve systems. According to Mary MacDonald, an attorney for the university system, "They [the AAP] clearly had a lawsuit in mind when they started contacting our office. . . . Their position was that the 'evidence' showed that we weren't following fair-use guidelines, that this was a national issue, and that the set of facts gave them a good platform from which to take legal action."[14]

As of the time of writing (Fall 2005), this case is unresolved. However, many copyright experts believe that fair use guidelines still apply to the world of electronic reserves. Attorney Georgia Harper, who is in charge of intellectual property law for the University of Texas System, has developed some guidelines based exclusively on fair use as described in section 107 of the Copyright Act:

> As a practical matter . . . we really only rely on fair use to excuse our use of others' materials for electronic reserves. Providing computer access to educational materials involves a performance or display of those materials, but it is not a "face-to-face" performance or display; rather, it is a "transmission." Section 110(2), [the TEACH Act, discussed below] explicitly excludes reserve readings from the scope of its coverage. Therefore, with only minor modifications, we would rely on [the fair use analyses to make materials] available to students via computer terminals in the library or remotely at other campus or off-campus locations. . . . As always, the hallmarks of fair use involve adequate protection of the copyright owner's interests. In electronic reserves, this usually means password protected storage; streaming media when practical; and getting permission after first semester use for text.[15]

Georgia Harper and Peggy Hoon, Scholarly Communications Librarian at North Carolina State University, have also been working with the American Library Association to develop a statement on the use of electronic reserves.[16] In the ALA statement, Harper and Hoon remind us that:

The number of electronic resources licensed by libraries has increased significantly over the past decade. The licenses to these resources often include the right to use them in e-reserves systems. In such cases, no permission is required and a fair use analysis is unnecessary.

To ensure, however, that electronic content is effectively incorporated into e-reserve systems, there must be cooperation among library staff acquiring the digital resources and those managing e-reserves operations. They must work together to be certain that the license agreements do not preclude rights to make materials available through e-reserve systems, and that no one pays additional permission fees for uses already covered by a license.[17]

The fate of the e-reserve systems is still in question. Although many libraries follow the CONFU guidelines, these guidelines have not been officially ratified. My recommendation is in line with that of Georgia Harper, namely, that you should rely solely on the fair use doctrine in deciding when to ask permission for electronic reserves. I would go further and suggest that:

(1) E-reserves should be password protected and only made available to students in a specific class.
(2) Items on e-reserve should be kept for limited amounts of time, up to one month, instead of being available for the entire semester.
(3) Multimedia reserves should use streaming audio/video.   NOT ACTUAL F[
(4) Libraries should monitor the items on e-reserve to make sure that the materials remain within the fair use guidelines and that the item on e-reserve does not use too much of the original. If the amount is greater than fair use allows, the library should obtain copyright permission.
(5) If the item is going to be reused in a subsequent semester, the library should obtain copyright permission.
(6) Libraries should adopt, distribute, and follow e-reserve policies which contain guidelines for faculty members, and which state that the teaching department must reimburse the library for any copyright permission fees.
(7) Whenever possible, e-reserve systems should link to licensed resources already in the library collection. For example, if an article appears in EBSCO*host* or LexisNexis, the e-reserve system should give the link to that article rather than reproducing it.

Libraries that follow these principles should have no problems with copyright. Although the status of e-reserves is not yet settled, professional groups are working to create guidelines that everyone can live with. Perhaps soon we will have an agreement; in the meantime, make sure to follow the fair use guidelines closely and be careful to monitor what you have online.

Distance Education and Copyright Law

The idea of distance education is not really new. Many institutions have had correspondence courses for a number of years. The University of South Africa has been a leader in the field of distance education, even granting a law degree to Nelson Mandela while he was in prison. Britain's Open University has helped large numbers of working adults gain college degrees. Today it is even possible to obtain a Ph.D. from a regionally accredited institution without ever setting foot on the campus.[18] There are, however, some principles of copyright law that need to be considered when dealing with distance education. This section will explain the copyright implications of distance education and the reforms provided by the TEACH Act.

A. The 1976 Copyright Act and Distance Education

When the 1976 Copyright Act was passed, distance education was in its infancy. Schools such as the University of Minnesota had extensive correspondence courses; however, these courses primarily consisted of written materials sent through the mail for individual study. The issue of performances only came up in connection with the few providers of live television broadcasts or with videotaped classes that were replayed in classrooms at remote locations.[19]

Under the law passed in 1976, educators could only transmit nondramatic literary or musical works if one of the following conditions applied: (1) the performance was received in classrooms or similar places normally devoted to instruction; (2) the performance was received by persons with disabilities or other special circumstances that prevented their attendance in classrooms; or (3) the reception was by officers or employees of governmental bodies as a part of their official duties or employment.[20]

The old rules for distance education began to break down in the 1990s with the maturing and widespread availability of the World Wide Web. The Web, along with technologies such as chat rooms and streaming A/V multimedia, opened up possibilities for individual and group study that had not been previously accessible. At the same time, the development of the Internet had led to computers being available in libraries across the country, and to an ever-larger percentage of the population who had dial-up service at home.

Because of the Web, distance education—once mostly provided by large land-grant universities and proprietary technical schools—became mainstream. By the end of the 1990s, the University of Phoenix had obtained regional accreditation and become the largest U.S. distance education provider. Meanwhile, traditional universities were entering the field with great zeal.

Unfortunately, the rules for transmission of performances found in section 110(2) had not kept up with the changes in technology and society. By the end of the 1990s, most distance education students were receiving materials via the Web in their homes or offices, rather than in a remote classroom facility. Because of this change in the structure of distance education, there were substantial differences between what an instructor could do in a classroom and what he or she could do in an online class.

For example, suppose that you are teaching a music appreciation class. One section meets on campus, and one section is taught via distance education on the Web. In the classroom, you may play any recording that you want. Although this is a performance, copyright is not a factor because of section 110(1) of the Copyright Act, as discussed above.

On the other hand, when you teach a class via the Web, you are transmitting the performance. Under the language of the 1976 Copyright Act, you could only transmit a performance if the transmission was received in "classrooms or similar places normally devoted to instruction."[21] Obviously, a student dialing the Web from home is not in a "classroom or similar place." Therefore, section 110(1) does not apply to this situation.

The legal status of educational copies and educational performances became one of the biggest problems that the budding Internet distance education market faced. After all, accreditation bodies would only recognize online programs if the education that the students received was substantially similar to what they would have gotten on campus in a face-to-face class. Yet without the ability to use copyrighted materials in online classes, the distance education class would never be substantially similar to a face-to-face course. It seemed as if online education was caught in a Catch-22 situation unless the law was changed. In order to rectify this problem, Congress passed the TEACH Act.

B. The TEACH Act and Transmission of Performances

Luckily for the distance education providers, the two top leaders of the Senate Judiciary Committee were major supporters of online education and were very interested in finding a solution to the copyright issues faced by online education. In 2001, Senator Orrin Hatch was the majority leader of the Senate Judiciary Committee, and Senator Patrick Leahy was the minority leader of the committee. These two influential senators were able to work together in a bipartisan manner to fix the problems that were keeping online education from developing to its full potential. Together with MaryBeth Peters, the Registrar of Copyrights, the two senators worked to create the TEACH Act. The acronym TEACH stands for "Technology, Education, and Copyright Harmonization." Senators Hatch and Leahy proposed the original bill (Senate Bill 487) in April 2001.

Unlike most legislative acts, this bill was a negotiated agreement from the very start. Copyright issues are always difficult, and the TEACH Act was no exception. Educators had one perspective; publishers had another. As with most copyright situations, librarians were caught in the middle. MaryBeth Peters, the Registrar of Copyrights, decided to bring the parties together.

In April and May 2001, Ms. Peters, with the cooperation of Senators Hatch and Leahy and their staffs, convened a summit meeting of all the interested parties. The purpose of the meeting was to create an agreement that would fix the problems with section 110. The meeting included librarians, publishers, educators, computer professionals, and copyright attorneys. The participants worked together to develop language for the bill which would satisfy everyone. On May 4, 2001, the participants came to a joint agreement on what the provisions of this bill should be.[22]

Senators Hatch and Leahy jointly introduced the language of the negotiated agreement as S. 487.[23] It was passed in the Senate, as amended, on June 7, and introduced in the House, where it was referred to the Judiciary Committee. On July 11, 2001, the House Subcommittee on Courts, the Internet, and Intellectual Property approved the bill for full committee action.[24] Unfortunately, the events of September 11, 2001, and the subsequent war in Afghanistan prevented the House from being able to consider the TEACH Act as quickly as might otherwise have been the case, and the bill remained buried in the House for some time.

Finally, on July 17, 2002, the Committee on the Judiciary ordered that S. 487 be reported to the full House.[25] The committee report[26] was filed, and the bill was reported in the House on September 25, 2002.[27] The House passed the bill, and it was signed into law (to the obvious relief of everyone in the distance education world) on November 2, 2002.

C. What the TEACH Act Covers

The TEACH Act applies to "the performance of a nondramatic literary or musical work or *reasonable and limited portions* of any other work . . . [and to the display] of a work in an amount comparable to that which is typically displayed in the course of a live classroom session."[28] This provision means that distance educators can use commercial works, as long as the use is "reasonable and limited."[29] The best way to determine what is reasonable and limited is to look at the principles of fair use (as discussed earlier).

The TEACH Act amends section 110(2) to eliminate the "face-to-face" requirement of the educational performance exception. The requirement that performances be received in "classrooms or similar places normally devoted to instruction" has also been removed. The new exception is available only to accredited nonprofit educational institutions. Only students who are officially enrolled may receive the performance. Since there are as many accrediting agencies as there are diploma mills, the Senate bill included a definition of what constitutes "accredited institutions." Section 110(11) states that:

> For purposes of paragraph (2), accreditation–
> (A) with respect to an institution providing post-secondary education, shall be as determined by a regional or national accrediting agency recognized by the Council on Higher Education Accreditation or the United States Department of Education; and
> (B) with respect to an institution providing elementary or secondary education, shall be as recognized by the applicable state certification or licensing procedures.[30]

The TEACH Act only applies to nonprofit educational institutions. This means that for-profit institutions such as the University of Phoenix are not covered by the TEACH Act. The exclusion of for-profit institutions was a key demand of the content owners. After all, these institutions are set up to obtain a financial benefit for their owners and stockholders. Since businesses and companies are not permitted to transmit copyrighted material, it makes sense that a for-profit educational institution also would not be allowed to transmit copyrighted material.

The TEACH Act only applies to educational institutions; it does not include performances by nonprofit libraries. Such performances were not included in the negotiated settlement or in S. 487. Nonprofit libraries, therefore, may only transmit materials if the organization obtains a valid license from the copyright holder. (Obviously, any for-profit library would also need permission from the copyright holder.) Since many public libraries (such as the New York Public Library) provide distance education classes, this situation has caused an increase in program costs to pay for copyright permissions.

In order for the TEACH Act to apply, the transmission must be "[m]ade by, at the direction of, or under the actual supervision of an instructor as an integral part of a class session."[31] The class must be a "regular part of the systematic mediated instructional activities."[32] It is important to remember that only students officially enrolled in the course for which the transmission is made, or governmental employees in the course of their duties, should be able to receive the transmissions.[33] In other words, for educators to be permitted to use a performance, it must be related to the content of a for-credit course. Section 110(11) states that:

> [T]he term "mediated instructional activities" with respect to the performance or display of a work by digital transmission under this section refers to activities that use such work as an integral part of the class experience, controlled by or under the actual supervision of the instructor and analogous to the type of performance or display that would take place in a live classroom setting. The term does not refer to activities that use, in 1 or more class sessions of a single course, such works as textbooks, course packs, or other material in any media, copies or phonorecords of which are typically purchased or acquired by the students. . . .[34]

This section is referring to instructional materials. The same type of material is considered to be one of the nine statutory categories that the *Work for Hire* doctrine applies to. For more information, see ***Chapter 3***, *Copyright and Patent Law*.

The TEACH Act also provides a safe harbor for institutions that have to make incidental copies of the materials while transmitting them. Every time you use a digital performance or a digital version of a document, you are also making a copy. The TEACH Act recognizes this fact and provides immunity, stating that:

[N]o governmental body or accredited nonprofit educational institution shall be liable for infringement by reason of the transient or temporary storage of material carried out through the automatic technical process of a digital transmission of the performance or display of that material as authorized under paragraph (2). No such material stored on the system or network controlled or operated by the transmitting body or institution under this paragraph shall be maintained on such system or network in a manner ordinarily accessible to anyone *other than anticipated recipients*. [Emphasis added.] No such copy shall be maintained on the system or network in a manner ordinarily accessible to such anticipated recipients for a longer period than is reasonably necessary to facilitate the transmissions for which it was made.[35]

One important part of the TEACH Act concerns the responsibilities that are required of the institutions. The TEACH Act exception only applies if the school creates and maintains policies regarding copyright. The school must provide educational sessions and informational material that explain copyright law. There must also be a notice to students that materials used in connection with the course may be subject to copyright protection.

For example, I sometimes teach an online class for the school library media program at Western Kentucky University. Based on this provision of the law, I posted the notice found in figure 5.1 on the front page of the course site.

The course and its components are copyright 2001-2003 Bryan M. Carson. This course also makes legal use of some copyrighted materials pursuant to Title 17 U.S.C. Sections 107 and 110. Copyrighted materials may not be reproduced without permission by the copyright holder.

Figure 5.1. Copyright Notice for Online Class.

Under the TEACH Act, the schools also have certain responsibilities for the transmissions. There must be technology in place which reasonably prevents students from retaining the work for longer than the class session, and the technology must not allow students to pass on the work to other individuals. In addition, the institution must not interfere with technological measures used by copyright owners to prevent retention or unauthorized further dissemination, such as those discussed in the Digital Millennium Copyright Act.[36]

For example, almost all DVDs contain software that only allows them to be played on certain machines. These machines are sold in particular zones of the world.[37] If you purchase a DVD in England, which is zone 2, it will only work in Europe, Japan, South Africa, Israel, Lebanon, and the Middle East. The English DVD will not work in the United States or Canada, which are in zone 1. The TEACH Act prohibits educators or institutions from removing the zone restrictions. The Digital Millennium Copyright Act also makes it a crime to interfere with technological measures such as the zone restrictions.

There are several categories of works that are excluded from transmission by the TEACH Act. These are works that are marketed "primarily for performance or display as part of mediated instructional activities transmitted via digital network."[38] This exclusion makes sense, since otherwise these kinds of instructional works would be in effect unprotected. The statute is talking about items such as instructional texts, tests, classroom guides, answer keys, etc. These same kinds of materials fall within the statutory definition of materials that may qualify for *Work for Hire* provisions in independent contractor agreements.

The TEACH Act also excludes performance or display of copies "not lawfully made and acquired."[39] Such a restriction is desirable since it would not serve the public purpose to reward people for violating copyright.

The TEACH Act does allow faculty members to convert analog works to digital formats under certain circumstances. For example, a performance that is contained on a VHS tape could be digitized for transmission provided that a digital version is not already available, or if the digital version is protected by a technological measure that prevents its being used in distance education. Also, you may not convert more material than you would be allowed to transmit under section 110(2) or under the fair use doctrine.[40]

One issue that is not specifically addressed by the law concerns handouts and other types of readings. Although handouts are not mentioned in the TEACH Act, Professor Kenneth Crews has discussed this issue extensively.[41] Professor Crews states that the TEACH Act's provision about displaying materials in quantity similar to the live classroom "would suggest that occasional, brief handouts—perhaps including entire short works—may be permitted in distance education, while reserves and other outside reading may not be proper materials to scan and display under the auspices of the new law."[42]

Crews' interpretation is also based on the fair use provisions in section 107, relating to multiple copies for classroom use. Fair use provisions apply to handouts and other types of materials used in class. According to intellectual property expert David Lange, fair use also applies to transmissions, even in the absence of the TEACH Act.[43] Of course, in order to be protected, you should not use more materials than fair use allows, whether you are teaching an in-person class or a distance education class. However, it appears that you can do the same things with handouts in a distance education class that you would be able to do in a face-to-face class.

The TEACH Act is an attempt to bring copyright law into harmony with the technological and social advances of distance education. The statute amends section 110(2) of the copyright law to allow "reasonable and limited" portions of performances to be transmitted via technological means to distance education students.

In order to use the distance education exception contained in the TEACH Act, educators must do the following:

- ◆ Transmit only legal copies of non-dramatic, literary, or musical works (or reasonable portions of other works).
- ◆ Transmit only to classes that are taught as part of the university's curriculum.
- ◆ Do not put material on an open Website; use course management software that will authenticate the student.
- ◆ Make sure that only students who are registered in the class (or graduate assistants) can access the course material.
- ◆ Make the performance available only for a limited time period.
- ◆ Make sure students can't copy or download materials or share materials with other people.
- ◆ Inform students that the material is copyrighted.
- ◆ Follow university rules.

Distance education holds the power to change lives by eliminating many of the social and geographical barriers to higher education. With the recent changes in copyright law and with the use of course management software, distance educators can finally do the same things online that they can do in a traditional classroom. These improvements may finally lead to the promise of distance education being fulfilled.

Conclusion

Librarians and other educators are obligated to follow the principles of fair use in the classroom, at the copy machine, and in the library reserve room. In addition, librarians need to be able to advise their colleagues on college campuses about how to stay within the law. This advisory role means that information professionals need to be well informed about changes in the intersection between copyright and education.

The passage of the TEACH Act has clarified for accredited non-profit educational institutions what they may do in their distance education programs; that is, they may do the same things in an online class as in an on-campus class. Thus, librarians and educators are becoming less bound by distance.

The TEACH Act provides important exceptions to copyright law. Even when the TEACH Act doesn't apply, librarians and other educators are still able to use some performance materials in distance education. After all, "Fair use still applies to distance education if you use reasonable and limited portions of a copy which has been legally obtained and the copies are lawfully made."[44]

It is especially important to be careful of copyright for materials on electronic reserve. Because the areas of e-reserves and distance education law are still evolving, librarians should pay careful attention to current developments. By staying aware of what is going on in your institution, you can help to avoid problems before they develop.

Information professionals strive to assist their patrons. In doing so, we must understand and remain within the restrictions (and exceptions) of copyright law, fair use, and the TEACH Act. Thus, in order to serve both their patrons and the law, librarians must be fully aware of copyright laws.

6

Trademark and Trade Secret Law

Most people think of trademark and trade secret law as being mainly related to commercial transactions and having nothing to do with libraries or archives. Yet nothing could be further from the truth. Librarians are often called upon to help conduct trademark searches.[1] Also, libraries themselves are users of trademarked goods, and need to make sure that these trademarks are used properly. Librarians were shocked and outraged in 2003 when OCLC[2] sued the Library Hotel in New York for infringing on the Dewey Decimal System. (This case got a lot of bad publicity in the newspapers, and the parties quickly settled the lawsuit.)[3] Finally, in this day of databases and Websites, some libraries are creators of products or services that are (or at least could be) trademarked. In order to stay out of court, information professionals need to understand trademarks.[4]

Trade secret law is even more important for librarians and archivists to understand. I believe that the principles of trade secret law provide an additional protection for library confidentiality duties beyond the protection established by state and territorial confidentiality laws. Although my theory has not been published by other researchers or tested in court, it is my opinion that we can use trade secret laws to help protect the confidentiality of our patron interactions.

In short, trademark law and trade secret law have a great deal of importance for librarians and archivists. The intellectual property system doesn't just stop with copyright and patent law. Intellectual property also encompasses goods, services, and trade secrets. Each of these forms of protection has implications in libraries and archives, and each type of protection has pitfalls that information professionals need to be aware of. Library professionals should know and understand the basic elements of each field, and understand that they are part of our day-to-day activities in the library.

Trademark Law

Trademark law is the overall term used for a variety of subfields, such as trademarks, service marks, and trade dress. (In this chapter, I will be using the term "trademark" or "mark" interchangeably to mean all forms of marks, including trademarks, service marks, and trade dress.) Trademarks are defined as "[w]ords, names, symbols, or devices used by manufacturers of goods and providers of services to identify their goods and services, and to distinguish their goods and services from [similar] goods manufactured and sold by others."[5] In order to obtain trademark protection, the mark must be "famous" and "distinctive."[6] One important requirement of trademark law is that the mark must be used in commerce. If the mark has not been used or has ceased to be used in commerce, it is not capable of being protected. Some examples of trademarks include:

- ◆ KODAK for cameras or BURGER KING for restaurant services;
- ◆ FLY THE FRIENDLY SKIES OF UNITED or GET A PIECE OF THE ROCK (Prudential Insurance);
- ◆ The Pillsbury Dough Boy and the Jolly Green Giant;
- ◆ The jingle used by National Public Radio;
- ◆ The shape of a Coca-Cola bottle. (Technically this type of trademark is called "Trade Dress.")[7]

Some of these examples ("FLY THE FRIENDLY SKIES" and "GET A PIECE OF THE ROCK") actually belong to a subdivision of trademark law known as service marks. The definition of a service mark is: "[A] mark used in the sale or advertising of services to identify the services of one person and distinguish them from the services of others. Titles, character names and other distinctive features of radio or television programs may be registered as service marks notwithstanding that they, or the programs, may advertise the goods of the sponsor."[8] Service marks may be designated by the [SM] symbol, but often are designated by the ™ or the ® symbol.

The goal of trademark protection is to protect the goodwill and investment of a business, while at the same time shielding consumers from misrepresentation and confusion as to the origin of the goods and services. "Trademark protection is available for words, names, symbols, or devices that are capable of distinguishing the owner's goods or services from the goods or services of others. A trademark that merely describes a class of goods rather than distinguishing the trademark owner's goods from goods provided by others is not protectible [sic]"[9] (e.g., words such as "pop" or "soda" can not be trademarked, while "Pepsi" or "Dr. Pepper" can be).

Once a trademark has been used in commerce, the mark's owner may use the ™ designation for a good or the SM designation for a service. The ® symbol for Registered may not be used until the mark has actually been registered with the U.S. Patent and Trademark Office (USPTO). Using the ® symbol before you have actually registered the mark is considered false and misleading advertising.[10]

In order to obtain Federal trademark protection, the person or entity must file an application with the USPTO. The USPTO will publish the mark in the *Official Gazette*.[11] Owners of similar trademarks have 30 days in which to oppose the proposed mark. If there is no opposition, the USPTO will issue the trademark.

Before the trademark application may be filed, the mark must have been used in commerce. The application contains the date of first use of the mark and the date of first use in commerce. "First use in commerce" is different from the first use of the mark, and means the first time that the mark was used in interstate commerce (i.e., the mark has been used in a different state from the one in which it was created). Sometimes, however, the mark is used for the first time in a different state from the one in which it was created. For example, a mark that was created by a Madison Avenue advertising agency in New York may be used for the first time in California. In this situation, the date of first use would be the same as the date of the first use in commerce. In trademark challenges, the mark that was used first is called the *senior mark*, and the mark that was used subsequently is called the *junior mark*.

Federal trademark protection is effective for 10 years; however, it may be renewed for an unlimited number of 10-year terms as long as the trademark is still being used. Federal trademark cases may be tried in U.S. District Court. There is also state trademark registration, which varies from state to state. In addition, there is a common law trademark, which continues as long as the trademark remains in use. However, state and common law trademarks do not qualify for Federal protection. Such cases may only be brought in state courts, and the amount of protection is limited.

In recent years, the Madrid Protocol has helped to facilitate international trademark protection. The World Intellectual Property Organization (WIPO) administers this trademark treaty. In the past, a mark owner had to file for protection individually in each country. The Madrid Protocol has streamlined this registration process by providing for a single application form for trademarks. The application for international registration may be sent to the USPTO. Mark owners may designate which countries they wish to register in. This single application process for all countries that signed the Madrid Protocol treaty has helped to facilitate the international registration of trademarks.

Trademark law is found in Title 15, Chapter 22 of the U.S. Code and is based on the Lanham Act,[12] supplemented by the Federal Trademark Dilution Act of 1995.[13]

There are four types of trademarks: *descriptive* marks, *suggestive* marks, *arbitrary* marks, and *fanciful* marks. Descriptive marks are exactly what they sound like, i.e., a trademark that describes the product or service being marketed. Descriptive marks are not creative and are more likely to describe the entire class of products. They are the weakest kind of trademark to protect. The USPTO will not register a descriptive mark unless it has some secondary meaning.[14] Some examples of descriptive marks include: "HONEY ROAST for roasted nuts, QUICK PRINT for printing services, BREADSPREAD for jellies and jams, and MOUNTAIN CAMPER for retail mail order of outdoor equipment and apparel."[15] Descriptive marks may also include surnames. Thus, names such as BRENDA'S BODY SHOP or JACKSON'S ORCHARD are not eligible for registration.

Sometimes a descriptive trademark will acquire a secondary meaning so that the public associates it with a particular product or service. For example, FORD for automobiles, McDONALD'S for hamburgers—these words mean something particular to the public, even though they are descriptive, and as a result they do qualify for Federal trademark protection.

In the old days, an entrepreneur named McDonald could start a restaurant and call it McDonald's. Since it was a descriptive surname, the restaurant name could not be protected. Today, calling a restaurant McDonald's creates an association with Big Macs, the golden arches, and Ronald McDonald. Because of this secondary association in the public's mind, the name McDONALD'S qualifies for trademark protection.

Suggestive marks require a creative leap on the part of the consumer, but appear to be only indirectly identified with the good or service. Suggestive marks, such as KRISPY KREME, are not very easy to protect, but are stronger than descriptive marks and are much more likely to receive trademark registration. These marks satisfy the trademark test of being inherently descriptive. Two additional examples of suggestive marks are "COPPERTONE for suntan oil, and WRAN-GLER for western boots and jeans."[16]

Arbitrary marks have "no mental connection"[17] with the good or service. These are common words that are used in a way that has nothing to do with their ordinary meaning. For example, BEST BUY is an ordinary phrase meaning that you have gotten the best deal; however, when applied to the consumer electronics industry, BEST BUY refers to a specific company. Another example is TARGET. In ordinary use, a target is either "[a]n object with a marked surface that is shot at to test accuracy . . . or [a] desired goal."[18] However, when applied to retail stores, the mark denotes a specific company. Arbitrary marks are easy to protect, since the ordinary meaning has nothing to do with the specialized meaning in commerce.

Fanciful trademarks are the strongest and the easiest to protect. These are marks that have been invented for the sole purpose of describing the particular good or service. "PEPSI for cola drinks, KODAK for film, EXXON for oil products, and XEROX for photocopiers"[19] are all examples of words that didn't exist before, but have been coined in order to create a trademark.

To register trademarks, the USPTO uses two separate registers: the *principal register* and the *supplemental register*. Marks that are listed on the principal register have the greatest amount of protection. The trademark is valid nationwide, rather than just in a specific geographical area.

There is a presumption in the law that marks on the principal register are valid. Once a mark has been registered on the principal register for five years, no challenges can be brought against the mark as being "not inherently distinctive" or as being "confusingly similar" to a senior mark. Another advantage of having a mark registered on the principal register is that if you win a case, the courts will award triple damages. (Your award will be three times the damages you prove—this triple award is known as *treble damages*.) In addition, the losing party will have to pay the winning party's attorney's fees.

The supplemental register does not provide as much protection as the principal register, but still allows the registrant to obtain the benefit of Federal trademark protection. The supplemental register is for marks that identify the good or service, but are not sufficiently distinctive to be placed on the principal register. "Thus, any would-be mark that is descriptive, geographically descriptive, primarily a surname or otherwise not inherently distinctive and that lacks secondary meaning may be registered on the supplemental register."[20]

For example, suppose that I run a chain of restaurants in Ohio, Indiana, and Kentucky called "Big Top Pizza." Since the mark has been used in commerce (in more than one state), I can file for Federal trademark protection. Because the word "Big Top" is not sufficiently distinctive to suggest my restaurant, I would not qualify for a listing on the principal register.

With the supplemental register, there is no presumption of validity of ownership, and the geographic area of the good or service is limited to that area in which it has been marketed. In order to be placed on the supplemental register, the mark must have been used in commerce for one year prior to the application date. The only real difference between the common law and the secondary register is that the registrant of a mark on the secondary register may use the Federal courts to sue.[21]

Although we usually don't think about it this way, trademark law is a type of consumer protection. The Lanham Act prevents imitations or forgeries from being sold as the real thing. For example, when I buy a Rolex watch, because of the Lanham Act I know that the watch I am buying is really made by Rolex rather than being a cheap knock-off. If there is a chance that the public might be confused or misled as to the origin of a product, the Lanham Act applies. Section 1125 of the Act states that:

> Any person who, on or in connection with any goods or services, or any container for goods, uses in commerce any word, term, name, symbol, or device, or any combination thereof, or any false designation of origin, false or misleading description of fact, or false or misleading representation of fact, which (A) is likely to cause confusion, or to cause mistake, or to deceive as to the affiliation, connection, or association of such person with another person, or as to the origin, sponsorship, or approval of his or her goods, services, or commercial activities by another person, or (B) in commercial advertising or promotion, misrepresents the nature, characteristics, qualities, or geographic origin of his or her or another person's goods, services, or commercial activities, shall be liable in a civil action by any person who believes that he or she is or is likely to be damaged by such act.[22]

Although protection of business assets is a secondary purpose of the Lanham Act, it is the primary purpose of the Federal Trademark Dilution Act. Section 1125(c)(1) of that Act permits remedies for infringement of a "famous mark" in order to prevent dilution. Dilution is the process by which people or companies begin to use the mark so that it is no longer distinctive. Some of the factors that help decide whether a mark is famous and distinctive include:

a) The degree of inherent or acquired distinctiveness of the mark;
b) The duration and extent of use of the mark in connection with the goods or services with which the mark is used;
c) The duration and extent of advertising and publicity of the mark;
d) The geographical extent of the trading area in which the mark is used;
e) The channels of trade for the goods or services with which the mark is used;
f) The degree of recognition of the mark in the trading areas and channels of trade used by the mark's owner and the person against whom the injunction is sought;
g) The nature and extent of use of the same or similar marks by third parties;
h) Whether the mark was registered under the Act of March 3, 1881, or the Act of February 20, 1905, or on the principal register.[23]

Owners of trademarks want their marks to become famous, but they don't want them to become so well known that the marks become generic. Trademarks become generic when a word or mark is so highly diluted that it is now synonymous with all of the competitors' products as well as with the original owner's product. Once a trademark becomes generic, it can no longer be protected. Some examples of marks that have become generic are ELEVATOR, ESCALATOR, ASPIRIN, THERMOS, TRAMPOLINE, and CELLOPHANE.[24] It is for these reasons, as well as because of the concept of dilution of trademarks (discussed in the section below) that companies such as XEROX or KLEENEX try to make sure that their trademarks don't become diluted or generic.

A. Dilution of Trademarks

Owners of trademarks must take aggressive actions to ensure that their marks are not infringed upon or diluted. Just as "use it or lose it" is necessary in order for a trademark to continue, "protect it or lose it" is also necessary. "A trademark . . . represents something that the mark's owner intends to protect: goodwill. Any person who uses a trademark in a way that is likely to cause confusion or dilute the mark's meaning is a potential infringer."[25] If the mark becomes diluted, it no longer carries the goodwill of the business and no longer represents that business to the public. If trademark owners do not enforce the use of their marks, they will lose them and the word or symbol will become a generic trademark.

There are two types of dilution. These are *blurring* and *tarnishment*. *Blurring* occurs when the junior mark, while not confusing, is a distraction to consumers. For example, if I opened a supermarket called BEST BUYS, this name would blur the mark of BEST BUY electronics and would result in my being sued by the electronics store.

On the other hand, *tarnishment* occurs when the junior mark creates aversion to the senior mark. An example of tarnishment involves the CABBAGE PATCH KIDS and the GARBAGE PAIL KIDS. In this case, the owner of the trademark for the CABBAGE PATCH KIDS won a lawsuit against Topps Chewing Gum, which had created a set of trading cards called the GARBAGE PAIL KIDS. Even though the only word in common between the two marks was the word "kids," the district court found that Topps' use was evocative of the senior mark and held the senior mark up to ridicule or aversion from consumers.[26]

The scope of tarnishment became uncertain after the U.S. Supreme Court decision in the case of *Moseley v. V Secret Catalog*.[27] This case involves the complexities of tarnishment and deserves detailed examination.

The *Moseley* case involved a store owned by Victor and Cathy Moseley in Elizabethtown, Kentucky. The store was called Victor's Secret. The Moseleys sold ladies lingerie, along with adult movies, novelties, and gifts. The Victoria's Secret chain sent the Moseleys a letter demanding that they cease and desist using the name Victor's Secret.[28]

The letter stated that the choice of the name "Victor's Secret" for a store selling lingerie was likely to cause confusion with the well-known VICTORIA'S SECRET mark and, in addition, was likely to "dilute the distinctiveness of the mark."[29] Victoria's Secret was not only concerned with the possibility of blurring, but also was worried that a store selling adult toys would tarnish the trademark. The Moseleys changed the name of their store to Victor's Little Secret, but this change was not satisfactory to Victoria's Secret, so the company filed a lawsuit.[30]

The plaintiff claimed that the junior mark infringed on the company's trademark because the Moseleys' use was "likely to cause confusion and/or mistake in violation of 15 U.S.C. § 1114(1)."[31] The complaint also claimed "unfair competition alleging misrepresentation in violation of § 1125(a), for 'federal dilution' in violation of the FTDA, and for trademark infringement and unfair competition in violation of the common law of Kentucky."[32] The complaint also alleged that the junior mark was "'likely to blur and erode the distinctiveness' and 'tarnish the reputation' of the VICTORIA'S SECRET trademark."[33]

At the trial, the District Court found that the Moseleys' store only derived 5 percent of their profits from lingerie. "Finding that the record contained no evidence of actual confusion between the parties' marks, the District Court granted a summary judgment for the Moseleys on the infringement and unfair competition claims, stating that: 'no likelihood of confusion exists as a matter of law.'"[34] With respect to the dilution claims, the District Court did not find any blurring, but did rule in favor of Victoria's Secret on the grounds of tarnishment. The 6th Circuit Court of Appeals affirmed this decision on the basis of both tarnishment and blurring.[35] The case was appealed to the U.S. Supreme Court.

The Supreme Court examined the statutory language and legislative history of the Federal Trademark Dilution Act. The statutory language was very important, since trademark dilution was not an action in the common law. In a unanimous opinion, the Court found that proof of actual dilution is required by the statute but that proof of actual loss of sales or profits is not required.[36] The Court stated that "where the marks at issue are not identical, the mere fact that consumers mentally associate the junior user's mark with a famous mark is not sufficient to establish actionable dilution."[37]

The most important part of the Supreme Court's opinion, however, was the surprise ruling that the Federal Trademark Dilution Act did not include a cause of action for tarnishment. This ruling "sent shock waves through the IP community."[38] After the case was over, Scot Duvall, one of the attorneys who wrote the brief for the Moseleys, said, "Nobody thought that tarnishment was not part of the FTDA except for me and my law partners and a couple of law professors who filed *Amicus* briefs on our behalf."[39] According to the Supreme Court:

> The District Court's decision in this case rested on the conclusion that the name of petitioners' store "tarnished" the reputation of respondents' mark, and the Court of Appeals relied on both "tarnishment" and "blurring" to support its affirmance. Petitioners have not disputed the relevance of tarnishment, presumably because that concept was prominent in litigation brought under state antidilution statutes and because it was mentioned in the legislative history. Whether it is actually embraced by the statutory text, however, is another matter. Indeed, the contrast between the state statutes, which expressly refer to both "injury to business reputation" and to "dilution of the

distinctive quality of a trade name or trademark," and the federal
statute which refers only to the latter, arguably supports a narrower
reading of the FTDA.[40] [Internal citations omitted.]

The unexpected decision in the *Moseley* case has led Congress to
create a new antidilution statute, the Federal Trademark Dilution Revision Act of 2006.[41] The Act was passed by the House in 2005, the Senate in 2006, and signed by the president on October 6, 2006, as P.L.
109-312, 120 Stat. 1730. The idea of the bill is to respond to the *Moseley* case by fixing the definitions. This bill was a compromise that was
agreed upon by a number of organizations, including the International
Trademark Association and the American Intellectual Property Law
Association. The language of the bill was established beforehand, and
the bill was passed without amendment. The definition of "tarnishment" in the bill is an "association arising from the similarity between a
mark or trade name and a famous mark that harms the reputation of the
famous mark."[42] The trademark bill also uses the following definition
for dilution by "blurring":

> "[D]ilution by blurring" is association arising from the similarity be-
> tween a mark or trade name and a famous mark that impairs the dis-
> tinctiveness of the famous mark.
>   In determining whether a mark or trade name is likely to cause
> dilution by blurring, the court may consider all relevant factors, in-
> cluding the following:
>   (i) The degree of similarity between the mark or trade name
>   and the famous mark;
>   (ii) The degree of inherent or acquired distinctiveness of
>   the famous mark;
>   (iii) The extent to which the owner of the famous mark is
>   engaging in substantially exclusive use of the mark;
>   (iv) The degree of recognition of the famous mark;
>   (v) Whether the user of the mark or trade name intended to
>   create an association with the famous mark;
>   (vi) Any actual association between the mark or trade name
>   and the famous mark.[43]

Attorney Scot Duvall, one of the lawyers who worked on the
Moseley case, helped to negotiate the trademark bill. While the main
purpose of the bill was to respond to the Court's decision in the *Moseley* case by fixing a cause of action for blurring, Duvall was also able to
strike a blow for First Amendment freedom of speech. This was done
through the inclusion of the copyright doctrine of fair use in the trademark bill.

In copyright law, "Fair use gives the Constitution breathing space between the limits on expression inherent in copyright, and the freedom of expression guaranteed by the First Amendment."[44] It is because of fair use that the intellectual property owner's monopoly does not trample on our First Amendment freedom of speech rights. Fair use includes parody and caricature, such as in a political cartoon, which:

> [I]s often based on exploration of unfortunate physical traits or politically embarrassing events—an exploration often calculated to injure the feelings of the subject of the portrayal. The art of the cartoonist is often not reasoned or evenhanded, but slashing and one-sided. One cartoonist expressed the nature of the art in these words:[45] "The political cartoon is a weapon of attack, of scorn and ridicule and satire; it is least effective when it tries to pat some politician on the back. It is usually as welcome as a bee sting and is always controversial in some quarters.[46]

Fair use has always been a copyright concept. There is nothing in trademark law that in any way resembled fair use. Trademark law does have the term "unfair use"; this refers to the use of a trademark for a "bad" purpose that results in confusion, mistake, or deception. Certainly dilution of trademark, including tarnishment, would be considered to be an unfair use. For example, the GARBAGE PAIL KIDS was considered to be an "unfair use" of the CABBAGE PATCH KIDS.

The new trademark dilution bill contains defenses to claims of tarnishment and blurring for:

> (A) Fair use of a famous mark by another person in comparative commercial advertising or promotion to identify the competing goods or services of the owner of the famous mark;
> (B) Noncommercial use of a designation of source;
> (C) All forms of news reporting and news commentary.[47]

Although Duvall was able to get the concept of fair use included in the new trademark dilution bill, he was not able to get the drafters to define what fair use means in the context of trademarks. At one point, Duvall had suggested a definition for fair use, or a statement that fair use was being defined as it would be in the context of copyright. Since these definitions were struck from the bill while it was being drafted, Duvall has expressed concern that "fair use" will be interpreted for trademark as simply the opposite of "unfair use."[48]

One of the other items that Duvall struggled unsuccessfully to have included in the bill was language dealing with the concept of parody in trademarks. Because parody has never been allowed in trademark law, the CABBAGE PATCH KIDS won their suit against the GARBAGE PAIL KIDS. Had this case been brought under copyright law, the GARBAGE PAIL KIDS would have probably won, since "[i]t is this joinder of reference and ridicule that marks off the author's choice of parody from the other types of comment and criticism that traditionally have had a claim to fair use protection as transformative works."[49] (For more information on parody and copyright law, see **Chapter 4**, *Fair Use and Intellectual Property Rights.*)

Although the new trademark dilution bill doesn't have a good definition of fair use, and doesn't include specific language relating to parody, the provisions for fair use are still effective. There is at least a good argument that a mark used for a noncommercial parody would fall within the tarnishment and/or blurring exceptions. I suspect that there will be substantial litigation in the future over the term "fair use" in order to decide how the copyright concept applies to trademark law. I also suspect that librarians and archivists (as the guardians of information access) will be in the forefront of this issue.

B. Palming and Reverse Palming

In trademark law, claiming the product of another as your own is called *palming off* (also known as *passing off*). A good definition of "palming off" is found in the case of *Dastar Corporation v. 20th Century Fox* (which will be discussed in greater detail below):[50] "Passing off . . . occurs when a producer misrepresents his own goods or services as someone else's.[51] Reverse passing off, as its name implies, is the opposite: The producer misrepresents someone else's goods or services as his own."[52]

Thanks to trademark laws, we know that the product or service we purchase is really the one we intended to purchase, rather than something that has been "palmed off" on the purchaser. For example, the trademark Subaru represents a certain level of quality automobiles. I can't just take a go-cart and sell it as a Subaru. By palming Subaru's trademark, I would be confusing consumers as to the origin and quality of my vehicle. I would also cause harm to the reputation of Subaru. If I sold a go-cart as a Subaru and the vehicle didn't work, consumers would begin to associate Subaru with sub-quality automobiles, even though Subaru had nothing to do with the inferior product.

Here is another example: In the past, I would go into a restaurant and order a Coke. The server would bring me a cola drink, and I wouldn't ask any more questions. Now the server will ask me if Pepsi is all right with me. This is being done to avoid palming off Pepsi as being Coca-Cola. Although the drinks are similar, there are differences in taste, calories, etc. And, of course, two different companies with two different trademarks created the drinks. Both the Coke and Pepsi companies have spent large sums of money on educating restaurant workers so that they will differentiate between the two products for customers.

Reverse palming consists of passing off another product as if it were your own. This is a type of plagiarism that is similar to some of the issues found in copyright law. One example of reverse palming comes from the case of *Federal Electric Co. v. Flexlume Corp.*[53] Professor John T. Cross describes this case as involving "a defendant who serviced signs that had been manufactured by the plaintiff. When servicing a sign, the defendant would replace the plaintiff's mark with defendant's own, thereby suggesting to passers-by that it had manufactured the sign. The court held that defendant's false representation constituted common law unfair competition."[54]

Courts have identified the following as necessary elements of reverse palming:

♦ The product must originate with the plaintiff.[55]
♦ Plaintiff must have attempted to take credit for the product in public.[56]
♦ Defendant falsely designates the origin of the product without plaintiff's permission.[57]
♦ The false designation is likely to cause consumer confusion.[58]
♦ Plaintiff (or plaintiff's business) must be harmed by the false statement.[59]

One interesting example of the concept of reverse palming occurred when Big O Tires marketed a tire called the Bigfoot. At the time of the case, however, Big O was a much smaller company than it is today.[60]

After Big O had already begun selling its Bigfoot tires, Goodyear launched a new product also called the Bigfoot tire. Goodyear asked Big O for a license to use the name, but Big O denied this request. Despite the refusal, Goodyear decided to go ahead with a national advertising campaign.[61]

What Goodyear was doing was using its market position as a leading manufacturer to make people think that the smaller company (Big O) was infringing on Goodyear's trademark, even though the truth was that Goodyear was the infringer. By engaging in reverse palming, Goodyear was also besmirching Big O's name. This case, naturally, led to a lawsuit. Big O won in court because the company was able to prove that it had used the mark first.[62]

C. The *Dastar* Case and the Relationship between Trademark and Copyright

In recent years, the relationship between copyright and trademark has been the subject of litigation. The general rule has always been that trademark and copyright are mutually exclusive. You can't use both; rather, you need to choose only one type of protection in order to shield your intellectual property. The U.S. Supreme Court recently reaffirmed this principle in the case of *Dastar Corporation v. 20th Century Fox Film Corporation*.[63] The case was decided 8-0 by the U.S. Supreme Court on June 2, 2003. (Justice Breyer did not take part in the consideration of the case.) Justice Scalia wrote the opinion of the Court. The case revolved around a trademark claim for some copyrighted materials that had passed into the public domain. Since copyright protection was not available for the product, the holder of the expired copyright attempted to protect the item under trademark law.

The basis of the *Dastar* case was General Dwight D. Eisenhower's book *Crusade in Europe*. This book was General Eisenhower's written account of the European campaign during World War II. After Doubleday published the book, exclusive television rights were granted to 20th Century Fox, which in turn licensed Time, Inc., to produce a television series. The series had 26 episodes and was first broadcast in 1949. Although Doubleday renewed the copyright on the book in 1975, Fox did not renew the copyright on the TV series. That copyright expired in 1977.[64]

In 1988, Doubleday again granted Fox exclusive rights to the book. Fox in turn licensed the rights of the book to New Line Home Video. The original television series was remastered and released on home video. What happened next is best quoted from the Supreme Court opinion:

> Enter petitioner Dastar. In 1995, Dastar decided to expand its product line from music compact discs to videos. Anticipating renewed interest in World War II on the 50th anniversary of the war's end, Dastar released a video set entitled *World War II Campaigns in Europe*. To make *Campaigns*, Dastar purchased eight beta cam tapes of the *original* version of the *Crusade* television series, which is in

the public domain, copied them, and then edited the series. Dastar's *Campaigns* series is slightly more than half as long as the original *Crusade* television series.[65]

Dastar made some editorial changes, none of them substantive. Then Dastar sold the video set "as its own product."[66] Naturally, Fox was not amused, and sued for trademark and copyright infringement, as well as for unfair competition under § 43(a) of the Lanham Act.[67]

The District Court found in favor of Fox, and the 9th Circuit Court of Appeals affirmed the decision. Basically, the District Court and the 9th Circuit ruled that Dastar had passed off Fox's work as its own. The District Court also held for Fox on copyright grounds, but the 9th Circuit reversed that portion of the claim.[68]

According to the 9th Circuit Court of Appeals, "Dastar copied substantially the entire *Crusade in Europe* series created by Twentieth Century Fox, labeled the resulting product with a different name and marketed it without attribution to Fox [and] therefore committed a bodily appropriation of Fox's series . . . Dastar's bodily appropriation of Fox's original [television] series is sufficient to establish the reverse passing off."[69] The Court of Appeals found that the misrepresentation created a risk of confusion in the mind of the consumer, which is one of the basic requirements of a suit for trademark infringement.

The Supreme Court, on the other hand, was not convinced by this argument and found for Dastar. According to the Supreme Court:

> The problem with this argument according special treatment to communicative products is that it causes the Lanham Act to conflict with the law of copyright, which addresses that subject specifically. The right to copy, and to copy without attribution, once a copyright has expired, like "the right to make [an article whose patent has expired] . . . passes to the public."[70] "In general, unless an intellectual property right such as a patent or copyright protects an item, it will be subject to copying."[71] The rights of a patentee or copyright holder are part of a "carefully crafted bargain,"[72] under which, once the patent or copyright monopoly has expired, the public may use the invention or work at will and without attribution.[73]

The Supreme Court summarized its decision as follows:

> In sum, reading the phrase "origin of goods" in the Lanham Act in accordance with the Act's common-law foundations (which were *not* designed to protect originality or creativity), and in light of the

copyright and patent laws (which *were*), we conclude that the phrase refers to the producer of the tangible goods that are offered for sale, and not to the author of any idea, concept, or communication embodied in those goods.[74] To hold otherwise would be akin to finding that § 43(a) (of the Lanham Act) created a species of perpetual patent and copyright, which Congress may not do.[75]

Some commentators also believe that *Dastar* was an example of plagiarism, and that the decision was the result of the Court refusing to get involved in defining what constitutes the act of plagiarism. Jonathan Band and Matt Schruers discuss the *Dastar* case in their article *Dastar, Attribution, and Plagiarism*.[76] These scholars read the *Dastar* case as dealing with the issue of whether plagiarism also constitutes a trademark violation, since the defendant didn't identify the origin of the *Campaigns* series as being *Crusade in Europe*. The article states that "in these circumstances it makes more sense to leave the regulation of plagiarism to social and professional norms rather than the law."[77]

There certainly is some merit in this view of the *Dastar* case. After all, it is undisputed that the defendant used material created by others but did not provide attribution. And, of course, plagiarism is an important issue for librarians and archivists, since the source of information is so important when making judgments as to the quality and reliability of an item. However, in my opinion the more important issue that the Supreme Court ruled on was the principle that creators of intellectual property must choose which type of safeguard they wish to use for protection, rather than relying on multiple forms of intellectual property to get around restrictions. Once the creator has chosen copyright, he or she is precluded from using another form of protection. As law professor Ronald Raitt has often said, "You get one pull on the litigation lever."[78]

The point of *Dastar* is that it would not be fair to allow unlimited choice of legal remedies. Allowing recovery for both copyright infringement and trademark infringement would basically permit the creation of an unlimited monopoly by the property owner. The intellectual property system is a monopoly, but it is a limited monopoly that allows for fairness and for reasonable use. Forcing creators to choose which type of protection they wish to obtain helps to avoid unlimited monopolies and helps to ensure the fairness of our legal system.

Trademarks, Domain Names,
and Cybersquatting

The Internet contains many types of information. In some ways, it might be called a "cyberspace library." This virtual library raises numerous challenges, questions, and concerns for librarians and archivists.

One area in which trademark law has resulted in litigation involves domain names on the Internet. How often do we think about the name that we enter into our computer in order to find a Website? Yet without the Domain Name System (DNS) currently in place, we would have links such as *255.15.543*.[79] Needless to say, this situation would make the Internet much more difficult to use. In order to ensure that the DNS registry runs smoothly, all of us need to understand how it operates and what the laws are that regulate domain name disputes. Libraries are at the forefront of the digital revolution, and the issue of domain names is every bit as important to information professionals as the materials that are actually on the Websites. The Internet is like the Wild West—there are many disputes, but there are also many attempts to introduce order.

Those of us who were early users of the World Wide Web remember when big corporations like McDonald's didn't have their own domain names. At that time, a large corporation might have had a web page somewhere within the directory of its Internet Service Provider, with a hard-to-remember URL something like: *www.internet-providers .net/members/business/corporations/mcdonalds*. This kind of domain name is practically unusable for web surfers because of its length and complexity. Of course, now McDonald's is very easy to find at *www.mcdonalds.com*.

The Internet was formed in 1969 by the U.S. Defense Department as a communications system that would be able to function in the event of a nuclear attack. It was originally called ARPANET (Advanced Research Projects Agency Network).[80] Around the same time, the National Science Foundation (NSF) developed the NSFnet. Eventually the two systems were merged under the control of the NSF. With the introduction of the World Wide Web in 1994, the Internet became increasingly popular and widely used.[81]

For many years, a company called Network Solutions maintained the Domain Name System (DNS) registry. As the Web grew, however, another system of management was needed.[82] In 1998, the Internet Corporation for Assigned Names and Numbers (ICANN) was formed as a nonprofit, private-sector corporation. "ICANN has been designated by the U.S. Government to serve as the global consensus entity to which the U.S. government is transferring the responsibility for coordinating four key functions for the Internet: the management of the domain name system, the allocation of IP address space, the assignment of protocol parameters, and the management of the root server system."[83] For Internet users, these key functions are as significant as the Dewey Decimal or Library of Congress systems are for information professionals and their patrons.

There are a number of Top-Level Domain Names (TLDs). The original TLDs consisted of **.com** for commercial businesses, **.org** for nonprofit organizations, **.edu** for educational entities, **.net** for network providers, **.gov** for agencies of the U.S. government, and **.mil** for the military. Using the wrong TLD can cause problems. For example, we must be careful to look for the official White House Website by entering www.whitehouse.gov/ instead of www.whitehouse.com/. Those who make the mistake of entering www.whitehouse.com/ are taken to a pornographic Website. This can be very embarrassing, especially when teaching research instruction classes!

Soon after the establishment of the World Wide Web, TLDs were approved for geographic entities, such as **.il** for Israel, **.cz** for the Czech Republic, and **.ky** for the state of Kentucky. For example, the URL for finding statutes, bills, and administrative regulations from the state of Minnesota is http://www.leg.state.mn.us/leg/legis.htm, and the city of Fresno, California, is at http://www.ci.fresno.ca.us. These geographic TLDs have proved to be very popular because they are useful and easy to remember.

In November 2000, ICANN granted approval in principle to seven new Top Level Domain Names. According to ICANN, "The selected TLD proposals are of two types. Four proposals (**.biz**, **.info**, **.name**, and **.pro**) are for relatively large, un-sponsored TLDs. The other three proposals (**.aero**, **.coop**, and **.museum**) are for smaller 'sponsored' TLDs."[84] The "un-sponsored" TLDS operate under policies established directly by ICANN. "Sponsored" TLDs are operated by a sponsoring organization representing a specialized community with specialized rules.[85] Currently, ICANN is in the process of negotiating the operating agreements.[86]

In the early days of the Internet, people would register the domain names of already established companies and then attempt to sell these names to the companies for large sums of money. This behavior is called *Cybersquatting* and is prohibited by the Anticybersquatting Consumer Protection Act of 1999,[87] as well as by trademark law. It is now illegal to register a name and then attempt to sell it to the trademark holder.[88] For example, if I registered the domain name "Wal-Mart.com" and tried to sell it to the Wal-Mart corporation, I would be violating the law. ICANN has also created dispute resolution rules for these and similar situations.[89]

There are, however, some companies that are actively trying to mislead the public. In December 2000, the Federal Trade Commission (FTC) issued a consumer alert entitled "What's Dot and What's Not: Domain Name Registration Scams."[90] I doubt that I am the only person who has received e-mail solicitations for domain name reservations. Some of these reservations are no doubt legitimate. However, the potential for consumer fraud or identity theft exists any time that people respond to a "spam" e-mail message from an unfamiliar company. Domain names are the newest area of opportunity for confidence games.

Domain names can also become a source of conflict and litigation, even in the absence of unethical intentions. One example that took place a few years ago in the area of legal research involved the dispute between legal researcher T. R. Halvorson and the LexisNexis Corporation. An experienced legal researcher and author of *Law of the Super Searchers: The Online Secrets of Top Legal Researchers*,[91] Halvorson created a free legal research Website entitled LexNotes.[92] LexNotes "is a new online resource for legal research professionals. It provides categorized and searchable links to research sources, bibliographies, pathfinders, articles, reviews, papers, legal news, and tips."[93] This Website is primarily aimed at lawyers and law librarians, although it is accessible by the general public as well.

On March 12, 2001, LexisNexis informed Halvorson that they believed LexNotes was infringing on the LEXIS trademark. LexisNexis requested that Halvorson cease and desist using the domain name www.lexnotes.com.[94] According to Halvorson, "While acknowledging that LEXIS never has used the mark LexNotes, LEXIS claims that my use of it infringes on a family of marks that begin with the Latin word lex, meaning law."[95] One issue involved in this dispute is whether "lex" is a generic word. LexNotes has compiled a partial listing of domain names beginning with "lex." The list contains over 4,000 domain names.[96] According to law librarian Karen Mahnk:

> Lex is not a name but a generic word for "law." Generic words are tough cookies to trademark, i.e. Agua/aqua/water. Note that there are numerous water companies with the name root Aqua (not to mention AquaVelva). Also, "Pizza Hut" certainly didn't have much luck

keeping "pizza" out of all the other restaurant names. So too any legal entity may include the word lex or law. So, unless "law" can be trademarked, I doubt they have much standing.[97]

Another product with a similar name is the luxury automobile "LEXUS." Mead Data Central, the previous owner of LexisNexis, sued Toyota, the producer of Lexus automobiles.[98] The 2nd Circuit ruled in favor of Toyota. According to the opinion:

> Mead introduced evidence that its president in 1972 "came up with the name LEXIS based on Lex which was Latin for law and I S for information systems." In fact, however, the word "lexis" is centuries old. It is found in the language of ancient Greece, where it had the meaning of "phrase," "word," "speaking" or "diction."[99] "Lexis" subsequently appeared in the Latin where it had a substantially similar meaning, i.e., "word," "speech," or "language."[100]

The court noted that many other companies had the root word "lex" in their name, comparing "LEXUS to NEXXUS, a nationally known shampoo, and LEXIS to NEXIS, Mead's trademark for its computerized news service. NEXXUS and NEXIS have co-existed in apparent tranquility for almost a decade."[101] The 2nd Circuit concluded that LEXIS as a computer research database did not dilute Toyota's mark of LEXUS for automobiles.[102]

In fact, there are 102 words in *Black's Law Dictionary* that begin with the root word "lex."[103] Several of these words are used in combinations. Some of the more important phrases include *lex loci delicti*, the "law of the place where the tort was committed," as well as *lex naturae*, which means "natural law," and *lex generalis*, "[a] law of general application, as opposed to one that affects only a particular person or small group of people."[104]

Eventually the dispute between Halvorson and LexisNexis was settled in a way which was satisfactory to both of the parties. Halvorson still runs the LexNotes Website, but his site contains the following disclaimer: "LexNotes™ is not affiliated with nor licensed, sponsored, endorsed, or otherwise approved of by LexisNexis or LEXIS, which are believed to be registered trademarks of Reed Elsevier Properties Inc."[105]

The Internet is still in the Wild West days of its beginning. The Domain Name System does provide a possibility for both abuse and unintentional conflicts. Sometimes disputes arise over domain names, even without bad faith on the part of anyone. However, ICANN and its allies—trademark law and the Anticybersquatting Consumer Protection Act of 1999—are trying to bring law and order to the system without being overly controlling. We who work with the Internet still have a hard road to travel, but the Wild West came to order, and even the most infamous territories were tamed. So, too, through the use of trademark law, through anticybersquatting regulations, and through teaching patrons how to evaluate Websites, information professionals are helping to bring civilization to the Internet.

Internet Linking and Framing in Copyright and Trademark Law

Linking and framing on Websites have received a great deal of attention in the recent past. One of the most important functions of the World Wide Web is the ability to link to other Websites. These links are invaluable to all users, but especially to librarians and archivists. Indeed, the three characteristics that separate the World Wide Web from what went before (Telnet, Gopher, etc.) are the ability to deliver multimedia, the use of a graphical interface, and the ability to link seamlessly to other sites. Without these three factors, the Web would not have obtained its current popularity and power.

Yet the idea of linking and framing is troubling to some specialists in intellectual property. There are multiple copyright and trademark issues involved in linking and framing. Also, there are some other concerns, such as libel, that need to be considered.

Does this mean that linking is dead? Is the Web destined to go away? Of course not! But there are definitely some things that librarians and archivists can do in creating Websites, and some things that librarians and archivists should not do in creating Websites. The following material will help to show the difference between what is permissible and what isn't.

A. Copying, Displaying, and Transmitting Files

One concern with copyright law and the World Wide Web is the issue of making copies. As we have already seen, section 106 of the Copyright Act provides that the copyright owner has certain exclusive rights:

♦ To reproduce the copyrighted work in copies;[106]

♦ To distribute copies or phonorecords of the copyrighted work to the public by sale or other transfer of ownership, or by rental, lease, or lending;[107]

♦ In the case of literary, musical, dramatic, and choreographic works, pantomimes, and pictorial, graphic, or sculptural works, including the individual images of a motion picture or other audiovisual work, to display the copyrighted work publicly;[108]

♦ In the case of sound recordings, to perform the copyrighted work publicly by means of a digital audio transmission.[109]

According to the Copyright Act, "'Copies' are material objects, other than phonorecords, in which a work is fixed by any method now known or later developed, and from which the work can be perceived, reproduced, or otherwise communicated, either directly or with the aid of a machine or device."[110]

The problem with copyright for Websites comes from the fact that each time you access a web page you are making a copy of the page on your computer. Of course, the creator of the Website knows that this is the case, and under normal circumstances this incidental copy is not an issue. After all, by placing an unencrypted page on the Web without password protection, the owner is in effect giving the public an implied license to view the page, even if that means making an incidental copy along the way.

Multimedia, sound, and graphics, on the other hand, are more difficult. With multimedia, you are not only making an incidental copy, but you are also displaying the work, which is also subject to copyright law. According to the Copyright Act, "To 'display' a work means to show a copy of it, either directly or by means of a film, slide, television image, or any other device or process or, in the case of a motion picture or other audiovisual work, to show individual images nonsequentially."[111]

Once again, if the copyright owner has placed the items on the Web without encryption or password protection, there is an implied license to use. The problem that crops up from time to time involves the downloading or display of multimedia works that are posted without the consent of the copyright holder. Since Website operators can't grant more rights than they have themselves, if the item is posted illegally an innocent user can't obtain legal rights to display the material. Because of this situation, users of Websites may in fact be illegally downloading multimedia without even realizing it.

This particular scenario frequently occurs with regard to music. A Website operator will sometimes place a digital audio file on his or her Website, despite not having permission from the copyright holder. If this file is then subsequently downloaded, the person who is listening to the file does not have legal rights. In effect, this problem was the basis for the finding in the *Napster* case, which involved a file transfer system whereby users could communicate with one another to exchange musical files.[112]

On the one hand, the *Napster* case stands for the proposition that cyberspace is subject to the same copyright restrictions as real space. On the other hand, however, a large part of the case rests on the fact that in this instance the copies were digitally transmitted.[113]

If the operator of a Website uses a link, he or she is not creating a digital transmission; rather, the operator is redirecting the user's browser to another site. The digital transmission comes from the other site. Thus, in terms of linking, a simple link on a Website does not rise to the level of copyright infringement. Nonetheless, Web developers should be advised to avoid linking to digital files unless they are certain that the linked file has no copyright problems. Thus, patrons are forewarned and forearmed.

B. Copyright and Trademark Issues with Deep Linking and Framing

Although a simple link doesn't generally rise to the level of a copyright violation, there are still significant problems with the inclusion of deep links and with frames. A deep link is a link to a page inside another Website, a page that can be reached without first going to the home page. According to attorney Randel S. Springer, framing is:

> [A] hybrid of linking which allows a Web site to display on a single screen content from its own site with content from another Web site simultaneously. In the usual case, the framing site's content appears in a "frame" which surrounds the content of another site. . . . In most instances, the "framing" site's Web address is listed at the top of the browser.[114]

Many copyright experts are troubled by deep linking that includes framing. These types of links sometimes imply that the content on the screen is original to that Website, when in fact some of the content is actually borrowed. This is a much larger problem with frames than with deep linking, but the possibility of misattribution is still an issue. As a result, some Websites do not allow interior pages to be linked. If you are at all in doubt, check the terms and conditions for Website use, and don't use more material than the terms allow.

The main case discussing deep linking is *Ticketmaster v. Tickets .com.*[115] In this case, a start-up company called Tickets.com employed a program called a spider to locate information about local events. *Spiders* are programs that automatically visit Websites and index them without human intervention. (Spiders are also called "crawlers" or "bots.")[116] Among other things, the Tickets.com spider indexed interior pages within the Ticketmaster Website. These interior pages were then linked from Tickets.com.

In the *Ticketmaster* case, the District Court identified three primary copyright issues. The first involved the incidental copy in computer memory; the court found that this was within fair use and was not a violation of copyright.[117] The second issue was whether the URLs were subject to copyright so that a linking site would not be allowed to copy them. The court ruled that URLs are not subject to copyright since they are a factual matter.

The third issue, however, is much more relevant to this discussion. In this portion of the case, the court had to decide whether deep linking was a violation of copyright. The District Court found that:

> [Tickets.com] did not try to disguise a sale by use of frames occurring on the Tickets.com website. [Tickets.com] further states that when users were linked to [TicketMaster] web pages, the [Ticket-Master] event pages were clearly identified as belonging to [Ticket-Master]. . . .[118]
> Moreover, the link on the [Tickets.com] site to the [TicketMaster] event page contained the following notice:
>> **Buy this ticket** from **another online ticketing company.** [Emphasis in original.] Click here to buy tickets. These tickets are sold by another ticketing company. Although we can't sell them to you, the link above will take you directly to the other company's web site where you can purchase them.
>> Even if the [TicketMaster] site may have been displayed as a smaller window that was literally "framed" by the larger [Tickets .com] window, it is not clear that, as matter of law, the linking to [Tickets.com] event pages would constitute a showing or public display in violation of 17 U.S.C. § 106(5).[119]

In effect, the District Court found that, since Tickets.com was careful to let users know that they were going to another Website, there was no copyright infringement. Tickets.com didn't palm off the pages as being their own material. In fact, Tickets.com was very careful to explain to customers that the browser was going to display material from another company's Website.

So far, the *Ticketmaster* case is the only major decision in the area of deep linking. This case appears to indicate that, as long as proper attribution is given, there should be no copyright problems with deep linking.

Framing, on the other hand, is almost by definition an issue both in terms of copyright and trademark. For copyright purposes, frames are problematic in that they appear to be passing off the work of someone else as if it were your own. According to Randel S. Springer, "Although there is little direct guidance on whether framing is legal, the practice certainly has the potential for causing consumer confusion, and thereby violating trademark laws and unfair competition laws."[120] As has been discussed above, one of the major purposes of trademark law is to protect the goodwill and investment of businesses while also protecting consumers against misrepresentation and confusion about the source of goods and services.[121] Therefore, it makes sense that framing would involve trademark issues.

The problem is that when frames are employed, it is difficult to tell the origin of the Website material. In effect, the framing Website is a type of reverse palming, claiming another's product as one's own. The most famous framing case involved a Website called *TotalNews* that framed stories from the *Washington Post* and other newspapers. Because the parties settled out of court before the case came to trial, the settlement document provides the only guidance on this issue.[122] The settlement states that:

> [TotalNews agrees] permanently not to directly or indirectly cause any [Washington Post] Website to appear on a user's computer screen with any material (e.g. Universal Resource Locator (URL), text, graphics, pop-up window, audio, video or other) supplied by or Associated with [TotalNews] or any third party, such as an advertiser. ... [Washington Post agrees] that [TotalNews] may link from the Totalnews.com Website or any other Website to [Washington Post's] Website, provided that:
> (a) [TotalNews] may link to [Washington Post's] Websites only via hyperlinks consisting of the names of the linked sites in plain text, which may be highlighted;
> (b) [TotalNews] may not use on any Website, as hyperlinks

or in any other way, any of [Washington Post's] proprietary
logos or other distinctive graphics, video or audio material,
nor may [TotalNews] otherwise link in any manner reasonably likely to:
  (i) imply affiliation with, endorsement or sponsorship by [Washington Post];
  (ii) cause confusion, mistake or deception;
  (iii) dilute [Washington Post's] marks; or
  (iv) otherwise violate state or federal law. . . .[123]

Even though the *TotalNews* case never reached trial, it provides
one of the few bits of legal guidance available on the legality of framing. As a result of the settlement, most authorities suggest that the way
to remain within the law is to follow the guidelines that were laid down
by the *TotalNews* settlement.[124] In other words, if you build a Website
with frames, clarify where the content came from, do not use trademarks without permission, and do not imply any type of sponsorship.
When using a frame, always read the framed site's terms and conditions, and obtain permission before creating the frame.

C. Other Legal Issues with Linking and Framing

In addition to copyright and trademark, there are other ways in
which linking and framing can get a Website operator into trouble.
Linking to a site that contains illegal material is a good way to attract
law enforcement attention and wind up in court. For example, a Webmaster who created a "directory of child pornography Websites" would
be sure to have a visit from the F.B.I. (Whether or not the charges
would finally stick depends on what the charges were and on the atti-
tude of the courts; however, I can think of a pretty good argument for
charging the Webmaster as an Accessory After the Fact.)

An example of this potential problem involves an online computer
publication called *2600 Magazine*. The magazine tried to publish a
story about computer codes that broke the encryption on DVDs. Under
the Digital Millennium Copyright Act,[125] it is a criminal offense to remove or disable an encryption device. A developer in Norway (where
the DMCA could not be enforced) had created a code that would disable encryptions, and had placed the code on a Website. In the story
about encryption, *2600 Magazine* attempted to place a link to the developer's Website. Because most DVDs contain movies, the Motion
Picture Association of America sued *2600 Magazine*—and won. The
ruling in this case barred *2600 Magazine* from placing a link on its

Website that would send users to the Website with the disabling code.[126]

Another potential problem with linking and framing involves the law of defamation. According to *American Jurisprudence*, the courts have defined defamation as including:

♦ A false publication causing injury to a person's reputation, or exposing him to public hatred, contempt, ridicule, shame, or disgrace, or affecting him adversely in . . . trade or business.

♦ The publication of anything injurious to the good name or reputation of another or which tends to bring him into disrepute.

♦ That which tends to injure reputation or to diminish the esteem, respect, good will, or confidence in the plaintiff or to excite derogatory feelings or opinions about the plaintiff.

♦ Communications made by a defendant to a third party that cause some injury to the plaintiff's reputation by exciting derogatory, adverse, or unpleasant feelings against the plaintiff or by diminishing the esteem or respect in which he is held.

♦ Repeating the false statements of others.[127]

In order to constitute defamation, the statement must be false. However, it *cannot* be something that is a matter of opinion. For example, one case found that "authors' description of plaintiff as 'drab and grey' and implication that she was 'unpleasant' were mere statements of opinion, not actionable as defamatory."[128]

In the case of linking and framing, one problem stems from the issue of "repeating the false statements of others." For example, newspapers are often sued for reporting defamatory statements that originated in sources. Even book reviewers are not exempt: "Assertions that would otherwise be actionable in defamation do not become nonactionable if they appear in [the] context of [a] book review."[129]

Linking to a Website that contains libelous information may constitute republishing the material for the purposes of defamation law. As a result, Website creators need to examine all the links they provide in order to determine whether there are potential problems.[130] This precaution includes examining online bibliographies and research guides, because the links may point to defamatory materials. Naturally, information professionals must ensure that—in advising patrons, writing book reviews, etc.—we do not act like a "link" to defamatory materials. Similarly, we must avoid acting as "links" to legally protected materials such as trade secrets.

Trade Secrets

Although less familiar than copyright, patents, and trademark, trade secrets are an important type of intellectual property. As such, they can be protected in a court of law. According to the definition used by the Uniform Trade Secret Act:

> "Trade secret" means information, including a formula, pattern, compilation, program, device, method, technique, or process, that:
>
>> (i) derives independent economic value, actual or potential, from not being generally known to, and not being readily ascertainable by . . . other persons who can obtain economic value from its disclosure or use, and
>>
>> (ii) is the subject of efforts that are reasonable . . . to maintain its secrecy.

The important point to remember about trade secrets is that the information must have some economic value that comes from being kept confidential. In addition, the person providing the information must make reasonable efforts to maintain the secret. A trade secret "provides the owner of the information with a competitive advantage in the marketplace, and is treated in a way that can reasonably be expected to prevent the public or competitors from learning about it, *absent improper acquisition or theft.*"[131] [Emphasis added.]

Some examples of trade secrets include the secret formula for Coca-Cola, the secret ingredients in Skyline Chili, the mix used by Colonel Sanders' Kentucky Fried Chicken, and other recipes. Trade secrets can also be: "a new invention for which a patent application has not yet been filed, marketing strategies, manufacturing techniques and computer algorithms."[132] Other types of trade secrets include a database of customer names and addresses, a new pharmaceutical drug, and even how much profit a private company makes. (Profit information from publicly traded companies is not a trade secret, since this information is required by law to be filed with the Securities and Exchange Commission and must be made available to the public.) In effect, a trade secret can be anything, as long as it contains *independent economic value.*

Since a trade secret is potentially unlimited in time, this form of protection is often used to maintain intellectual property rights in a product if the producer is worried about patent rights expiring. When a patent application is filed, the applicant must not only disclose complete details of the invention, but must also provide the Patent and Trademark Office with a working model. Patent protection is complete and total—but only for a limited time. Once the patent has expired, the invention becomes available for anyone to copy without payment of royalties.

Trade secrets, on the other hand, do not involve any kind of filing. Rather, the owners simply take steps to keep the information confidential. As a result, misappropriation of a trade secret is grounds for a lawsuit.

Trade secret protection is generally the subject of state law, although there are some Federal statutes that apply as well. Many states have adopted all or parts of the Uniform Trade Secrets Act, which offers a valuable overview of the field.[133] In addition, the Economic Espionage Act of 1996 also provides for criminal penalties in the event of misappropriation of trade secrets.[134] Of course, information professionals must respect the protection of trade secrets when we advise researchers. In addition, archivists and records managers who deal with corporate documents should be careful that the documents in their archives do not reveal trade secrets.

A. The Case of the "Ancient Family Secret!"

Let's analyze how information becomes a trade secret. Do you remember the 1972 advertisement for Calgon laundry detergent? Here is the ad in slightly modified form: A customer asks the manager of a laundry how he gets the shirts so clean. The manager replies (paraphrased), "Ancient family secret!" The manager's wife reveals the "ancient family secret" when she calls across the room to her husband, "We need more Calgon!" The customer then says to the manager (paraphrased), "Ancient secret, huh!"[135] Does this information qualify as a trade secret?

The brand of detergent that a laundry uses may indeed be something that the owner would not want his competitors to know. However, in order to find out whether this is in fact a trade secret or simply a regular secret, we need to use the two-part test given above. We need to be able to show that there is independent economic value to the information, and that the person with the secret has taken reasonable steps to maintain secrecy.

In this case, the brand of detergent that a laundry uses may very well have independent economic value. After all, if the competitors know which detergent is being used, they may be able to use the same product and lure customers away. So this information satisfies the first part of the requirements for being a trade secret.

However, there are two parts to the trade secret test. The individuals must also make reasonable efforts to keep the information confidential. In the Calgon ad, the wife shouts across the room, "We need more Calgon!" This scenario doesn't sound like a reasonable effort to keep the information secret. As a result, the Calgon ad fails the second part of the test. The use of Calgon in the laundry is not a trade secret.

B. Reasonable Efforts to Maintain Secrecy

What would be a reasonable effort to maintain secrecy? According to Findlaw, the following groups of people can be prevented from using or disclosing a trade secret:

- ◆ People who are automatically bound by a duty of confidentiality not to disclose or use trade secret information, including any employee who routinely comes into contact with the employer's trade secrets as part of the employee's job;

- ◆ people who acquire a trade secret through improper means such as theft, industrial espionage or bribery;

- ◆ people who knowingly obtain trade secrets from people who have no right to disclose them [such as learning a trade secret from a librarian];

- ◆ people who learn about a trade secret by accident or mistake, but had reason to know that the information was a protected trade secret; and

- ◆ people who sign nondisclosure agreements (also known as "confidentiality agreements") promising not to disclose trade secrets without authorization from the owner.[136]

In order to make sure that trade secret status is maintained, documents should be marked "Confidential," secrets should be locked away, and they should only be shared with those who have a "need to know." (In effect, this is what James Bond is doing when he says, "I can tell you, but then I'll have to kill you!") However, the best way to protect your secrets is to have everyone who works with the confidential material sign a nondisclosure agreement saying that the information will not be given out. Nondisclosure provisions are routinely included in employment contracts and business agreements. Many highly compensated employees also sign a covenant not to compete with their previous business. In their contracts, the employees specify that they will not reveal trade secrets if they go to work for a competitor. I firmly recommend that anyone who is in possession of trade secret information should make use of appropriate nondisclosure and noncompetition agreements.

C. Legal and Equitable Remedies for Trade Secrets

The law provides a multitude of remedies in the event that a trade secret is disclosed. These remedies include getting an injunction to prevent further disclosure, asking for financial damages, and other types of legal and equitable solutions. In some circumstances (such as the *Redmond* case discussed below), courts have prevented former employees from taking new jobs because of the "inevitable disclosure" of confidential knowledge; however, this type of ruling is very unusual.

The idea of the inevitable disclosure doctrine is that the former employees learned secrets of a type that they could not help but rely upon in their new job. The most famous example of this situation is the case of *PepsiCo v. Redmond*.[137] In this case, William Redmond, Jr., was a high-level employee at PepsiCo. As part of his employment, he was acquainted with numerous trade secrets, including strategic marketing plans for the All-Sports drink, which was produced by PepsiCo. This product was in direct competition with Gatorade, which was produced by the Quaker Oats Company.

On November 8, 1994, Redmond was offered a job with Quaker Oats as chief operating officer for the Gatorade/Snapple division. PepsiCo asked the court to block Redmond's employment on the grounds that his knowledge of the All-Sports strategic marketing plan would constitute an inevitable disclosure of trade secrets. The parties were from two different states, so the case wound up in Federal court.

The court looked at the idea behind the inevitable disclosure doctrine, which is that "an employee with knowledge of a former employer's trade secrets would 'inevitably' disclose the [information] to the new employer since the nature of the new job would lead to such disclosures, given that the new and old employers were competitors."[138]

The 7th Circuit Court of Appeals explored the delicate balance between trade secret protection and freedom of choice. According to the Circuit Court:

> The question of threatened or inevitable misappropriation in this case lies at the heart of a basic tension in trade secret law. Trade secret law serves to protect "standards of commercial morality" and "encourage invention and innovation" while maintaining "the public interest in having free and open competition in the manufacture and sale of un-

patented goods." Yet that same law should not prevent workers from pursuing their livelihoods when they leave their current positions. It has been said that federal age discrimination law does not guarantee tenure for older employees. Similarly, trade secret law does not provide a reserve clause for solicitous employers. . . . This tension is particularly exacerbated when a plaintiff sues to prevent not the actual misappropriation of trade secrets but the mere threat that it will occur.[139] [Citations omitted.]

Nevertheless, the 7th Circuit found in favor of PepsiCo, ruling that:

> [W]hen we couple the demonstrated inevitability that Redmond would rely on PCNA trade secrets in his new job at Quaker with the district court's reluctance to believe that Redmond would refrain from disclosing these secrets in his new position (or that Quaker would ensure Redmond did not disclose them), we conclude that the district court correctly decided that PepsiCo demonstrated a likelihood of success on its statutory claim of trade secret misappropriation. . . . [W]e also agree with . . . the likelihood of Redmond's breach of his confidentiality agreement should he begin working at Quaker.[140]

The type of noncompetition action found in the *Redmond* case is very unusual, and generally only applies to executives and managerial employees who are very high in the organizational chart and who have been offered jobs at a similar level by a competitor. Most state courts have refused to adopt the inevitable disclosure doctrine for fear that it would restrict economic freedom of action. For example, California rejected the doctrine in the case of *Whyte v. Schlage Lock Co.*[141] The court in *Whyte* stated that:

> The chief ill in the covenant not to compete imposed by the inevitable disclosure doctrine is its after-the-fact nature: The covenant is imposed *after* the employment contract is made and therefore alters the employment relationship without the employee's consent. . . .
>
> Schlage and Whyte did not agree upon a covenant not to compete. We decline to impose one, however restricted in scope, by adopting the inevitable disclosure doctrine. *Lest there be any doubt about our holding, our rejection of the inevitable disclosure doctrine is complete.* If a covenant not to compete . . . is part of the employment agreement, the inevitable disclosure doctrine cannot be invoked to supplement the covenant, alter its meaning, or make an otherwise unenforceable covenant enforceable.[142] [Emphasis added.]

Once again, the best way to avoid problems would have been with nondisclosure and noncompetition agreements written into the employment contracts. As the court in the *Whyte* case so eloquently stated, if the employer wanted to avoid competition a nondisclosure agreement should have been included in the employment contract.

Another potential penalty for violating trade secrets is found in the Economic Espionage Act (EEA) of 1996. This statute provides for criminal penalties in the event of misappropriation of trade secrets.[143] According to Findlaw, "The EEA punishes intentional stealing, copying or receiving of trade secrets 'related to or included in a product that is produced for or placed in interstate commerce.'"[144]

Violation of the EEA is a major felony, involving both large fines and lengthy prison sentences. If the individual is performing a theft on behalf of a U.S.-based company, he or she may be fined up to $500,000 and receive a prison sentence of up to 10 years. Corporations that are found guilty of industrial espionage may be fined up to $5 million. Performing an act of industrial espionage on behalf of a foreign government or a foreign agent may cause the fines to double and the jail time to increase to 15 years.[145] Sections 1831 and 1834 of the EEA also allow both the item and the proceeds that resulted from industrial espionage to be confiscated by the government and then sold.[146] Obviously, librarians and archivists must be careful to ensure that they do not unwittingly assist a client in the commission of a felony.

The passage of the Economic Espionage Act was an unprecedented change in the trade secret law. For the first time, criminal penalties could be given for trade secret violations. The EEA has been subject to both praise and criticism from different sources, but whether you love it or hate it, information professionals must be aware of the provisions of this important statute.

D. Librarian Confidentiality and Trade Secret Law

The materials in this chapter are important for librarians and archivists. Trade secret law is directly applicable to the rules of patron confidentiality in the library setting. As professionals, our ethical principles require us to keep confidential the questions our patrons ask. Most states have legal provisions for keeping this type of information confidential. (For more information, see *Chapter 9*, *Search Warrants, Investigations, Library Records, and Privacy*.)

Trade secret laws and patron confidentiality laws are clearly related to one another. For example, if an inventor comes into the library, the questions asked and resources consulted could reveal to a competitor what the inventor is working on. As a result, it is imperative from the perspective of trade secrets for librarians to keep this kind of information confidential.

Remember that trade secret protection is lost completely if the confidential information is disclosed. After all, if the information is no longer secret, there is no point in having protection. Giving information to a professional who is covered by a confidentiality policy does not cause any problems with trade secret protection. The professional is not supposed to reveal the information, so there are no problems about disclosure of the secret. Library ethics ensure confidentiality, and trade secrets are included in this policy.

I believe that trade secret law gives library patrons an additional protection beyond that of professional ethics and state nondisclosure laws. My theory is that, under trade secret law, courts could enjoin librarians from revealing patron information. (Librarians and archivists could also be subject to the provisions of the Economic Espionage Act if protected information was deliberately leaked.)

The principles of trade secret protection give our library patrons an extra level of security beyond that contained in state laws. Indeed, as we will see in *Chapter 9*, not all states have mandatory duties of confidentiality; some jurisdictions only protect public libraries or circulation records. Trade secrets, on the other hand, are based on the confidential information given during a reference interview, so the rules of trade secret law protect the reference question (and the answer) from disclosure—exactly the type of interaction that has the least type of protection under some state privacy laws.

By using both library confidentiality laws and trade secret law, patrons can feel assured that their research will not lead to their competitors learning secrets. After all, this type of information can have great economic impact. This is why it is important to have trade secret protection. Information often does have economic value, and when it comes to keeping confidences, a wink really is as good as a nod.

Conclusion

Trademarks and trade secret laws form an important part of our system of intellectual property. Trademarks and service marks help ensure that goods and services will retain their value in the marketplace. The trademark laws help guarantee that consumers are really buying what they think they are buying.

Trademarks help to protect domain names and prevent cybersquatting. Trademark law also applies to Websites that use deep links and frames, since there is a possibility of misattribution in these situations.

While less complex in detail than trademarks, trade secret laws are also important. Trade secret laws protect property that would otherwise not fall within the traditional copyright, patent, and trademark classifications. Trade secret laws also protect property that would lose its value if the confidential information became widely known.

It is important for organizations to choose carefully what type of intellectual property protection they will use. The system should not be manipulated by using trademark laws to get around an expired copyright or patent. After all, as Professor Ronald Raitt says, "You get one pull on the litigation lever."

Librarians may also possibly be able to use trade secret law as another form of protection for patron confidentiality. Finally, libraries and archives that produce materials, Websites, and services will want to use trademarks in order to protect their investment in intellectual property. The various laws relating to intellectual property help protect everyone, from the creator to the patron, from the library to the consumer. For these reasons, all information professionals need to find their way through the thickets of trademark and trade secret laws.

7

Licensing of Intellectual Property

Metro University has an excellent collection of letters, diaries, and manuscripts related to the Second World War. The library and archives have scanned these items and created an online database of primary sources. Metro University would like to provide this database—for a fee—to subscribers at other universities. How do they go about doing this? What kinds of rights do the subscribers receive? What licensing laws pertain to these transactions?

Licensing agreements allow an individual or an organization the legal right to use a product of intellectual property without buying it. A license to use a product is nothing more or less than a contract that specifies permission to use the product, giving each party certain rights and privileges. To this end, basic contract laws apply to licenses. (For more information about contract laws, see **Chapter 2**, *Contracts: A Meeting of the Minds*.)

Remember the Scooby Doo lunch box that you used in elementary school? How about the Star Wars light sabers? And how many of us have eaten Babe Ruth bars? What you didn't know then was that all of these items came about as a result of the licensing of trademarks. Most people think of licensing in terms of technology transfer and patents; however, another common use of licensing consists of the agreements that we all sign for EBSCOhost, Lexis, Microsoft Word, etc.[1]

A license is "a written authority granted by the owner of a patent [or copyright or other type of intellectual property] to another person empowering the latter to make or use the [intellectual property] article for a limited period or in a limited territory."[2] In effect, the person who owns the intellectual property—whether it is something as mundane as a Scooby Doo lunch box or as vital to library services as a database—signs a contract granting limited rights to the product. In other words, the intellectual property (the name or the product) is "rented" to the user.

As with any contract, there must be a meeting of the minds, and the requirements of contract formation must be observed. Naturally, consideration is needed for the licensing agreement to be enforceable. That is where the terms of the contract and the payment of money come in.

A license for intellectual property is first and foremost a contract, and as such it is similar to any other type of contract.[3] A license can be as broad or as narrow as the parties wish. Some types of licenses, such as those given to a library subscribing to a database, are very basic. "In its simplest form, a license means only leave to do a thing which the licensor would otherwise have a right to prevent."[4] Thus, a library subscribes to a database; in exchange for payment of money, the provider allows the library to use the database for a certain period of time. This type of basic license has all the regular elements of a contract—offer, acceptance, consideration, etc.

In the example of a library database, the licensee (the library) then passes on the right to use the property to a sub-licensee (in this case, the library's patrons). It is important to remember that, as with any type of contract, the licensees can only pass on the rights that they actually have themselves. (If you think about it, this makes a lot of sense.)

Other types of licenses, such as those that are often granted for patents, "may be accompanied by the patent owner's promise that others shall be excluded from practicing it within the field of use wherein the license is given leave."[5] These types of licenses are called exclusive licenses. Once an exclusive license has been granted, the licensor has "'assigned' all its existing rights to exclude [granting new licenses] . . . and only one having the right to exclude can grant a license to enjoy."[6] This situation has happened with library databases as well. In 2003, the producers of the database Sociological Abstracts, formerly carried by a number of aggregators (including EBSCOhost and FirstSearch) signed an exclusive license with Cambridge Scientific Abstracts (CSA). The license agreement stated that Sociological Abstracts would only be available on the CSA service.

It is important to understand the differences between a licensing agreement and a sale. In order to illustrate these differences, let's look at what happens when a library gets a book versus what happens when the library gets a database.

Under most circumstances, libraries (and consumers) purchase their books outright. According to section 106 of the Copyright Act, the purchaser of any copyrighted work is entitled to sell, loan, give away, or otherwise dispose of his or her copy without any further consent from the copyright owner.[7] Once the copy has been sold the first time, the copyright owner no longer has any rights in that particular copy.[8] This transaction is governed by section 109 of the Copyright Act. The section reads: "[T]he owner of a particular copy or phonorecord lawfully made under this title, or any person authorized by such owner, is entitled, without the authority of the copyright owner, to sell or otherwise dispose of the possession of that copy or phonorecord."[9]

This legal provision is known as the *First Sale doctrine*. (It is because of the First Sale doctrine that used bookstores exist.) The First Sale doctrine allows owners of a copy of a book or phonorecording to further transfer their rights to another person or entity. In effect, this doctrine puts books in the same position as any form of tangible property. I can loan, sell, or give away a hammer that I bought; I can also loan, sell, or give away a book that I bought.

On the other hand, computer software and databases are not sold. Instead, the organization or consumer that wants the software pays money in exchange for a limited assignment of the rights under contract law. This assignment may be limited to only one use at a time, as with software programs, or it may be limited by the amount of time, such as a yearly subscription to a database. The license agreements usually restrict further transmission of the item, and in fact section 109 of the Copyright Act prohibits the rental, lease, or lending of computer information for direct or indirect commercial advantage.[10] (The law does contain an exception authorizing lending by noncommercial libraries or educational institutions.)[11] As one source stated:

> Unlike most goods, but like other intellectual property (such as books, movies, and music), computer software is generally regarded as being licensed, not bought. (The person who purchases a book normally owns the atoms, but not the text.) This means that the licensee has fewer rights than someone who has purchased the underlying creative work. (A publisher who buys a book (the text) may typically republish it under a new title, but a consumer who buys a book (the atoms) may not.)[12]

In effect, when you wish to use intellectual property, you rent it instead of buying it, just as the car you get when you vacation is rented rather than bought. The rental agreement is similar to a license agreement in that you consent to the terms and conditions of the owner (the car rental company) in exchange for being allowed to use the product. Licensing may or may not involve the payment of a fee (for example, there are some free software downloads), but licensing will always include conditions of use that are set by the owner of the product.

Licensing has always been an important issue in the world of special libraries and archives, since many special collections charge fees to individuals who wish to publish materials from their holdings. If the archive or library has been able to acquire copyright, it is able to control duplication and publication, just as a commercial publisher would. One reason that special collections give for charging licensing fees involves "value-added" situations, the care and preservation that items are given in libraries, archives, and museums. According to Georgia Harper, the intellectual property expert for the General Counsel's Office at the University of Texas System:

> These services are expensive. Publication fees charged to offset such expenses are not within the scope of copyright. Instead, they are a legitimate prerogative of management of an archive. . . . Were the same works unprotected by copyright, a repository would still need to charge fees to users of the works because the cost of maintaining the archive, not the status of their protection under copyright law, forms the basis of the fees. Fees are charged, pursuant not to law but to a repository's need to conduct a service that needs to operate in the black rather than in the red. . . . Special collections value and support the sharing of their holdings with the public and a publication fee policy and structure is not intended to discourage such sharing. Rather, the intent is physically and fiscally to manage collections so that they continue to exist in excellent condition and to be available . . . when today's copyrights will play absolutely no part in their value at all.[13]

By now, you should appreciate the necessity for information professionals to understand licensing and licensing laws. Librarians and archivists are both the users and the providers of numerous licensed materials. We use these materials through agreements (contracts) with the copyright owners. Licensing agreements in the world of libraries and archives may cover more than just databases and e-journals. Organizations often sign licensing agreements for equipment such as photocopiers and computer systems, and some libraries have even licensed shelving systems.

At this time, ordinary contract law applies to most licensing agreements. The law does not distinguish between licensing a database and renting a car. However, there are some proposals to change this situation by creating new statutes. The next section of this chapter will discuss this effort.

The Uniform Computer Information Transactions Act and the Attempt to Create a Special Law of Licensing

Under normal circumstances, ordinary contract law applies to license agreements. A license agreement is merely the contract between parties. Some legal analysts feel that the current laws covering software, databases, and Websites are sufficient to protect the rights of publishers but need to be expressly applied to software and databases. However, other analysts are concerned that the existing laws are not sufficient to protect vendors and publishers.

The Uniform Computer Information Transactions Act (UCITA) is an attempt to codify current practices and to add protections that some vendors and publishers feel are necessary. Unfortunately, even those people who believe a new law is necessary find certain provisions of the proposed law unpalatable. Almost everyone agrees that we need to standardize the laws concerning software, databases, and Websites. However, there are a number of disagreements on how to address these issues.

A. What Is UCITA?

The Uniform Computer Information Transactions Act (UCITA) is a proposed uniform law dealing with software and database licensing issues. The scope of this proposed law is to cover contracts involving computer software, documentation, databases, Internet sites, digitized books, movies, and audio recordings.[14] As a proposed uniform law, UCITA must be adopted by the states in order to go into effect.

At this time, only two states (Maryland and Virginia) have adopted the uniform act.[15] Several other states have rejected the proposed law, and many states have not made any serious attempts to pass UCITA.[16] The reason that proponents have not been successful in getting UCITA passed is because of serious opposition from an unlikely group of organizations (discussed below). These organizations have serious problems with various sections of the proposed law.

UCITA is intended to codify and standardize the laws for using signed licenses, shrink-wrap licenses, and "click-through" licenses on software, databases, and Websites.[17] The shrink-wrap license allows the vendor to set the terms of the license without any input or negotiation from the licensee. This license becomes effective as soon as the plastic shrink-wrap over the installation disk is broken. The click-through license becomes effective when Website users click a button that says that they agree with the license terms.

Software and database vendors use shrink-wrap licenses for a variety of reasons. According to database producers, shrink-wrap licenses allow producers to get the software to the end user more quickly, without the hassle of obtaining a signed licensing agreement. The shrink-wrap process also saves money for both the vendor and the licensee. Click-through licenses give Internet Website vendors the ability to issue a license at the time that an individual or organization accesses the product.[18]

In the early years of computing, programmers working for large organizations usually wrote software for their employers. If a company needed a word processing program, one was created. These programs did not require any special changes in the law. With the advent of the personal computer, however, the production and sale of software for the mass market has developed into a big business. Software producers and database vendors became concerned that the existing laws were not sufficient to protect their businesses.

As a result of the concern over copying of software, the American Law Institute (ALI) and the National Conference of Commissioners on Uniform State Laws (NCCUSL) began working working together on uniform laws for software licensing. The *Uniform Commercial Code* seemed to be a logical place for these new laws.[19] In 1992, the two entities began working on an amendment to the *Code* covering the topic of contracts for computer software and databases. This amendment would be known as *Uniform Commercial Code* Article 2(B) (hereafter referred to as UCC2B).[20] Like the other articles of the *Uniform Commercial Code*, both the NCCUSL and the ALI would propose the amendment, but each state would need to adopt the article for it to become law.

B. Objections to UCC2B and the Withdrawal of the American Law Institute

As the drafting process for UCC2B began, a number of objections were voiced by legal analysts. The American Law Institute itself began to have doubts about UCC2B. The main areas that the ALI was concerned about were the provisions dealing with shrink-wrap licenses.[21] Groups such as the American Association of Law Libraries were opposed to the language of the proposal.[22] On May 10, 1999, the ALI received a letter of opposition from a broad coalition made up of the Motion Picture Association of America, the Recording Industry Association of America, the Newspaper Association of America, the National Association of Broadcasters, the National Cable Television Association, and the Magazine Publishers of America.[23]

Finally, in April 1999, the American Law Institute ended its sponsorship of UCC2B.[24] Since new amendments to the *Uniform Commercial Code* require adoption by both the ALI and the NCCUSL, this withdrawal by the ALI meant that the new amendment would not be a part of the UCC. According to attorney Cem Kaner, "ALI is a very conservative organization. In many ways, it IS the Establishment in American law. [Emphasis in original.] UCITA represents a radical change in contract law. The ALI called for fundamental revision of UCITA (Article 2B), and the drafting committee refused. The fact that ALI walked away underscores the extent to which UCITA is biased against customers."[25]

C. UCITA Rises from the Ashes

Once the ALI withdrew from the drafting process, UCC2B was finished. However, like the phoenix that rises from its own ashes, the NCCUSL took the final draft of UCC2B and proposed it in substantially the same form as a uniform law under the name "Uniform Computer Information Transactions Act."[26] Many supporters of UCC2B threw their support behind the new act, reasoning: "the UCITA still offers the promise of a consistent approach to fundamental legal issues, which is necessary to facilitate e-commerce."[27]

UCITA has the support of many software and database vendors. However, there are still a number of outspoken critics, including many library organizations. The American Library Association, the Association of Research Libraries, the American Association of Law Libraries, the Special Libraries Association, and the Medical Library Association are united in their opposition to the proposed law,[28] as is the Association for Computing Machinery.[29] In addition, the Attorneys General of 32 states sent letters to the NCCUSL opposing the adoption of UCITA.[30]

UCITA was approved by the NCCUSL's delegates in July 1999 by a vote of 43 to 6, with delegates from two states abstaining.[31] Now the legislatures of each state and territory will individually consider the proposed law and decide whether or not to enact it.[32] According to James Love of the Consumer Project on Technology, "The fight pits several industries against each other . . . and will be played out before the 50 state legislatures. . . . At stake is whether laws for Internet transactions will be uniform in all states or will become a hodgepodge of regulations that differ depending on the jurisdiction."[33]

Some experts believed that it didn't matter whether all the states adopted UCITA, as long as at least one state did. "Any one state will do, and the ability of a state's Uniform Law Commissioners to obtain enactment in her or his state is far more important [than] industry prominence. If having a presence is of importance to other states' courts in deciding whether to give effect to a choice of law clause, a major player will simply move a substantial business unit to the enacting jurisdiction."[34]

However, in the wake of UCITA's adoption in Maryland and Virginia, a number of states moved to exclude choice-of-law provisions that would expose their citizens to those provisions of UCITA that exist in Maryland and Virginia.[35] At the same time, the language of UCITA has been used in judicial decisions by other states, even without adoption of the statute.[36] In short, at the time of this writing (Fall 2005), nothing much has really happened, even though Maryland and Virginia have adopted UCITA.

D. Objections to UCITA

Why are the opponents of UCITA so negative about the proposal? Critics of the act have cited a variety of reasons, including intellectual property issues. Other controversial provisions of UCITA include:

- ◆ Allowing the vendor to choose which court it can be sued in (and under what law);
- ◆ Allowing the producer to make significant changes to the product, without allowing the licensee to cancel the contract;
- ◆ Giving software manufacturers the right to disclaim all warranties of sale;
- ◆ Providing immunity from lawsuits for defects in the program, even if the manufacturer knew about the defect but declined to fix the problem;
- ◆ Intellectual property issues;
- ◆ Restrictions on lending and transferring of software and databases;

♦   Legalization of "self-help" procedures;

♦   Self-determination of the type of products that are covered by
    UCITA, i.e. the scope of the term "Information."[37]

One criticism of UCITA is that the proposal would allow software
companies to restrict the giving of information about the product. Several companies currently restrict the giving of information as part of
their licensing agreement, but UCITA would give this practice a legal
grounding. For example, UCITA would let companies prohibit the publication of criticisms of their product by any source. According to one
critic of UCITA, in 1999 McAfee VirusScan included the following
restrictions in its standard license: "The customer shall not disclose the
results of any benchmark test to any third party without McAfee's prior
written approval" and "The customer will not publish reviews of the
product without prior consent from McAfee."[38] Many writers and librarians are rankled by the thought that they might not be able to write
product reviews because of these restrictions. (There also seem to be
some issues of freedom of speech and freedom of the press in these
provisions.)

Another issue of importance to librarians is that the license can restrict lending of the item.[39] Suppose for example that you had purchased a copy of Bill Gates' book *The Road Ahead*.[40] This particular
title, like so many others, comes with a CD-ROM. If you lend a patron
the book *with the CD-ROM*, you may have just violated the terms of
your licensing agreement. Lending the CD-ROM on interlibrary loan
may also be a violation.

UCITA allows the publisher to restrict lending by libraries, but
there are many gray areas that will take years of litigation to work out.
For example, suppose that *The Road Ahead* comes with a license stating that use of the CD-ROM means that the user accepts the license for
both the CD *and the book*. If you lend this book to a patron or send it
through interlibrary loan, have you violated the license? Only time—
and the courts—will tell.[41]

Another gray area not addressed by UCITA directly is the situation
in which software is kept on reserve. If you check out software to a
patron for use in a database, have you loaned the software? Again,
there is no way to tell at this time, since the proposed law does not specifically address this topic.

If you violate your license under UCITA, the software or database
vendor is allowed to use *self-help* procedures to deal with the violation.
Self-help means that a library could have a database taken away or de-

activated summarily without warning.[42] In jurisdictions that have not adopted UCITA, the database producer would normally have to notify the library of the violation and then give the licensee a chance to correct the violation. However, under the provisions of UCITA, the product can be deactivated without notice.[43]

One question that many businesses and consumers ask is whether software should be treated differently from other products. Commissioner Stephen Y. Chow says that he "would like to see the more generalized rules for online and off-line goods sales (laid out in UCC Article 2) apply to information technologies."[44] On the other hand, some vendors believe that the current laws don't go far enough to protect the intellectual property rights of software creators.[45]

The motion picture industry has been outspoken in its opposition to UCITA. The proposed legislation includes movies on DVD, sound recordings on CD, and similar types of products. Hollywood legal analysts believe that these controversial provisions result in the changing of laws that have worked well for many years. In effect, they contend that UCITA is attempting to fix what is not broken.[46]

The main objection that the media have to the proposed law is the way the term "information" is defined in UCITA. According to John F. Sturm, president and CEO of the Newspaper Association of America, "If UCITA is passed by the state legislatures, what we'll see are different sets of rules governing our print and online products—despite the fact that both the content and the means by which we acquire the right to publish them are the same."[47] According to a letter written by the members of the Working Group on Consumer Protection of the American Bar Association:

> Section 103(e) allows a seller of goods to opt into UCITA if the transaction involves "information." "Information" is a term defined in Section 102(a)(37) to include data, text and images. Any goods with text or images, from books and magazines to T-shirts and plates, would qualify under this language, permitting opt-in to UCITA. When asked about use of the term "information". . . the drafting committee chair and reporter indicated that "computer information" was the term intended. But the NCCUSL annual meeting draft continues to use the term "information."[48]

In fact, the American Bar Association eventually voted to advise against the adoption of UCITA, and every state (except Maryland and Virginia) that has considered the proposed law has voted against it.

One final bone of contention with UCITA is that there is no way to know who broke the shrink-wrap or clicked the Agree button. For example, is a corporation or a library bound by a license if the custodian broke the shrink-wrap, or a five-year-old clicked the Agree button?[49] These are issues that concern critics of the law and that need to be addressed before any licensing laws are passed.

The Uniform Commercial Information Transactions Act appears to be dead in all states other than Maryland and Virginia. Although these two states have passed UCITA, many of the promised benefits (and few of the feared problems) have actually come about. Most states do not have any serious initiatives to pass this uniform law. However, the opponents of UCITA are not able to rest for fear that the phoenix will once again rise from its ashes. In the meantime, libraries are in a limbo of uncertainty about some types of "information"!

Licensing Freelance Articles for Databases: The Case of *Tasini v. New York Times*

One of the most important copyright licensing cases of the past 30 years is the case of *Tasini v. New York Times Co.*, which was decided by the U.S. Supreme Court in 2001.[50] This case is about the question of when reproducing material constitutes fair use, and when that reproduction constitutes a copyright violation. The case is even more about the scope of licensing agreements, and the relationship between compilations and derivative works. *Tasini* involved the granting of copyright clearance to publications and the licensing of articles to research databases. The *Tasini* case is of major importance to librarians because of the nature of the information contained in the library's subscribed databases.

In the *Tasini* case, six freelance authors sold their works to various newspapers and magazines, including *The New York Times*, *Newsday*, and *Sports Illustrated*.[51] The publishers in turn licensed the articles to LexisNexis and to UMI's *New York Times OnDisc*.[52] Since these types of transactions have become increasingly common over the last few years (leading to the so-called Information Revolution), this situation sounds like a routine transaction that should cause no problems. However, the plaintiffs in the *Tasini* case have pointed out that there are still many unanswered questions about the licensing of intellectual property.[53]

The *Tasini* case is about the relationship between compilations (collective works) and derivative works. (For more information on copyright law, see **Chapter 3**, *Copyright and Patent Law*.)[54] The basis of the *Tasini* claim is that the publishers had no right to license the authors' work for inclusion in a database. According to the authors, only the writer of an article may license its subsequent use. The authors are freelance writers, and their work does not constitute "work-for-hire."[55] The authors base their claim on section 103 of the copyright law, which grants the individual authors the exclusive rights for their own contributions in the compilation.[56]

The issues in the trial court (hereinafter "*Tasini I*") revolved around whether the databases constituted "revisions" of the original works,[57] since both collective works and derivative works are based upon other works (the efforts of individual authors) that are already copyrighted.[58] The database companies claimed that their products were compilations, while Tasini and the other authors claimed that the databases were derivative works.

Derivative works transform the preexisting works into a new creation, as with the movie adaptation of the novel *Gone with the Wind*. Although a collective work is entitled to copyright protection for the item as a whole, each individual contribution is itself protected. Thus, an anthology of short stories can be copyrighted as a collection or compilation, but the authors of each story retain their copyrights to the individual stories.

In order for a compilation to become an independent work, the compiler's effort must be more than minimal or trivial. The compiler must demonstrate "[o]riginality in . . . selectivity, or independent original effort in collecting, assembling . . . and compiling the pre-existing materials."[59] For example, "a compilation of selected scenes from movies featuring a particular actor has been held to constitute a protectable work under the Copyright Act, to the extent that the [compiler] exercised skill and creativity in selecting and arranging the scenes."[60]

The District Court found in favor of the defendants; however, the 2nd Circuit Court of Appeals reversed this decision and found in favor of the authors. The U.S. Supreme Court then took up the issues of *Tasini* and the question of whether a database was a compilation or a derivative work.

A. *Tasini* in the Supreme Court

Once the *Tasini* case reached the U.S. Supreme Court,[61] the various copyright communities knew exactly where they stood. Representatives of the author, publisher, and library communities filed briefs and gave arguments. Finally, the Court came to a decision, finding in favor of the authors by a vote of 7 to 2. Justice Ginsburg delivered the Opinion of the Court. The dissenting opinion was written by Justice Stevens and was joined by Justice Breyer. According to the majority opinion, inclusion of a work within a database does not constitute a medium-neutral compilation, but rather a republication of the work. In order to decide how databases fall under the law, the justices took a look at how the end user sees the information.

The case of the publishers rested in part on a provision in the copyright law that states that copyright in original works does not depend on the format of the works.[62] The publishers used the analogy of microfilm and microfiche, which have been popular methods of preserving newspapers and magazines since the 1930s.[63] The Court did not agree with this argument. According to the decision:

> We find the analogy wanting. Microforms typically contain continuous photographic reproductions of a periodical in the medium of miniaturized film. Accordingly, articles appear on the microforms, writ very small, in precisely the position in which the articles appeared in the newspaper. The Times, for example, printed the beginning of Blakelys Remembering Jane Article on page 26 of the Magazine in the September 23, 1990, edition; the microfilm version of the Times reproduces that same Article on film *in the very same position*, within a film reproduction of the entire Magazine, in turn within a reproduction of the entire September 23, 1990, edition. True, the microfilm roll contains multiple editions, and the microfilm user can adjust the machine lens to focus only on the Article, to the exclusion of surrounding material. Nonetheless, the user first encounters the Article *in context*. In the Databases, by contrast, the Articles appear *disconnected from their original context*. In NEXIS and NYTO, the user sees the Jane Article apart even from the remainder of page 26. In GPO, the user sees the Article within the context of page 26, but clear of the context of page 25 or page 27, the rest of the Magazine, or the remainder of the day's newspaper. In short, unlike microforms, the Databases do not perceptibly reproduce articles as part of the collective work to which the author contributed or as part of any revision thereof.[64] [Emphasis added.]

The court went on to compare, in a creative manner, the databases to an imaginary library.[65] In this library:

> Rather than maintaining intact editions of periodicals, the library would contain separate copies of each article. . . . The library would store the folders containing the articles in a file room, indexed based on diverse criteria. . . . In response to patron requests, an inhumanly speedy librarian would search the room and provide copies of the articles matching patron-specified criteria. . . .

> Viewing this strange library, one could not, consistent with or-
> dinary English usage, characterize the articles as part of a revision of
> the editions in which the articles first appeared. . . . The crucial fact is
> that the Databases, like the hypothetical library, store and retrieve ar-
> ticles separately within a vast domain of diverse texts. Such a storage
> and retrieval system effectively overrides the Authors exclusive right
> to control the individual reproduction and distribution of each Arti-
> cle.[66] [Internal citations in endnotes.]

In other words, the Supreme Court effectively found that when the
works were entered into a database, they were taken out of the context
of their original publication and thus constituted unauthorized copies.
The fact that one criterion of retrieval was the name of the publication
was found not to be relevant.[67]

Now that the authors have won their case, what happens? Are we
left with gaping holes in the electronic history of time, as the publishers
have suggested?[68] According to the *Amicus* brief filed by Advance Publications, Inc., the Supreme Court's decision will have devastating effects, causing publishers to remove freelance articles from their databases.[69] Advance Publications also noted that: "The modest phrase
'freelance contributions,' moreover, covers a large territory: for newspapers, for example, it extends past such traditional 'freelance' works
as travel pieces and book reviews to news stories sent in by stringers,
letters to the editor, Op-ed pieces and other articles sent in 'over the
transom' by political officials and public spirited citizens, among others."[70]

On the other hand, the American Library Association and the
Association of Research Libraries stated that the publishers' claims of
harm to the historical record were exaggerated.[71] The ALA/ARL brief
states that:

> [T]he terms "electronic libraries" and "electronic archives" are
> misnomers. Despite the utility and wide availability of commercial
> electronic databases, they are collections of information designed to
> meet particular market demands and do not fulfill the traditional roles
> of libraries and archives. Further, access restrictions and licensing
> practices of many commercial electronic database publishers are de-
> signed *to limit access* to digital copies of works. These restrictions
> perpetuate a system of payment by end-users of ongoing subscription
> fees and/or "pay per use" fees to obtain access to works, often to the
> detriment of legitimate fair use and archival concerns.[72] [Emphasis
> added.]

In reality, the practical effects of *Tasini* have been much less drastic. Some articles that had previously been available electronically are now only available in print. This situation is not really a significant change, since many articles were not available electronically before. In contrast to students who think that everything is available for free on the Internet, librarians know that databases do not replace the collections of a library. Most databases only go back to the early 1990s or the late 1980s for the very practical reason that computers were not in wide use before that time.

An additional problem with database coverage has always been the selective nature of the materials included in library databases. "Full-text" coverage of a journal in a database does not really mean full text cover-to-cover. Often it means selected full text. One missing item that historians and genealogical researchers lament are the paid obituary notices. To find these items, you must look at the paper itself or at the microform. And what about miscellaneous contributions such as "travel pieces and book reviews[,] news stories sent in by stringers, letters to the editor, Op-ed pieces . . ." and so on.[73] Have these items disappeared from databases? In most cases, they were never included in the databases to begin with, making irrelevant their freelance status under *Tasini*.

In addition to selection of text, sometimes a journal will be included in a database for a while, but if the contract is not renewed that journal will no longer be included. This means that sometimes articles will just "disappear" from the database. These "disappearances" have nothing to do with *Tasini*; rather, this has been going on since the electronic database industry began developing in the late 1980s and early 1990s.

Since the *Tasini* case, publishers have re-worked their consent forms to reflect this new reality. Some publishers that previously did not require copyright assignment from the authors are now requesting the rights. Other periodicals have simply asked the authors if they consent to the article being used electronically. If the author says no, the article is only available in print.

The results of the *Tasini* decision have been felt mostly in those databases where the years of coverage were reduced. For example, Newsbank used to provide access to the Louisville (KY) *Courier-Journal* from 1988 to the present. Now Newsbank only provides online access to the newspaper from 1999 to the present. However, the subscribing library can deal with this issue by letting patrons know that they can use the microfilm version of the paper for articles prior to 1999.

Thus, the results of *Tasini* have been far less disastrous than the publishers claimed they would be. Effective research techniques require the use of databases, print indexes, library catalogs, books, journals, and microform items. Other types of research involve the use of archival records, manuscripts, letters, etc. The real answer to the legacy of *Tasini* is that we must work to educate patrons about the limits of databases, the proper resources to use, and the reality of effective research using a combination of materials. Giving patrons the skills to find appropriate information will help to avoid *Tasini* problems with database searches and will lead to better results for researchers. And this is a challenge which librarians must accept.

The Process of Getting Permission

Since we need a license in order to use intellectual property, the process of getting permissions is very important for information professionals. In many cases, such as when we subscribe to a database, it is clear with whom we need to negotiate in order to obtain a license. However, there are other situations where the waters are much more murky. For example, suppose that you wish to create a derivative work. Let's say that the Greentown Public Library wishes to create a play based on a poem in one of its books. The library would have to first contact the appropriate party in order to obtain a license to use the copyright.

This requirement begs the question: how do you find the appropriate person? It may not be the publisher; after all, the author may have only granted the publisher the rights to use his or her materials without granting the right to authorize derivative works.

One way to obtain rights is by using the Copyright Clearance Center (CCC).[74] The CCC has permission to grant rights to over 1.75 million titles from over 9,800 publishers.[75] You can fill out a form online to obtain copyright, and the CCC will take care of tracking down the rights for you. The CCC has extensive experience in working with libraries and archives and has done a great deal of work with library reserves, course packs, etc.[76]

The Copyright Clearance Center is not the only place to go if you wish to license copyrighted material. There are several other organizations that handle rights for copyrighted materials. Some of the agencies that handle intellectual property rights include:

- The American Society of Composers, Authors, and Publishers (ASCAP).[77] ASCAP handles the rights to music from over 200,000 U.S. composers, songwriters, lyricists, and music publishers. In addition, ASCAP can help obtain the rights to music from other countries through agreements with other agencies.

- Broadcast Music International (BMI).[78] BMI represents over 300,000 songwriters, composers, and music publishers. Like ASCAP, BMI has reciprocal arrangements with agencies in other countries. BMI collects license fees for the public performance of music, particularly for music that is going to be broadcast, used in restaurants and stores, etc.

- Society of European Stage Authors and Composers (SESAC).[79] Like ASCAP and BMI, SESAC represents songwriters and publishers. SESAC is a much smaller organization than the other two entities.

- The Harry Fox Agency.[80] This agency also represents the music industry. Fox's list includes the largest concentration of digital music of any agency.

- Motion Picture Licensing Corporation (MPLC).[81] According to its Website, MPLC is "an independent copyright licensing service exclusively authorized by major Hollywood motion picture studios and independent producers to grant Umbrella Licenses® to non-profit groups, businesses and government organizations for the public performances of home videocassettes and DVDs ('Videos')."[82]

- Movie Licensing USA.[83] This organization serves public libraries and schools by providing public performance rights for movies.

- The American Association of Community Theatre.[84] This organization helps community theatre groups obtain necessary permissions, as well as providing other types of resources and information. According to its Website, "AACT is the central resource for theatre information and resources, connecting not only members in an information network, but providing data and information to non-members, businesses, other arts and not-for-profit organizations, and the media, as well as to members of local, state and federal governments."[85]

- Dramatists Play Service, Inc.[86] This organization has the largest catalog of plays in the English language and helps to provide performance rights in the United States.

- ◆ Baker's Plays.[87] This organization provides performance rights for plays in the eastern part of the United States.

- ◆ Samuel French, Inc.[88] This agency provides performance rights for plays in the western part of the United States.

By using the agencies listed above, librarians and archivists can quickly and easily obtain licenses for many types of materials. Information professionals can also advise clients to obtain appropriate permissions. These agencies facilitate the legal use of information.

Conclusion

License agreements are contracts between parties that allow *the use of* intellectual property without selling the property. Although most librarians and archivists use the terms "licenses" and "licensing" on a regular basis, we don't always think about the underlying concepts. Usually, basic contract laws apply to these licensing transactions. Although some commentators feel that current laws are sufficient, other commentators urge the adoption of special statutes, such as the Uniform Computer Information Transactions Act, which is aimed at the licensing of computer information.

UCITA is an attempt to clarify the laws pertaining to computer software, databases, and Websites. Publishers and vendors believe that these changes are necessary in order to protect their business, while librarians are concerned with the intellectual property issues surrounding shrink-wrap licenses and click-through licenses. There are also issues relating to the copyright of freelance articles in databases. Most of these issues can be resolved by using well-written consent forms.

Licensing of intellectual property is an area of law that has become extremely important in recent years. It is crucial that information professionals understand these topics in order to avoid problems. With the spread of technology, licensing means more than just lending or playing the latest Partridge Family album. For information professionals, awareness is synonymous with safety.

8

Information Malpractice, Professionalism, and the Unauthorized Practice of Law and Medicine

It was a dark and stormy night, and a crime was about to be committed.

The scene: a library reference desk.

The characters: a well-meaning librarian and an upset patron.

PATRON: *I need your help, please! I wrecked my car, and the police officer gave me a ticket. I got these forms in the mail from the court. What do I do? Is there some sort of form I can use to respond?*

LIBRARIAN: *How long do you have to respond? What kind of ticket did you get?*

PATRON: *I have 20 days, so that makes the response due on the 5th. The officer said that I must have been going too fast, or else I wouldn't have slid into his lane. I was only going 25, but the ice was very thick and I just lost control! He said that I must be in control of my car at all times and under all conditions. Is that right?*

LIBRARIAN [taking PATRON to law books]: *Well, let's see. Let's take a look at* West's Digest *for this state. O.K., here we are—a case on the liability of a driver on a patch of ice. The case is* Smith v. Jones. *It was a case where someone was killed, and the court said that drivers couldn't be prosecuted for problems that occur as a result of weather.*

PATRON: *Oh, I'm so glad to hear that. I guess it means that I can fight the ticket. I know that if I challenge the ticket in court and lose I will have to pay court costs and an even higher fine. How do I respond to the court?*

LIBRARIAN [taking PATRON to State Form Book]: *Well, here is a form for replying to a traffic violation. I hope this helps you.*

PATRON: *You have really helped me a lot. I feel better, and now I know what the law is. Thank you very much.*

LIBRARIAN: *Good luck.*

Librarians and archivists are not only subject to ethical guidelines, but also—like other professionals—they must uphold a duty of ethics to their clients. Information professionals are subject to certain legal restrictions. Because of these restrictions, sometimes librarians and archivists cannot provide as much assistance to their patrons as they would like to give. The most important of these restrictions involves answering legal and medical questions. There is also a debate as to whether librarians can be sued for information malpractice. Certainly a librarian who gives incorrect legal or medical answers is at risk for a malpractice lawsuit.

There are two problems with the answer that the librarian gave in the above scenario. Not only was the answer wrong (more about this later in the section on information malpractice), but the librarian also crossed a line in the reference interview by practicing law without a license. By engaging in the Unauthorized Practice of Law (UPL), the librarian committed a crime.

Avoiding the Unauthorized Practice of Law and Medicine

Whenever library workers are dealing with legal or medical information, they have to be careful not to substitute themselves for licensed legal or medical professionals. What the librarian in the above scenario did wrong was to find the law for the patron, explain the law to the patron, and recommend a form. This behavior would have been acceptable if the question had involved literature or history. However, by answering the patron's question about the law, the librarian stepped over the line.

In all 50 states, it is a crime to practice law or medicine without a license! It doesn't matter whether the perpetrator is actually treating a patient or representing a client in court. Just giving advice is a violation of the law. In a reference interview, the librarian may ask the patron what kind of information he or she needs and how the patron plans to use the information. The problem comes from the personal interview between the librarian and the patron. During a *reference interview*, the librarian gathers information, and the patron's particular set of circumstances is applied to *the research*.

During a *legal interview*, lawyers gather information, and the client's particular set of circumstances is applied *to the legal procedures*. The interview process is very much like an intensive library reference interview. However, if a librarian applies the patron's circumstances to specific legal procedures, he or she is engaging in the unauthorized practice of law. Similarly, a medical professional conducts a personal interview to discuss the patient's symptoms, previous illnesses, and remedies that have already been tried. The medical professional then uses this information to give a diagnosis, provide treatments, and answer questions about the condition. If a librarian makes a diagnosis, recommends a remedy, or explains a health condition, he or she has committed the Unauthorized Practice of Medicine (UPM).

When librarians work with legal or medical questions, we face the possibility of crossing the line. Yet this is not an inevitable problem. There is a difference between answering a reference question and giving legal or medical advice.

A. What Kinds of Assistance May Librarians Provide?

Here is the essential caveat: librarians may help a patron find legal or medical information, but they should not analyze or discuss the relationship of the information to the patron's own situation. Librarians should *not* point out the relevant decision or recommend the use of a specific form for a particular situation. Librarians should *absolutely never* give any interpretation or advice about the law or about legal opinions, or about medicine and medical options. In other words, the librarian must not do legal or medical research or give advice about any kind of legal or medical issue.

In order to avoid UPL or UPM, librarians should show the patron the text of a requested law or give the patron a book dealing with the issue in question. Librarians can safely send the patron to the right place, give him or her the location of the information, check library holdings and materials, assist in locating material, and provide an explanation about how to use a digest or index. The patron, not the librarian, must personally go to the index or digest. The patron must personally select the material, and must be the one who decides upon the proper form, case, statute, or medical information. The patron, *not the librarian*, should interpret and draft all legal documents, and should apply and interpret all medical advice.

Pro se library users—patrons who are planning to represent themselves in court without an attorney—can sometimes be the cause of problems for librarians. According to Paul Healey, a law librarian at the University of Illinois Urbana-Champaign and an expert on librarians and UPL:

> Pro se library users can . . . approach the law library with a number of misapprehensions. In addition to being unfamiliar with legal materials, pro se users often misunderstand essential aspects of law and the legal process. The fluid nature of the law often comes as a surprise, including the lack of a clear answer to most legal questions. They often underestimate the skill required for effective representation in almost any legal matter, as well as the value of a dispassionate, but fully informed, point of view on a legal case. This often results in frustration for the pro se user, a condition that they hope the law librarian will help alleviate.[1]

The unauthorized practice of law is a crime, and an individual can go to jail for committing UPL.[2] Library workers must be very careful to avoid giving legal advice and committing UPL. For example, in Kentucky the unauthorized practice of law is discussed in Kentucky Revised Statutes section 524.130. This statute makes UPL a misdemeanor punishable by a fine or imprisonment. In the event that a librarian gives incorrect legal advice, he or she may also be sued for malpractice. A good discussion of this problem is found in Yvette Brown's article "From the Reference Desk to the Jail House: Unauthorized Practice of Law and Librarians."[3] Some of the following scenarios may help explain what librarians may do and what they may not do.

- ◆ A Certified Public Accountant who researched case law before having a meeting with the Internal Revenue Service engaged in the unauthorized practice of law. The type of research the CPA did was similar to what a librarian might (but should not) do.[4]

- ◆ A man was found to have practiced law when he showed someone a motion to quash and told the person to go to the library and look at formbooks. Showing specific forms, explaining how a law or rule applies to a specific person, or interpreting cases is a clear violation of the laws against the unauthorized practice of law.[5]

- ◆ A non-attorney who . . . resolves legal questions for another at his request by giving him advice is "practicing law" if difficult or doubtful legal questions are involved which, to safeguard the public, reasonably demand the application of a trained legal mind.[6]

These are some examples of the complexities a librarian might encounter in assisting a patron. However, as the next section will illustrate, there are many questions that librarians can answer without practicing law.

B. The Virginia Bar Association Weighs In

Although there are no cases of UPL which specifically involve librarians, the Virginia State Bar has given some relevant guidance through three opinions about the unauthorized practice of law.[7] (For the text of these opinions, see *Guidelines and Opinions on the Unauthorized Practice of Law,* available at the Scarecrow Press support Website for this book.) The Virginia opinions dealt with specific scenarios that described what kinds of information could legally be provided to patrons. The biggest distinction involved whether the patron was in the legal field, whether the patron was a student with an academic assignment, or whether the patron was searching for legal information for himself or others as a *pro se* patron. The first Virginia opinion (opinion 127) came to the following conclusions:

♦ Retrieving and copying specific citations for cases, statutes, articles, etc. does not constitute the unauthorized practice of law, no matter who the patron is.

♦ Doing research when the patron simply gives an outline of the legal issue does not constitute UPL if the patron is a lawyer. "[S]ince the non-lawyer researcher . . . is providing assistance to a licensed attorney who retains an attorney-client relationship with the ultimate beneficiary of the research materials, and since it is the licensed attorney who will assess the legal case and select from among the materials provided by the non-lawyer researcher . . . [the situation] does not constitute the practice of law."[8]

♦ Doing research when the patron simply gives an outline of the legal issue constitutes UPL if the patron is a member of the general public. "The Committee believes that in order for appropriate legal research to be done for members of the general public, it is essential that legal training provide the researcher with the ability to assess the inquirer's legal training and to then determine which cases, statutes or other legal materials are applicable to the case. Thus, the Committee opines that provision of legal research services to the general public by non-lawyer personnel constitutes the unauthorized practice of law."[9]

The Virginia Opinions 152 and 161 (the second and third Virginia opinions) involved the "Policy for Information Service to the Public" adopted by a local bar association library that is open to the public.[10] This policy is contained in Opinion 152 in its entirety.

Opinion 161 contains further discussion of this policy, with examples of what can and can't be done.[11] Opinion 161 also analyzes the services that could be provided to different types of patrons. (The text of all three Virginia opinions can be found at the Scarecrow Press support Website for this book.) According to Opinion 161, there are three categories of questions from non-lawyers. Two types of questions are permissible, but one type is not acceptable:

> The first category is the patron who seeks assistance in legal research for academic, historical, employment or other non-legal purposes. Since a legal opinion or advice is not being requested and the patron does not intend to use the assistance to affect his legal or constitutional rights or to advise others, provision of assistance would not constitute the unauthorized practice of law. Upon adequate verification of these purposes, such a patron may be given any assistance that the library policies permit.
>
> The second general category would be the law student, clerk, summer associate, paralegal, etc., who is performing legal research under the supervision of a licensed attorney. The committee is of the opinion that the supervising attorney retains the ultimate responsibility for his own work product and the accuracy of his advice. Therefore, assistance to his agent or employee would not constitute the unauthorized practice of law. Upon the library staff being satisfied that the patron is acting under the supervision of a licensed attorney, then assistance may be provided without limitation . . . .
>
> The third category would be inquiries from *pro se* litigants or members of the public seeking legal advice and opinion without the involvement of an attorney. The committee is of the opinion that responses to such inquiries must of necessity be limited since the patron would presumably intend to take positions or actions or advise others in a manner that would affect their legal and/or constitutional rights and which might have grave consequences.[12]

The basic premise of the three Virginia opinions is that librarians can do almost any research for a lawyer, paralegal, law student, or other person who is employed by (or under the supervision of) an attorney. In this situation, UPL will not be an issue. If the work is of an academic nature, there are no restrictions on the nature of the help the librarian can provide. However, if the individual is a *pro se* patron, the amount of assistance is limited. As Opinion 161 indicates:

> For example, if the patron sufficiently identifies a case, statute, regulation or other legal material by name, citation or other unambiguous description, the library staff may either provide the requested

document or direct the patron to the place in which it might be found. This would include showing the patron how to locate the material if they are unfamiliar with the index or other locator. However, the library staff should caution such a patron that other decisions, statutes, regulations, etc., may exist that would affect or alter the effect of the material actually identified and provided. Likewise, the staff may provide [database searching] if the inquiry is formulated by the patron without assistance from the staff. . . .

If the request by the non-lawyer patron is nonspecific or general in nature, the committee is of the opinion that the librarian and staff may only direct the patron to the general location of the materials and instruct the patron in the use of indexes or other finding tools. The committee does believe, however, that questions relating to the meaning of legal citations, to the extent that they will assist the patron in locating materials from indexes or citators, may be answered since this is a proper function of a library of any description.[13]

Opinion 161 does emphasize that the library is responsible for verifying the status of the patron, although the verification methods are left to the individual library.[14] The opinion also indicates that there is the possibility of liability if the librarian provides incorrect advice. (See the section on information malpractice below.)

Another issue involving UPL comes up when patrons are doing patent searches in the library. Since patent searching involves a legal issue, giving too much assistance could constitute the unauthorized practice of law. For example, Harry Moatz, who works with Enrollment and Discipline at the U.S. Patent and Trademark Office, stated in a talk that "if library staff suggest keywords, synonyms, or specific search strategies to a patron conducting a search, such suggestions could be unauthorized practice."[15] In order to avoid getting into the specific search request, Moatz recommended using a generic search example with generic keywords, rather than performing the patron's own database search.[16]

C. How to Keep Out of Trouble

So how do we do our jobs as librarians without falling into the UPL trap? Should we just avoid all questions involving the law entirely? Of course not! Librarians can still answer directional and holdings questions. The issue of UPL is more likely to arise when a librarian is answering a reference question. This does not mean we should not answer reference questions, but that we should take care with what we do.

Directional questions involve a patron asking about the location of library material or the location of something in the facility. Besides the most frequently asked question—"Where is the restroom?"—some examples of directional questions include:

- ◆ Where do I find the *Federal Reporter*?
- ◆ Where is the *Code of Federal Regulations* located?
- ◆ I need to look at the *Physician's Desk Reference.* Where can I find it?
- ◆ Where do I go to search MEDLINE?

It is perfectly acceptable to answer this kind of directional question.

Holdings questions involve a patron trying to find out whether the library owns a particular item. These questions involve using the library catalog to answer the question. Some examples include:

- ◆ Does the library subscribe to the *University of Toledo Law Review*?
- ◆ What is the call number of the *Merck Manual*?
- ◆ How far back does the library have the *New England Journal of Medicine*?

There is no problem in answering these questions. An answer to this type of holdings question will not cause liability for UPL or UPM.

The third type of inquiry, the *reference question*, involves the use, recommendation, or instruction in the use of information sources, including books, the Internet, and databases. There is a very thin line between answering a reference question and answering a legal or medical question, but the distinction can be made. Some examples of reference inquiries include:

- ◆ I'm looking for cases on the right to die.
- ◆ I need to find Minnesota laws on driving while intoxicated.
- ◆ How do I use the *Federal Practice Digest*?
- ◆ I need information about drug interactions.
- ◆ How do I lance a boil?
- ◆ I need help with LexisNexis, EBSCOhost, MEDLINE, Internet, or CD-ROMs.

You can safely send patrons to the right place, give them the location of books, and provide an explanation about how to use the materials. However, the patron must select the proper form, case, statute, medication, treatment, etc. Only if the reference question goes too far does UPL or UPM become a problem.

For example, suppose that a patron came into the law library and said that he had an order from a judge for a jury trial to begin on a certain date. His adversary's counsel withdrew from the case five days before the trial. The patron asked "Isn't the judge's order for a trial date more important? He can't do that—he is violating the judge's order." You must *not* tell the patron any information about continuances or withdrawal of counsel, even though you may know the answer. The most that a librarian can do is to show the patron the rules of civil procedure, digests, legal encyclopedias, and other sources. The patron must read through the books personally to find the law for himself or herself.

The same types of restrictions apply to medical questions. For example, suppose a patron is looking for information about which medications to take for a headache. You may *not* recommend any type of medication, not even an aspirin. This recommendation would constitute the unauthorized practice of medicine. Instead, you could suggest that the patron look at a general medical encyclopedia or search for headache information on WebMD or MEDLINE.

The Virginia statements are the best indicators of what information is acceptable to give and what is not acceptable. Since there have not been any legal cases involving librarians, there really is not that much precedent to help draw the line between good library practice and the unauthorized practice of law or medicine.

There is some controversy about UPL, and a few scholars believe the whole idea is overblown. For example, Paul Healey in his article "Chicken Little at the Reference Desk: The Myth of Librarian Liability," expresses the opinion that UPL is more myth than reality.[17] However, librarians should understand how far is too far, not only to avoid the unauthorized practice of law, but also to avoid being sued for malpractice.

Just as we can serve patrons who have legal reference questions, so too can we assist patrons with medical and health-related questions. The Virginia Bar Association guidelines can be applied by analogy to medical questions. If the patron is a healthcare professional, there are no restrictions on the type of information that can be given. Similarly, if the patron is a student working on an academic assignment, we can provide as much assistance as necessary. It is only when the patron is looking for consumer health information for himself or herself (or others) that librarians need to be careful not to give *too much* information.

Potential problems can be avoided by doing a proper reference interview without crossing the line. Patrons may have questions about the symptoms of a disease, about the meaning of a diagnosis, or about various methods of treatment. Remember that, like the *pro se* legal patron, a person coming to the library for health-related information does not necessarily realize that the librarian cannot give medical advice. It is therefore up to us to remind patrons of our own limitations. Barbara Beattie, author of the article *A Guide to Medical Reference in the Public Library*,[18] advises that:

> [Librarians] must remain especially cognizant of their obligation to provide information, make resources available, direct patrons to those resources, and allow patrons to study independently. It is not the librarian's task to assist individuals in *understanding* the material they read. . . . We must also refrain from attempting to interpret information or apply it to a patient's situation. As librarians, we must fulfill our role as impartial suppliers of information. If we do, we are staying within the bounds of our profession and need not fear negative legal consequences.[19] [Emphasis added.]

Ms. Beattie's article provides excellent guidelines and limitations.

D. The Library Profession's Ethical Code

So far we have discussed the unauthorized practice of law and medicine in the context of decisions from other professions. But what does our own code of ethics have to say about this situation? The Reference and User Services Association (RUSA), a division of the American Library Association, has created a set of guidelines, not only for legal and medical assistance but also for responses which relate to business matters.[20] (The full text of the guidelines is included on the Scarecrow Press support Website for this book.) These guidelines establish the standards which we, as professionals, need to meet.

According to the RUSA guidelines, library staff members should have enough knowledge to satisfy the routine needs of our patrons. Library workers should refer more difficult questions to subject specialists. Each library should prepare a written policy outlining the level of assistance for legal, medical, or business questions. RUSA recommends that information professionals make their roles clear when they are asked for assistance, especially on legal, medical, or business questions.

The RUSA guidelines also state that libraries should strive to carry the most current materials, should indicate when materials are not up to date, and should let patrons know that more current information may be available elsewhere.[21]

Besides following the RUSA guidelines, another service that librarians should provide involves the accuracy of materials. This service is especially important when advertisements may be mistaken for objective information. For example, if a patron is looking up medication information on the Web and is using the pharmaceutical company's Website for that information, the librarian should refer the patron to a more objective source. If a patron questions the accuracy of materials, we should not comment on whether or not we think the materials are correct, as this would constitute UPL or UPM. However, we can help the patron find other materials that might help to answer the question.

If necessary, librarians should refer patrons to agencies that provide the professional services they need. "Staff may not make recommendations to specific lawyers, legal firms, doctors, other medical care providers or business professionals but may provide access to other information that may help the user identify and locate those resources."[22] Of course, librarians may suggest governmental and nonprofit agencies that might be of assistance to the patron.

Finally, if the user is off-site and requesting information via telephone, e-mail, or live chat, special care should be taken. The RUSA guidelines recommend that each library develop a written policy as to what can be provided to an off-site patron. Creating a remote-use policy is very important because of such factors as the complexity of statutes, because of the existence of prescription drugs that have similar-sounding names, and because of other situations in which mistakes may occur.

My recommendation is that librarians should never read over the telephone any legal cases, laws, or materials about pharmaceutical drugs. Complex financial information is similarly problematic, especially if the information is contained in chart form. Also, it is more difficult for the librarian to identify over the phone whether the patron is an attorney, a healthcare worker, or a member of the general public. Instead, remote patrons should be told that the information is in the library, and they should be invited to come in to complete their research. In this way, librarians can avoid errors, ambiguity, and the possibility of information malpractice.

We should not interpret information; rather, we should help patrons find appropriate tools, we should explain the use of these tools, and then we should get out of the way. Our professional response to the problems of the unauthorized practice of law or medicine is to do what our profession requires—help the patrons to discover for themselves the information they need.

Is there such a thing as the "Unauthorized Practice of Engineering" or the "Unauthorized Practice of Business"? These "unauthorized practices" do not really exist as such. But if we tell patrons what we think the standard is for engineering specifications, we may still be committing UPL by interpreting the building code. Our job as librarians is not to interpret, but to guide. By giving advice, we may be committing UPL or UPM. We may also be setting ourselves up for the potential of a malpractice lawsuit.

Does Information Malpractice Exist?

Let us now return to the scenario at the beginning of this chapter. Besides the other problems, the librarian's answer was wrong. The patron asked whether the police could give a ticket to someone who lost control of his or her vehicle on ice. The librarian researched the issue (in the process committing UPL) and found a case where someone was killed, and the court said that drivers couldn't be prosecuted for problems that occur as a result of weather.

In fact, the librarian's answer was wrong in several ways. To begin with, most states specify that the driver must be in control of the vehicle at all times.[23] While a case involving someone who died might indeed say that the person can't be held responsible for vehicular homicide, that situation has nothing to do with a driver being given a traffic ticket. So our librarian not only committed the *crime* of UPL, but also gave improper advice—which might eventually cause the patron to pay a higher fine. Unfortunately for the librarian, he or she has also committed legal malpractice.

Lawyers fulfill their duties to the client by "performing the legal services for which they have been engaged with such skill, prudence and diligence as lawyers of ordinary skill and capacity commonly possess. . . ."[24] If a librarian commits UPL, he or she will be held to the same standard of care as an attorney. A librarian who commits UPL can be sued for legal malpractice if he or she "failed to possess and apply the knowledge, skill and ability that a reasonably careful professional in the field would exercise under the circumstances."[25]

A librarian who gives the wrong answer while committing UPL is subject to a lawsuit for legal malpractice. Similarly, a librarian committing UPM will be held to the standard of care provided by an ordinary medical professional. The librarian in the opening scenario certainly committed legal malpractice, but did he or she also commit information malpractice? Read on for the answer.

In the late 1980s, independent information brokers began to talk about the possibility of lawsuits for information malpractice.[26] There are two theories of malpractice in the professional literature. One theory involves old material on the library shelves. When a patron uses outdated materials, he or she is hurt because the library did not collect more recent information.[27] In order to avoid this problem, libraries should make sure to collect the most up-to-date materials and to mark outdated materials appropriately. The second issue involves the librarian actually providing incomplete or inaccurate information.

The legal requirements for a charge of professional malpractice are that there be a duty owed by the professional to the client and that the duty is breached, thus causing actual damage to the client.[28] A professional may not be sued for negligence, only for malpractice. This distinction is important because the standard of proof for negligence is lower than that of malpractice. A professional may not be sued for malpractice as long as his or her actions conform to the standards of the profession. It takes a lot more evidence to obtain a malpractice verdict than it does to obtain a negligence verdict. Thus, professionals want to be eligible for malpractice claims instead of negligence claims.

There is an important question of whether librarians are considered to be professionals. In addition, we need to examine the nature of the relationship between librarians and patron-clients, and to investigate the nature of the duty that information workers owe to the patron-client.

A. What Is a Professional?

Let us start with the question "What is a professional?" There are many different ideas about what constitutes being a professional. If the person is not a professional, then he or she cannot be sued for malpractice, but can be sued instead for negligence. Several court cases have dealt with the issue of who is considered a professional.[29]

In the common law, only law, medicine, and theology were originally considered professions; everything else was a trade. This narrow reading has been superceded by changes in modern life.[30] At times, courts have gone one by one through careers, saying that one individual is a professional and another isn't. However, this type of case-by-case reasoning is difficult and futile, so courts are starting to write some specific rules to decide about professionalism. As author Michael Polelle pointed out:

> With an increasing number of lawsuits filed for malpractice (more accurately called professional negligence), it is critical to be able to determine just who is a "professional." A number of significant legal rules depend on whether a court classifies a defendant sued for negligence as a professional. . . . Sociologists have already noted the rise of "semi-professions," such as nursing, library science, pharmacy, stockbrokering, advertising and business management, which strive for the same social and legal status as the fully recognized professions of law and medicine.[31] Unless either legislatures or courts develop a more unified definition of what constitutes a professional, this uncertainty creates the risk of capriciousness. . . .[32]

Certainly librarians consider themselves to be professionals rather than "semi-professionals." But whether or not other people consider librarianship a profession, there are some standards that have been set by the courts. Martha J. Dragich points out that the role of librarians as information providers has been changing considerably over the past few decades:

> While in the past the librarian may have been the "organizer and dispenser of books and documents," the role of information providers today is more often to advise the client on information needs. . . . While in our earlier role it was improper for a librarian to interpret information for a patron, information professionals now are required to evaluate requests for information, determine the best databases for searching, translate the request into the appropriate search language, evaluate the results during and after the search, and determine whether the results are appropriate.[33]

Dragich argues that this change in the role of the information professional helps to establish librarians as professionals, with the "duty to assume responsibility for the accuracy of the information we provide."[34] Dragich goes on to say:

> The client's increased reliance on our knowledge and judgment increases our duty to assume responsibility for the accuracy of the information we provide and for the manner in which it was obtained. Even though we gather and use data originating with an author, database producer, publisher or agency, we are called upon specifically to employ our knowledge and judgment to retrieve accurate and up-to-date information relevant to the client's information needs. We are not only the finders but also the evaluators and interpreters of the in-

formation—roles formerly performed by the client. Thus, it will be much easier for courts to find a duty sufficient to sustain liability in cases filed against us by disgruntled clients.[35]

Dragich's point is an important one. The new role of librarians and archivists means that we are holding ourselves out as experts. This role as professionals may make us liable for complaints of professional negligence. As a result, we must make changes in the way we approach our duties.

There are several tests that courts have used to determine who is a professional. For example, Michael J. Polelle contends that:

> [T]he central criterion of a profession should be whether the occupation or trade involved has a credible code of fiduciary ethics [i.e., a duty of care and a duty of loyalty towards patron/clients] that is effectively enforced. [For more information on fiduciary duties, see **Chapter 11**, *Employment and Workplace Law*.] In the United States, medicine and law are the prime models of such professionalism. Applying this ethical standard, other occupations can only merit the same classification of professionalism to the extent [that] they resemble medicine and law in creating and effectively enforcing explicit ethical norms for the governance of their members.[36]

As suggested by Polelle's article, the New York courts have adopted a test based on the qualities that professionals share. These standards are articulated by the case of *Chase Scientific Research, Inc. v. NIA Group, Inc.*:[37]

> The qualities shared by such groups guide us in defining the term "professional." In particular, those qualities include extensive formal learning and training, licensure and regulation indicating a qualification to practice, a code of conduct imposing standards beyond those accepted in the marketplace and a system of discipline for violation of those standards. . . . Additionally, a professional relationship is one of trust and confidence, carrying with it a duty to counsel and advise clients.[38] [Citations omitted.]

Although librarians do not have a professional licensure or certification, they do have educational requirements. In order to be recognized by the national associations as a professional librarian, an individual must have a master's degree in library science. In order to be recognized as an archivist, an individual must have formal credentials, i.e., either a master's degree in library science or a master's degree in history. These educational prerequisites meet the *Chase Scientific Research* standard of "extensive formal learning and training."[39]

Librarians and archivists are also subject to a "code of conduct imposing standards beyond those accepted in the marketplace."[40] Although librarians do not have a system of discipline beyond that of the employer, the librarian-patron relationship is indeed "one of trust and confidence, carrying with it a duty to counsel and advise clients."[41] Thus, librarianship meets most (but not all) of the tests laid out in the *Chase Scientific Research* case.

Some states have statutes that discuss professional services, but these statutes are often in the context of limited liability companies, and so they don't provide much help in determining who is really a professional.[42] A very good statement of the difficulty of determining who is a professional comes from the recent case of *Gardiner Park Development v. Matherly Land Surveying*. The *Gardiner Park* case analyzed the various tests for being a professional and summarized them, saying:

> There are three main tests that states have used to determine who is a professional. . . . The first adopts the view of the common law and restricts the statute's application only to those engaged in the professions of law, medicine, or divinity. A second approach simply defines professional and professional services as all licensed occupations. The third approach follows what has been termed the "dictionary" definition of professional.[43] Yet a fourth approach appears to be followed by Florida[44] where that state's Supreme Court has created a bright-line test [a necessary test] requiring that any vocation that wishes to be considered a profession must require, at a minimum, a four-year college degree before licensing. If alternative methods may be used to practice the vocation it is not [considered] a profession.[45]

The most helpful cases about professionalism are those that use the dictionary definition and those that require educational attainment before entering the field. For example, in North Dakota, the case of *Jilek v. Berger Electric, Inc.* used the dictionary definition of the word *profession*:

> Webster's New World Dictionary[46] defines "profession" as "a vocation or occupation requiring advanced education and training, and involving intellectual skills such as medicine, law, theology, engineering, teaching, etc." Black's Law Dictionary[47] similarly defines "profession" and explains that "the labor and skill involved in a profession is predominantly mental or intellectual, rather than physical or manual." These definitions, at least implicitly, distinguish a profession from a trade. . . .[48]

The opinion in the *Jilek* case also notes that the U.S. Code contains a statutory definition of "professional employee" for purposes of collective bargaining. (For more information on collective bargaining, see ***Chapter 11, Employment and Workplace Law***.) The collective bargaining statute reads:

> The term "professional employee" means —
>
> (a) any employee engaged in work (i) predominantly intellectual and varied in character as opposed to routine mental, manual, mechanical, or physical work; (ii) involving the consistent exercise of discretion and judgment in its performance; (iii) of such a character that the output produced or the result accomplished cannot be standardized in relation to a given period of time; (iv) requiring knowledge of an advanced type in a field of science or learning customarily acquired by a prolonged course of specialized intellectual instruction and study in an institution of higher learning or a hospital, as distinguished from a general academic education or from an apprenticeship or from training in the performance of routine mental, manual, or physical processes; or
>
> (b) any employee, who (i) has completed the courses of specialized intellectual instruction and study described in clause (iv) of paragraph (a), and (ii) is performing related work under the supervision of a professional person to qualify himself to become a professional employee as defined in paragraph (a).[49]

The definition of a "professional" which is used in collective bargaining can be very helpful, as it attempts to differentiate between professions and trades. The approach in Florida is also useful, with its emphasis upon the attainment of a college degree in the specific field.[50] This is what distinguishes a skilled trade from a profession. As the opinion in the *Jilek* case stated, "an electrician may be trained in a technical area and may perform skilled work, but he or she is not engaged in an occupation that requires a college degree. . . . In short, an electrician practices a trade, not a profession."[51]

Ultimately, the question of whether librarians are professionals will need to be settled on a state-by-state basis. Under many of the tests, librarians would be considered to be professionals, because of the educational standards for entering the field, the application of intellectual discretion, and the librarian's code of ethics. However, the question of who is a professional is subject to a great deal of interpretation.

Does all this mean that librarians or archivists can be sued for professional malpractice? Not necessarily, since it still has to be determined whether the information professional used reasonable care according to the duty owed to the patron. The duty of care that should be used by librarians and archivists in providing information will be discussed in the next section.

B. Defining the Information Professional's Duty of Care to Patrons

When a patron claims that he or she was harmed by the information in a book or a database, it is fairly easy for librarians to escape legal responsibility. After all, we didn't create the book. Fortunately, there have been no cases involving this type of liability.

A case similar to our situation concerned a video store that was sued for distributing a libelous videotape.[52] In *EWAP v. Osmond*, the court found in favor of the video store, since the store was similar to "one who merely plays a secondary role in disseminating information published by another, as in the case of libraries, news vendors, or carriers. . . ."[53]

Relying upon the Restatement (Second) of Torts, the *EWAP* case stated that "vendors or lenders" are not required to examine items that come from reputable publishers.[54] However, if a particular author or publisher "has frequently published notoriously sensational or scandalous books," there may be a duty to examine the materials to ensure that they are reputable.

The other U.S. case involving the provision of information, *Brocklesby v. Jeppesen*,[55] can probably be distinguished from the general library situation because it involved product liability law. The Jeppeson company took data in chart form from the FAA and created maps. The company sold a map that failed to show a mountain. The original mistake was in the FAA data, but Jeppesen was found to be liable. However, the reason that they were liable had more to do with products liability law than with malpractice. The court found that the charts were mass-produced, and emphasized that "Jeppesen had a duty to test its product and to warn users of its dangers."[56] Since librarians, of necessity, provide individualized services to patrons, we are not going to be judged by product liability law. But it certainly is important to make sure that the information we provide is accurate.

The situations in which librarians have the greatest possibility of being the subject of malpractice suits are those in which the librarian acts as an expert and gives advice to patrons, rather than just helping them find information. In other words, the very same scenarios that lead to the unauthorized practice of law or the unauthorized practice of medicine are the circumstances that have the greatest potential to expose librarians to legal liability.

Some states do have statutes that may help to limit liability. For example, Illinois has a statute that limits liability for the provision of information:

> A public employee acting in the scope of his employment is not liable for an injury caused by his negligent misrepresentation or the provision of information either orally, in writing, by computer or any other electronic transmission, or in a book or other form of library material.[57]

Although there have not been any cases of this type of informational malpractice in the United States, there was a case in Britain. The case was *Vacwell Engineering v. B.D.H. Chemicals Ltd.*[58] Vacwell, a manufacturer of transistors, ordered a chemical called boron tribromide from B.D.H. Both parties understood that when boron tribromide came in contact with water, a toxic vapor was emitted. However, neither party knew that the contact with water would cause a violent explosion. The shipping container warned about "harmful vapour."[59] A Vacwell scientist accidentally dropped a container into water, and the chemical exploded violently. One scientist was killed, the other one was seriously injured, and there was extensive damage.[60]

Some of the earlier scientific works on boron tribromide had information about the explosion risk, but more recent books did not mention the danger.[61] According to the British court's opinion: "The scientific literature contained warnings of this explosion hazard as long ago as 1878, when a French scientist named BERTHELOT described it in the ANNALES DE CHIMIE ET DE PHYSIQUE."[62] Articles and books containing warnings about the danger of explosions were also published in 1899, 1924, 1926, and 1938.[63] The court continued: "Against this background of scientific literature . . . it is surprising to find that there is no reference to the explosion hazard of boron tribromide on contact with water in at least four more modern scientific works."[64]

The books that B.D.H. consulted included *Lange's Handbook of Chemistry,*[65] the *C.R.C. Handbook of Chemistry and Physics,*[66] the *Merck Index,*[67] and *Sax's Dangerous Properties of Industrial Materials* (which is hailed by the publishers as "the Bible of Safety Information").[68] Each of these books is a standard reference work, and all four books are still among the most-consulted materials in the library collection. These works are generally the first place that chemists and librarians go for information.[69] It turned out that B.D.H. had consulted the four modern books. However, none of the researchers from B.D.H. had looked at any of the older works, even though *three of these works were available in B.D.H.'s own library*. This piece of evidence was relied upon heavily in the opinion. The judge stated:

> My conclusion on the whole of the evidence is that it was the duty of B.D.H. to have established and maintained a system under which adequate investigation and research into the scientific literature took place in order to discover . . . what hazards were known. . . . I am satisfied that this duty was never complied with. . . . [T]here was a breach of duty of care and skill on the part of those responsible in B.D.H. to carry out an adequate and proper research into the scientific literature. . . . [R]esearch which covered only the four books mentioned . . . was plainly inadequate. If a proper research had been undertaken, [it] would have revealed the explosion hazard in relation to water on boron tribromide.[70]

The result of the *Vacwell* case was that B.D.H. was found responsible for the damage because the company did not do a proper job of researching the risks. Although the sources consulted are standard works that most libraries have and that are consulted on a regular basis, a complete search by a trained information professional would probably have revealed the existence of the explosion risk *in the materials held in B.D.H.'s own library*. Because of this negligent research, B.D.H. was held liable for the death, injuries, and damages from the explosion.

Although the researchers were not trained librarians, they were in fact chemists trained to perform research, and the court ruled that they should have done a more thorough job of looking through the scientific literature. Unlike *EWAP* or *Jeppesen*, the *Vacwell* case turns directly on whether the appropriate amount of research was done. As a result, the *Vacwell* case is very relevant for librarians. Had a librarian made this error of insufficient research, he or she might be liable for information malpractice.

If a court were to find liability for information malpractice, what standards would be used? The statements of our profession as to appropriate levels of service would become the minimum standard to which we would be held.

For example, the RUSA *Guidelines for Medical, Legal, and Business Responses*,[71] discussed above, explains the standards by which high-quality library services should be judged. A copy of the guidelines is available at the Scarecrow Press support Website for this book.

RUSA guidelines are also available for other subject areas, including electronic services, virtual reference, professional competencies for reference and user services libraries, guidelines for library services to Hispanics, and guidelines for library services to older adults.[72]

Other divisions of the American Library Association have further statements that may be relevant, such as the *Guidelines for Library and Information Services for the American Deaf Community*. This statement was created by the Association of Specialized and Cooperative Library Agencies (ASCLA).[73] The broader ALA itself has guidelines, as do the Special Libraries Association, the Medical Libraries Association, and other specialized library organizations. Finally, the Association of Independent Information Professionals has formulated a series of standards, including a *Code of Ethical Business Practices*.[74] Together these guidelines from the professional associations indicate the collective standards to which the library profession should be held.

One way to avoid information malpractice is to keep your knowledge up to date. "The importance of keeping up to date . . . [will not only] make legal proceedings less likely to arise in the first place; it may also provide a partial defense."[75] Having current knowledge shows that you are engaging in good professional conduct and are trying to meet the standards of the profession.

The best way to avoid problems is to restrict the relationship to *providing* information. Then let the *patron* interpret the information himself or herself. Don't define, don't recommend for particular situations, just direct the patrons to the appropriate information and let them make up their own minds.

The guidelines of the Virginia Bar Association for avoiding UPL also have a corresponding use in avoiding professional malpractice. If the information professional follows these guidelines, he or she will be acting within the standards of the profession.

The best policy is to follow the practices used by school and academic librarians in assisting students who are researching a topic. If the students need a librarian's assistance in finding the materials, the school and academic librarians direct them to the materials, then leave the patrons alone, allowing the students to complete their assignments. If you do this, you won't stray over the line to commit the unauthorized practice of law or the unauthorized practice of medicine. Allowing the researcher to come to his or her own conclusions will also help librarians and archivists to avoid exposing themselves to the potential of malpractice lawsuits.

Conclusion

While helping patrons, librarians must be careful not to commit the unauthorized practice of law or of medicine. Don't interpret information, don't give definitions, and don't apply the data to the patron's personal situation. These are the basics of the unauthorized practice of law and medicine.

The three Virginia Bar Association opinions on the unauthorized practice of law and the RUSA *Guidelines for Medical, Legal, and Business Responses* provide a good summary of the types of services librarians can legally perform. (For the text of these opinions and the RUSA guidelines, see *Guidelines and Opinions on the Unauthorized Practice of Law*, available at the Scarecrow Press support Website for this book.)

Remember the principles of effective reference service and apply them to the situation. There is a way to fully satisfy our patrons without crossing the line into UPL or UPM. Performing a proper reference transaction also helps to protect us from being sued for information malpractice. Do not, however, shy away from helping with reference questions if the patron has a legal or medical issue.

Although there have been no cases in the United States that have found liability for librarians or archivists in the provision of their services, the *Vacwell* case in Britain provides a cautionary warning to information professionals. There is a real risk of liability if people are harmed as a result of incomplete research.

Although there are some questions as to whether librarians and archivists are professionals, many states do indeed define professionals in such a way as to include the information field. The inclusion of librarians and archivists within the ranks of professionals allows us to be held to the malpractice standard whereby a professional may not be sued for malpractice as long as his or her actions conform to the standards of the profession. These standards are defined by the guidelines and statements of our professional bodies, as well as by outside groups such as the Virginia Bar Association. Under the laws of malpractice, if a librarian or archivist adheres to these standards, he or she would not be liable for damages to a patron. Since malpractice is much harder to prove than ordinary negligence, it is very important that librarians and archivists be defined as professionals.

How should the librarian in our opening scenario have dealt with the patron? Let's turn back in time and see how the transaction should have been handled.

PATRON: I need your help, please! I wrecked my car, and the police officer gave me a ticket. I got these forms in the mail from the court. What do I do? Is there some sort of form I can use to respond?

LIBRARIAN: What kind of ticket did you get?

PATRON: The officer said that I must have been going too fast, or else I wouldn't have slid into his lane. I was only going 25, but the ice was very thick and I just lost control! He said that I must be in control of my car at all times and under all conditions. Is that right?

LIBRARIAN [taking PATRON to law books]: Well, let's see. Why don't we take a look at West's Digest *for this state. In a nutshell, the* Digest *puts cases together by topic with a numbering system. It is kind of like the Library of Congress Classification System or the Dewey Decimal Classification System. So you can look up your topic in the index, and find out what number it is under. When you look under that number, you will find cases on your topic.*

PATRON: Thank you very much! I'll take a look at this and decide whether to fight the ticket or pay it. If I challenge the ticket in court and lose I will have to pay court costs and an even higher fine. How do I respond to the court?

LIBRARIAN [taking PATRON to State Form Book]: Well, here are the form book and court rules for our state. Take a look at this and see if anything looks applicable to your situation. I hope this helps you.

PATRON: You have really helped me a lot. I feel better, and now I know where to find the law. Thank you very much.

LIBRARIAN: Good luck.

9

Search Warrants, Investigations, Library Records, and Privacy

> You are working at the circulation desk one rainy night when a man walks into the library. He comes up to the desk and shows you a police badge. The officer explains that he is investigating a suspected methamphetamine manufacturer, and he would like to find out whether the person has checked out any books about manufacturing meth. You inform the officer that your professional ethics and the library's policy demand the privacy of circulation records. In return, the officer explains that if you do not turn over the records, he will arrest you as an accessory to the crime. What do you do? If he has a search warrant, does that make any difference? What are your rights, and what are your patron's rights?

This chapter will begin by discussing search warrants. Librarians, archivists, and bookstore workers need to understand what a search warrant is and what it means. You need to understand search warrants in order to balance the need for security and the need for privacy, both of which are important interests in our society. This chapter will discuss what a valid search warrant is and what is covered by a search warrant. I will then discuss library confidentiality laws in the United States, as well as the Family Educational Rights and Privacy Act (FERPA), and the USA PATRIOT Act.[1] Following these discussions are two charts which will provide a visual overview of the library privacy laws in each jurisdiction. The actual text of each state's library privacy laws can be found on the Scarecrow Press support Website for this book. By the end of this chapter, you should understand how search warrants work, and you will know what to do in the event that "the law" comes knocking on your library's door. The final section of this chapter will explore those times when librarians and archivists *should* disclose information about patrons. The last section will also discuss how to deal with patrons who are dangerous to themselves or to others.

The Basics of Search Warrants for Libraries and Archives

A. The FBI Library Awareness Program

In June of 1987, agents from the Federal Bureau of Investigation visited the libraries at Columbia University. According to Paula Kaufman, director of Academic Information Services at Columbia University, the FBI agents "explained that they were doing a general 'library awareness' program in the city and that they were asking librarians to be alert to the use of their libraries by persons from countries 'hostile to the United States, such as the Soviet Union' and to provide the FBI with information about these activities."[2] In other words, the FBI was asking librarians to inform the FBI about which patrons were using which materials.

The FBI Library Awareness Program created an enormous uproar. Following the FBI's visit to Columbia, more accounts of FBI "interviews" began to emerge. Apparently, during the years 1986 and 1987, the FBI had visited libraries at a number of institutions of higher education across the country, including the libraries at New York University, the University of Maryland, SUNY Buffalo, George Mason University, and the Universities of Cincinnati, Michigan, Wisconsin, and Utah. Public libraries were also included in the FBI "program."[3]

The Library Awareness Program turned out to be a public relations nightmare for the FBI. Questions were asked in Congress, and the issue of privacy relating to library circulation was discussed on the front page of the *New York Times*.[4] Suddenly the media were interviewing librarians about their institutions' privacy policies, and librarians were shown to be protecting their patrons' confidentiality. According to Vartan Gregorian, who at the time was the president of the New York Public Library, "We consider reading a private act, an extension of freedom of thought. And our doors are open to all. We don't check IDs."[5]

In the wake of the FBI's Library Awareness Program, many states have adopted library privacy laws. Some of these laws relate only to public libraries while some laws cover other types of libraries as well. Librarians and archivists need to know about the privacy laws in their own states in order to respond to questions from law enforcement officials and the media, as well as to respond to Freedom of Information and Open Records requests. Every library worker needs to be aware of the laws regarding what type of library is covered, what kinds of library records are private, and what happens in the event of a disclosure of information. Library and archival workers also need to know the basic laws about search warrants in order to understand when they should respond to a request for information, and when they should refuse to respond.

B. The Fourth Amendment and Search Warrants

In order to conduct searches or investigate private records, police and other law enforcement officials are required by the Fourth Amendment of the U.S. Constitution to obtain a search warrant. The Fourth Amendment states: "The rights of the people to be secure in their persons, houses, papers, and effects, against unreasonable searches and seizures, shall not be violated, and no warrants shall issue but upon probable cause, supported by oath or affirmation, and particularly describing the place to be searched, and the persons or things to be seized."[6] Time and again, the U.S. Supreme Court has decided that, with only a few exceptions, searches that are not based upon search warrants are illegal.

The basis of the Fourth Amendment is the idea that privacy is one of the paramount concerns in our society. The goal of the Fourth Amendment is to prevent government officials and the police from going on "fishing expeditions."[7] According to the Supreme Court, "In so doing the Amendment does not place an unduly oppressive weight on law enforcement officers but merely interposes an orderly procedure under the aegis of judicial impartiality that is necessary to attain the beneficent purposes intended. Officers instead of obeying this mandate have too often, as shown by the numerous cases in this Court, taken matters into their own hands and invaded the security of the people against unreasonable search and seizure."[8] [Citations omitted.]

Although there have not been many cases of "unreasonable search and seizure" within the context of archives, libraries, or bookstores, the principles of Fourth Amendment law apply to all types of situations. For example, one of the key cases used in discussing the necessity of search warrants is *Johnson v. United States*.[9] In the *Johnson* case, police searched a hotel room after smelling opium in the hallway. The Supreme Court suppressed the evidence on the basis of the Fourth Amendment. According to the Court's decision:

> The point of the Fourth Amendment, which often is not grasped by zealous officers, is not that it denies law enforcement the support of the usual inferences which reasonable men draw from evidence. Its protection consists in requiring that those inferences be drawn by a

neutral and detached magistrate instead of being judged by the officer engaged in the often competitive enterprise of ferreting out crime. Any assumption that . . . will justify the officers in making a search without a warrant would reduce the Amendment to a nullity and leave the people's homes secure only in the discretion of police officers. . . . *When the right of privacy must reasonably yield to the right of search is, as a rule, to be decided by a judicial officer, not by a policeman or government enforcement agent.*[10] [Emphasis added.]

One interesting point about the *Johnson* case is that the police had sufficient grounds to obtain a valid search warrant but chose not to get one. According to the Supreme Court, the odor of burning opium provided probable cause to believe that a crime was being committed in the hotel room.[11] Nevertheless, the police didn't obtain a warrant. Therefore, the evidence was obtained illegally and could not be used in court.

The *Johnson* case emphasizes the Supreme Court's insistence that law enforcement officials obtain search warrants. Because of the Fourth Amendment and its reinforcement by Supreme Court decisions, police investigators must obtain a search warrant before they can legally examine circulation or business records. Libraries, archives, bookstores, and other organizations are not only within their rights to deny access to investigators who do not have search warrants or subpoenas, but in fact these entities may be legally required to deny access to their records. (A subpoena is a court order requiring a person to appear in court. A *subpoena duces tecum* requires that the person or entity bring something—such as business records—to court. This type of order is often referred to simply as a subpoena.) The bottom line is that police officers must obtain search warrants or subpoenas first before requesting records.

C. Probable Cause

In order to obtain a valid search warrant, the Fourth Amendment requires *probable cause*. For probable cause to exist, it "must be supported by substantial evidence: [1] that the items being sought are in fact seizable by virtue of being connected with criminal activity, and [2] that the items will be found in the place to be searched."[12] The officer who wants to get a search warrant needs to be able to show that he or she has a reasonable basis for believing a crime has occurred, that there is a reasonable basis for believing the person being investigated has committed the crime, and that there is a reasonable chance the evidence will be found in the area to be searched. According to the Supreme Court, if "the affiant had reasonable grounds at the time of his affidavit . . . for the belief that the law was being violated on the premises to be searched; and if the apparent facts set out in the affidavit are such that a reasonably discreet and prudent man would be led to believe that there was a commission of the offense charged, there is probable cause justifying the issuance of a warrant."[13]

One problem that comes up occasionally is what to do if the library's circulation records are needed in order to establish probable cause for the search warrant. If there is no probable cause in the first place, the records can't be searched. However, information that is available to everyone through the library catalog can be used to establish probable cause.

This type of probable cause question usually occurs when a suspect is in possession of a large number of library books which appear to be stolen. Police would need to determine that the books were not checked out to the suspect before they could obtain a search warrant. Yet without circulation information, the investigators would be unable to show probable cause that a crime had been committed. After all, the suspect might have checked the books out legally.

Since there is no search warrant, the police are not allowed to look at the patron's circulation record. However, many online library catalogs show whether books have been checked out, although the catalog does not specify who has the book. If this information is available to the public via the library catalog, investigators can look at the catalog to determine whether or not the books are listed as being checked out. If the books in the suspect's possession are not listed as being checked out, the police have established probable cause to believe that a crime has been committed and that the suspect has committed the crime.

D. Particularity

One of the most important parts of the Fourth Amendment is the concept of particularity. The Fourth Amendment provides for two different types of particularity, stating that warrants shall particularly describe "the place to be searched, and the persons or things to be seized."[14] The point is to leave as little to the discretion of the officer as possible. Instead, the decisions are to be made by an impartial judge or magistrate.

Particularity of location means that the search warrant must identify the *place* where the search will take place. The search must take place at the location that was given in the warrant, and investigators are not allowed to search other places without obtaining a new warrant. Usually the requirement of particularity means that the warrant will include the specific address of the location to be searched.

If investigators want to look at library circulation records or bookstore business records, the search warrant must specify the location of the records. For example, a search warrant to look at computer sign-in logs at one library branch does not allow the police to look at the logs at another branch. Investigators must obtain a search warrant for each location, or at least they must identify in the search warrant each location to be searched. However, if circulation or sales records are available at any location, the warrant doesn't need to specify all branches; it need only name the location where the search will physically take place.

Particularity of items is potentially a more important area for libraries, archives, and bookstores than particularity of location. Thus, "the requirement that warrants shall particularly describe the things to be seized makes general searches under them impossible and prevents the seizure of one thing under a warrant describing another. As to what is to be taken, nothing is left to the discretion of the officer executing the warrant."[15] In effect, the officers are bound by the terms of the search warrant.

The particularity requirement means that libraries, archives, and bookstores are only allowed by law to show officers the items named in the search warrant or subpoena. If the warrant asks for the circulation records of John Doe, it must state what kinds of records are included. For example, a search warrant authorizing a search of circulation records for John Doe means that only that patron's circulation records can be given to the investigator. The warrant does not mean that computer sign-in logs are also available to the investigators. Those records would have to be named separately in the search warrant.

The search warrant must also be specific about what dates are covered. If the warrant authorizes a search of the circulation records from June 1 to July 1, 2005, the police are not allowed to look at records from May 2005. The date is not usually a major issue with library circulation records, since most automated circulation systems delete the record as soon as the book is returned.

Finally, the particularity requirement means that the warrant must specifically *name the person* who is being investigated. If the judge issues a warrant to look at the circulation records of John Doe, the officer is not allowed to look at the library's circulation records in general and find information about Jane Doe. The police would need a separate search warrant if they wanted to obtain information about Jane Doe. In order to avoid disclosing confidential patron information to the police in the midst of a search, library and archival workers should themselves obtain the specific information that was requested, rather than allowing law enforcement agents to look up the records. If an automated circulation system is being used, the librarian should make a printout of the patron record for the police officer.

E. Due Process in the Library Setting

The Fourteenth Amendment states: "No State shall make or enforce any law which shall abridge the privileges or immunities of citizens of the United States; nor shall any State deprive any person of life, liberty, or property, without due process of law; nor deny to any person within its jurisdiction the equal protection of the laws."[16] The due process clause of the Fourteenth Amendment has applied to the states the search warrant requirements of the Fourth Amendment. However, there is more to Fourteenth Amendment due process than just the necessity for search warrants, and several of the Fourteenth Amendment's provisions also apply to libraries, especially since many libraries are governmental or quasi-governmental organizations.

One provision that has caused a great deal of litigation involves holding patrons who may have been trying to steal library materials. Most of the cases in this area come from stores, including bookstores, that are investigating potential shoplifting cases. The rule is that an officer may "stop and briefly detain a person for investigative purposes" if the officer has "a reasonable suspicion supported by articulable [sic] facts that criminal activity may be afoot."[17] The stop must be for a reasonable and limited amount of time. According to the U.S. Supreme Court, "an investigatory detention must be temporary and last no longer than is necessary to effectuate the purpose of the stop."[18]

Another issue that relates to investigating a theft involves the methods that are used. The U.S. Supreme Court has stated that "investigative methods employed should be the least intrusive means reasonably available to verify or dispel the officer's suspicion in a short period of time."[19] In the case of a library, that means determining whether or not the book has been checked out. Once it has been discovered that the book was checked out, the investigative stop must end. If the library material is not checked out or is noncirculating, the inquiry would continue.

One Website has summarized the situation with respect to a shop-lifting stop as follows:

> A store owner or someone who works for the owner generally has the right to detain a person they suspect of shoplifting in order to investigate the possible crime. This investigation must take place in a reasonable amount of time. Generally, the owner or employee can't look inside the person's bag without permission, unless they actually saw the person steal something, or the item is in plain view. If this is not the case, the store would either have to let the person go or call the police to conduct any further investigation. The owner or employee can't loudly accuse the suspect in front of other customers and must not be rude or offensive during questioning.[20]

For example, suppose that the gate alarm goes off when a patron is walking through the exit. It is reasonable for the library worker to stop the patron and ask to look through his or her bag. If the patron refuses to cooperate, the worker should call the police. However, the library worker should be polite at all times and should avoid accusations or insults.

Another area of due process that applies to libraries involves suspension of library privileges. There is a case from New York in which a library failed to follow its own procedures when suspending library privileges. In the case of *Hewlett-Woodmere Public Library v. Phyllis Rothman*, a patron returned a film that had been destroyed.[21] The public library was a direct unit of the local government, meaning that the Fourteenth Amendment applied to the library. According to the library, the film had been in good condition when it was borrowed; the patron claimed that the film was damaged when she received it. The library charged the patron for replacement of the film. When the patron refused to pay, her borrowing privileges were suspended. Sounds pretty straightforward, right? Wrong!

It seems that the library had a written procedure that allowed for a hearing in front of the library board in the event of a suspension of privileges. Because the library did not inform the patron of her rights, the court ruled that the patron had been denied due process of law. The court further ruled that this denial of due process existed regardless of whether the public library was a municipal unit or a nonprofit organization. The court's decision stated: "A public library which is supported by public taxation regardless of whether it is a municipal corporation or some other legal entity is a person subject to liability under section 1983 of title 42 of the United States Code."[22]

The lesson of the *Hewlett-Woodmere* case is that libraries and archives should follow their own procedures. Any deviation from written procedure has the possibility of being viewed later as a violation of due process. Therefore, libraries and archives must not only write these kinds of policies, but they must also adhere to them.

State Privacy Laws for Libraries and Archives

The records kept by libraries have always been given a reasonable expectation of privacy, and most state laws recognize this expectation.[23] As early as 1973, it was realized that "an individual's personal privacy is directly affected by the kind of disclosure and use made of identifiable information about him in a record."[24] In addition, the American Library Association's Code of Ethics states that librarians must "protect each library user's right to privacy and confidentiality with respect to information sought or received and resources consulted, borrowed, acquired or transmitted."[25] Nonetheless, libraries have always been subject to court orders which require disclosure of patron records. State privacy laws allow disclosure of private information when there is a valid subpoena or court order.

Many states' privacy laws have features in common. There are four types of legal provisions for library privacy in the various jurisdictions: an open records exemption, a separate library privacy statute, rules of evidence, and Attorney General opinions. In addition, Idaho has a Supreme Court rule providing for privacy for the State Law Library.[26] Most of the states have provisions in their statutes for library privacy. These provisions are written either separately or in the context of open records exemptions. Some statutes contain exceptions for the parents of minor children, while other statutes contain penalties for disclosing protected information.

The privacy provisions in Georgia and New York are contained in the evidence code for each state. In Idaho, the entire open records act is contained within the evidence code.[27] Kentucky and Hawaii have provisions for library privacy in Attorney General opinions. Arkansas, Massachusetts, New Mexico, and the District of Columbia have the most detailed code provisions, while Mississippi, Oklahoma, Oregon, Pennsylvania, South Dakota, and the Virgin Islands have the briefest statutes. American Samoa and the Commonwealth of the Northern Marianas do not have any library privacy statutes. (For the text of each jurisdiction's library privacy laws, see the Scarecrow Press support Website for this book.)

A. What Type of Library Is Covered?

In order to understand privacy laws, one must first determine to which libraries the statutes apply. Several states provide library privacy only for public libraries; however, most jurisdictions apply their privacy laws either to all libraries that are open to the public, or to all libraries that receive government funding. A small group of states apply their privacy laws to all libraries, regardless of status.

The library privacy law in Tennessee is typical of many such laws in the rest of the country. According to the Tennessee Code Annotated, "'Library record' means a document, record, or other method of storing information retained by a library that identifies a person as having requested or obtained specific information or materials from such library. 'Library record' does not include nonidentifying material that may be retained for the purpose of studying or evaluating the circulation of library materials in general."[28]

Tennessee law applies confidentiality provisions to:

(A) Libraries that are open to the public and established or operated by:
    (i) The state, a county, city, town, school district or any other political subdivision of the state;
    (ii) A combination of governmental units or authorities;
    (iii) A university or community college; or
(B) Any private library that is open to the public.[29]

Most states also apply their library privacy laws to a variety of types of organizations, although there are some states that only recognize privacy of circulation records in public libraries. For example, in South Carolina the records of "users of public, private, school, college, technical college, university, and state institutional libraries and library systems, supported in whole or in part by public funds or expending public funds, are confidential information."[30] The statute in Illinois applies to "any public library or library of an educational, historical or eleemosynary [the word means "charitable"] institution, organization or society."[31] Nevada's law applies to all libraries.[32] Kentucky's Attorney General opinions apply to all libraries supported at least 25 percent by public funds; these Kentucky decisions will be discussed in *Section E.* For a listing of states that provide for circulation privacy in a variety of library settings, see table 9.1, Sources of State and Territorial Library Privacy Laws, located at the end of this chapter.

B. What Type of Information Is Private?

The states and territories are generally in agreement that registration and circulation records are confidential. The difference among the statutes is that some jurisdictions also protect additional services, while others do not. Georgia's evidence code deals with "[c]irculation and similar records of a library,"[33] but does not mention issues such as reference transactions. Many other states are similarly focused on registration and circulation records. The Virginia statute deals with "[l]ibrary records which can be used to identify both (i) any library patron who has borrowed material from a library and (ii) the material such patron borrowed."[34] Louisiana similarly protects records which indicate "which of its documents or other materials, regardless of format, have been loaned to or used by an identifiable individual or group of individuals."[35] Louisiana gives additional protection to "records of any such library which are maintained for purposes of registration or for determining eligibility for the use of library services."[36]

On the other hand, several states protect not only the circulation records, but also books used within the library. For example, in Colorado "a publicly-supported library shall not disclose any record or other information that identifies a person as having requested or obtained specific materials or service or as otherwise having used the library."[37] In Iowa, the law protects "The records of a library which, by themselves or when examined with other public records, would reveal the identity of the library patron checking out or requesting an item or information from the library."[38] The language of these laws may be broad enough to include requests for reference assistance and certainly would include sign-up sheets for computer use.

Rhode Island has also included other types of transactions beyond library interactions. The law states that: "It shall be unlawful for any person to reveal, transmit, publish, or disseminate in any manner, any records which would identify the names and addresses of individuals, with the titles or nature of video films, records, cassettes, or the like, which they purchased, leased, rented, or borrowed, from libraries, book stores, video stores, or record and cassette shops or any retailer or distributor of those products. . . ."[39]

The Arkansas statute contains the most detailed definition of what library information is confidential. In fact, the statute contains so much detail that it answers many of the questions that are raised by laws in other jurisdictions and provides a substantial amount of protection to the library patron. The statute reads:

"Confidential library records" means documents or information
in any format retained in a library that identify a patron as having requested, used, or obtained specific materials, including, but not limited to, circulation of library books, materials, computer database
searches, interlibrary loan transactions, reference queries, patent
searches, requests for photocopies of library materials, title reserve
requests, or the use of audiovisual materials, films, or records.[40] [Em-
phasis added.]

In addition to state library privacy laws, a Federal statute—the
Family Educational Rights and Privacy Act (FERPA)—covers student
records at colleges and universities. FERPA prohibits the release of
student records without the express written consent of the student involved. Although FERPA does not specifically mention library records,
many institutions have interpreted the statute as including library records. As a result, librarians and archivists at academic institutions have
an additional law to follow in protecting the privacy rights of their patrons.[41]

FERPA applies to all institutions, public or private, which receive
Federal funding. Violations of this statute may result in the revocation
of Federal funding, so FERPA is an important restriction to keep in
mind if you are at a school or academic library in a state that provides
privacy only for public libraries.

Another restriction on disclosure of information comes from the
law of trade secrets. Under some conditions, the restrictions of trade
secret law may apply to disclosure of patron information, and the librarian or archivist may be liable for civil damages if information is
released. This topic is covered in more detail in *Chapter 6*, *Trademark
and Trade Secret Law*.

C. What Types of Information May Be Disclosed?

As with other issues, the various jurisdictions generally agree on
what information can be released and what information cannot be released. However, there are still many differences in the various statutes.
Arizona's laws are typical, stating that records may be disclosed (1) if
necessary for the reasonable operation of the library, (2) on written
consent of the user, and (3) on receipt of a court order. Otherwise, the
library records are confidential.[42]

Library officials may use patron records while working within the
scope of their duties, such as when the records are "used to seek reim-

bursement for or the return of lost, stolen, misplaced or otherwise over-due library materials."[43] In order to provide additional protection, Arkansas requires that: "Public libraries shall use an automated or Gaylord-type circulation system that does not identify a patron with circulated materials after materials are returned."[44]

Some states allow the parents of minor children to have access to their children's records, although other states do not permit this. For example, the Alaska law says: "Records of a public elementary or secondary school library identifying a minor child shall be made available on request to a parent or guardian of that child."[45] Some states make all library records available to the parents, regardless of what type of library it comes from. For example, Ohio law provides that: "If a library record or patron information pertaining to a minor child is requested from a library by the minor child's parent, guardian, or custodian, the library shall make that record or information available to the parent, guardian, or custodian. . . ."[46]

Some states do not specifically mention inspection for parents of minors, but do have in their statutes legal provisions that suggest the parents would be able to get access to the records. In Georgia, the parents or guardian of a minor child may waive the child's rights of privacy. Naturally, this means that the parents would be able to inspect the records. Minnesota also has a provision allowing libraries to release materials for pickup by family members or others who live with the patron.[47] Obviously, this provision implies that the person picking up the material will know what is being checked out of the library.

A number of states don't have a separate library privacy statute; instead, circulation records are exempted from disclosure under the states' open records acts. Although most states make this nondisclosure mandatory, several states such as Virginia and Kentucky do not prohibit library officials from releasing the records, thus giving library officials the discretion to determine whether or not to disclose records. It is also unclear whether libraries in Virginia would be required to turn over their records upon subpoena; the state open records act is silent on this issue.

One of the most detailed library privacy statutes comes from the District of Columbia.[48] The D.C. statute ensures confidentiality of circulation records except for information related to the operation of the library, or except for releases of information in response to a court order. However, the D.C. statute goes on to provide provisions for challenging court orders. A further provision requires that D.C. public libraries send a copy of the subpoena by certified mail to the affected patrons, along with the following notice:

Records or information concerning your borrowing records in
the public library in the District of Columbia are being sought pursuant to the enclosed subpoena.

In accordance with the District of Columbia Confidentiality of
Library Records Act of 1984, these records will not be released until
10 days from the date this notice was mailed.

If you desire that these records or information not be released,
you must file a motion in the Superior Court of the District of Columbia requesting that the records be kept confidential, and state your
reasons for the request. A sample motion is enclosed. You may wish
to contact a lawyer. If you do not have a lawyer, you may call the
District of Columbia Bar Lawyer Referral Service.[49]

According to the D.C. statute, the required notice may be waived
by court order. In order to waive the notice, the presiding judge must
find that:

(A) The investigation being conducted is within the lawful jurisdiction of the government authority seeking the records;
(B) There is reason to believe that the records being sought are relevant to a legitimate law enforcement inquiry; or
(C) There is reason to believe that the notice will result in:
(i) Endangering the life or physical safety of any person;
(ii) Flight from prosecution;
(iii) Destruction of or tampering with evidence;
(iv) Intimidation of potential witnesses; or
(v) Otherwise seriously jeopardizing an investigation or official proceeding.[50]

It is interesting that the District of Columbia has such detailed requirements for the execution of search warrants. The issue of reading
records came to the forefront in D.C. several years ago during the Bill
Clinton/Monica Lewinsky scandal. As part of the investigation, special
prosecutor Kenneth Starr requested records of the books Ms. Lewinsky
had purchased from the D.C. bookstore KramerBooks. KramerBooks
appealed the order, and the request was eventually withdrawn. Had this
request been for library circulation records, there would have been
greater guidance and privacy protection. However, the D.C. statute has
been affected by the antiterrorism legislation passed by Congress in the
wake of the terrorist attacks on September 11, 2001. This legislation
will be discussed in detail later in this chapter.

D. Privileged Communication for Libraries in Georgia and New York

Georgia and New York have taken a unique approach to the issue of library privacy. In both states, confidentiality of library records is included within the evidence code and involves the concept of privileged communications. However, the statutes read like those of many other states, and there is some question as to whether the placement within the evidence code does in fact make library records privileged.[51]

Privileges are exceptions to the general rule that a witness must answer any questions that are asked. Unless the witness has a valid privilege, he or she must testify and cannot remain silent. "Privileges only exist to serve important interests and relationships, they are construed narrowly, and new ones are rarely created, at least by the courts."[52]

The person whose information is being kept confidential can waive some privileges. The question is: Who holds the privilege and, therefore, who can consent to waive it? Only the holder of the privilege can allow a witness to testify to privileged information. Courts from most Federal and state jurisdictions recognize the following privileges:

♦ *The privilege against self-incrimination*: This privilege is guaranteed by the Fifth Amendment to the U.S. Constitution.

♦ *The attorney-client privilege*: The attorney may not disclose any information without the consent of the client.

♦ *Spousal and marital privileges*: The spousal privilege and the marital privilege are two different things. A married person is not required to testify against his or her spouse. The witness can decide whether or not to testify; the spouse can't prevent the witness from testifying. Some states also recognize a privilege for confidential marital communications.[53]

♦ *The physician-patient privilege*: The patient holds this privilege, so the physician is not allowed to testify without the patient's permission. However, most states require physicians to report suspected child abuse and molestation.

♦ *The psychotherapist-patient privilege*: This privilege applies to any type of counselor, including psychiatrist, psychologist, social worker, etc. As with the physician, this privilege is held by the patient. An exception to this rule is when the patient threatens harm to another person. The psychotherapist must disclose such a threat to the authorities.

♦   *The clergyman-penitent privilege*: Both parties hold this privilege jointly, which means that both have to agree before the communication can be divulged.

♦   *The journalist's privilege*: This privilege is a recent addition to the law of evidence, and is the subject of a great deal of litigation.

Journalists claim that they do not have to reveal their sources. Not all courts recognize this privilege.[54] Unlike many other states, the California constitution recognizes journalistic privilege:

> A publisher, editor, reporter, or other person connected with or employed upon a newspaper, magazine, or other periodical publication, or by a press association or wire service, or any person who has been so connected or employed, shall not be adjudged in contempt by a judicial, legislative, or administrative body, or any other body having the power to issue subpoenas, for refusing to disclose the source of any information procured while so connected or employed for publication in a newspaper, magazine or other periodical publication, or for refusing to disclose any unpublished information obtained or prepared in gathering, receiving or processing of information for communication to the public.[55]

Nonetheless, journalistic privilege is not universally accepted. There has been a great deal of litigation over journalistic privilege in relation to the 2003 revelation by Robert Novak that Valerie Plame, wife of ambassador Joseph Wilson, was a CIA agent. In the recent past, it was revealed that W. Mark Felt (former assistant director of the FBI) was the "Deep Throat" source for Watergate. Many journalists have used "Deep Throat" as an example of the importance of protecting sources.

In many ways, librarians and archivists enjoy more legal protections than journalists, thanks to the Fourteenth Amendment, FERPA, and state privacy laws. Trade secret law also helps to protect confidential information that is learned during a reference transaction.

The inclusion of library privacy in the Georgia and New York evidence codes implies that information in library records is privileged communication. Although the statutes are written in the context of evidence law, the wording does indicate that the statute might have broader application. If there is indeed a library privilege, the holder of the privilege (the person who has the power to waive privilege) is the patron, or the patron's parent or guardian. The only exception to the privilege would be upon an order of the court.[56]

The important issue raised by the library privacy laws in Georgia and New York is whether a witness may legally refuse to testify on the grounds that he or she has a privilege. Since the statutes are written in the context of evidentiary privilege, it would imply that a witness might permissibly refuse to testify. However, the statutes go on to state that disclosures may be made upon court order or subpoena. The statutes contain no annotations to help resolve this problem, nor does a current search of case law and Attorney General opinions from Georgia and New York. My analysis is that the legislatures may have intended to draft general statutes, similar to those of other states, regardless of their inclusion in the evidence code.

E. Kentucky, Hawaii, and the Attorney General Opinions

Kentucky and Hawaii are the only states that do not have statutory provisions relating to library records. Instead, both states have Attorney General opinions on the topic. In both states, the Attorney General opinions are considered to be binding law in the absence of legislative action or court interpretations. Public entities in both states are required to follow these Attorney General rulings. As a result, these opinions constitute the laws of Kentucky and Hawaii in relation to library records.

On April 21, 1981, the Kentucky Attorney General responded to a question submitted by the state librarian (James A. Nelson, director of the Kentucky Department for Libraries and Archives) regarding library records. The Attorney General determined that library records are not subject to disclosure under the state's open records laws because they fall under the exception for "public records containing information of a personal nature where the public disclosure thereof would constitute a clearly unwarranted invasion of personal privacy. . . ."[57] The Attorney General opinion goes on to say:

> We think that the individual's privacy rights as to what he borrows from a public library (books, motion picture film, periodicals and any other matter) is overwhelming. In fact we can see no public interest at all to put in the scales opposite the privacy rights of the individual. We would point out, however, that Kentucky has no privacy statute and that the exceptions to mandatory disclosure of public records are permissive and no law is violated if they are not observed by the custodian. In summary, it is our opinion that the custodian of

the registration and circulation records of a public library is *not* required to make such records available for public inspection under the Open Records Law.[58] [Emphasis added.]

This decision was followed by a second Attorney General opinion the following year.[59] Since the initial opinion used the term "public libraries," Nelson sought a clarification about what types of libraries were included in the opinion. The reply stated:

Our opinion applies to any library which is subject to the Open Records Law as defined by KRS 61.870. This includes all tax supported libraries and all private libraries which receive as much as 25 percent of their funds from state or local authority. It does not include, of course, a private library receiving less than 25 percent of its funds from state or local authority. Our opinion, in effect, places tax supported libraries in the same position as private libraries which would not be governed by the Open Records Law. In other words, all libraries may refuse to disclose for public inspection their circulation records. As far as the Open Records Law is concerned, they may also make the records open if they so choose; *however, we believe that the privacy rights which are inherent in a democratic society should constrain all libraries to keep their circulation lists confidential.*[60] [Emphasis added.]

Since this opinion interpreted the law within the context of Kentucky's Open Records Act, there was no discussion of penalties or of exceptions to disclosure. Kentucky libraries are in fact free to open their records if they wish, but are also free to keep their records closed. However, the Attorney General made it very clear in both opinions that the privacy interests of the individual were extremely strong.

Besides Kentucky, Hawaii is the only other state to have library privacy in an Attorney General opinion rather than in a statute. Like Kentucky, the question in Hawaii involves an exception to the state's open records laws. However, that is where the similarities end. The Kentucky Attorney General (AG) was primarily concerned with answering the direct question in front of him. In Hawaii, the eight-page Attorney General opinion discusses the privacy laws of various states, looks at court and Attorney General decisions nationally (including the Kentucky opinion), and generally does an excellent job of analyzing the trends. The Hawaii AG also made note of policies by the American Library Association and reviewed a number of pertinent law review articles on the subject.

The Hawaii AG decision found that the public disclosure of library circulation records would "constitute a clearly unwarranted invasion of personal privacy."[61] However, the opinion went further, protecting other interactions that indicate which materials a patron has used. (Of course, since the opinion was in the context of open records laws and most reference transactions are oral, reference transactions cannot be obtained by a records request anyhow.) The conclusion of the AG was that:

> In our opinion, individuals have a significant privacy interest in information that reveals the materials that they have requested, used, or obtained from a public library. . . . [The] Hawaii Supreme Court noted that . . . the Constitution of the State of Hawaii was intended to protect individuals from unwarranted governmental intrusion in activities or matters which reveal an individual's "activities, associations and beliefs," such as an individual's choice of reading materials.[62]

Interestingly enough, the Hawaii AG opinion quotes authorities from other jurisdictions that relate the right to library privacy to our First Amendment rights under the U.S. Constitution. For example, the Hawaii decision quotes with favor a 1981 case from the Oregon Attorney General, which stated:

> In our society, the private thoughts of individuals comprise the most sacred bastions of privacy. The development of these thoughts is commonly nourished by reading. These private thoughts frequently develop as reflections of, or reactions to the literature an individual selects. The knowledge that the disclosure of library circulation records showing the use of specific library materials by named persons may occur, may intimidate individuals in the selection of library materials. Such disclosure could permit inferences to be drawn as to the private thoughts of individuals. *We therefore conclude that the disclosure of such circulation records would clearly constitute an unreasonable invasion of privacy. . . .*[63] [Emphasis added by Hawaii AG opinion.]

Another opinion that the Hawaii Attorney General relied on came from the Texas Attorney General's office. This opinion discusses some of the U.S. Supreme Court cases dealing with information, including:

- ♦ The right to receive information;[64]
- ♦ The anonymity of the author;[65]

◆ Anonymity of members of organizations;[66]

◆ The right to ask persons to join a labor organization without registering to do so;[67]

◆ The right to dispense and to receive birth control information in private;[68]

◆ The right to have controversial mail delivered without written request;[69]

◆ The right to go to a meeting without being questioned as to whether you attended or what you said;[70]

◆ The right to give a lecture without being compelled to tell the government what you said;[71]

◆ The right to view a pornographic film in the privacy of your own home without governmental intrusion.[72]

After extensive analysis, the Hawaii Attorney General concluded that there was no significant public interest in releasing library circulation records; rather, the release would be a significant invasion of privacy, since:

> [T]he public interest in the disclosure of library records reflecting materials requested, used, or obtained by a Library patron, does not outweigh a Library patron's significant privacy interest in such information. Accordingly, we conclude that the public disclosure of this information would, under most circumstances, result in a clearly unwarranted invasion of personal privacy.[73]

On the other hand, the Hawaii Attorney General found that the public interest was clearly served by a release of information about overdue items and fines, as long as the library does not disclose information that identifies the materials. The opinion stated that:

> Unlike the disclosure of patron circulation records, the disclosure of amounts owed by library patrons for overdue materials would open up agency actions to the light of public scrutiny. Specifically, the disclosure of such information would indicate whether Library personnel diligently collect unpaid fines, show favoritism in the assessment or collection of such penalties, or allow patrons to exceed fine maximums set by the Library. As such, disclosure of patron fine information would significantly further one of the [open records statute's] central policies, that the "decisions, and actions of government agencies . . . shall be conducted as openly as possible."[74]

Although the Hawaii Attorney General opinion analyzed the laws of other states, it did not rule specifically on whether library records were to be released for a subpoena or search warrant. Nonetheless, the opinion of the Hawaii Attorney General is certainly one of the most important places for information on national trends in library privacy.

Interestingly enough, there was a later case in which the Hawaii Attorney General's office decided that it is permissible for a library to send postcards through the mail with overdue information, even though people other than the patron could read the postcards.[75]

The USA PATRIOT Act

The September 11, 2001, terrorist attacks on the World Trade Center and the Pentagon have caused the Federal government to revise many of its laws. On October 25, 2001, Congress passed the Uniting and Strengthening America by Providing Appropriate Tools Required to Intercept and Obstruct Terrorism Act (USA PATRIOT Act).[76] This statute makes many changes in the way that search warrants are issued for business records, broadens the way in which electronic surveillance can be conducted, and authorizes some seizure of records without a warrant. The PATRIOT Act made many changes in existing laws, most notably with amendments to the Foreign Intelligence Surveillance Act (FISA), which was originally passed in 1978. One of these changes is an expanded definition of business records that affects libraries and archives. The reason that the Foreign Intelligence Surveillance Act now applies to libraries and archives is because circulation records and patron transactions are considered to be business records. Commentators often describe this provision as being a part of the PATRIOT Act, which indeed it is; however, the PATRIOT Act is actually a much broader statute. The provisions that are usually discussed in the context of libraries and archives are those parts of the PATRIOT Act that amended the Foreign Intelligence Surveillance Act; thus, it is helpful to analyze these sections in the context of FISA.

Although many portions of the PATRIOT Act are helpful to law enforcement,[77] several parts of the Act have become controversial.[78] Perhaps the most controversial portions of the statute are the sections that relate to libraries, as well as those parts of the statute relating to the issuance of National Security Letters. The parts of the PATRIOT Act relating to libraries include the following sections:

♦ *Section 216* amended the authorities governing the use of pen registers, so that federal courts must now issue a pen register order for real-time interception of noncontent information from computers, not just from telephones.

♦ *Section 214* amended the Foreign Intelligence Surveillance Act (FISA), broadening the reasons the government may apply to the FISA court for a pen register order for real-time interception of noncontent information from computers and telephones.

♦ *Section 218* allowed a FISA wiretap of content information on any computer where a "significant purpose" of the investigation is to gather foreign intelligence. The FISA court must issue the warrant if the government certifies that certain conditions are present.

♦ *Section 206* made this FISA wiretap a roving wiretap, to be attached to any computer a suspect uses, including a library computer.

♦ *Section 215* amended FISA and now includes libraries as entities subject to a FISA warrant for records and any tangible thing.

♦ *Section 505* allowed *national security letters*, which are issued administratively and come with a gag order, to be issued by a broader range of government personnel and to require a lower standard of relevancy.[79]

According to some commentators, section 215 of the PATRIOT Act is also problematic from a Fourth Amendment standpoint. This issue will be discussed in more detail in *Section C* below.

A. The FISA Court

Under the PATRIOT Act, jurisdiction for court orders and search warrants is given to the special court set up by the Foreign Intelligence Surveillance Act.[80] Unlike a regular court, the FISA court can only issue a search warrant in cases involving foreign intelligence. In addition, the FISA court meets in secret, and its records are not open to the public. According to author David Jonas:

> The Foreign Intelligence Surveillance Act . . . was enacted in 1978 when the issue of terrorism was gradually emerging on the domestic and international scene. FISA is important because it codifies the legal basis for foreign intelligence surveillance operations separate and distinct from routine law enforcement surveillance. FISA comes into play in foreign intelligence or counterintelligence investi-

gations. The unique aspect of FISA is that, while requiring judicial approval of surveillance, it authorizes such surveillance to be conducted without prior authorization from a traditional probable cause search warrant as in the case of criminal investigations.[81] [Citations omitted.]

The original standard of the Foreign Intelligence Surveillance Act was that "the purpose" of the warrants issued by the FISA court must be to obtain foreign intelligence information.[82] When the PATRIOT Act was passed, the new statute amended FISA, changing the standard for judicial review to allow the court to issue warrants when a "significant purpose" of the investigation involves foreign intelligence.[83] According to David Jonas, "Many are concerned that without the requirement of a primary purpose of foreign intelligence surveillance, the government will utilize FISA in criminal investigations, where judicial deference is not as likely."[84]

B. Pen Register and Wiretap Provisions of the PATRIOT Act

The pen register and wiretap provisions of section 216 allow the government to monitor computers. These provisions have direct implications for libraries.[85] Prior to the PATRIOT Act, these laws were mostly concerned with telephone transactions.

Law enforcement officials have used pen registers for many years. A pen register is a device that attaches to a telephone and records the numbers that have been dialed. Unlike a wiretap, a pen register does not record the conversation.

Wiretaps are subject to great scrutiny by the courts, and in the past have been restricted to specific situations where the person under investigation was using a particular phone. For example, the FBI routinely obtains warrants to tap the home and office telephones of reputed mobsters.[86] In the past, the Fourth Amendment requirement of particularity has kept wiretaps from being attached to payphones on the off chance that someone would say something illegal. However, if a payphone is routinely used for the sale of illegal narcotics, police may apply for a court order to attach a pen register device. When attached to a telephone, the pen register does not indicate the *content* of the conversation, only the phone number that was dialed.

Under the PATRIOT Act, pen registers may now be attached to computers as well as telephones.[87] This change is significant to libraries for two reasons. First, since libraries provide the public with computers for Internet access, a pen register now means that libraries may be required to assist law enforcement with monitoring library patrons. Of more significance, however, is the fact that a pen register connected to a computer indicates which Websites have been visited by the patron. This is the type of content that was formerly the subject of wiretaps. In effect, the new pen register provisions allow the government to monitor, without any particularity, what people read—provided that they read it online.[88]

The standard that the FISA court must use for approving a pen register is that the device is needed for: "foreign intelligence information not concerning a United States person or is relevant to an ongoing investigation to protect against international terrorism or clandestine intelligence activities, provided that such investigation of a United States person is not conducted solely upon the basis of activities protected by the First Amendment to the Constitution."[89] Despite the prohibition in the previous sentence, the use of a pen register device records activities that are protected by the First Amendment.

The wiretap provisions of the PATRIOT Act have also been the subject of controversy. The roving wiretap provisions in section 206 of the PATRIOT Act appear to have eliminated the need for particularity. Under the new law, wiretaps can be attached to any telephone or computer that is routinely used by the subject of surveillance—including library computers. The roving wiretap may be left active at all times. Thus, all patrons using the tapped computer are subject to surveillance, not just the actual subject of the investigation. According to former U.S. Representative Bob Barr:

> First, when Congress created foreign intelligence roving wiretap authority in the USA PATRIOT Act, it failed to include the checks against abuse present in the analogous criminal statute. This is troubling because, as roving wiretaps attach to the target of the surveillance and not to the individual communications device, they provide a far more extensive and intrusive record of a person's communications.
>
> Accordingly, criminal roving wiretaps require agents to "ascertain" that the target, rather than a third-party, is in fact using the telephone before they begin recording. They also require that, if the FBI does not actually know the identity (or an alias) of the target, but knows that he or she will be using a particular phone, the wiretap can attach to a single phone and all its users.
>
> In creating roving wiretap authority under FISA, the USA PATRIOT Act did away with this ascertainment requirement. Then, shortly thereafter, the intelligence authorization bill for FY2002 took

away the requirement that the applicant specify either the identity of the target *or* the particular communications device.

The result, today, is a "John Doe" general warrant, issued secretly under FISA, that permits electronic surveillance irrespective of the communications device being tapped *or* the person being eavesdropped on.[90]

From a library standpoint, the roving wiretap is problematic because patrons who are not related to the investigation may still be placed under surveillance if a public-access computer in a library is tapped. In many ways, the roving wiretap provision helps to accomplish what the FBI's Library Awareness Program failed to do in the 1980s—namely, to make known to law enforcement officials the content and materials being accessed in the library.

C. The Standard for Search Warrants in Section 215

Section 215 of the PATRIOT Act states that the FBI "may make an application for an order requiring the production of any tangible things (including books, records, papers, documents, and other items) for an investigation to protect against international terrorism or clandestine intelligence activities, provided that such investigation of a United States person is not conducted solely upon the basis of activities protected by the first amendment to the Constitution."[91]

The main issue that most commentators have identified when discussing section 215 is that it reduces the standard of proof necessary for the issuance of a search warrant—section 215 does not require the judge or magistrate who issues the search warrant to find probable cause.[92] The law reads: "Upon an application made pursuant to this section, the judge *shall* enter an ex parte order as requested, or as modified, approving the release of records if the judge finds that the application meets the requirements of this section."[93] [Emphasis added.]

Since the Fourth Amendment to the U.S. Constitution states that no warrants shall be issued without "probable cause,"[94] there is an apparent conflict between the terms of this statute and constitutional principles that the Supreme Court has continually upheld. This conflict has led one court to issue dicta finding section 215 to be unconstitutional.[95]

D. Section 505 and National Security Letters

One of the most controversial parts of the PATRIOT Act is section 505, which authorizes the FBI to issue an administrative order known as a *national security letter* (NSL). Prior to the passage of the PATRIOT Act, the FBI could issue an order to telephone companies, Internet providers, and credit card companies, asking that they turn over the records of specified individuals. These letters, "which serve as non-judicial subpoenas issued at the sole discretion of the FBI," were voluntary.[96]

When the PATRIOT Act was passed, section 215 expanded the types of entities that were subject to national security letters. With the passage of the PATRIOT Act in 2001, any entity that collected business records was subject to the provisions of FISA search warrants and national security letters. This provision has become known as the "library provision" because it made libraries and archives into entities that could be required to produce business records.[97] The PATRIOT Act also marked a change in that section 505 makes compliance with these orders mandatory, and also reduces the standards for their issuance.[98]

Before the passage of the PATRIOT Act, FBI agents had to apply to the Assistant Director for a National Security Letter. Section 505 removed that requirement, allowing the Special Agent in Charge of an FBI field office to issue an NSL.[99] This change made NSLs easier to obtain than in the past.

The second change made by the PATRIOT Act is a relaxation of the standard required to issue an NSL. Under the original standard, the requesting agent had to certify to the FBI that the NSL referred to a specific person and that the person was acting on behalf of a foreign power. The new standard applied by section 505 allows NSLs to be issued as long as "records sought are relevant to an authorized investigation to protect against international terrorism or clandestine intelligence activities, provided that such an investigation of a United States person is not conducted solely on the basis of activities protected by the first amendment to the Constitution of the United States."[100]

The NSL process is not subject to court supervision as a search warrant would be. In the case of *Doe v. Ashcroft*, the U.S. District Court for the Southern District of New York found that this provision was unconstitutional.[101] According to the court's opinion:

> While the Fourth Amendment reasonableness standard is permissive
> in the context of administrative subpoenas, the constitutionality of the
> administrative subpoena is predicated on the availability of a neutral

tribunal to determine, after a subpoena is issued, whether the subpoena actually complies with the Fourth Amendment's demands. In contrast to an actual physical search, which must be justified by the warrant and probable cause requirements occurring before the search, an administrative subpoena "is regulated by, and its justification derives from, [judicial] process" available after the subpoena is issued.[102]

It was this lack of subsequent judicial review that the District Court criticized. According to the District Court's opinion, the language of the statute "has the effect of authorizing coercive searches effectively immune from any judicial process, in violation of the Fourth Amendment."[103] Technically, the judge in the *Doe* case was dealing with the Foreign Intelligence Surveillance Act rather than the PATRIOT Act. However, the provisions he dealt with were amendments to FISA that were made by the PATRIOT Act.

E. The Nondisclosure Provisions of the PATRIOT Act

In addition to the section on national security letters, the *Doe* opinion also invalidated the section of the Foreign Intelligence Surveillance Act that prohibits NSL and search warrant recipients from disclosing that the FBI has performed a search. These provisions were added to FISA by section 215 of the PATRIOT Act.

Section 215 states that: "No person shall disclose to any other person (other than those persons necessary to produce the tangible things under this section) that the Federal Bureau of Investigation has sought or obtained tangible things under this section."[104] The judge in the *Doe* case was presented with the question as to whether this restriction was a violation of the Freedom of Speech provisions of the First Amendment.

Whenever the constitutionality of a law is challenged using First Amendment, equal protection, or due process theories, the court must decide what kind of scrutiny to give that law. The courts will generally defer to the legislative branch on laws; however, not all laws are constitutional. In looking at statutes that have been challenged, the Supreme Court has come up with three types of scrutiny that should be applied when reviewing the constitutionality of a statute. The three types of scrutiny are:

♦ *Strict scrutiny*: the law is unconstitutional unless it is the "least restrictive means" of serving a "compelling" government interest. Deference to Congress is at its most minimal here.

♦ *Intermediate scrutiny*: the law is unconstitutional unless it is "substantially related" to an "important" government interest.

♦ *Rational basis test*: the law is constitutional as long as it is "reasonably related" to a "legitimate" government interest.[105] This test has the highest level of deference to the legislative branch.

The Supreme Court has generally given *strict scrutiny* to laws that affect race, as well as to issues related to freedom of speech in a public forum. *Intermediate scrutiny* has been traditionally given to decisions involving gender. (Note: the term "gender discrimination" came into general use in the late 1980s. Before that time, many cases used the terms "sex" or "sex discrimination.") Most laws are decided on the *rational basis test*. Often, the results of the three tests are that most laws will be found constitutional if the rational basis test is applied, while most laws that are looked at with strict scrutiny will be found unconstitutional. That is why lawyers challenging a law try to avoid the rational basis test, urging the court to apply strict scrutiny, or at least intermediate scrutiny.

In the *Doe* case, the government urged the judge to apply intermediate scrutiny, while the plaintiff urged the court to use strict scrutiny. When courts are confronted with a First Amendment issue, they must ask whether the government is issuing a *prior restraint* on speech. A prior restraint means that the speech has been prohibited before it has occurred. When there is a prior restraint, the court will apply strict scrutiny and will only allow the restriction if it is the least restrictive alternative.[106]

The other factor that will cause a court to apply strict scrutiny is when the speech is being regulated *because* of the content. Whenever speech is regulated on the basis of what it contains, courts will apply strict scrutiny.[107]

The judge in the *Doe* case analyzed the two forms of scrutiny in order to determine the appropriate standard of review. According to the *Doe* opinion:

> The difference is crucial. A speech restriction which is either content-based or which imposes a prior restraint on speech is presumed invalid and may be upheld only if it is narrowly tailored to promote a compelling Government interest.[108] If "less restrictive alternatives would be at least as effective in achieving the legitimate

purpose that the statute was enacted to serve," then the speech restriction is not narrowly tailored and may be invalidated.[109] Under intermediate scrutiny, a speech restriction may be upheld as long as "it advances important governmental interests unrelated to the suppression of free speech and does not burden substantially more speech than necessary to further those interests."[110]

In the *Doe* case, the judge ruled that the nondisclosure provisions in the Foreign Intelligence Surveillance Act constituted both a prior restraint on speech and a restraint on speech because of the content.[111] Because the court found that the nondisclosure provisions of FISA failed both the prior restraint test and the content test, the judge applied strict scrutiny to the restrictions.

Once strict scrutiny was applied, the judge needed to analyze whether the governmental purpose was compelling, whether the restrictions were narrowly tailored, and whether the restrictions were the least restrictive alternatives available. As the opinion stated: "The question of how narrow is narrow enough is not amenable to scientific measurement, nor can it be reduced to articulable facile tests. Rather, it depends largely on context and perspective."[112] The court found that prohibiting disclosure of an ongoing investigation was a compelling government interest. However, the judge went on to compare this statute with other laws requiring secrecy, and found that the unlimited time period indicated in the FISA amendments rendered it unconstitutional because, according to the opinion:

> The relevance of this doctrine reaches its limit, however, when the Court considers that the NSL statutes . . . impose a permanent bar on disclosure in every case, making no distinction among competing relative public policy values over time, and containing no provision for lifting that bar when the circumstances that justify it may no longer warrant categorical secrecy. . . . This feature . . . is extraordinary in that the breadth and lasting effects of its reach are uniquely exceptional, potentially compelling secrecy even under some decidedly non-sensitive conditions or where secrecy may no longer be justifiable under articulable national security needs.
>
> The Government's claim to perpetual secrecy surrounding the FBI's issuance of NSLs . . . neither restrained by the FBI's own internal discretion nor reviewable by any form of judicial process, presupposes a category of information, and thus a class of speech, that, for reasons not satisfactorily explained, must forever be kept from public view, cloaked by an official seal that will always overshadow the public's right to know. . . .[113]

The holding in the *Doe* case was appealed to the 2nd Circuit Court of Appeals, where it was consolidated with the Connecticut *John Doe* case which is discussed below. The court of appeals overturned the district court decision, which means that the controversial provisions of FISA and the PATRIOT Act are still the law of the land, and must be followed. The next section will discuss what you should do if law enforcement officials come to the library.

F. How to Handle a Law Enforcement Visit

The American Library Association has addressed the issues raised by the new statute. On October 26, 2001, Don Wood, program officer with the ALA's Office of Intellectual Freedom, distributed a statement interpreting the PATRIOT Act. This statement was especially concerned with the provisions relating to the nondisclosure of search warrants and NSLs. According to the ALA's interpretation:

> The existence of this provision does not mean that libraries and librarians served with such a search warrant cannot ask to consult with their legal counsel concerning the warrant. A library and its employees can still seek legal advice concerning the warrant and request that the library's legal counsel be present during the actual search and execution of the warrant.[114]

Because of potential conflicts with local laws and since there are some constitutional issues involved, the ALA has made an arrangement with a law firm to assist libraries and librarians in the event that a search warrant or national security letter is served under the PATRIOT Act or the Foreign Intelligence Surveillance Act. According to the ALA statement:

> If you or your library are served with a warrant issued under this law, and wish the advice of legal counsel but do not have an attorney, you can still obtain assistance from Jenner & Block, the Freedom to Read Foundation's legal counsel. Simply call the Office for Intellectual Freedom and inform the staff that you need legal advice without disclosing the reason you need legal assistance. OIF staff will assure that an attorney from Jenner & Block returns your call. *You do not and should not inform OIF staff of the existence of the warrant.*[115] [Emphasis added.]

The PATRIOT Act has been used to obtain library records. On August 9, 2005, after receiving a national security letter, a librarian filed a case under seal (a legal term meaning that the name of the plaintiff will not be released publicly) in the District Court of Connecticut. The lawsuit challenged the nondisclosure provisions of the PATRIOT Act. The reason that the plaintiff's name is not being released is because of the nondisclosure provisions of the PATRIOT Act. According to the *Washington Post*:

> [T]he edited lawsuit reveals that the plaintiff is a member of the libraries association, that [the library] provides "circulation and cataloging of library materials," and that it allows "library patrons . . . to search library collections and check the status of their accounts." The complaint also says the institution "provides Internet access for use by staff and patrons" and that the FBI was seeking "subscriber information, billing information and access logs" related to an unidentified target.[116]

The district court ruling was kept under seal while the case was appealed to the 2nd Circuit Court of Appeals. The Connecticut *John Doe* case was consolidated with the New York *Doe* case. After the hearing, but before the court of appeals had ruled, the FBI announced that they were dropping the case because of the amendments to the PATRIOT Act. On Friday, June 23, the FBI officially closed the case and lifted the gag order in its entirety.

John Doe turned out to consist of four individuals—George Christian, Barbara Bailey, Peter Chase, and Janet Nocek—from the Library Connection cooperative in Connecticut. The FBI was looking for Internet access logs related to a specific computer.[117] (For a complete description of the Connecticut *John Doe* case and an analysis of the consolidated ruling in the New York and Connecticut cases, see my "Legally Speaking" column in the September 2006 issue of *Against the Grain*.[118])

By filing a case under seal, a library can challenge the NSL, while avoiding any disclosure of information. Thus, the Connecticut *John Doe* case did not violate either the privacy of the patron or the nondisclosure provisions of the PATRIOT Act.

G. Renewal of the PATRIOT Act

Although the library community was the first group to protest the PATRIOT Act, many of the provisions have become increasingly unpopular. As a result, there was a fierce battle in Congress during the waning days of 2005. Sixteen provisions of the Act were due to expire on December 31 of that year. The House and Senate passed competing versions of the renewal bill, resulting in conflict between the two chambers and a filibuster in the Senate.[119] In order to resolve this conflict, Congress agreed to temporarily extend the PATRIOT Act, first until February 3, and then until March 10, 2006.[120]

On March 2, 2006, the Senate passed the PATRIOT Act reauthorization by a vote of 89 to 10.[121] On March 7, 2006, the House approved the bill by a vote of 280 to 138, "just two more than needed under special rules that required a two-thirds majority."[122]

The reauthorization bill made permanent all but two sections of the PATRIOT Act. The two sections of the original PATRIOT Act that still have sunset provisions are the roving wiretaps allowed by section 206 and the production of business records in section 215 of the PATRIOT Act. These sections are now effective for only four years, and unless renewed by Congress will expire on December 31, 2009.[123] Some of the changes in the PATRIOT Act include:

♦ Section 215 has been amended to require that only the Director, the Deputy Director, or the Executive Assistant Director for National Security may apply to the FISA court for "an order requiring the production of library circulation records, library patron lists, book sales records, book customer lists, firearms sales records, tax return records, educational records, or medical records containing information that would identify a person . . . ."[124]

♦ Recipients of national security letters will be able to request judicial review, and may also challenge the nondisclosure provisions of the NSL.[125]

♦ The revised act clarifies that recipients of an NSL may consult with other individuals in their organization in order to carry out the requested actions.[126] The names of all individuals consulted must be disclosed to the FBI. However, the recipient may also consult an attorney,[127] and does not need to disclose the attorney's name to the FBI.[128]

♦ "Libraries functioning in their 'traditional capacity'"[129] will generally be exempt from the national security letter provisions of section 505. This exemption is accomplished through a tighter definition of when an NSL may be used. The definition of an NSL in section 118(D) of the renewal defines a National Security Letter as being available only for specific legal provisions:

(1) Section 2709(a) of title 18, United States Code (to access certain communication service provider [tele-communications and Internet] records).

(2) Section 1114(a)(5)(A) of the Right to Financial Privacy Act (12 U.S.C. 3414(a)(5)(A)) (to obtain financial institution customer records).

(3) Section 802 of the National Security Act of 1947 (50 U.S.C. 436) (to obtain financial information, records, and consumer reports).

(4) Section 626 of the Fair Credit Reporting Act (15 U.S.C. 1681u) (to obtain certain financial information and consumer reports).

(5) Section 627 of the Fair Credit Reporting Act (15 U.S.C. 1681v) (to obtain credit agency consumer records for counterterrorism investigations).[130]

Although there are many people who feel that the PATRIOT Act should not have been renewed, there are some additional protections that have been included. Under the new provisions, most libraries will not be presented with national security letters requiring the disclosure of circulation records. However, those libraries that provide Internet services may still be subject to the NSL provisions of the PATRIOT Act. Only time and judicial interpretation will determine whether the changes in the Act have really removed libraries from the jurisdiction of national security letters.

The PATRIOT Act has created some new issues for librarians. However, you should remember that, under the laws that existed before September 11, 2001, libraries already had to turn over circulation records if served with a valid subpoena or search warrant. If you are faced with a problem relating to circulation records, the best thing to do is to consult with legal counsel.

Patron Confidentiality and Duty to Society: An Ethical Quandary

Now that we have discussed the laws relating to library privacy, you should understand how to protect patron information. In brief, patron records may be released when the library or archive is presented with a search warrant or subpoena. However, there is still one more question: when should a librarian or archivist disclose information in the absence of a court order?[131]

What do you do if a patron appears to be suicidal? What if a patron requests a book about how to build a bomb? What if a patron threatens someone? Should the librarian provide the information to the patron and keep the request confidential, or should the librarian reveal the information to the appropriate authorities? Of all the ethical dilemmas in the field of librarianship, the balance between confidentiality and societal interest is the most difficult to decide. This section will take a look at the problem and at the ALA Code of Ethics, and will make suggestions based on the ethical principles used by other professions.

I am a very strong advocate of library privacy rights. There are many reasons why it is in the interest of the individual and of society to protect information about the materials that patrons may read. I am also concerned about the effects of the USA PATRIOT Act. As Richard Rubin has stated:

> [O]ne could argue there are many acts of speech that should be protected regardless of whether *harm* arises. After all, a cardinal reason why free speech is protected is that it can indeed produce substantive results that some would consider harmful while others would consider the same results salutary. Similarly, what if *harm* arises from truthful speech? Shouldn't such speech be protected regardless of *harm*? The point is that if people are to speak freely, speech must generally be protected regardless of its consequences; otherwise a chilling effect on speech would result.[132] [Emphasis in original.]

Along with the importance of preserving free speech, there is also a duty to the greater society. And in some cases there is a responsibility to the patron as well. Thus, there are two competing ethical principles involved in the situation of the potentially harmful patron. One principle is intellectual freedom, but the other is a duty to society. For example, Robert Hauptman poses the question: "Must one simply respond as a librarian who is there to serve, or does one have a higher duty 'to society in general' . . . to make a professional judgment and refuse to help the patron, if detrimental effects are suspected?"[133]

What are the circumstances under which librarians should disclose information about patron requests? This is one of the most difficult issues for library practitioners to resolve. Some people would argue that national security is one such situation. However, in the face of vague concepts such as national security, I would not disclose information without a search warrant, as discussed above.

A. The Ethical Background

As professionals, it is crucial for us to have an ethical code of conduct and to follow this code to the greatest extent possible. There are three basic codes for the library and information profession: the *ALA Code of Ethics*, the *Library Bill of Rights*, and the joint *Freedom to Read Statement* from the American Library Association and the Association of American Publishers.[134] Together, these codes are strongly protective of individual rights. At the same time, other professional standards, such as collection development policies, place librarians and archivists in the role of impartial information provider. Yanqing Li summed up this dilemma as follows:

> There is a paradox in current librarianship regarding the censorship of controversial materials. On the one hand, librarians tend to depoliticize or neutralize their role in the process of information provision, considering themselves just as "custodians of information" rather than "judges of what is and what is not acceptable. . . ." On the other hand, however, librarians strongly politicize and moralize the issue of censorship. We seem to treat the Library Bill of Rights as unquestionable or unchallengeable.[135]

Our ethical decisions can affect people's lives.[136] We have a special duty to our patrons and our profession to follow the ethical guidelines. (For more information on this issue, see *Chapter 8, Information Malpractice, Professionalism, and the Unauthorized Practice of Law and Medicine*.) In fact, the very definition of a profession involves following ethical guidelines. According to the New York Court of Appeals:

> A profession is not [just] a business. It is distinguished by [1] the requirements of extensive formal training and learning, [2] admission to practice by qualifying licensure, [3] [a] code of ethics imposing standards qualitatively and extensively beyond those that prevail or are tolerated in the marketplace, [4] a system for discipline of its members for a violation of the code of ethics, [5] duties to subordinate financial reward to social responsibility, and, notably, an obligation on its members, even in non-professional matters, to conduct themselves as members of a learned, disciplined and honorable occupation.[137]

It is because of these considerations that we have the *ALA Code of Ethics*, the *Library Bill of Rights*, and the ALA's *Freedom to Read Statement*. These ethical guidelines are a large part of what distinguishes information workers as being professionals rather than technicians. (For more information on this issue, see ***Chapter 8***, *Information Malpractice, Professionalism, and the Unauthorized Practice of Law and Medicine.*) Yet the ALA's ethical rules do not cover every situation. As Robert Wengert has said:

> Insisting that one's obligation is merely to follow the rules leads [to] a life of avoiding the blame of having broken any rules. But in our ethical lives we need to attend not only to the rules [and] the principles of our professional or personal lives; we also need to be attentive to what effects following those rules may have on those with whom we live. . . . Our sole goal ought not be to be morally blameless; we would also like to contribute to making better the lives of those . . . who share our communities.[138]

Although ethical standards, library privacy laws, and trade secrets should be adhered to, sometimes it is necessary for professionals to disclose information. For example, most state library privacy statutes contain exceptions for criminal activity occurring in the library. In order to prosecute a patron for accessing illegal child pornography in the library, there would have to be a disclosure of what site the patron used. The librarian should not decide whether the site was legal or illegal; that is the responsibility of investigators, prosecutors, and ultimately the judge and jury. However, if a patron is charged with a crime in regard to illegal child pornography sites which he accessed in the library, the library worker who witnessed the act would certainly be called upon to testify, and should do so.

B. The Suicidal Patron

The issue I will be dealing with in this section involves patrons who pose an immediate and identifiable risk to themselves or to others. Richard Rubin has effectively framed the moral quandary of the suicidal patron. In a popular library-school textbook, Rubin presents a case study dealing with this important issue.[139] Rubin's scenario involves a teenage patron who is known to have "problems."[140] She comes up to the reference desk crying and asks for the book *Final Exit*,[141] which is a manual on how to commit suicide. You know that the book is on a cart waiting to be reshelved. What do you do?[142]

This type of situation is one in which the reference interviewing process becomes crucial. If you do the right type of reference interview, it should become apparent why the person is requesting information.

She could be a student with a problem, or the request could be academically related. There is also a limit on what the librarian can do. We don't want to go too far and practice medicine or psychology without a license. Such behavior is not the job of the information professional, and it might be illegal under state laws, as well as possibly exposing the librarian to the risk of information malpractice.

In the reference interview, you should ask the student what kind of information she is looking for, to see whether there is anything else she may need. If the patron is working on an academic project, she will probably want to find other articles, books, statistics, etc. She might also want to find materials on prevention of suicide. In the course of the reference interview, it would probably become clear eventually whether she is looking solely for a book to help her commit suicide, or whether she has other purposes.

Suppose, however, that the patron states that she is going to commit suicide. I don't have any hard-and-fast answers, but I do have some suggestions. First of all, the answers to these questions depend on what type of library we are talking about. By law, K-12 school libraries have a different standard which they are required to follow. "Unlike public libraries, [K-12] school libraries do assume some *in loco parentis* responsibilities, or duties to act on behalf of children 'in the place of a parent.'"[143] [Emphasis added.] According to *Words and Phrases*, "a person assuming the parental character or discharging parental duties" is *in loco parentis*.[144] In other words, by law a K-12 school is responsible for the students while they are under school care. The schools have a legal duty to protect their students in a different way from public or academic libraries. (Since *in loco parentis* only applies to minors, this issue is generally reserved for K-12 schools; colleges and universities usually are not considered *in loco parentis*.)

In a K-12 school setting, there is a special duty to report potentially dangerous behavior to the school guidance counselor or principal. Educators have a legal duty to report students who may have been abused, appear suicidal, or in any way appear to be at risk.[145] This is a duty which school personnel must always perform. Indeed, in the aftermath of the school shootings in Columbine and West Paducah, there has been a great deal of discussion about reporting potentially violent behavior. Therefore, in a school setting, potentially harmful or violent behavior should *always* be reported to the appropriate school authorities. Other types of libraries and archives need to consider whether they also have an obligation to report potentially violent behavior under other statutory provisions.

C. The Immediate Threat of Physical Violence

Suppose that you are not in a school setting and don't have the special duty that comes with being *in loco parentis*. What should you do? I would suggest that you would have another type of duty.

My solution is not something that comes from our professional associations, but rather from my background in law. What I would recommend is that librarians adopt the standard that psychologists, psychiatrists, clergy, and other professionals use. What a patient says to a counselor is confidential, but if the person is a danger to himself or others, the counselor has a duty to report this situation to the potential victim and to the appropriate authorities. For example, the Louisiana State Board of Examiners of Psychologists states that:

> A. When a patient has communicated an immediate threat of physical violence against a clearly identified victim or victims, coupled with the apparent intent and ability to carry out that threat, a psychologist or psychiatrist treating such patient and exercising reasonable professional judgment, shall not be liable for a breach of confidentiality for warning of such threat or taking precautions to provide protection from the patient's violent behavior.
> B. A psychologist's or psychiatrist's duty to warn or to take reasonable precautions to provide protection from violent behavior arises only under the circumstance specified in Subsection A of this Section. This duty shall be discharged by the psychologist or psychiatrist if he makes a reasonable effort to communicate the immediate threat to the potential victim or victims and to notify law enforcement authorities in the vicinity of the patient's or potential victim's residence.
> C. No liability or cause of action shall arise against any psychologist or psychiatrist based on an invasion of privacy or breach of confidentiality for any confidence disclosed to a third party in an effort to discharge the duty arising under Subsection A of this Section.[146] [Citations omitted.]

Of course, the Louisiana statute may not be the operative law in your jurisdiction. But it does provide some suggestions and some guidelines to consider.

The premier case on this topic was *Tarasoff v. Regents of the University of California*.[147] In the *Tarasoff* case, a patient named Prosenjit Poddar told his psychologist that he was planning to kill Tatiana Tarasoff, a young woman with whom the patient had become obsessed. The psychologist asked the campus police to go to Poddar's dorm room, but because of confidentiality limitations did not tell them why. The police left the room because Poddar appeared to be rational.

A few hours after the police visit, Prosenjit Poddar killed Tatiana Tarasoff. After the murder, her family sued the psychiatrist, saying that he had a duty to warn Tarasoff that she was in danger. In deciding the *Tarasoff* case, the California Supreme Court stated:

> [O]nce a therapist does in fact determine, or under applicable professional standards reasonably should have determined, that a patient poses a serious danger of violence to others, he bears a duty to exercise reasonable care to protect the foreseeable victim of that danger. While the discharge of this duty of due care will necessarily vary with the facts of each case . . . "the ultimate question of resolving the tension between the conflicting interests of patient and potential victim is one of social policy, not professional expertise. . . . In sum, the therapist owes a legal duty not only to his patient, but also to his patient's would-be victim. . . ."[148] [Citations omitted.]

The standard that is generally used in such cases involves the immediate and identifiable danger of harm to oneself or others. This principle has become law in many jurisdictions. For example, in 1999 the Supreme Court of Canada[149] adopted similar reasoning,[150] stating:

> [E]ven the fundamentally important right to confidentiality is not absolute in doctor-patient relationships. . . . When the interest and the protection of the . . . accused and the safety of members of the public is engaged, the privilege will have to be balanced against these other compelling public needs. In rare circumstances, these public interests may be so compelling that the privilege must be displaced. . . . Danger to public safety can, in appropriate circumstances, provide the requisite justification. . . .[151]

In a library setting, the question involves the potential for the person committing harm against himself or others. Many professions have had to struggle with this question, and most of them have come to the same conclusion: if the person appears likely to commit immediate and identifiable harm to himself or others, the professional has a duty to report the situation to the appropriate authorities. I would argue that this is how librarians should handle the situation as well, whether we are talking about a suicidal patron or a patron planning to build a bomb, or the possibility of some other immediate and identifiable harm.

Attorney William Clark explains that, in deciding whether disclosure of confidential information is justified, courts and professional bodies in the United States, Canada, the United Kingdom, Australia, and other common-law countries generally consider three factors:[152] (1)

Is there a clear risk to an identifiable person or group of persons; (2) is there a risk of serious bodily harm or death; and (3) is the danger imminent?[153]

The duty to report potentially dangerous situations to the appropriate authorities does not mean that librarians should attempt to make determinations about the sanity of an individual or that librarians should try to undertake counseling sessions. Care should always be taken to avoid practicing psychology or medicine without a license. When I refer to the duty to inform, I am not discussing vague situations where a patron asks for books about bombs, Marxism (as in the McCarthy cases of the 1950s), or any other subject. I am discussing the limited situation that Clark explains—where there is a *clear risk to an identifiable person or group of persons*, where there is a *risk of serious bodily harm or death*, and where the *danger is imminent*. This is a very specific situation, one that most librarians will never have to face. Nonetheless, this issue is very important and needs to be considered.

With all this in mind, let us return to Richard Rubin's case study of the patron asking for *Final Exit*. If we change the scenario a bit, we may come up with an answer which differs from Rubin's principle.

For example, suppose that the student comes up to the reference desk calmly and rationally, without any evidence of crying or depression, and asks for *Final Exit*. At this point, we should use our reference interview to ascertain what type of research she is working on. This may just be a school project, and if so we should give her the book. But if she says that she is going to commit suicide, we *should not* give her the book; instead, we should refer her to the suicide prevention hotline. In fact, if we are at all in doubt about the patron's motives, we might want to make an anonymous call ourselves to the suicide prevention hotline.

As I stated above, this answer does not come from the guidelines of the ALA, AASL, or any other professional association for librarians. The writers of these guidelines might disagree with my opinion that library confidentiality should not extend to those patrons who pose a clear, identifiable, and imminent danger to themselves or others. Other commentators might disagree, but I believe that as professionals, we have a duty to the patron as well as a duty to society. Sometimes our ethical principles require us to balance these duties accordingly.

Conclusion

Patron privacy is extremely important for libraries and archives. Patrons must be able to trust librarians with confidential information in the course of their research. Most state and territorial governments provide library patrons with privacy protections. While there are some similarities between the laws, there are also many differences. All of the states, as well as the District of Columbia, Guam, and the Virgin Islands, have developed some form of privacy protection for library records, either as statutes, rules of evidence, or Attorney General opinions. Only Puerto Rico, American Samoa, and the Commonwealth of the Northern Marianas do not have any library privacy provisions.

In order to guard patron privacy, information professionals should understand the basics of search warrants and the laws of their own jurisdiction. The requirements of probable cause and particularity help to keep patron records private, while still providing a way for investigators to do their jobs. The purpose of the Fourth Amendment is to establish search and seizure rules by which everyone must live. These rules help our society achieve the delicate balance between the need for security and the right of privacy.

Finally, there may indeed be some times when the professional librarian or archivist *should* reveal confidential patron information. Great caution should be taken when disclosing. Disclosure should only be made if the reference interview reveals that: (1) there is a clear risk to an identifiable person or group of persons; (2) there is a risk of serious bodily harm or death; and (3) the danger is imminent. If these three factors exist, I believe that the librarian must disclose information in order to protect the potential victims.

The laws that are on the books are a good start; however, more needs to be done. The states should standardize and strengthen library privacy statutes, and include language applying the law to all types of libraries and to all types of library services. (The Arkansas law is a very good model for library privacy statutes.) Puerto Rico, American Samoa, and the Commonwealth of the Northern Marianas need to adopt laws to protect their library patrons.

While there could be improvement in library privacy laws, almost all jurisdictions have provided protection from unwarranted intrusion. Information professionals need to be aware of those state and federal laws which relate to privacy. Librarians who understand privacy laws need no longer fear the rainy night and the inquisitive visitor.

Table 9.1. Sources of State and Territorial Library Privacy Laws [A]

Jurisdiction	Exempt from Open Records Laws	General Privacy Law	Attorney General Opinion	Applies to Public Libraries	Libraries Open to Public or Receiving Public Finances
Alabama	X	X			X
Alaska					X
Arizona					X
Arkansas		X			X
California[B]	X	X			
Colorado					X
Connecticut	X			X	
Delaware	X			X	
District of Columbia		X		X	
Florida		X		X	
Georgia	X				X
Guam		X			X
Hawaii	X		X	X	X
Idaho[C]	X				X
Illinois[D]	X	X			X
Indiana	X				X
Iowa[E]	X				X
Kansas	X				X
Kentucky	X		X		X
Louisiana		X			X
Maine[F]					X
Maryland[G]		X			X
Massachusetts		X		X	
Michigan		X			X
Minnesota[H]		X			X
Mississippi		X			X
Missouri		X			X
Montana		X			X
Nebraska	X				X
Nevada		X			X
New Hampshire	X	X			X

Jurisdiction	Exempt from Open Records Laws	General Privacy Law	Attorney General Opinion	Applies to Public Libraries	Libraries Open to Public or Receiving Public Finances
New Jersey		X			X
New Mexico		X			X
New York[I]		X			X
North Carolina		X			X
North Dakota	X				X
Ohio[J]		X			X
Oklahoma		X			X
Oregon	X				X
Pennsylvania		X			X
Rhode Island	X	X			X
South Carolina		X			X
South Dakota	X	X		X	
Tennessee		X			X
Texas	X				X
Utah	X				X
Vermont	X				X
Virgin Islands	X	X			X
Virginia	X				X
Washington	X				X
West Virginia		X		X	
Wisconsin		X			X
Wyoming	X				X

Table 9.2. Types of Library Materials Protected by State and Territorial Privacy Laws [A]

Jurisdiction	Excepts Records of Minors	Circulation Records Only	Other Transactions Protected	Penalty for Disclosure
Alabama	X		X	
Alaska	X	X		
Arizona			X	X
Arkansas			X	X
California[B]		X		
Colorado	X		X	X
Connecticut		X		
Delaware		X		
District of Columbia		X		X
Florida	X	X		X
Georgia	X		X	
Guam			X	X
Hawaii			X	
Idaho[C]		X		
Illinois[D]		X	X	
Indiana		X		
Iowa[E]			X	
Kansas		X		
Kentucky		X		
Louisiana	X		X	
Maine[F]			X	
Maryland[G]			X	
Massachusetts			X	
Michigan			X	X
Minnesota[H]			X	
Mississippi			X	
Missouri			X	
Montana			X	X
Nebraska			X	
Nevada		X		
New Hampshire			X	

Jurisdiction	Excepts Records of Minors	Circulation Records Only	Other Transactions Protected	Penalty for Disclosure
New Jersey			X	
New Mexico	X		X	X
New York[I]			X	
North Carolina			X	
North Dakota			X	
Ohio[J]	X		X	
Oklahoma			X	
Oregon			X	
Pennsylvania		X		
Rhode Island		X		X
South Carolina		X		
South Dakota		X		
Tennessee			X	
Texas			X	
Utah				
Vermont		X		
Virgin Islands			X	
Virginia		X		
Washington			X	
West Virginia	X		X	
Wisconsin	X		X	
Wyoming	X		X	

Notes for Table 9.1 and Table 9.2

[A] American Samoa, Puerto Rico, and the Commonwealth of the Northern Marianas do not have library privacy laws.

[B] California has three separate provisions for library privacy. One law is in the context of the state open records exceptions. A more complete library privacy statute is also included in the Open Records Act, and another statute is included in the Health & Safety Code.

[C] Idaho's statute is an Open Records Act exception. The state Open Records provisions are contained within the evidence code. In addition, there is an Idaho Supreme Court rule prohibiting disclosure of information for patrons of the State Law Library. (This provision is important because prisoners often use materials from the State Law Library to challenge their convictions.)

[D] Illinois has both a library privacy statute and an Open Records Act exception.

[E] Iowa has a separate provision for records from educational institutions. There is no exception for minors. It could be argued that this provision also includes library records.

[F] Maine's statute includes only "Records maintained by any public municipal library, the Maine State Library, the Law and Legislative Reference Library and libraries of the University of Maine System and the Maine Maritime Academy." There is no mention of records from other publicly supported entities or from public schools.

[G] Maryland has one statute that applies specifically to public libraries, and another statute that applies specifically to libraries in schools, colleges, and private associations.

[H] Minnesota contains an exception allowing "a family member or other person who resides with a library patron [to pick] up the material on behalf of the patron. A patron may request that reserved materials be released only to the patron [himself or herself]."

[I] New York's library privacy statute is included in the state's evidence code, but does not mention privilege. The LexisNexis database contains a complete annotation by the Law Revision Commission that discusses this statute.

[J] Ohio has a complete library privacy statute, but it is included in the Public Records section of the Ohio Revised Code.

10

Internet Use Policies
and the Filtering Debate

A well-known university professor is using a library computer to access the Internet for his research. The web site he is trying to access is blocked by an Internet filter. The professor requests removal of this filter. He also objects to the library's use of such blocking devices. How do you respond to his request and his objection?

In a previous chapter, I discussed legal restrictions on library services. These restrictions assist librarians to avoid the unauthorized practice of law or medicine, and to escape legal liability for information malpractice. However, there are other types of legal restrictions on the information that librarians can provide.[1] For example, the library world has been the center of heated discussion recently over the issue of installing filtering software on Internet terminals.

The Children's Internet Protection Act[2] (CIPA) requires that libraries receiving funding under the Library Services and Technology Act (LSTA) or receiving the E-rate (a discount on Internet service for schools, libraries, and museums) must use filtering software on their public Internet terminals. Although the American Library Association challenged this restriction in court, the challenge was unsuccessful.[3] As a result of this case, libraries of all types need to reevaluate their Internet use policies.

The CIPA Case, its background, and the District Court Opinion will be discussed in the first section of this chapter. The second section will analyze the U.S. Supreme Court plurality decision in *United States et al. v. American Library Association*.[4] The third section will discuss Internet use policies and what the Supreme Court's decision means to libraries. This section will also provide some resources and Websites concerning library Internet use policies.

247

The CIPA District Court Decision

When the Children's Internet Protection Act (CIPA) was passed in December 2000, the statute included a provision requiring all libraries that receive federal funding to install filtering software on Internet terminals used by minors.[5] This provision was included because some patrons were using public access Internet terminals to view pornographic Websites. Any library that did not comply with the CIPA provisions was precluded from receiving an E-rate telecommunications discount[6] or any funding under the Library Services and Technology Act (LSTA).[7]

The American Library Association promptly challenged CIPA in Federal court.[8] The District Court ruled in favor of the ALA, stating: "any public library that complies with CIPA's conditions will necessarily violate the First Amendment."[9] The District Court's reasoning was based upon the argument that filtering software restricts access to constitutionally protected speech in two ways. The first restriction involved the fact that filtering software can block access to sites that have nothing to do with pornography, thus making the restrictions overly broad.[10]

The second part of the ruling by the District Court was based upon the reasoning that public access Internet terminals in a library constitute a public forum.[11] When the government imposes a restriction on a public forum based upon the content of the speech, the law is subject to strict scrutiny, and is permitted only if the law is narrowly tailored to further a compelling state interest.[12] Furthermore, the law must be the least restrictive alternative available. (For more information on strict scrutiny, see the section on the USA PATRIOT Act in *Chapter 9*, *Search Warrants, Investigations, Library Records, and Privacy*.)

In the CIPA case, the ALA argued that libraries were a public forum. Since speech issues in a public forum are subject to strict scrutiny, this was an important part of the ALA's case. The District Court agreed, stating that:

> In providing even filtered Internet access, public libraries create a public forum open to any speaker around the world to communicate with library patrons via the Internet on a virtually unlimited number of topics. Where the state provides access to a "vast democratic forum," open to any member of the public to speak on subjects "as diverse as human thought," the state's decision selectively to exclude from the forum speech whose content the state disfavors is subject to *strict scrutiny*, as such exclusions risk distorting the marketplace of ideas that the state has facilitated. Application of strict scrutiny finds further support in the extent to which public libraries' provision of

Internet access uniquely promotes First Amendment values in a manner analogous to traditional public fora [sic] such as streets, sidewalks, and parks, in which content-based restrictions are always subject to strict scrutiny.[13] [Emphasis added; citations omitted.]

The District Court ruled that, although the government has a compelling interest in preventing the dissemination of obscenity, child pornography, or material harmful to minors, the use of software filters is not narrowly tailored to further that interest. According to the District Court, CIPA was unconstitutional because the law was overly broad and did not survive strict scrutiny.

The CIPA Plurality Ruling by the U.S. Supreme Court

After the decision by the District Court, the government appealed to the U.S. Supreme Court. In a plurality opinion, the Supreme Court ruled in favor of the government, finding that the filtering provisions of the Children's Internet Protection Act are constitutional.[14]

A plurality opinion is the most difficult type of decision to read and understand. In a traditional opinion, if a majority of the justices vote the same way, the opinion becomes law. Thus if at least five out of nine justices agree, you have a straightforward majority opinion that announces a rule of law. However, sometimes there is a situation in which more than five justices agree on which party should win the case, but fewer than five justices agree on why that party should prevail. In that situation, you have a plurality opinion.[15]

In a plurality opinion, there may be separate parts of the decision. Some parts may be joined by five or more justices, while other parts may be joined by fewer justices. "Very often . . . the only way to determine the holding in a plurality decision is to head-count."[16]

There are important questions concerning the authority of a plurality decision, and whether it establishes a precedent for future cases. The Supreme Court attempted to answer this question in *Marks v. United States*.[17] In the *Marks* case, the Supreme Court wrote that "when a fragmented Court decides a case and no single rationale explaining the result enjoys the assent of five Justices, 'the holding of the Court may be viewed as that position taken by those Members who concurred in the judgments on the *narrowest grounds* [i.e., the court will read the

plurality opinion to represent the most narrow possible rule].'"[18] There
are still questions about plurality decisions, however, and the Supreme
Court itself has not always followed the *Marks* rule.[19]

In the CIPA Case, there was no single majority opinion. Instead,
there were five separate opinions. Six justices asserted that the CIPA
was constitutional. Chief Justice Rehnquist, joined by Justices
O'Connor, Scalia, and Thomas, decided the opinion of the Court. Justices Kennedy and Breyer each filed separate opinions concurring in
the judgment, but not agreeing upon the reasons. Justice Stevens wrote
a dissenting opinion, and Justices Souter and Ginsburg each wrote a
separate dissenting opinion. In order to determine what, exactly, the
Court decided, we have to analyze each opinion and then do a head
count.

A. Chief Justice Rehnquist's Opinion

Chief Justice Rehnquist's opinion (joined by Justices O'Connor,
Scalia, and Thomas) relied in large part on the nature of collection development, since the selection of materials is necessarily a content-based decision.[20] Chief Justice Rehnquist's analysis included analogies
to the decisions of public television stations and the National Endowment for the Arts (NEA) in selecting items based on "artistic merit." [21]
According to the Chief Justice's opinion:

> The principles . . . apply to a public library's exercise of judgment in selecting the material it provides to its patrons. Just as forum
> analysis and heightened judicial scrutiny are incompatible with the
> role of public television stations and the role of the NEA, they are
> also incompatible with the discretion that public libraries must have
> to fulfill their traditional missions. Public library staffs necessarily
> consider content in making collection decisions and enjoy broad discretion in making them.[22] [In other words, libraries already use discretion in deciding what materials to make available or not to make
> available to their patrons.]

The Chief Justice's opinion stated that public access Internet terminals are not a public forum and are not subject to strict scrutiny.[23] He
also stated that the filtering provisions in CIPA are not overly broad.[24]
According to the opinion:

> A public library does not acquire Internet terminals in order to
> create a public forum for Web publishers to express themselves, any
> more than it collects books in order to provide a public forum for the

authors of books to speak. It provides Internet access, not to "encourage a diversity of views from private speakers," but for the same reasons it offers other library resources: to facilitate research, learning, and recreational pursuits by furnishing materials of requisite and appropriate quality. As Congress recognized, "[t]he Internet is simply another method for making information available in a school or library."[25] [Citations omitted.]

One interesting provision of the plurality decision is that "the justices ultimately ruled that the law was constitutional only if adult library users were able to readily request and receive unfiltered access to the Internet."[26] This point was very important in getting the divergent justices to agree upon the results of the case, and was based on provisions in CIPA that allow libraries to disable the filtering software "to enable access for bona fide research or other lawful purposes."[27] Although plurality decisions are usually limited in their scope, the fact that a majority of the justices agreed to this interpretation makes it the law of the land. According to Chief Justice Rehnquist:

> [A]ny such concerns [about accessing blocked material] are dispelled by the ease with which patrons may have the filtering software disabled. When a patron encounters a blocked site, he need only ask a librarian to unblock it or (at least in the case of adults) disable the filter. . . . [T]he Solicitor General stated at oral argument that a "library may . . . eliminate the filtering with respect to specific sites . . . at the request of a patron . . . [and] can, in response to a request from a patron, unblock the filtering mechanism altogether. . . ."[28] [Citations omitted.]

The argument that libraries can disable the filtering software was ultimately used in all three of the concurring opinions, making it an important part of the decision. This provision will become even more important as libraries begin to draft and revise their Internet use policies.

The second part of the Chief Justice's opinion involved a discussion of statutory analysis and the powers of Congress. According to the opinion:

> The E-rate and LSTA programs were intended to help public libraries fulfill their traditional role of obtaining material of requisite and appropriate quality for educational and informational purposes. Congress may certainly insist that these "public funds be spent for the purposes for which they were authorized." Especially because public libraries have traditionally excluded pornographic material from their

other collections, Congress . . . could reasonably impose a parallel limitation on its Internet assistance programs. As the use of filtering software helps to carry out these programs, it is a permissible condition. . . . [29] [Citations omitted.]

B. Justice Breyer's Concurring Opinion

The opinion by Justice Breyer, like the opinion by Chief Justice Rehnquist, finds that strict scrutiny does not apply; however, Justice Breyer would apply the principles of "heightened scrutiny" to the issue of filtering. According to Justice Breyer's decision:

> I would apply a form of heightened scrutiny, examining the statutory requirements in question with special care. The Act directly restricts the public's receipt of information. And it does so through limitations imposed by outside bodies (here Congress) upon two critically important sources of information—the Internet as accessed via public libraries. For that reason, we should not examine the statute's constitutionality as if it raised no special First Amendment concern—as if, like tax or economic regulation, the First Amendment demanded only a "rational basis" for imposing a restriction. Nor should we accept the Government's suggestion that a presumption in favor of the statute's constitutionality applies [i.e., we should not defer to Congress].[30]

In discussing the case, Justice Breyer questions "whether the harm to speech-related interests is disproportionate in light of both the justifications and the potential alternatives. . . ." Justice Breyer's concurring opinion also explores "the legitimacy of the statute's objective, the extent to which the statute will tend to achieve that objective, whether there are other, less restrictive ways of achieving that objective, and ultimately whether the statute works speech-related harm that, in relation to that objective, is out of proportion [to the situation it proposes to remedy]."[31]

Justice Breyer found that the restrictions were legitimate, and that they were in fact of the same nature as the ordinary collection development which libraries routinely perform. Although Justice Breyer found that the restrictions of the filtering software were overly broad and did indeed restrict protected speech, he noted that:

> At the same time, the Act contains an important exception that limits the speech-related harm that "overblocking" might cause. As the plurality points out, the Act allows libraries to permit any adult patron access to an "overblocked" Web site; the adult patron need

only ask a librarian to unblock the specific Web site or, alternatively, ask the librarian, "Please disable the entire filter. . . ." The Act does impose upon the patron the burden of making this request. But it is difficult to see how that burden (or any delay associated with compliance) could prove more onerous than traditional library practices associated with segregating library materials in, say, closed stacks, or with interlibrary lending practices that require patrons to make requests that are not anonymous and to wait while the librarian obtains the desired materials from elsewhere. Perhaps local library rules or practices could further restrict the ability of patrons to obtain "over-blocked" Internet material.[32] But we are not now considering any such local practices. We here consider only a facial challenge to the Act itself [i.e., the Court is considering whether the statute itself is void on its face].

Given the comparatively small burden that the Act imposes upon the library patron seeking legitimate Internet materials, I cannot say that any speech-related harm that the Act may cause is disproportionate when considered in relation to the Act's legitimate objectives. I therefore agree with the plurality that the statute does not violate the First Amendment, and I concur in the judgment.[33] [Citations omitted.]

C. Justice Kennedy's Concurring Opinion

The concurring opinion by Justice Kennedy also relied upon the ability of the librarians to remove the filter when necessary. According to Justice Kennedy:

If, on the request of an adult user, a librarian will unblock filtered material or disable the Internet software filter without significant delay, there is little to this case. The Government represents this is indeed the fact. . . . If some libraries do not have the capacity to unblock specific Web sites or to disable the filter or if it is shown that an adult user's election to view constitutionally protected Internet material is burdened in some other substantial way, that would be the subject for an as-applied challenge. . . . There are, of course, substantial Government interests at stake here. The interest in protecting young library users from material inappropriate for minors is legitimate, and even compelling, as all Members of the Court appear to agree. Given this interest, and the failure to show that the ability of adult library users to have access to the material is burdened in any significant degree, the statute is not unconstitutional on its face. For these reasons, I concur in the judgment of the Court.[34]

D. Justice Stevens' Dissent

Justice Stevens accepted one of the arguments that the ALA used. This premise was that "[a] federal statute penalizing a library for failing to install filtering software on every one of its Internet-accessible computers would unquestionably violate [the First] Amendment."[35] The argument is that "the provision of Internet access within a public library . . . is for use by the public . . . as a designated public forum"[36] that "promotes First Amendment values. . . ."[37]

Justice Stevens also discussed the discretion of libraries to make decisions about what to include and exclude from their collections. Unlike the plurality decisions, his dissent did not accept the argument that this discretion in collection policy should be a reason to deny public forum status to Internet terminals. According to Justice Stevens' opinion, "Given our Nation's deep commitment 'to safeguarding academic freedom' and to the 'robust exchange of ideas,' a library's exercise of judgment with respect to its collection is entitled to First Amendment protection."[38]

Justice Stevens was not impressed by the plurality argument that some computers could be left unblocked: "A federal statute penalizing a library for failing to install filtering software on every one of its Internet-accessible computers would unquestionably violate [the First] Amendment. I think it equally clear that the First Amendment protects libraries from being denied funds for refusing to comply with an identical rule [identical to the rule that would violate the First Amendment]."[39]

In addition, Justice Stevens did not agree with the contention of the Chief Justice that the First Amendment was not harmed simply because libraries lost funding. According to Justice Stevens, "This Court should not permit federal funds to be used to enforce this kind of broad restriction of First Amendment rights, particularly when such a restriction is unnecessary to accomplish Congress' stated goal. The abridgment of speech is equally obnoxious whether a rule like this one is enforced by a threat of penalties or by a threat to withhold a benefit."[40]

E. Justice Souter's Dissent

Justice Souter (joined by Justice Ginsburg) used a different type of analysis in dissenting. According to Justice Souter's dissent, although patrons may request that the filtering software be disabled, the nature of the filtering software still constitutes governmental censorship. Speaking to the collection development argument used by the plurality, Justice Souter states:

> Public libraries are indeed selective in what they acquire to place in their stacks, as they must be. There is only so much money and so much shelf space, and the necessity to choose some material and reject the rest justifies the effort to be selective with an eye to demand, quality, and the object of maintaining the library as a place of civilized enquiry by widely different sorts of people. Selectivity is thus necessary and complex, and these two characteristics explain why review of a library's selection decisions must be limited: the decisions are made all the time, and only in extreme cases could one expect particular choices to reveal impermissible reasons (reasons even the plurality would consider to be illegitimate), like excluding books because their authors are Democrats or their critiques of organized Christianity are unsympathetic. . . .
>
> At every significant point, however, the Internet blocking here defies comparison to the process of acquisition. Whereas traditional scarcity of money and space require a library to make choices about what to acquire . . . blocking is the subject of a choice made *after* the money for Internet access has been spent or committed. Since it makes no difference to the cost of Internet access whether an adult calls up material harmful for children or the Articles of Confederation, blocking (on facts like these) is not necessitated by scarcity of either money or space. In the instance of the Internet, what the library acquires is electronic access, and the choice to block is a choice to limit access that has already been acquired. Thus, deciding against buying a book means there is no book (unless a loan can be obtained), but blocking the Internet is merely blocking access purchased in its entirety and subject to unblocking if the librarian agrees. The proper analogy therefore is not to passing up a book that might have been bought; it is either to buying a book and then keeping it from adults lacking an acceptable "purpose," or to buying an encyclopedia and then cutting out pages with anything thought to be unsuitable for all adults.[41] [Emphasis added; citations omitted.]

Justice Souter discussed in detail the history of intellectual freedom in libraries, tracing the development of the *Library Bill of Rights* and the intellectual freedom documents of the American Library Association. He looked at the ALA's policies against labeling, at policies against removal of materials from the shelf, etc. Justice Souter stated that:

Amidst these and other ALA statements from the latter half of
the 20th century, however, one subject is missing. There is not a
word about barring requesting adults from any materials in a library's
collection, or about limiting an adult's access based on evaluation of
his purposes in seeking materials. If such a practice had survived into
the latter half of the 20th century, one would surely find a statement
about it from the ALA, which had become the nemesis of anything
sounding like censorship of library holdings, as shown by the history
just sampled. The silence bespeaks an American public library that
gives any adult patron any material at hand, and a history without
support for the plurality's reading of the First Amendment as tolerat-
ing a public library's censorship of its collection against adult enquiry. . . .

[T]here is no preacquisition scarcity rationale to save library
Internet blocking from treatment as censorship, and no support for it
in the historical development of library practice. To these two reasons
to treat blocking differently from a decision declining to buy a book,
a third must be added. Quite simply, we can smell a rat when a library blocks material already in its control, just as we do when a library removes books from its shelves for reasons having nothing to
do with wear and tear, obsolescence, or lack of demand. Content-
based blocking and removal tell us something that mere absence from
the shelves does not.

There is no good reason, then, to treat blocking of adult enquiry
as anything different from the censorship it presumptively is. For this
reason, I would hold in accordance with conventional strict scrutiny
that a library's practice of blocking would violate an adult patron's
First and Fourteenth Amendment right to be free of Internet censorship, when unjustified (as here) by any legitimate interest in screening children from harmful material. On that ground, the Act's blocking requirement in its current breadth calls for unconstitutional action
. . . and is itself unconstitutional.[42]

In other words, Justices Souter and Ginsburg believed that the library filtering provisions of CIPA constituted governmental censorship.
The Justices would have therefore applied strict scrutiny, and believed
that the CIPA statute was unconstitutional under the First and Fourteenth Amendments. However, through the counting of heads, the
plurality opinion prevailed: the Supreme Court upheld the constitutionality of the Children's Internet Protection Act. The CIPA decision
means that libraries must follow the law and install Internet filtering on
computers that are accessed by minors.

The CIPA decision has many implications for libraries and archives, and for the policies that we follow. These implications will be
discussed in the next section of the chapter.

Reviewing Internet Use Policies

What does the plurality opinion by the Supreme Court mean to libraries? In light of the opinion, *all* public libraries, school libraries, and special libraries which serve patrons who are under the age of 18 need to reevaluate their Internet use policies.

Because the three plurality opinions all discussed the right of patrons to request that the filtering software be disabled, this provision in the statute becomes key to the revision of Internet use policies. Both the E-rate Internet discount for libraries and the Library Services and Technology Act guidelines for grants allow the software to be disabled. According to the statute, the E-rate program allows disabling "during use by an adult,"[43] while the LSTA grant guidelines allow disabling upon request "by any person."[44]

The CIPA does not require filtering for adults, which means that public libraries don't have to filter in the adult sections or with adult users. This provision allows adult users to have access to materials without restrictions so that their First Amendment rights are protected. This situation may be the basis of another case in the future, but for the present all material is available to adults. An individual library could decide to filter everything on the Internet for every patron. However, it appears from the dissenting opinions of both Justice Souter and Justice Stevens and the plurality opinion of Justice Kennedy that this type of universal filtering might be subject to greater scrutiny than a mere blocking of computers operated by children.

Although the CIPA Case specifically involved public libraries, it applies equally to school library media centers and special libraries serving children. Of course, school libraries are also subject to additional regulations from the U.S. Department of Education and from state educational bodies. Yet the principles laid down in the plurality opinion should be considered by all types of libraries that serve minors under the age of 18.

Libraries should have—and follow—a written policy covering the questions and procedures concerning filtering. This policy should be posted or otherwise made available to patrons.

One of the most important provisions that libraries should make in their Internet use policies is to state specifically who is eligible to ask for filters to be disabled, and under what circumstances the request may be made. It is of special importance that Internet use policies discuss whether only adults may request disabling, or whether minors may do so as well. The policy should state whether minors must have parental permission to disable the filtering software, and whether that parental permission should be in writing.

Libraries must also develop procedures to be followed when a patron requests that the filtering software be disabled. For example, does the patron have to fill out a form, or is it sufficient to ask orally? The policy should state whether the patron has to indicate a reason for the request, or whether requests should be granted with no questions asked.

Another procedural issue that should be resolved in advance is the question of at what level may a disabling decision occur. For example, the policy should spell out whether a decision to disable may be made by paraprofessionals, or whether only professional librarians should decide about disabling the filtering software. In addition, the policy should state whether the person on duty has the discretion to disable the filter, or whether he or she has to forward the request to an appropriate person. (The policy should clearly state who that appropriate person is.) Finally, the policy should give the time period within which a decision will be made, and indicate routes of appeal up to and including a hearing by the library board.

Remember that library policies are not just pretty pieces of paper. Policies should be adhered to at all times, and the procedures that are included should always be observed. Obviously, all library personnel will need detailed briefing about these policies. There is a case in New York indicating that a library that doesn't follow its own procedures is violating the due process requirements of the Fourteenth Amendment.[45] (For more information, see *Chapter 9*, *Search Warrants, Investigations, Library Records, and Privacy*.) In order to avoid violating due process, libraries should always follow their own written policies. If the policy doesn't work, change it, but be sure to always follow what is written.

In addition to procedural issues, Internet use policies should specify whether computers in the adult section will be filtered or unfiltered. If a decision is made not to filter adult computers, the Internet use policy needs to be specific as to whether children may use those computers and under what circumstances. For example, I would suggest that minors under the age of 18 not be allowed to use unfiltered computers in the adult section unless they have written permission from their parents. That seems to me to be the easiest solution to the problem of filtering, thus allowing adult users to have unfiltered access to materials—while still protecting children.

Necessary Resources Discussing Internet Use Policies

Here are some resources on the Web relating to Internet use policies. These Websites contain both explanatory material and samples of use policies. Libraries that are revising their policies should remember, however, that some of these policies were written before the Supreme Court decision.

♦ American Library Association, *Guidelines and Considerations for Developing a Public Library Internet Use Policy* (November 2000), *available at* http://www.ala.org/alaorg/oif/Internetusepolicies.html.

♦ American Library Association, *Libraries & the Internet Toolkit: Tips and guidance for managing and communicating about the Internet* (October 16, 2002), *available at* http://www.ala.org/alaorg/oif/Internettoolkit.html.

♦ Library Research Center, *Survey of Internet Access Management in Public Libraries* (University of Illinois Graduate School of Library and Information Science June 2000), *available at* http://www.lis.uiuc.edu/gslis/research/Internet.pdf.

♦ Division of Technology, *Acceptable Use Policies—A Handbook* (Virginia Department of Education 2002), *available at* http://www.pen.k12.va.us/go/VDOE/Technology/AUP /home.shtml.

♦ InfoPeople Project, *Library Internet Use Policies* (California State Library and Peninsula Library System September 16, 2002), *available at* http://www.infopeople.org/about/policies.

♦ Develop an "Acceptable Use Policy" (AUP) for Schools and Public Libraries, Internet Advocate (May 11, 2000), *available at* http://www.monroe.lib.in.us/~lchampel/netadv3.html.

♦ *CDT releases proposed guidelines for library filtering*, 53-2 Newsletter on Intellectual Freedom 43 (March 2004).

♦ *Selecting a Filter*, 40-2 Library Technology Reports 26 (March/April 2004).

♦ *Internet Use Policies*, 40-2 Library Technology Reports 64 (March/April 2004).

♦ B. Crane, *Issues Surrounding Internet Use: Acceptable Use Policies*, 15-2 Information Searcher 13 (2004).

♦ C. H. Helms, *Internet Safety Policy Guidelines*, 40-2 Georgia Library Quarterly 19 (Summer 2003).

◆ Joan Miller, *Intellectual Freedom and the Internet: Developing Acceptable Use Policies*, 23-3 School Libraries in Canada 1 (2004). [Note: Although written in Canada, this article does not contain anything specific to Canadian libraries; rather, it provides general advice on writing Internet use policies for a school library.]

◆ Cynthia K. Richey, *Molding Effective Internet Policies*, 22-6 Computers in Libraries 16 (June 2002).

◆ John Alita, *Creating an Internet Policy by Civic Engagement*, 32-11 American Libraries 48 (December 2001).

◆ Mike Rusk, *Acceptable Use Policies: Four Examples from Community College Libraries*, 10-2 Community & Junior College Libraries 83 (2001).

Conclusion

The plurality opinion from the United States Supreme Court, one of the most complicated opinions written by the Court in many years, brings up as many issues as it resolves. A large part of the decision revolved around the ability of adult users to request that filtering software be disabled. This decision increases the importance of having written policies. This decision also means that libraries must review and then revise their Internet use policies as soon as possible.

When looking at an Internet use policy, the most important part of the policy involves the procedure that a patron should follow when he or she wishes to have the filtering software disabled. In addition, libraries that decide to provide unfiltered access to adult computers should look at their policies concerning the use by minors of computers in the adult room.

Every decision has its nuances, but a plurality decision from the Supreme Court is even more complicated to interpret than most. As a result, I definitely recommend that organizations should consult with their library, city, or school board attorneys before finalizing their written Internet use policies.

11

Employment and Workplace Law

Metro University would like to hire a new business librarian. The library is also looking for a few high school students to shelve books and for someone to cut the grass. How should the search committee write these advertisements, and what laws do they need to know in order to hire someone? What do they need to do in order to avoid discrimination or harassment? How does the library's personnel handbook affect the employment relationship?

Libraries and archives depend on two factors—their collections and their employees. Without good people, the collections are useless. As a result, librarians and archivists need to understand the basic elements of employment law. The employment relationship is a two-way street. Organizations need to know how to properly hire workers while following applicable laws. Employees need to know their rights and how the employment relationship is structured. This chapter will provide a basic overview about these topics.

Agency Law

In order to understand employment law, one must first understand the concepts of agency law. The idea of agency law is ingrained in the English Common Law system that the United States has adopted (except in Louisiana and Puerto Rico). The basic idea of agency law in England was to help determine when a servant was acting on behalf of his master.

In England during the Renaissance, a master would sometimes send a servant to sell or purchase goods or to negotiate business on the master's behalf. The servant would be acting for the master, rather than for himself. In the case of a sale of goods, a legal device was needed so that the proceeds of the sale would go to the master. At the same time, since the person selling the goods (the servant) was not the actual owner, the buyer needed a legal assurance that he or she would actually receive the purchased goods.

Agency law evolved so that there would be a mechanism through which a servant who was acting with the master's permission could sign a contract that would bind the master. If goods were being sold, the master had to give them up. If goods were being bought, the master would be responsible for the debt and would receive the benefit of the goods. It was for these reasons that the law of agency was created.

Agency law is based on a duty of trust towards the person on whose behalf the actions are being taken; this duty is known as a "fiduciary relationship." According to the Restatement (Second) of Agency, the formal definition of "agency" is: "the fiduciary [trust relationship] which results from the manifestation of consent [given] by one person to another that the other shall act on his behalf and subject to his control, and consent by the other so to act."[1] Another way of stating this idea is that "one person (the agent) agrees to act on behalf of another (the principal) to carry out the principal's affairs under the principal's control."[2]

For example, suppose that the director of the Largetown Public Library signed a contract to purchase furniture. The Largetown Public Library (as the principal) would be responsible for the debt and would get the benefit of the goods. The director (as the agent) would not be personally responsible for paying the bill and could not have the goods sent to his or her home instead of to the library.

Agency law is a basic part of corporation law and employment law. Agency law is also very important in the world of nonprofit organizations. Because corporations and nonprofits are artificial persons, they are considered principals, and the board members, executive officers, management, and staff are considered to be agents of the organization. Today we no longer use the archaic words "master" and "servant" to describe the employment relationship. Instead we use the words "employer" and "employee," although employees sometimes humorously say that they feel that they are being treated like servants. (See the section below for the distinction between an employee and an independent contractor.)

One important result of agency law is that a principal can be sued for acts committed by his or her agent. In the same way, a modern employer can be sued for acts committed by an employee. This legal doctrine is called *Respondeat Superior*.

For example, suppose that the Largetown Public Library hires a bookmobile driver. The bookmobile driver runs through a red light and hits another car. The driver of the other car can sue both the driver and the Largetown Public Library for negligence because the bookmobile driver was an agent of the library.

An agency relationship contains the following elements:

♦ The parties have a contract, either express or implied, which governs their relationship, and which both of the parties understand.

♦ The agent has the power to bind his principal as to third persons [i.e., the agent can make contracts with other people, and these contracts will be binding upon the principal].

♦ There exists a fiduciary relationship between principal and agent.

♦ The principal has the right to control the conduct of the agent with respect to matters entrusted to him/her.[3]

In order to have an agency relationship, the principal must give his or her agent the authority to act. There are two types of authority: *actual authority* and *apparent authority*.

Actual authority occurs when the principal gives consent to the agent to act on his or her behalf. Authority may also be "implied or inferred from the words used, from customs and from the relations of the parties."[4] Actual authority generally involves a contract between the parties. To decide whether there is indeed a contract, the normal factors for contract formation apply. These factors include offer, acceptance, and consideration.

The second type of authority, *apparent authority*, occurs when the actions of the principal suggest to third parties that an agency relationship exists, even if it does not. This situation is similar to the concept of promissory estoppel in contracts. According to the Restatement (Second) of Agency, "One who represents that another is his servant or other agent and thereby causes a third person justifiably to rely upon the care or skill of such apparent agent is subject to liability to the third person. . . ."[5]

The representation of apparent authority can be communicated either directly or through advertising that makes the third party believe that the authority exists.[6] "An agency relationship may be established by words or conduct of a principal, communicated to a third party, that gives rise to an appearance and reasonable belief by the third party that an agency has been created and the agent possesses the authority to enter into a transaction. . . ."[7] However, the third party's reliance on apparent authority must be reasonable. There are some situations in which the principal may be prevented from denying the authority of the agent, including:

>   (a) acts of commission or omission, instructional or negligent, by the principal [which] create the appearance of authority in his agent;
>   (b) the third party acts in reliance upon such appearance of authority, reasonably and in good faith; and
>   (c) the third party changes his position to his detriment in reliance upon the appearance of authority.[8]

A principal can also later adopt the acts of a purported agent who has been acting without authority. This adoption is called *ratification*. If the principal ratifies the acts of the purported agent, the relationship will be retroactive and the principal will be bound by the agent's prior actions.[9]

The agent owes his or her principal a number of duties. These duties include:

- The duty to use reasonable skill, care, and diligence in all that is done under the authority as an agent;
- The duty to obey instructions of the principal;
- The duty to account for all money or property the agent receives on behalf of the principal;
- The fiduciary duties of loyalty and good faith towards the principal;
- The fiduciary duties not to compete with the principal and to avoid self-dealing or making any secret profits in connection with the agency;
- The affirmative duty of the agent to give advice on the subject matter of the agency, to disclose all relevant information affecting the subject matter of agency, and to keep the principal's affairs confidential. As such, an agent cannot represent both parties to a transaction (dual agency) unless there is full and complete disclosure, including advising the principal as to the consequences of the dual agency.[10]

The agent must act for the benefit of the principal at all times when the agent is conducting business on behalf of the principal. This is known as the *fiduciary* duty or the *fiduciary relationship*. This stipulation is necessary in order to protect the principal from the misdeeds of a dishonest agent. An example of a fiduciary responsibility involves the board of directors of a nonprofit organization, such as a library or an archive. The directors must act on behalf of the organization, without any self-dealing, and they must avoid conflicts of interest. (For more on the fiduciary duties of board members, see **Chapter 12**, *Forming a Nonprofit Organization*.)

In addition, the principal must have the ability to direct the agent in the performance of his or her duties. "The right of control by the principal may be exercised by prescribing what the agent shall or shall not do before the agent acts, or at the time when he acts, or at both times."[11] The principal can tell the agent exactly how to do something, and the agent should not do anything without the permission of the principal.

For example, suppose that the director of the Largetown Public Library wanted to order green furniture, but the purchasing agent wanted to order red furniture. The purchasing agent doesn't have the power to go ahead and order red furniture without permission; he or she must follow the director's (the principal's) instructions. The issue of the principal's control over the agent's actions becomes especially important in trying to determine whether a worker is an employee or an independent contractor.

The Employment Relationship

A. Employee or Independent Contractor?

One very basic issue of employment law is the distinction between whether a worker is an employee or an independent contractor. When a library hires a staff person or librarian, he or she is an employee. However, if the library hires someone who is not a regular employee to cut the grass, that person is an independent contractor.

The distinctions between an employee and an independent contractor are crucial because the laws that apply to each relationship are totally different. This distinction between the two types of workers is also important for other areas of law, such as copyright law, withholding taxes and social security, and liability for wrongdoing. (For more information, see **Chapter 3**, *Copyright and Patent Law*.)

The relationship between an employer and an employee relies to a large extent on agency law and on the master-servant relationship, which "arises when the person charged as master has the right to direct the method by which the master's service is performed."[12] Some of the differences between an employee (the servant or agent) and an independent contractor include:

♦ An employee gets a salary or wage, rather than being paid on a per project basis.

♦ An employee is furnished the equipment used in the performance of the work; the independent contractor [usually] supplies his or her own.

♦ An employer controls, directs, and supervises an employee in the performance of his or her work, whereas when an independent contractor is hired a company merely specifies the result to be achieved, and the individual uses personal judgment to achieve that result.[13]

The Restatement (Second) of Agency lays out a number of factors that help to determine whether the worker is an employee or an independent contractor, including:

(a) The extent of control which, by agreement, the master may exercise over the details of the work;
(b) Whether or not the one employed is engaged in a distinct occupation or business;
(c) The kind of occupation, with reference to whether, in the locality, the work is usually done under the direction of the employer or by a specialist without supervision;
(d) The skill required in the particular occupation;
(e) Whether the employer or the workman supplies the instrumentalities, tools, and the place of work for the person doing the work;
(f) The length of time for which the person is employed;
(g) The method of payment, whether by the time or by the job;
(h) Whether or not the work is part of the regular business of the employer;
(i) Whether or not the parties believe they are creating the relation of master and servant; and
(j) Whether the principal is or is not in business.[14]

Many of the provisions of employment and labor law discussed below do not apply to independent contractors. For example, the Fair Labor Standards Act (FLSA), which establishes minimum wage, overtime pay, and child labor standards for employees, does not apply to independent contractors. The work-for-hire doctrine in copyright law also relies to a certain extent on the distinction between employees and independent contractors, although there are some exceptions. (For more information, see *Chapter 3*, *Copyright and Patent Law*.)

Worker's compensation is another area that is only available to employees. An independent contractor who is hurt on the job is responsible for his or her own medical bills, unless there is a lawsuit for negligence. For example, suppose that the library hires a painter who falls off his ladder and breaks both of his arms. The worker's compensation insurance from the library would not pay for the painter's medical treatment. However, if the library had created an unsafe condition that led to the accident, the painter could sue the library for negligence.

Finally, since the independent contractor is not an agent, he or she can't bind the organization as a principal. The independent contractor has no authority to conduct business on behalf of the principal. For example, a lawn service can't order databases for the library. The distinction between an employee and an independent contractor is a basic element in many areas of law.

B. Employment-at-Will and Employment Contracts

Most employees fall under the doctrine of employment-at-will. The only situations where employment-at-will does not apply are if there is a union collective bargaining agreement or a governmental civil service merit system, or if the employees have a specific written employment contract with their employer. If the worker can't show the existence of a contract, the courts will assume that the relationship is one of employment-at-will. Basically, employment-at-will means that the worker can be fired at any time, for any reason, as long as it is not an illegal reason such as discrimination, punishment for whistle-blowing, etc.

Attorney John Leidecke provides a helpful explanation of employment-at-will:

> *Employment-at-will* is a common law (judge-made law) doctrine that defines the employer-employee relationship. It permits the employer wide latitude in deciding how [to] conduct business, including whom [to] employ and for how long. With respect to discharges, the *employment-at-will* doctrine provides for the termination of employment by either the employer or the employee at any time and for almost any reason. *At-will* employment is contrasted with employment governed by a contract for a definite term or employment covered by a collective bargaining agreement. . . . [15]

In other words, an employee-at-will may be fired for "good reason, bad reason, or no reason at all, but not [for] an *illegal* reason."[16] [Emphasis in original.]

Workers may have heard about terms such as "just cause"; however, this concept only applies to situations involving employment contracts, collective bargaining, or a determination of whether the organization will have to pay unemployment compensation. Some organizations do have an "employment contract" that governs the relationship; however, there are also times when the employment contract states that the employee is in an employment-at-will relationship. As has been already indicated, in the employment-at-will situation, the courts will allow an employer to fire the worker at any time, for any reason, as long as it is not an illegal reason.

If the employee is covered by an employment contract, an employer must follow the provisions of that contract in order to fire the employee. An employment contract usually takes one of three forms—individually negotiated contracts, personnel manuals, and collective bargaining agreements.

One type of employment contract consists of an agreement that the individual employee negotiates with his or her employer. In this situation, all of the normal rules of contract formation apply. There must be an offer, an acceptance, and consideration. The consideration for employment contracts usually consists of the employer paying money in exchange for the employee's labor, although sometimes employment contracts will specify other types of compensation. For example, an apartment complex may hire a manager who gets free rent instead of being paid.

Note that the Statute of Frauds applies to employment contracts. As was discussed in **Chapter 2** on contracts, the Statute of Frauds requires certain types of contracts to be stated in writing in order to be legally enforceable. These include contracts that can't be performed within one year, along with contracts for personal services.[17] "However, a contract for at-will employment, where either party can terminate the relationship at any time, is not subject to the Statute of Frauds because it has the potential of being completed in less than one year."[18] Basically, if the worker does not have a written employment contract, he or she will be considered to be an at-will employee.

The second type of employment contract consists of an organization's personnel manual. The personnel manual or handbook is not negotiated with individual employees, although sometimes the employer will convene a committee with employee representatives. If the employer has voluntarily adopted a personnel manual that states the terms of continued employment and specifies how employees are to be termi- nated, the courts will consider this handbook to be an employment con- tract.

For example, academic institutions usually have guidelines for faculty hiring, tenure, promotion, and termination.[19] If the employer doesn't follow the rules stated in the personnel manual, the employee may sue in court for wrongful termination. In order to decide whether a personnel manual is legally enforceable, courts will generally consider the following issues:

♦ Whether there was a promise in return for the employer's prom- ise; that is, the offer contained in the handbook constituted, in effect, a promise;

♦ Whether there was some benefit or detriment bargained for and in fact conferred or suffered, sufficient to create a unilateral con- tract [in other words, whether there was consideration such as a salary for contract formation];

♦ Whether the action or inaction, the benefit, or the detriment was done or not done in reliance on the employee's offer or promise;

♦ Whether the alleged agreement was so lacking in "mutuality" as to be insufficient for contractual purposes; that is, whether the fundamental requirements of contract have been met.[20]

In addition to personnel manuals that apply to an entire organiza- tion, there are also unit or departmental policies.[21] Often these depart- mental policies will clarify how the broader organizational policy ap- plies to the individual unit. Sometimes departmental policies may be more specific or have higher standards than the overall organizational policy.

For example, Western Kentucky University's *Faculty Manual* states that appointment to each faculty rank requires "[d]emonstrated achievement appropriate for this rank in teaching effectiveness, re- search/creative activity, and university/public service."[22] Using the dictionary definition of "teaching effectiveness," this criterion doesn't seem to relate to academic librarians. However, the WKU Department of Library Public Services has taken this term and given it a definition that applies to professional librarians:

Teaching Effectiveness as an Academic Librarian
    Each librarian is expected to perform at an outstanding profes- sional and academic level in areas which enable the faculty member to contribute to the educational, research, and service missions of the

University. The term "teaching effectiveness," when applied to a librarian, is meant to be interpreted as fulfillment of the wide variety of functions defined by each individual's library—and instructional—related job descriptions. These functions may include, but are not limited to, all or some of the following:

1. Outstanding performance in academic librarianship;
2. Extensive technical knowledge of academic librarianship;
3. Distinctive contributions to librarianship;
4. Outstanding performance of library duties, including management of staff, equipment, and time resources;
5. Outstanding performance in reference assistance, collection development, bibliographic instruction, computer-assisted literature searching, or collection management;
6. Teaching college-level courses outside of the library, or guest lectures.[23]

Another source of material for a contract is the employee's offer letter. The terms of employment offered in a letter can in fact constitute a portion of the employment contract. A notorious example of the offer constituting a contract occurred in 1992, when Bo Schembechler sued former Detroit Tigers owner Tom Monaghan for wrongful termination of employment. After retiring as head coach of the football team at the University of Michigan, Schembechler had accepted a job as the president of the Detroit Tigers. The offer of employment came during a lunch between Schembechler and Monaghan. Unfortunately, the two men had different ideas about how to manage the organization, and in July 1992 Monaghan sent Schembechler a two-word fax saying: "You're fired!"[24] (Monaghan had simultaneously put out a news release saying that he was firing Schembechler. Schembechler actually did not receive the fax until after he had been called by a reporter asking for a comment on the news release.) Schembechler's most important exhibit in his case was a paper napkin on which Monaghan had written the terms of their relationship. In May 1994, the two parties reached a settlement, and the case was dropped.[25]

Obviously, employment contracts are not often written on napkins, but this case does show how an offer letter can constitute an employment contract. Personnel policies, employment handbooks, and formal offer letters are more conventional sources for employment contracts, although the existence of a personnel policy or an employment handbook does not prevent the employer from making changes in the workers' situations:

When an employer distributes a new handbook, the [new handbook constitutes] a new offer of employment to the at-will employee. This new offer is limited to the new handbook's or employment policy's contents and becomes effective on the date [the new handbook] is distributed. When [employment policies] are withdrawn, the new offer becomes effective on the date that the employer notifies the employee of the withdrawal. At-will employees accept the new offer and provide consideration by continuing their employment. As long as the employer does not deprive the employee of benefits already earned, the employer can unilaterally change its terms and conditions.[26]

Basically, any time an employer changes the personnel manual, the at-will employee has the option of accepting the new policies or terminating employment. If the worker continues his or her employment, the courts will deem the worker to have accepted this new employment offer.

One issue that most librarians and archivists do not have to deal with in their employment contracts is a covenant not to compete. However, some librarians working in special libraries in the corporate setting may have this clause in their contracts. Under most circumstances these clauses are not enforceable; however, if the clause has consideration valid for the formation of a contract, it may be enforceable. Generally only highly compensated employees or executives can be held to such a covenant.[27] On the other hand, trade secret law may prevent an employee from using the secrets of his or her employer to compete. This is a valid type of noncompetition agreement. (For more on this topic, see *Chapter 6, Trademark and Trade Secret Law*.)

C. Terminating an Employee

Sometimes, employment must be ended and an employee fired. While this is an unpleasant subject, it is also very important. Terminating employment requires strict adherence to well-defined procedures.

In order to terminate an employee without being sued, there are three things to remember: (1) document everything, (2) treat each employee by the same standards, and (3) if the organization has a policy handbook, make sure that the written policies have been followed.

The three basic rules of termination are document, *document*, and *document*. Every time that an employee does something problematic, write him or her a warning letter and keep a printed copy in the employee's personnel file. (Wisdom dictates that the memo should inform the employee that a copy of the memo is being placed in his or her file.) These copies may be needed later in a lawsuit, or to prevent a lawsuit.

There is a myth that tenured faculty members, union members, and civil servants can't be fired. This is not true. However, there are usually specific procedures that need to be adhered to in order to remove an employee in these situations. Most lawsuits are successful not because the employees can't be fired, but rather because supervisors did not follow the stated procedures or didn't document the workers' problems.

The memorandum to the employee should indicate what he or she did that was wrong and when the incident took place. The memo should include all pertinent information, along with citations to the appropriate workplace policies. The memo should also include a corrective plan of action with details as to what is expected from the employee in the future (such as suggestions as to how a situation should have been handled differently). Finally, the letter should include information about the procedures that will be taken if improvement does not occur.

The memorandum should contain a place for the recipient to sign indicating that he or she has received a copy of the letter and that the contents of the memo have been explained to the worker. The supervisor should explain that signing the letter does not indicate that the employee agrees with the contents, only that he or she has received a copy. If there are institutional procedures for appeal, these procedures should be indicated in the warning letter.

For example, suppose that Ronald comes to work drunk. Figure 11.1 contains a sample letter of warning for this scenario. This letter can be modified to reflect the appropriate institutional policies.

The courts will treat the totality of an organization's policies, procedural manuals, offer letters, memoranda, and general practices as being the employment contract. Courts will use these documents for determining working conditions and termination procedures, as well as for unemployment compensation. Thus, the organizational policies should be reviewed carefully to ensure that they are consistent with one another.

In order to avoid problems, all of the organization's policies should be followed carefully, and all employees should be treated in the same way. Playing favorites is a bad idea, not only from a managerial standpoint but also from a legal perspective. Disparate treatment of workers can be a legal issue that will come back to haunt the organization. Policies are not just pretty words on a page; they should be strictly applied. If the policy doesn't reflect practice, either the policy or the practice needs to be changed.

Dear Ronald:

On September 16, 2005, you came to work while inebriated. When you arrived at work, your clothing was untidy, your breath smelled of alcohol, and you were staggering while you walked. In addition, you were talking in a loud and aggressive voice, and one of the librarians observed you drinking from a beer can.

Library Workplace Policy 20.1(a) states: "Substance abuse of whatever type, legal or illegal, shall not be permitted on the job, and shall be grounds for termination of employment." In addition, Library Workplace Policy 20.77(b) states: "Employees shall follow all state, local, and national laws while at work. Violation of a criminal statute while on the job shall be grounds for termination of employment." Since you are under the age of 21, and it is illegal in this state to consume alcohol while under the age of 21, you have violated a state law.

This letter constitutes a first warning. According to the library's Disciplinary Policy, once an employee has received two warnings within a 24-month period, he or she may be terminated immediately. This letter may also be considered when making decisions on raises or promotions. A copy of this letter will be placed in your personnel file and will be kept in your file in the supervisor's office.

In the future, you are expected not to use or abuse any intoxicating substances—legal or illegal—such as alcohol while at work or immediately prior to coming to work. You are expected not to be in an intoxicated state while working. You are also expected to obey all state, local, and national laws while at work, including laws relating to the legal age for drinking alcohol. Any further violations will result in a second letter of warning, which may be followed by immediate termination.

If you disagree with the statements contained in this letter, you may file a written response with your supervisor (with copies to the Division Manager and Human Resources) within ten (10) working days from the date of your signature on the warning letter. The supervisor must consider your response and make any justified modifications to the warning letter within ten (10) working days. Should you continue to disagree with the supervisor's allegations, you may make a final appeal to the Divisional Manager within five (5) working days of receiving the supervisor's response. The Divisional Manager will make a final determination regarding the status of this warning letter.

_____   _____   _____   _____
Supervisor Signature   Date   Employee Signature   Date

NOTE: Your signature does not indicate that you agree with the contents of this letter, only that you have received a copy.

Figure 11.1. Sample Letter of Warning for an Employee.

D. Labor Unions and Collective Bargaining

Some librarians and archivists belong to labor unions. In this situation, their contracts are a collective bargaining agreement between the employer and the labor union. The individual worker does not negotiate the terms of employment, and must accept the contract as presented and approved by the union membership. Once a labor union has been certified, the employer can only deal with the union and not with the individual worker. In addition, all employees who are part of the group represented by the union are bound by the collective bargaining agreement that the union has negotiated. Individual employees are not able to opt out of the contract, even if they decide not to join the union (the legal term is "opting out of membership").

There are certain steps that have to be taken before a labor union can represent the employees of an organization. These steps are known as certification of a labor union. According to the rules of the National Labor Relations Board (NLRB), the process is begun when at least 30 percent of the employees in the bargaining unit sign a petition asking for a union certification election. Before holding a certification election, however, the union must determine what the bargaining unit will be. The NLRB rules explain:

> A bargaining unit is a group of two or more employees who share a "community of interest" and may reasonably be grouped together for collective-bargaining purposes. The NLRB is responsible for ensuring that any election in a representation case is conducted in an appropriate unit. A unit is usually described by the type of work done or job classification of employees.[28]

For example, in a public library setting a bargaining unit might consist of all the professional librarians, while another bargaining unit might include the custodial staff. In a university library setting, the professional librarians and archivists might be included in the bargaining unit with teaching faculty, while library assistants and clerical workers might be placed in a different bargaining unit. In many academic libraries and archives, the bargaining unit consists of the entire organization. Frequently, librarians are included in the same bargaining unit as teaching faculty. In some cases, however, the bargaining unit may be limited to the library itself. This is the case with many large urban library systems such as the New York Public Library. Some bargaining units include professional librarians and library staff together, while others separate professionals and paraprofessionals into two separate units.

Other considerations may also affect the certification election:

> In some cases, the number of facilities to be included in a bargaining unit is at issue, and a unit may be described by the number of locations to be involved. . . . Generally, the appropriateness of a bargaining unit is determined on the basis of the community of interest of the employees involved. The NLRB may also consider factors such as any history of collective bargaining and the desires of the affected employees.[29]

Not all workers are eligible to join unions. For example, agricultural and domestic workers are not eligible to join unions. Another situation where the employee may not join a union is if the person is employed by a member of his or her family.

The National Labor Relations Board oversees unions in most private organizations and companies.[30] However, people who work for airlines or railway companies are subject to the Railway Labor Act instead of the National Labor Relations Act.

The Railway Labor Act would apply to some special librarians who are employed by railroad or airline companies. For example, Northwest Airlines has "jet librarians" who work with maps and charts. Their work is crucial because the pilots rely on these maps and charts to fly their planes. The jet librarians are part of a bargaining unit with the ticket agents, gate workers, and baggage handlers.

The other groups of workers that are not covered by the NLRB are those who work for Federal, state, or local governments. Each state has its own labor relations laws that cover these employees. Librarians and archivists who work for state universities, schools, and state governmental libraries would fall within the purview of these state laws. In addition, the U.S. Department of Labor deals with labor unions that represent U.S. government workers, including governmental librarians. Nonprofit organizations and private universities are subject to the jurisdiction of the NLRB.

In the case of libraries and archives, not all workers are eligible for union representation. Unions cannot represent supervisory employees and independent contractors. However, there are some rank-and-file supervisors who are not considered to be management. The idea is that these people are more like crew foremen at a factory rather than managers.

For example, at the New York Public Library, the union represents staff and librarians together in one bargaining unit. The ranks of librarian that are included are entry-level librarian, Senior Librarian, Supervisory Librarian, and Assistant Department Head. The Department Heads, however, are considered managerial employees and are not part of the union.

In order for a labor union to win a certification election, over 50 percent of the membership must vote in favor of the union. Once the certification election has taken place and the union has been certified, that union will represent the membership until the bargaining unit is decertified or until another union is certified. In order to hold an election for certification of a new union or decertification of an existing union, at least 30 percent of the employees of the bargaining unit must sign a petition. The NLRB will oversee this election, which requires a majority vote in order for the decertification to pass or for the new union to be certified.

After the union is certified and the bargaining unit is established, the union will represent all the members of that bargaining unit (as previously defined) in negotiations with the employer. When the union reaches a collective bargaining agreement with the employer, a ratification election will be conducted. If a majority of the employees in the bargaining unit vote for the contract, it will become effective for all employees. Members of the bargaining unit will not be able to change this agreement, and will be bound by the negotiations of the labor union.

E. The Fair Labor Standards Act (FLSA)

The FLSA covers a number of issues relating to employees.[31] (The Act does not apply to independent contractors.) The FLSA contains the minimum-wage law, provisions about child labor, and equal pay requirements. The statute also includes provisions for overtime entitlement and compensation.

Needless to say, libraries and archives must pay employees at least minimum wage.[32] One major issue for libraries and archives involves the overtime provisions of the FLSA. The Act divides employees into two categories, "exempt" employees and "non-exempt" employees. Unless specifically exempted, all employees are covered by the provisions of the FLSA and are considered to be non-exempt. The Act does not apply to salespeople, agricultural workers, computer programmers making at least $27.63/hr,[33] or "any employee employed in a bona fide executive, administrative, or professional capacity (including any employee employed in the capacity of academic administrative personnel or teacher in elementary or secondary schools). . . ."[34]

One of the most important differences between an exempt employee and a non-exempt employee involves the way in which the workers are paid. If the worker is paid by the hour and is subject to having money taken away if he or she doesn't work all of the scheduled hours, the employee is considered to be non-exempt. Salaried employees, on the other hand, are considered exempt as long as they make at least $455 per week and fall within one of the categories outlined in the statute. These categories include executives, administrative workers, professional employees, and outside salespeople.[35]

In order to be considered a professional employee, the worker must be doing work which requires advanced intellectual knowledge in a field of science or learning "which has been acquired by a prolonged course of specialized intellectual instruction."[36] (See the discussion of what constitutes a professional employee below, as well as the discussion of what is a professional in *Chapter 8, Information Malpractice, Professionalism, and the Unauthorized Practice of Law and Medicine*.)

Most, although not all, professional librarians and archivists are exempt from the FLSA because they are considered to be learned professional employees. On the other hand, most library and archival staff are non-exempt workers. (K-12 school librarians are also exempt, but under a separate provision; the FLSA definition of an educational administrator specifically includes K-12 school librarians.)[37] To be considered a professional employee, the worker must either be in a learned field or a creative field. The regulations are contained in the Code of Federal Regulations, Title 29, section 541.[38] Professional employees are defined as:

♦ *Learned*—Generally . . . the employee must perform work that requires advanced knowledge typically acquired by a prolonged course of specialized academic instruction. Learned professional employees can be found in law, medicine, teaching, engineering, science and other similar fields.

♦ *Creative*—To qualify . . . the employee must perform work that requires invention, imagination, originality or talent. The work is in a recognized field of artistic or creative endeavor such as music, writing, acting, the graphic arts and other similar fields.[39]

Most librarians and archivists fall within the learned professional employee category, although some large library systems (such as the New York Public Library) pay rank-and-file librarians by the hour. These workers are covered by the FLSA and are considered to be non-exempt.

The most important difference between exempt employees and non-exempt employees involves overtime compensation. According to the FLSA, non-exempt employees must be paid 1½ times their normal wage rate for all work beyond 40 hours a workweek.[40] The overtime pay must be awarded in the next regular paycheck. The FLSA defines the workweek as being any seven consecutive days; the workweek does not have to coincide with the calendar week.[41] By contrast, exempt employees do not have to be paid for overtime, no matter how many hours they work in the same week. For example, a survey of young lawyers in Nevada showed that the average lawyer had 1,881 billable hours per year.[42] The general rule is that lawyers work two hours for every hour that they are able to bill. Using this calculation, the average lawyer works approximately 72.35 hours per week. However, as professional employees, lawyers don't get overtime.[43]

F. Child Labor Laws under the FLSA

In addition to wages and overtime compensation, the Fair Labor Standards Act also contains laws relating to child labor. These are minimum rules; states can adopt more stringent regulations if they choose. Child labor rules are important for libraries and archives, since high school students are often hired to shelve books. Thus, it is very important for libraries and archives to keep informed about the various Federal and state laws that relate to employment of minors.

Under the FLSA, the minimum age for employment is 14 years for nonagricultural work. The only exceptions are if the parents own the business, if the child is an actor or delivers newspapers, and "[y]outh working at home in the making of wreaths. . . ."[44] The statute does not cover yard work and babysitting, so children under 14 may also do these jobs. However, since minors are prohibited from operating heavy machinery, there are some types of yard work that young children may not be allowed to perform.

According to the FLSA, children who are 14 or 15 years old may only work:

- ♦ Before and after school hours, except in a Work Experience and Career Exploration Program;
- ♦ After 7:00 a.m. or before 7:00 p.m., except from June 1 through Labor Day when they can work until 9:00 p.m.;
- ♦ Not more than 3 hours a day on school days, including Fridays;
- ♦ Not more than 18 hours per week in school weeks;

♦ Not more than 8 hours a day on non-school days;
♦ Not more than 40 hours per week when school is not in session.[45]

The FLSA also specifies which kinds of jobs young adults who are 14 or 15 may hold and what types of tasks and duties they may perform. (For more details, see the U.S. Department of Labor's Website.)[46] Children who are 16 or 17 may work for any number of hours on any day in any occupation, except for certain hazardous occupations that are designated by the Department of Labor.[47] Once the young adults turn 18, the child-labor provisions of the FLSA no longer apply, and there are no restrictions whatever on their work.[48] Understanding the FLSA will assist you when you undertake the hiring of new employees.

G. Hiring New Workers

When you are hiring a new librarian or staff member, there are a few legal principles to keep in mind. There are a lot of myths about the hiring process that are not correct. In this section, my intention is to correct these myths. Also keep this in mind: to attract the best candidates for the position, you should advertise the job as broadly as possible.

Many libraries, schools, and academic institutions are equal employment opportunity/affirmative action (EEO/AA) employers. The myth is that EEO/AA is a quota, namely, that you are *required* to hire a member of a minority group. This is not true. What EEO/AA means is that the organization should advertise as broadly as possible, with a national search for professional positions. The goal is to hire the best candidate for the job—which is exactly what the employer wants to do anyhow!

Under both state and Federal laws, it is illegal to take race or gender into consideration in the hiring process.[49] In addition to race or gender, when making a hiring decision you may not consider marital or parental status, religion, national origin, age, or membership in political organizations.[50]

The Equal Employment Opportunity Commission enforces these laws about hiring. Most states also have their own civil rights offices with regulatory powers. In addition to the EEOC, the U.S. Department of Education Office of Civil Rights enforces civil rights laws for "all state education agencies, elementary and secondary school systems, colleges and universities, vocational schools, proprietary schools, state vocational rehabilitation agencies, libraries, and museums that receive U.S. Department of Education funds."[51]

Because employers are prohibited from using illegal considerations in the hiring process, they are limited in the questions that they may ask during a hiring interview. Questions involving illegal factors are themselves illegal. In some cases, these kinds of questions may be permissible *after* the candidate has been hired. Table 11.1, contained at the end of this chapter, provides some examples of inappropriate and appropriate questions.

Before you reach the interview stage, you need to attract candidates. The most common methods of securing applicants are advertisements and listings with professional organizations. When advertising or listing a position, the first thing to do is to separate the stated qualifications into two categories—the *required qualifications* and the *desired qualifications*.

Required qualifications are the absolute minimum that a candidate must have, while *desired qualifications* would be helpful but are not necessary. For example, a professional librarian position would normally require an M.L.S., and a professional archivist position would normally require either an M.L.S. or an M.A. in history.

The best way to hire candidates is to read the applications or résumés while also looking at the job advertisement. First, determine how many years of experience each candidate has. Decide how experience will be determined, and be consistent for each applicant. For example, when hiring a professional librarian, are you going to count paraprofessional experience? What about student worker experience while in library school? For a staff position, do you count bookstore experience? These are questions that must be decided upon before beginning to screen applications. When I chair a search committee, I usually create a sheet with all of the definitions that each member of the committee can refer to as he or she is reading applicant files. In addition to helping with the screening process, this list of definitions is necessary in the event that there is later litigation. As a result, this definitional sheet should be retained even after the search has been completed.

Figure 11.2 contains an example of the structure and wording of an effective position advertisement. The required and desired qualifications are clearly stated, as are the duties of the position. A prospective candidate reading this advertisement would understand clearly what is required for the position and what criteria the search committee will be applying.

Metro University is seeking applicants for a business reference librarian position. This is a tenure-track reference/subject specialist position at the starting faculty rank of Assistant Professor. The successful candidate will work in a team-oriented environment of fifteen professionals in the Services Department. Duties include: (1) assisting patrons at the reference desk in the use of reference and periodical resources, databases, and microforms; (2) performing collection development for assigned departments; (3) teaching research instruction classes for assigned departments and participating in library rotation for Freshman English classes; (4) being involved in professional associations; and (5) other duties as assigned. Research and publication are required for promotion and tenure.

Required qualifications: (1) ALA-accredited MLS (completed at the time of employment); (2) master's degree in business, public administration, or healthcare administration, or J.D. degree; (3) ability to communicate well, relate well, and work well with faculty, staff, students, and library patrons; (4) experience using computer applications such as word processing; (5) ability to work with Internet and CD-ROM databases.

Desired qualifications: (1) At least three years library experience working with business or law materials; (2) Web authoring skills; (3) ability to work with numbers and statistics and to use spreadsheets and database programs.

Review of applications will begin June 1, 2006. Starting salary $38,000. Please send letter of application, résumé, and names/addresses/phone numbers of three references to: Chair, Librarian Search Committee, Metro University Library, Largetown, Anystate 10101.

All qualified individuals are encouraged to apply, including women, minorities, persons with disabilities, and disabled veterans. Metro University is an Affirmative Action/Equal Opportunity Employer.

Figure 11.2. Sample Advertisement for Job Opening.

Once you have determined how much experience each candidate has, you must then determine whether each candidate meets the required or desired qualifications. At Western Kentucky University, we score the applicants according to the following scale:

(1) Meets all required qualifications and all desired qualifications;
(2) Meets all required qualifications and some desired qualifications;
(3) Meets all required qualifications but none of the desired qualifications;
(4) Meets some of the required qualifications and all of the desired qualifications;

(5) Meets some of the required qualifications and some of the desired qualifications;
(6) Meets neither the required qualifications nor the desired qualifications.[52]

Normally, you should only interview those candidates who are in categories 1, 2, or 3. If none of those candidates is satisfactory, or if you don't have any candidates who are in categories 1-3, you will need to re-advertise the position. This scoring system helps to ensure that you will have candidates who meet your requirements and your needs. In addition, the scale helps to rank each candidate in a neutral and fair manner.

Let's say that the following applicants sent résumés for the Business Librarian position at Metro University:

♦ *Courtney*: MLS, MBA, three years of experience with business materials, good communication skills, experience with word processing, spreadsheets and statistical software, Internet and CD-ROM databases, and Web authoring skills.

♦ *James*: MLS, J.D., ten years of experience with law materials, good communication skills, experience with word processing, spreadsheets and statistical software, Internet and CD-ROM databases, and Web authoring skills.

♦ *Lacey*: MLS, MBA, good communication skills, experience with word processing, spreadsheets and statistical software, Internet and CD-ROM databases, and Web authoring skills. Lacey just graduated from library school and has no library experience. Before she went to library school, however, she was a marketing research analyst for 10 years in a consulting firm.

♦ *Tom*: MLS, J.D., good communication skills, experience with word processing, Internet and CD-ROM databases. Tom just graduated from library school and has no library experience. He also does not work with spreadsheets or statistical software and has never learned Web authoring skills.

♦ *Bob*: MLS, six years of experience with business materials, good communication skills, experience with word processing, spreadsheets and statistical software, Internet and CD-ROM databases, and Web authoring skills.

♦ *Sarah*: MLS, good communication skills, experience with word processing, spreadsheets and statistical software, Internet and CD-ROM databases, and Web authoring skills. Sarah just graduated from library school and has no library experience.

♦ *George*: B.A., just graduated from college, has no experience and no computer skills.

Before reading the following analysis, you should use the rating system to rank these applicants. See how well your ratings match the evaluations given below.

Courtney meets all of the required qualifications (MLS, MBA, good communication skills, experience with word processing, knowledge of Internet and CD-ROM databases). She also meets all of the desired qualifications (three years of experience with business materials, works with spreadsheets and statistical software, and has Web authoring skills). Therefore, using the rating system, Courtney would be rated a **1**.

James, like Courtney, meets all of the required qualifications (MLS, J.D., good communication skills, experience with word processing, knowledge of Internet and CD-ROM databases. He also meets all of the desired qualifications (10 years of experience with law materials, works with spreadsheets and statistical software, and has Web authoring skills). Therefore, using the rating system above, James would be rated a **1**.

Lacey has a pretty good record. She meets all the required qualifications, but because she has no library experience she only meets some of the desired qualifications. Therefore, Lacey is rated a **2**.

Tom meets all of the required qualifications for the job; however, he doesn't meet any of the desired qualifications. Therefore, Tom will be rated as a **3**.

Bob has a pretty good record, but he does not have a second master's degree in a business-related field. As a result, he only meets some of the required qualifications. However, he does meet all of the desired qualifications. Therefore, Bob will be rated as a **4**.

Sarah only meets some of the required qualifications and only meets some of the desired qualifications. She doesn't have a second master's (a required qualification). In addition, she doesn't have any library experience (a desired qualification). Therefore, Sarah will be rated as a **5**.

George shouldn't have even applied for this job. He doesn't meet any of the required qualifications or any of the desired qualifications. As a result, George is rated as a **6**.

By the time the résumés have been evaluated, it will be clear that the only candidates who can be hired (based on the standards set by the advertisement) are Courtney, James, Lacey, and Tom. All of the other candidates will be eliminated because they don't meet the requirements for the job. At this point, the search committee would probably want to talk on the telephone with Courtney and James—the two candidates who have all the required qualifications and all the desired qualifications—to see if the committee wishes to interview these two candidates.

The library doesn't have to hire someone whose rating is a **1**; the committee could decide that other factors are more important. For example, suppose that James is unpleasant on the telephone; the committee might eliminate him from consideration and interview Courtney and Lacey. The committee might also decide that Lacey's experience in marketing research makes up for her lack of library experience.

Hiring a candidate who doesn't have all the required qualifications can lead to a lawsuit. There are two types of potential plaintiffs who might sue. If a candidate without the required credentials is hired, an applicant who has those credentials but didn't get the job might have a case against the employer. However, most organizations don't think about the second class of potential plaintiffs, namely, people who didn't apply because the advertisement contained certain requirements.

For example, suppose that Metro University hires Bob, who has an M.L.S., but does not have an M.B.A. If Metro University hires Bob, Courtney might sue. However, Susan, who didn't even apply for the job, might also sue the university. Susan could say that she saw the ad, but didn't apply because she only has an M.L.S. and not an M.B.A. Susan's case would be that, if she had known that Metro University didn't really require an M.B.A., she would have applied for the job.

We have already seen that in judging our candidates, we are not required by EEO/AA to establish a quota. So what does EEO/AA mean in the hiring process? First, you rank all candidates as discussed above, determine their experience, and look at the qualities they possess. Then, if you are having trouble deciding between two equal candidates, you may look at the *voluntary* affirmative action information that each candidate has provided.

The *only* permissible use of race or gender is to help *decide between two equal candidates*. If one of the two equal candidates is a member of a minority group, you may choose that person over the other equal candidate. (Of course, you may not eliminate any candidate because of race or gender.) Once again, you may *only* look at race or gender if you have two *absolutely equal* candidates between whom you cannot decide. *This circumstance is the only legal use of race or gender in the entire hiring process.* Now you know what it means when an institution indicates that it is an Equal Employment Opportunity/ Affirmative Action employer.

H. Drug Testing in the Workplace

One issue that has come up many times in recent years involves drug testing. This issue is relevant both for the institution in terms of hiring candidates and for the employee in terms of retaining a job. The three main types of job-related drug testing are preemployment testing, random testing of existing employees, and drug testing after an accident.

Preemployment screening is usually legal if it applies to all applicants equally. Once an offer has been extended, organizations can make one of the conditions of employment a physical examination, including a drug test. This examination must be done with as much privacy and as little intrusiveness as possible.[53] Thus, a urinalysis test would be preferable to a blood test.[54]

Once the individual has been hired, the employer can only do random drug testing. The courts will not uphold a policy of regular drug testing.[55] Regular drug testing would be considered a violation of the employee's privacy.[56] With only a few exceptions, a random drug test must be based on a reasonable suspicion that the employee is using drugs.[57] The exceptions "are limited to instances where employees work in positions critical to public safety or the protection of life, property or national security (e.g., truck drivers and aviation personnel)."[58] Library workers generally would not fall under this classification; however, a bookmobile driver might be included in this category because he or she is driving a motor vehicle.

An employer might have sufficient reasonable suspicion to do a random drug test because of one or more of the following reasons:

> [A]lcohol on the breath, unusually slurred speech, lapses in performance, inability to respond to questions and physical symptoms of alcohol or drug influence. . . . Employers should consider requiring a designated individual, or individuals, to pre-approve drug testing to help ensure the procedures are followed properly and uniformly . . . pursuant to an established written policy. . . . Failure to prove actual reasonable suspicion for testing may lead to liability.[59]

The other type of drug testing involves doing a test after an on-the-job accident. This testing should occur only after a serious accident, and the employer must have reasonable suspicion that the employee was under the influence of drugs or alcohol at the time of the accident. In other words, there has to be some sort of a link between drug or alcohol use and the accident. For example, if a bookmobile driver is involved in a serious accident, the library could require testing for drug or alcohol use.[60]

It is very important to remember that drug-testing policies should be applied to all employees in the same way, and all policies should be in writing and distributed to the employees. These policies must be followed rigorously. As attorney Sue M. Bendavid-Arbiv has indicated, employers should always adhere to the following guidelines:

- ◆ Have a written drug and alcohol policy in their employee handbooks;

- ◆ Require employees to sign an acknowledgment of receiving and reading the employee handbook;

- ◆ Identify safety-sensitive positions and have the documentation necessary to support these designations;

- ◆ Identify legitimate interests for drug testing and have the documentation necessary to support those interests;

- ◆ Train supervisors on what factors constitute sufficient grounds for reasonable-suspicion testing and the importance of applying the policy evenhandedly;

- ◆ Train supervisors on the ramifications of taking action against employees who use prescription drugs as treatment for a disability covered by the ADA.[61]

Once again, it is critically important to remember that policies need to be applied as written and that all employees need to be treated in the same way. Treating one worker differently from another worker can cause claims of discrimination. Fair treatment of everyone not only makes for a better workplace environment but also helps the employer to avoid being sued.

I. Discrimination and Harassment

In the employment relationship, certain factors are illegal, and firing or demoting employees on the basis of these factors can be grounds for a lawsuit. These are the same restrictions that apply to hiring an employee. Any type of employment decision or harassment made on the basis of race, color, religion, sex or gender, national origin, disability, or age is illegal, and the U.S. Equal Employment Opportunity Commission or the Department of Education Office of Civil Rights will investigate accordingly. Even employees at will are protected against discrimination or harassment. An at-will employee can be fired at any time for any reason, *as long as it is not an illegal reason.*

In addition to hiring and firing decisions, the EEOC will generally investigate the following types of employment situations:

♦ Compensation, assignment, or classification of employees;

♦ Transfer, promotion, layoff, or recall;

♦ Job advertisements;

♦ Recruitment;

♦ Testing;

♦ Use of company facilities;

♦ Training and apprenticeship programs;

♦ Fringe benefits;

♦ Pay, retirement plans, and disability leave; and

♦ Other terms and conditions of employment.[62]

The laws involving discrimination are found in Title VII of the Civil Rights Act of 1964,[63] the Pregnancy Discrimination Act,[64] the Americans with Disabilities Act,[65] and the Age Discrimination in Employment Act.[66] The courts have interpreted these laws as also applying to situations where a worker is fired for a pretext, but is able to show that the real underlying reason was illegal discrimination.[67]

In addition, the Equal Employment Opportunity laws protect whistle-blowers and prohibit "retaliation against an individual for filing a charge of discrimination, participating in an investigation, or opposing discriminatory practices."[68] (Some other laws also protect whistle-blowers, including the Occupational Safety and Health Act.) Other types of discrimination that are prohibited by civil rights laws include:

♦ Harassment on the basis of race, color, religion, sex [gender], national origin, disability, or age;

♦ Employment decisions based on stereotypes or assumptions about the abilities, traits, or performance of individuals of a certain sex [gender], race, age, religion, or ethnic group, or individuals with disabilities;

♦ Denying employment opportunities to any person because of marriage to, or association with, an individual of a particular race, religion, national origin, or an individual with a disability; and

♦ Discrimination because of participation in schools or places of
   worship associated with a particular racial, ethnic, or religious
   group.[69]

Religious worship has sometimes led to discrimination claims.
Usually these claims involve not letting the person take time off for
worship. For example, suppose that Susan is one of four reference librarians at Metro University. Susan belongs to a religious group that
meets on Wednesday nights. The library can't force Susan to work on
Wednesday night if another librarian is available to take that time. On
the other hand, if all of the librarians worship on Wednesday night, it is
permissible for the organization to require that the four reference librarians take turns working on Wednesday nights.

Many states also have laws prohibiting discrimination or harassment on the basis of marital or parental status. Although Title VII of
the Civil Rights Act does not include these two classes of individuals,
some courts have found that discrimination on the basis of marital or
parental status can fall within the broader category of gender discrimination (discrimination on the basis of sex).

Although many people do not realize it, gender discrimination also
includes sexual harassment. If you are looking for laws about this topic,
you would need to use the words "gender," "gender discrimination," or
"sex discrimination," as well as "sexual harassment." The following
definition of sexual harassment comes from the Oshkosh, Wisconsin,
Public Library's policy:

> Sexual harassment is unwanted sexual attention of [a] persistent
> or offensive nature made by a person who knows, or reasonably
> should know, that such attention is unwanted. Sexual harassment in-
> cludes sexually oriented conduct that is sufficiently pervasive or se-
> vere to unreasonably interfere with an employee's job performance or
> create an intimidating, hostile, or offensive working environment.
> While sexual harassment encompasses a wide range of conduct, some
> examples of specifically prohibited conduct include:
>
> ♦ Promising, directly or indirectly, an employee a re-
>   ward if the employee complies with a sexually ori-
>   ented request;
>
> ♦ Threatening, directly or indirectly, to retaliate against
>   an employee if the employee refuses to comply with a
>   sexually oriented request;

♦ Denying, directly or indirectly, an employee an em-
ployment-related opportunity if the employee refuses
to comply with a sexually oriented request;

♦ Engaging in sexually suggestive physical contact or
touching another employee in a way that is unwelcome;

♦ Engaging in indecent exposure;

♦ Making sexual or romantic advances toward an employee and persisting despite the employee's rejection
of the advances;

♦ Deliberately displaying, storing, or transmitting pornographic or sexually oriented materials using . . . Library equipment or facilities in such a way as to harass
another employee.[70]

The Oshkosh policy is fairly typical of (and an excellent example
of) the definition of sexual harassment. The EEOC considers conduct to
be sexual harassment when:

(1) Submission to such conduct is made either explicitly or im-
plicitly a term or condition of an individual's employment,
(2) Submission to or rejection of such conduct by an individual
is used as the basis for employment decisions affecting such individual, or
(3) Such conduct has the purpose or effect of unreasonably inter-
fering with an individual's work performance or creating an intimidating, hostile, or offensive working environment.[71]

Courts have found two different types of harassment, namely *quid
pro quo* harassment and harassment that creates a *hostile work environment*. *Quid pro quo* harassment involves an explicit demand for sex
in exchange for promotion or continued employment. *Quid pro quo*
harassment also can involve job termination because of refusal to have
sexual relations. This request can be made by either gender to either
gender; the harassment is not limited to a male propositioning a female.

Harassment that creates a *hostile work environment* occurs when
the employee is made to feel unwelcome because of repeated sexual
jokes or references. In this situation, the worker is not fired or demoted,
but he or she is forced to be intolerably uncomfortable in the workplace. Pornographic images, sexual jokes or cartoons, and constant references to sex create a hostile work environment.

> Hostile work environment harassment is sexual harassment that
> . . . [is] severe or pervasive, offensive to the plaintiff, offensive to a
> reasonable person in the plaintiff's situation, and unwelcome. . . .
> [The] context matters.[72]

The problem with a hostile work environment is that the employee
is made to feel uncomfortable. The gender of the employee becomes an
issue because of constant comments, jokes, viewing of pornography,
and other inappropriate workplace actions. An example of hostile work
environment occurs in the case of *Harris v. Forklift Systems, Inc.*:[73]

> [T]he president of a company continually insults an employee
> because of her gender, suggests that her success with customers may
> be due to promises of sexual activity, and suggests that her salary
> could be negotiated with him in a motel room. . . . Even though no
> tangible job detriment occurred—the employee quit rather than con-
> tinue to endure the behavior—the gender-based conduct created an
> atmosphere in which the harasser's conduct may have made the
> plaintiff's job significantly more difficult to do because of her gen-
> der. The plaintiff suffered harm to be sure, but there did not appear to
> be a tangible job detriment.[74]

In a unanimous opinion, the U.S. Supreme Court found in favor of the
plaintiff, stating that this behavior did indeed form a hostile work environment.[75]

Under some circumstances, the employee may resign rather than
being fired. However, under certain circumstances, the resignation can
be considered to be similar to having been fired. If an employee quits
rather than face an intolerable situation, the law considers this to be a
constructive discharge.

> Constructive discharge has long been discussed in the context of
> employment discrimination and . . . resistance to union organizing.
> Constructive discharge may also be claimed in sexual harassment
> cases. An employee is constructively discharged if he or she resigns
> because "working conditions become so intolerable that a reasonable
> person in the employee's position would have felt compelled to re-
> sign. . . ."[76]

In recent years, there has been a great deal of litigation over the issue of whether an organization can be held responsible for the harass-
ing actions of its employees. Of course, if the harassment involves employment actions (such as terminating employment), the organization
can be held responsible. When job actions are not involved, employer

liability depends on how the situation has been handled. The general rule is that if an organization takes claims seriously by investigating them and punishing the perpetrators, there is no liability. However, if the organization knows or should have known about the harassment and does not take action, it can be held responsible.[77]

One recent case in the library world helps to illustrate the responsibility of management for a hostile work environment. In 2000, 12 librarians (known popularly as the "Minneapolis 12") at the central branch of the Minneapolis Public Library filed a complaint with the EEOC, stating that they were subjected to a hostile work environment.[78] The basis of their complaint was that library patrons were using computers to access pornography on the Internet, printing out pictures and leaving pornographic images on the computer screens.[79]

At the time of the complaint, the position of the American Library Association was that filtering was not acceptable, and the Minneapolis Public Library agreed with this stance. This case occurred just as the American Library Association was challenging the filtering requirements of the Children's Internet Protection Act.[80] (For more information on this issue, see *Chapter 10, Internet Use Policies and the Filtering Debate.*) In 2001, the Minneapolis 12 won their case before the EEOC, and eventually reached a settlement with the Minneapolis Public Library.

There were two reasons why the Minneapolis 12 were successful. One reason involved the filtering debate; the other reason, however, was because (unlike most libraries) the Minneapolis Public Library did not enforce a policy against patron use of pornography. Librarians were instructed to "avert their eyes" when they were near patrons who were accessing pornography.[81] According to the EEOC, this is simply not an acceptable way to handle these types of situations. The EEOC ruled that the library should have taken steps to help insure that patrons were not viewing pornography. Although this case became ensnared in the filtering debate, the EEOC noted that there were other steps that the library could have taken, such as more aggressive enforcement of the Minneapolis Public Library's existing policies against viewing pornography in the library.

The lesson for libraries is that they can be held responsible for the actions of patrons in creating a hostile work environment if the library does nothing to alleviate the situation. Even beyond the filtering issue, libraries need to have a written policy banning pornography. Libraries should enforce this policy, not only to protect their patrons, but also to avoid the creation of a hostile environment for the library workers.

J. The Americans with Disabilities Act

Congress passed the Americans with Disabilities Act (ADA) in 1990. Together with the Workforce Rehabilitation Act of 1973 (as amended), the ADA has done much to help people with disabilities to become part of the mainstream of American society. The idea of these two laws is that organizations such as libraries and archives must make their facilities handicapped-accessible, must treat individuals with disabilities fairly, and must make reasonable accommodations for individuals with disabilities.

The ADA and the Workforce Rehabilitation Act apply both to employees and to patrons. "An individual with a disability under the ADA is a person who has a physical or mental impairment that substantially limits one or more major life activities, has a record of such an impairment, or is regarded as having such an impairment. Major life activities are activities that an average person can perform with little or no difficulty such as walking, breathing, seeing, hearing, speaking, learning, and working."[82] It is illegal to discriminate against a qualified applicant who is able to perform the duties of the job simply because he or she has a disability. A disability is a factor that can't be considered at all, for any reason, provided that the worker is able to perform the functions of his or her job.[83] If the applicant is able to do the job with a reasonable accommodation, then the employer must make that accommodation.[84]

The employer is prohibited from asking questions about "the existence, nature, or severity of a disability" prior to making an employment offer.[85] The offer can be contingent on a medical examination, but only if the organization requires a medical examination for *all* employees in the same job category. This examination must be "job-related and consistent with business necessity."[86] As we have seen above, the medical exam may include a preemployment drug test.[87]

If the individual has a disability that prevents him or her from performing the job, but that disability can be alleviated with a reasonable accommodation, the organization is required to provide this reasonable accommodation. The only exception is if the accommodation would impose an undue hardship on the employer. Most of the time, this requirement means that very small organizations with limited budgets can claim an undue hardship if the accommodation is extremely expensive.[88] However, most organizations are able to make reasonable accommodations for their employees without incurring enormous expense. Some accommodations, such as making the building wheelchair accessible and adding ramps or lifts, should be done anyhow in order to serve the patrons of libraries and archives. Occasionally, if an accommodation is expensive compared to the entire budget of the organization, the employer might offer to split the cost with the worker. This is considered to be a reasonable accommodation under the ADA.[89]

Some additional examples of reasonable accommodations include: "job restructuring; modification of work schedules; providing additional unpaid leave; reassignment to a vacant position; acquiring or modifying equipment or devices; adjusting or modifying examinations, training materials, or policies; and providing qualified readers or interpreters."[90]

There are some myths about the ADA. For example, while the statute does cover people with mental illnesses, it does not require that the organization lower its expectations for workers. If an organization requires workers to be collegial and not to intimidate or harass other employees, mental illness is not an excuse for hostile behavior. The worker cannot claim that he or she is behaving in an intimidating manner because of mental illness.

In addition, alcoholism and drug abuse are not protected by the ADA, and in certain circumstances the employer can require and enforce a drug-free workplace policy. (See the section above on drug testing.) However, the employer is prohibited from discriminating against people *who are recovering* alcoholics or drug addicts. The fact that an employee has had a problem with substance abuse *in the past* is not a legal reason to discriminate. However, should such an employee "fall off the wagon," he or she would be subject to the same sanctions as other workers. As with mental illness, the organization can and should hold workers with such disabilities to the same standards of behavior and performance in the workplace as all other employees.[91]

A major ADA issue for libraries and archives involves making Websites accessible to patrons with disabilities. This is important both for employees and for patrons, and is required by section 508 of the Rehabilitation Act.[92] All organizations that receive Federal funding must follow these accessibility provisions. In most cases, the necessary changes are very easy to make, and frequently can be done at the time the Website is built just by using good site design.

The basic premise of the ADA in the employment situation can be summed up as follows:

> The lesson . . . is that an employer cannot put its head in the sand and ignore requests for an accommodation. Rather, when a request for accommodation is received, an employer must analyze that request and

enter into an interactive process to determine whether a reasonable accommodation exists or is appropriate. Ignoring the situation or saying no without doing anything more may land an employer in court.[93]

In addition to employment law, the ADA also has provisions that apply to serving library patrons with disabilities. There are many resources available on this topic. The Scarecrow Press support Website for this book lists several valuable sources that discuss serving library patrons with disabilities. In addition, the Website lists articles about Website accessibility under section 508, as well as articles about the ADA and employees with disabilities.

K. The Family and Medical Leave Act

The Family and Medical Leave Act (FMLA)[94] was passed in 1993. The purpose of the law is to help employees who need to take time off from work because of their own illness or the illness of a close family member. Organizations that employ 50 or more people are subject to the provisions of this law, as are employees of public agencies and of public or private schools (regardless of the number of employees).[95]

Since most libraries are either public agencies, part of a school, or employ over 50 people, the Family and Medical Leave Act would apply to them. A more difficult question is whether a small nonprofit library or archive is covered by the Act. The courts have not yet addressed this question, but I suspect that such a decision will be based upon whether or not the organization is considered to be a public entity because of public support.

Employers who are covered by the Family and Medical Leave Act must grant leave to their employees. The FMLA allows workers to take an unpaid leave for up to 12 weeks during any 12-month period. The FMLA provides for leave for the following reasons:

- ♦ For the birth and care of the newborn child of the employee;
- ♦ For placement with the employee of a son or daughter for adoption or foster care;
- ♦ To care for an immediate family member (spouse, child, or parent) with a serious health condition; [or]
- ♦ To take medical leave when the employee is unable to work because of a serious health condition.[96]

During the time that an employee is on leave under the Family and Medical Leave Act, he or she will still be covered by all of the normal employment benefits. The employee will get his or her previous position back when the leave has ended. Employment contracts, collective bargaining agreements, and personnel policies may also provide for additional time off for family or medical situations, so it is very important to check with your employer as to how their policies are structured.

Sometimes employment benefits can be coordinated with the FMLA in order to help provide an income while taking time off of work. Some employers ask the worker to use up sick leave and vacation time first, since those are paid leaves. These provisions are for the benefit of the worker, as they help to keep income during the period taken off.

The FMLA applies to all covered employees, regardless of whether they accumulate any vacation time or sick leave. The FMLA helps to protect workers who qualify to take time off because of a new child, their own illness, or the illness of an immediate family member. The FMLA is also economically important, as it helps to preserve employment for those who need temporary leave and might otherwise be tempted to quit their jobs.

Employers should be careful to distinguish leaves under FMLA from worker's compensation situations. Worker's compensation pays for injuries suffered on the job and includes provisions for disability leave while the injured person recovers. This type of leave is different from the FMLA and is subject to different laws.

Worker's compensation is entirely a state issue, except for Federal employees or employees of railroads. Each state has its own worker's compensation laws. The Federal government also has worker's compensation laws that pertain to Federal employees, as well as a separate disability provision for railroad workers. Librarians and archivists should check their state laws to determine what the procedures are and what kinds of events will trigger a worker's compensation claim. Some librarians working for railroad companies may fall within the provisions of the Federal railroad disability policies.

Just as the Americans with Disabilities Act helps to level the playing field for workers with disabilities, the Family and Medical Leave Act helps those workers who are ill, those workers who have family members who are ill, and those workers who are bringing a new child into their family. The Family and Medical Leave Act provides a mechanism for a worker to take time off from work when temporary situations occur while not putting his or her job at risk.

Conclusion

Employment law is a complicated field, but it is one that every employer and every employee should understand. Librarians and archivists must abide by employment law. Some of the guidelines of employment law, such as the difference between independent contractors and employees, are important in other areas of law as well. For example, the work-for-hire doctrine in copyright law makes a distinction between employees and independent contractors, and the ownership of intellectual property rights depends on whether an individual is an employee or an independent contractor. The elements of agency law are also important for understanding the responsibilities of officers and board members of for-profit and nonprofit organizations.

A supervisor who plays favorites is helping to create a management problem, since workers usually notice and disapprove of disparate treatment. Moreover, this type of behavior may lead to the creation of legal issues. All policies should be adhered to as written, and all workers should be treated equally.

By understanding legal requirements, libraries and archives will be able to stay within the law when hiring and firing workers. It is vital that organizations provide *written* policies relating to hiring and firing, as well as to discrimination and sexual harassment. These policies should be adhered to without fail, and should be changed if they are not practical. Finally, problems with workers should always be documented, and the employee should be told what he or she did that was wrong.

A library or archive that follows these rules will be much less likely to be sued and will operate more efficiently. Knowledge of employment and workplace law will go a long way towards helping to make the workplace both efficient and legal. Thus, libraries and archives will be places of learning and not arenas for contention.

Table 11.1. Inappropriate and Appropriate Uses of Personal Questions

Question	Inappropriate	Appropriate
Marital Status	◆ Are you married? ◆ Is this your maiden or married name? ◆ With whom do you live?	◆ After hiring, marital status must be indicated on tax and insurance forms.
Parental Status	◆ How many kids do you have? ◆ Do you plan to have children? ◆ Are you pregnant?	◆ After hiring, dependent information must be indicated on tax and insurance forms.
Age	◆ How old are you? ◆ What year were you born? ◆ When did you graduate from high school [or college]? ◆ What year did you get your MLS?	◆ Before hiring, asking if [the candidate is] over the legal minimum age for the hours or working conditions to comply with state or Federal labor laws. ◆ After hiring, verifying legal minimum age with a birth certificate or other ID, and asking age on insurance forms. ◆ Asking for information on degrees, licensure, or certification.
National Origin	◆ Where were you [or your parents] born? ◆ What is your heritage?	◆ Verifying legal U.S. residence or work visa status.
Race or Skin Color	◆ What race are you? ◆ Are you a member of a minority group? ◆ Are you married to a member of a minority group?	◆ [Giving a] general indication that you are an equal opportunity employer. ◆ Asking race only as required for affirmative-action programs.

Question	Inappropriate	Appropriate
Religion or Creed	◆ What religion are you? ◆ Which religious holidays will you be taking off? ◆ Do you attend church regularly?	◆ Contacting religious or other organizations related to the candidate's beliefs that are listed as employers or references.
Criminal Record	◆ Have you ever been arrested? ◆ Have you ever been in jail?	◆ [Asking] about convictions by civil or military courts, if accompanied by a disclaimer that the candidate's answers will not necessarily cause loss of job opportunity. ◆ [Asking] about specific convictions, if related to fitness to perform the job. Except for law enforcement and security clearance, employers can ask only about convictions and not about arrests.
Disability	◆ Do you have any disabilities? ◆ What's your medical history? ◆ How does your condition affect your abilities?	◆ Asking if the candidate can perform specific duties of the job. ◆ After hiring, asking about medical history on insurance forms.

Source: J. Steven Niznik, *Illegal Interview Questions*, About.com (2003), *available at* http://jobsearchtech.about.com/od/interview/l/aa022403_2.htm.

12

Forming a Nonprofit Organization

Many libraries and archives are founded as nonprofit agencies. In order to organize a new nonprofit library or archive, information professionals need to be aware of the legal requirements for these types of organizations. The principles of forming a nonprofit association can also come in handy when dealing with fund-raising issues. As governmental units look for ways to reduce their deficits, charitable groups such as the Friends of the Library become more important. In addition, many libraries and archives have established private foundations to solicit and handle donations. (Although governmental entities may accept donations, private foundations are often used because the money does not go away at the end of the fiscal year.) Because of these various situations, librarians and archivists need to understand the basic formation of a nonprofit organization.

Nonprofit associations are "private, self-governing, non-profit-distributing, voluntary, and of public benefit."[1] Nonprofit organizations are chartered by the states in which they are located. Most nonprofit organizations fall within the categories of education, health, religion, social services, arts and recreation, advocacy or legal services, or international aid. Libraries, naturally, fit within the educational category.

Being chartered as a nonprofit is not the same thing as being tax-exempt. The term "tax-exempt" refers to a status granted by the Internal Revenue Service. Once the IRS grants tax-exempt status, the nonprofit association will not have to pay income tax. Most nonprofit organizations that are tax-exempt fall within the provisions of section 501(c)(3) of the Internal Revenue Code.[2] Individuals or corporations that donate to tax-exempt 501(c)(3) organizations will be able to deduct the donations on their income tax returns.

Once an organization is recognized as tax-exempt under section 501(c)(3), it is then classified either as a foundation or as a public charity. According to *Black's Law Dictionary*, a foundation is a "Permanent fund established and maintained by contributions for charitable, educated [sic], religious or other benevolent purpose."[3] For example, a library or archive would be classified under section 501(c)(3) as being a foundation.

A subdivision within the realm of foundations is known as a *private foundation*. Private foundations usually distribute their money to other nonprofits or to individuals in the form of grants. An example of a private foundation would be an organization such as the Carnegie Foundation or the Ford Foundation.

Sometimes a private foundation is established to support a single organization. Instead of giving grants to applicants, the private foundation only gives grants to one organization. Libraries that are governmental, such as public libraries or academic libraries at a state university, sometimes establish private foundations in order to handle donations and provide more flexibility.

For example, the Louis and Anne Abrons Foundation is a private foundation in New York. This foundation does not accept applications; instead, it gives gifts only to preselected organizations. At the time the foundation was set up, the donors decided which nonprofit associations would receive money. One of the organizations that receives money from the Abrons foundation is the New York Public Library. In 2002 (the most recent year for which data is available at the time of writing), the foundation gave the New York Public Library a $25,000 grant for operating support.

It is important to note the distinctions between a private foundation and a public charity:

> [P]ublic charities generally derive their funding or support primarily from the general public, receiving grants from individuals, government, and private foundations. Although some public charities engage in grantmaking activities, most conduct direct service or other tax-exempt activities. A private foundation, on the other hand, usually derives its principal fund from a single source, such as an individual, family, or corporation, and more often than not is a grantmaker. A private foundation does not solicit funds from the public.[4]

Thus, public charities and private foundations differ both in the source and the destination of their funding. Friends of the Library groups would be considered to be public charities because they conduct direct service. These groups "generally derive their funding or support primarily from the general public, receiving grants from individuals, government, and private foundations."[5]

According to the Minnesota Council on Nonprofits, most nonprofit organizations typically go through four stages of development. These stages are not always exclusive, and can sometimes overlap. However, the Minnesota model provides a general overview of the birth of many nonprofits:

1. Many organizations start out as an informal organization. Your organization can continue with programs and activities informally as long as revenues do not exceed $25,000 per year and the organization does not employ anyone.

2. As donations and activities grow, the organization may find a fiscal sponsor to aid with reporting requirements, [to perform] administrative tasks, and to lend their tax-exempt status. This allows the organization to continue to focus its attention on programs.

3. An organization may then incorporate at the state level and . . . begin to establish itself on its own.

4. Finally, the organization may apply for tax-exempt status from the Internal Revenue Service. If accepted, the organization is now able to accept tax-deductible donations and is responsible [for] following regulations set by the IRS and the state, and for reporting annually to the IRS [and] Secretary of State's Office. . . .[6]

When an organization incorporates, it becomes an artificial person. The association can buy and sell property, take out loans, and pay employees. Furthermore, informal organizations are not able to get tax-exempt status without being incorporated. Many grantmakers, foundations, and donors won't work with organizations that are not incorporated.

Incorporating also limits personal liability. A nonprofit organization is really a form of corporation; just as businesses incorporate to limit their liability, so do nonprofits. Since the nonprofit is an artificial person, it incurs liability for lawsuits separate from the people who operate it.

Once an association makes the decision to incorporate, an officer or director should obtain specific information about how the process works in his or her state. In most states, incorporation is a function of the Secretary of State's office. Sometimes a great deal of information can be found on the Secretary of State's Website. It is often wise to consult with an attorney during the incorporation stage.[7]

Since obtaining nonprofit status from the state is different from obtaining tax-exempt status from the IRS, there are some differences in the requirements for preparing operating documents. Officers and directors need to read the IRS Website and consult the local IRS office before incorporating. Advance research will help avoid the need to re-write the articles of incorporation or bylaws.

Forming a Mission Statement and Selecting a Board

The first two steps in establishing a nonprofit association take place almost simultaneously. These steps are the selection of a board of directors (sometimes also known as a board of trustees), and the creation of a mission statement. Since the board of directors is responsible by law for the governing of an incorporated organization, the directors should be individuals who can bring expertise to their tasks. Often this means finding board members who are dedicated to the mission of the organization or who are involved with similar organizations. For example, when founding a public library, certain professionals can prove highly valuable as board members. School administrators, museum directors, the president of the local historical society, an accountant, or a lawyer could greatly assist in the formation of a library. By including professionals with an expertise in the area of the nonprofit, the new board will be able to take advantage of the knowledge that the board members bring with them. Of course, nonprofits should always have a written code of ethics that determines, among other things, how board members will handle conflicts of interest.[8]

When choosing a board, be sure that the people you select are willing to roll up their sleeves and work. Many organizations grant board membership to someone they wish to honor, or to philanthropists who they hope will give large donations. I would not recommend this practice. It is especially important at the very beginning to have a governing board that is composed of people who will work together to advance the mission of the organization.

There is a significant difference between a governing board and an advisory board (also sometimes called an advisory group). Advisory groups function to provide guidance to an organization. An advisory group does not have legal responsibility for governing the organization. Instead, an advisory group can be thought of as a type of focus group:

> An advisory group is a collection of individuals who bring unique knowledge and skills which complement the knowledge and skills of the formal board members. . . . Advisory groups are some-

times used, too, to provide membership which gives status to people, for example, retired CEOs, board chairs or major contributors.

The advisory group does not have formal authority to govern the organization. . . . Rather, the advisory group serves to make recommendations and/or provide key information and materials to the formal board of directors.

The advisory group can be standing (or ongoing) or ad hoc (one-time) in nature.[9]

Forming an advisory group is a good way to bring expertise to an organization. Libraries that are part of a larger organization (school or academic libraries, governmental public libraries, etc.) will find value in using the experience of experts in related fields. As a secondary benefit, many libraries have found that advisory groups are also good for public relations.

At the same time that the board of directors is being recruited, the organization should also be working on a mission statement. Ultimately the board of directors will need to ratify the mission statement. "Draft a mission statement that further refines your broad charitable purpose while providing your founding body of individuals with some realistic and concrete objectives toward which the body may direct its collective energies."[10]

The mission statement is very important because it helps to proclaim to the world what the organization does. The statement should be general and brief, no more than a few paragraphs long. The mission statement explains what the nonprofit organization is trying to do, and how the organization will impact society. "A mission statement should be brief, timeless, and descriptive of what the organization is trying to accomplish. This statement will guide the organization through its initial formation, program development, growth and change."[11]

The following example from the New York Public Library illustrates an effective mission statement:

The New York Public Library is one of the cornerstones of the American tradition of equal opportunity. It provides free and open access to the accumulated wisdom of the world, without distinction as to income, religion, nationality, or other human condition. It is everyone's university; the scholar's and author's haven; the statesman's, scientist's, and businessman's essential resource; the nation's memory. It guarantees freedom of information and independence of thought. It enables each individual to pursue learning at his/her own personal level of interest, preparation, ability, and desire. It helps ensure the free trade in ideas and the right of dissent.

The mission of The New York Public Library is to use its available resources in a balanced program of collecting, cataloging, and conserving books and other materials, and providing ready access directly to individual library users and to users elsewhere through cooperating libraries and library networks. The New York Public Library's responsibility is to serve as a great storehouse of knowledge at the heart of one of the world's information centers, and to function as an integral part of a fabric of information and learning that stretches across the nation and the world.[12]

Note how effectively the New York Public Library's statement analyzes its goals, defines whom it seeks to serve, and explains how it will affect and enhance society—all this in a well-written, idealistic document. A mission statement should always be brief, yet should explain to the world what the organization does. Notice also that the New York Public Library's mission statement was revised in 2001. An organization's board of directors should review the mission statement every few years to ensure that it is still relevant to the goals and activities of the organization.

Having established a board and developed a mission statement, the association needs to obtain an Employer Identification Number (EIN). The EIN functions in the same way for an organization that a social security number does for an individual. An association must have an Employee Identification Number in order to open a bank account, to incorporate, or to hire employees. The Internal Revenue Service is the entity that assigns the EIN.[13]

Another step that must be taken prior to incorporation is to select a name and to make sure that the name is available. Since a specific name can only be used by one specific organization, the name's availability needs to be established. The Secretary of State's office can assist the board members in determining whether the selected name is available. Some states have placed their incorporation database on the Web.

Once the organization has selected a name, it should be reserved with the Secretary of State. This will help to ensure that no other entity will take the name that has been selected. Watch out for names that are confusingly similar to the names of other organizations, as there might be some trademark implications to the name that has been selected. (For more information, see *Chapter 6*, *Trademark and Trade Secret Law*.) Only after the name has been selected and reserved should the organization begin to prepare articles of incorporation and bylaws.

Creating the Governing Documents

A. Articles of Incorporation

After selecting the board, writing the mission statement, and deciding on a name, the next step is to create the articles of incorporation and bylaws for the organization. Each state has different requirements for the format of the articles of incorporation (sometimes called a charter or a constitution). Once again, the Secretary of State's office can assist with the preparation of these documents. Most states require that the articles of incorporation contain the legal name of the organization, its location, and its purpose, as well as a statement about how the nonprofit is to be managed.

The articles of incorporation should also explain what would happen to the organization in the event that it is dissolved. Although not required by most states, this language is required by the Internal Revenue Service in order to obtain tax-exempt status under section 501(c)(3) of the Internal Revenue Code. The dissolution section of the articles of incorporation must state that after all of the debts are completely paid, all property and money remaining should be given to another tax-exempt organization, or should be distributed by the court of general jurisdiction in the county of incorporation. Here is an example of a dissolution clause from the Greater Cincinnati Library Association:

> Upon the dissolution of the corporation, or in case the work of the corporation should be abandoned, all title to real and personal property of the corporation remaining after the debts of the corporation have been paid shall be distributed as the trustees may determine for one or more exempt purposes within the meaning of Section 501(c)(3) of the Internal Revenue Code of 1986, or the corresponding section of any future tax code, or shall be distributed to the federal government or to a state or local government for a public purpose. Any of such assets not so disposed of shall be disposed of by the Court of Common Pleas of the county in which the principal office of the Corporation is then located, exclusively for such purposes, or to such organization or organizations as such Court shall determine which are organized and operated exclusively for such purpose.[14]

The articles of incorporation must give the name and address of an agent for the service of legal notices. The articles must also state how the organization is going to be governed. There are two different types of governance for nonprofit organizations—membership organizations and self-perpetuating organizations. In a membership group (such as a Friends of the Libraries chapter or the Special Libraries Association), the members elect the board and the officers. In a self-perpetuating group, the board of directors selects the officers and also nominates future board members. Most libraries use the self-perpetuating form of government. In some states, the board may actually be designated as the sole member of the organization for purposes of governance.[15]

In order to gain tax-exempt status, the articles of incorporation must also state that the association is organized and operated exclusively for one of the purposes (charitable, scientific, or educational) within the meaning of section 501(c)(3) of the Internal Revenue Code. In addition, the following clause must be included in the articles of incorporation:

> No substantial part of the activities of this corporation shall consist of carrying on propaganda, or otherwise attempting to influence legislation, and the corporation shall not participate or intervene in any political campaign (including the publishing or distribution of statements) on behalf of any candidate for public office.[16]

In other words, the organization must avoid involvement in political activities. If the IRS determines that the entity is really a political action committee (PAC), tax-exempt status will be denied. This restriction will be discussed in greater detail below in the section on obtaining and retaining tax-exempt status.

The other statement that the IRS requires in the governing documents is that the earnings of the corporation will not be distributed to the directors, officers, or members of the association. In other words, the entity must not make and distribute profits. This is the basic difference between a for-profit corporation and a nonprofit corporation. The statement about non-distribution of profits may be placed either in the articles of incorporation or in the bylaws. (I recommend placing this required statement in the articles of incorporation, so that it is immediately clear that the organization is in fact a nonprofit.) Here is an example of a statement about non-distribution of profits:

> No part of the net earnings of the Library shall inure to the benefit of, or be distributable to its directors, officers, or other private persons except that the Library shall be authorized and empowered to pay reasonable compensation for services rendered and to make payments and distributions in furtherance of the purposes set forth herein. . . .[17]

B. Creating Bylaws

Once the articles of incorporation have been created, the next step is to draft the bylaws. The bylaws are the governing rules for the association. They must not be in conflict with the articles of incorporation. The articles of incorporation are very difficult to amend, and changes must be filed with the Secretary of State's office. For that reason, specific points, such as how officers are elected or how committees are created, should be placed in the bylaws.

Bylaws usually are relatively easy to change, and generally contain a process for amendment. The following items should be included in the bylaws:

◆ Membership—if the organization will have members, who they are, how/when membership meetings will occur, what notice is required for meetings, requirements of a special meeting, quorum, and voting;

◆ Board of directors—number, election process, meetings, length of term, number of terms allowed, vacancies, removals, quorum, officers, and standing committees;

◆ Fiscal management—fiscal year, and committee/officer responsibilities, compensation of directors, reporting requirements and dues;

◆ Amendments—how will amendments be made and approved.[18]

Sometimes bylaws enumerate what the organization is allowed to do, and what it is not allowed to do. Provisions that direct what the association may do can limit the board, officers, and staff of the organization, so I recommend not including this type of provision in the bylaws. If the bylaws don't have enumerated duties, the board, officers, and staff will have the maximum amount of flexibility to do their jobs.

Another item that is often included in the bylaws is a statement about which committees may be formed. (I recommend that this statement be limited to the most important board committees, such as the long-range planning, personnel, nominations, and finance/audit committees. For more information on the formation of an audit committee, see the section below on the Sarbanes-Oxley Act.) It is a good idea to maintain flexibility with a general statement allowing the board to create whatever committees or task forces it deems necessary, whether standing or ad hoc.

Finally, the bylaws must clearly state what the process is for amendment. For example, the bylaws of the Greater Cincinnati Library Consortium have the following provisions for amendment:

> Any member of the Directors' Council may propose amendments to these By-Laws by submitting the proposed changes in writing for consideration at a meeting of the Council. All proposed changes shall be submitted to the membership by mail at least fifteen (15) days before the final vote. The amendments may be adopted by a two-third (2/3) vote at the next consecutive meeting of the Council.[19]

Effective bylaws are an important part of an organization. Because these are the rules by which the organization is governed, the bylaws must be clear, and they must be followed. Of course, if parts of the bylaws are not working, then these sections should be amended.

C. Ethics for Board Members

Because the board is ultimately responsible for the governance of the organization, there is a *fiduciary duty* for board members to act in an ethical fashion. (The term "fiduciary duty" means that there is a legal duty for the board member to act in the best interests of the organization.) There are three main fiduciary duties that a board member owes to the association: (1) the duty of care, (2) the duty of loyalty, and (3) the duty of obedience.

The *duty of care* means that when the trustee is working on behalf of the organization, he or she should "exercise the care an ordinary person would employ in dealing with that person's own property."[20] The duty of care includes the following elements:

> A director must actively participate in the management of the organization including attending meetings of the board, evaluating reports, reading minutes, reviewing the performance and compensation of the Executive Director. . . . [The director has] the duty to protect, preserve, invest and manage the corporation's property and to do so consistent with donor restrictions and legal requirements. . . .
>
> A director should have general knowledge [and insure the accuracy] of the books and records of the organization as well as its general operation. . . . This may mean the director must take steps to require regular audits by an independent certified public accountant . . . .
>
> A director has a duty to investigate warnings or reports of officer or employee theft or mismanagement . . . [and] to report misconduct to the appropriate authorities, such as the police or the Attorney

General. Where appropriate, a director should consult an attorney or other professional for assistance.[21]

One of the most important duties a board member has is to evaluate the performance of the chief officer of the organization. As one commentator has stated:

> [D]irectors are legally responsible to oversee organizational affairs. This responsibility includes evaluation of the chief officer. It even includes reprimanding the chief officer or terminating his or her employment if circumstances warrant. . . . If a chief officer acts unethically or illegally he or she should be confronted. . . . If abuses are not curtailed when discovered, more abuses will occur. Soon, the integrity of the entire organization will be compromised. . . .
>
> Chief officers should be selected at least in part for their administrative skills. The chief officer should also have the ability to attract and maintain generous donors and to be skilled in carrying out the organization's mission.[22]

The second duty that a board member has is the *duty of loyalty*. This means that the board member must be acting in the best interests of the organization at all times. "It is a duty which embraces fairness, good faith and honesty. It is the intention to advance and protect the organization free of any conflicts of interest or self-dealing. . . . It requires directors to act without contemplating any direct or indirect personal financial gain or business opportunity."[23]

A director must refrain from self-dealing and avoid conflicts of interest. An example of self-dealing would be when a board member votes himself a salary or a loan. (This is where many of the problems have occurred in the recent corporate scandals.) Self-dealing is usually an intentional dereliction of duty.

On the other hand, however, conflicts of interest can arise in an innocent way. For example, if the director of the local historical society is a member of a library board, there may be times when both institutions are applying for the same grant or are approaching the same donor. In these situations, the board member should disclose the conflict and recuse himself or herself from participating in any discussion as well as from voting on the issue.

Sometimes a board member might decide (or be requested) to be absent while a decision is being discussed that could present a potential conflict of interest. By not attending the meeting where a conflict of interest is being discussed, the board member helps to reduce the conflict. Other examples of conflicts of interest include:

- ◆ Performing professional services for a fee for the organization;[24]
- ◆ Proposing that a relative or friend be considered for a staff position;[25]
- ◆ A board member serving on two boards . . . who finds himself in the position of approaching the same donors on behalf of both organizations;[26]
- ◆ A staff member receiving an honorarium for conducting a workshop for another group in the organization's field of interest.[27]

In some cases, association members or donors can challenge a decision in court on the grounds that there has been a conflict of interest and that the directors have violated their fiduciary duties. The basic argument in this type of a lawsuit is that the directors have not had the best interests of the organization in mind. Careful monitoring of potential conflicts and adherence to board policies relating to conflicts can help to avoid this type of problem.

If a conflict of interest is disclosed and the board makes a decision in an objective manner, there should be no problems. However, in the absence of disclosure, these kinds of actions can lead to two important problems, namely, "legal challenges and public misunderstanding."[28]

Board members must avoid conflicts of interest and the appearance of such conflicts. "Like Caesar's wife, board members must be 'above suspicion.'"[29]

If the board members have conflicts of interest, the public or the members of the group will lose confidence in the organization. In addition, donors and foundations often will not provide funds to organizations that are not well managed. Foundations will frequently ask for copies of the articles of incorporation, the bylaws, and the policies for handling conflicts of interest before they will consider a grant proposal.

Some of the steps that boards should take to avoid even the appearance of problems include:

- ◆ Adopting a conflict-of-interest policy that prohibits or limits business transactions with board members and requires board members to disclose potential conflicts;
- ◆ Disclosing conflicts when they occur so that board members who are voting on a decision are aware that another member's interests are being affected;

◆   Requiring board members to withdraw from decisions that present a potential conflict;

◆   Establishing procedures, such as competitive bids, that ensure that the organization is receiving fair value in the transaction.[30]

The third duty that directors have is the *duty of obedience* to the organization's mission and to the law. The directors must be aware of, understand, and support the organization's mission and its nonprofit goals. Obedience to the law requires directors to "ensure that board policies and decisions obey the law. Management is responsible to ensure that its actions obey the law."[31]

While the board is responsible for the legal governance of an organization, the officers and staff are in fact responsible for the day-to-day workings. The board should allow the officers and the staff to do their jobs without being micromanaged. The board must govern and the staff must manage.[32] When a board tries to manage, conflict and tension can result. While the board has ultimate responsibilities for the actions of the officers, under most circumstances board members need to let the officers do their jobs. The board has specific duties, the officers have specific duties, and these duties are separate.

> Directors do not have power or authority individually. A board's decision-making ability lies in its group structure. While at times an individual board member may become extensively involved with one particular program area and be working with staff, this is usually temporary, and information regarding the need for increased attention by that board member should be relayed regularly to the full board. . . .[33]

The duties of the board of a nonprofit organization include:

> [S]electing and working with the executive director, amending bylaws, approving the annual budget and long-term strategic plans, and ensuring its own succession.[34]

The board may create committees, subgroups, or working groups for certain areas such as finances, auditing, fund-raising, long-term planning, and personnel:

> Through such committees, the board assists management in policy formation and strategic planning. While nonprofit staff may conceive, develop and implement the organization's plan, the board will often monitor the process and provide counsel. However, it is often

true that in smaller, younger nonprofits with limited staff positions or experience, or in more grass-roots type organizations, board duties may include more tasks typically associated with management.[35]

The best way to manage an organization is for the board and the officers to work together. The board often contains people with great expertise whose knowledge can be used to help provide guidance. Some ways in which an executive officer can help to foster good board relations include:

- ◆ Use a comprehensive strategic plan that has been developed in conjunction with the board, and supplement it with regular progress reports. . . . Regular reports based on this plan will keep board members apprised of progress toward organizational goals, and provide part of the basis for evaluation of the executive director.

- ◆ Provide the board with relevant materials before board meetings. . . . Let board members know how specific agenda items relate to the organization's larger mission, and what kind of action or discussion is desired of the board on each item.

- ◆ Facilitate board and board committee discussions so that the board stays focused on the larger issues. Refer to set policies that define the limits of the board's decision-making power, and strive to engage the board in a dialogue among themselves that leads to consensus-building.[36]

Good communication between the executive officers and the board will help to prevent problems, while allowing everyone to fulfill his or her duties. Board members have legal and ethical duties to the organization, but the executives and staff are responsible for day-to-day management. When the board and the management work together, the organization is better able to pursue its mission.

D. The Sarbanes-Oxley Act and Nonprofits

One very important duty of the board is to review the financial transactions of the organization in order to help identify potential problems before they arise, or to help alleviate problems once they have occurred. In the wake of the Enron collapse and the accounting scandals that came to light in 2001 and 2002, Congress passed the Sarbanes-Oxley Act of 2002.[37] Although this statute was crafted for profit-making companies, many auditors have applied the law to nonprofits as well.

The Sarbanes-Oxley Act states that organizations should have an audit committee, chaired by an outside director (i.e., one who is not also an officer of the organization). The audit committee must have the ability to request any financial records or documents it wishes. The audit committee also has the right to conduct investigations, including hiring an outside auditor or attorney, if needed. Nonprofits can satisfy the requirements of the Sarbanes-Oxley Act by doing the following:

♦ Create an audit committee (if you do not already have one), and ensure it is active and aware. In a smaller organization, the finance committee can also function as the audit committee. [Remember that this is the *board's* finance committee, *not* the financial committee of the officers and staff.]

♦ Have your CEO and CFO publicly attest to the accuracy, completeness, and fairness of your financial statements (Form 990, if you use that as a public financial statement), and to the adequacy of your internal accounting controls.

♦ Publicly disclose that you have adopted, and follow, a code of ethics for senior management and the governing board. If you do not have such a code, adopt one at once!

♦ Consider very carefully all transactions between your organization and any "insider," including executive compensation and fringe benefits and perks. "Insiders" (sometimes called Related Parties) include: organization officers, directors, trustees, and management in decision-making positions, major donors, and members of the immediate families of any of the preceding; controlled and affiliated organizations and trusts; and businesses in which any of the preceding are in significant positions of authority (owner or manager). Would you be even slightly embarrassed to read details of these transactions in your local newspaper?[38]

According to Sherron Watkins (the accountant who pointed out Enron's financial and ethical problems), "Corporate governance on paper means jack all. . . . Procedures mean jack all. It's more about the relationship between the board and upper management."[39] The proper way to handle this type of relationship is, as former President Ronald Reagan often said, to "Trust, but verify."[40]

Although the provisions of the Sarbanes-Oxley Act are not yet required for nonprofit organizations, every association should consider adopting these provisions. The Sarbanes-Oxley Act provides a useful model for good fiscal governance. More and more funding agencies and organizations are demanding compliance with the Sarbanes-Oxley Act, since these provisions help to assure transparency. In addition, the Attorney General of New York has proposed regulations for nonprofits that mirror Sarbanes-Oxley.[41] As a result, a wise nonprofit will follow these new rules.

Obtaining and Maintaining Tax-Exempt Status

Once an association has been registered with the state as a nonprofit, it is time to apply for tax-exempt status from the IRS. This is a very important step for an organization. If the nonprofit fails to obtain tax-exempt status, it will have to pay income tax on any revenues. In addition, individuals or corporations that donate money to non-tax-exempt organizations will not be able to take an income tax deduction. Finally, most foundations will only award grants to tax-exempt nonprofits.

The main rules for tax-exempt status are found in sections 501 and 509 of the Internal Revenue Code. The rules for private foundations are contained in section 509.[42] Most nonprofits, however, operate under the rules of section 501(c)(3). Only donations to 501(c)(3) organizations are deductible on the donor's income tax return.

In order to apply for tax-exempt status, an officer of the organization must fill out IRS form 1023, *Application for Recognition of Exemption*.[43] The application must include copies of the articles of incorporation and bylaws, and these documents must contain certain required clauses. (For more details, see the sections above on articles of incorporation and bylaws.) The application must also include a narrative description of the activities and history of the organization, along with financial data and balance sheets. The IRS also asks for financial and compensation information for officers, directors, trustees, employees, and independent contractors. This requirement ensures that profits are not being distributed in the same manner as in a for-profit organization.

Filing for tax-exempt status as soon as possible is essential. If form 1023 is filed within 27 months from the date the organization is incorporated, the IRS will consider the association to be tax-exempt *from the date of formation*. Otherwise, the tax-exempt status will not begin until the date that the IRS receives the form.[44]

In order for libraries to obtain and maintain tax-exempt status under section 501(c)(3) of the Internal Revenue Code, the type of activities and amount of money spent on lobbying or political advocacy must be limited.[45] Political action committees are not eligible for tax-exempt status. Section 501(c)(3) only grants tax-exempt status if:

> No substantial part of the activities [consists of] carrying on propaganda, or otherwise attempting, to influence legislation (except as otherwise provided in subsection (h)), and [the organization] does not participate in, or intervene in (including the publishing or distributing of statements), any political campaign on behalf of (or in opposition to) any candidate for public office.[46]

This is an important point for librarians and archivists to remember. A tax-exempt association such as a library or archive must *never* endorse candidates or engage in political campaigns. Activities associated with elections will cause the organization to lose its tax-exempt status, which means that potential donors will not be able to deduct contributions.

In order to remain within the law and avoid the appearance of endorsing a candidate, libraries should open their meeting rooms to all groups. If the Republican candidate can use the meeting room, the Democratic candidate should be able to use it as well. This type of balance is in accordance with the *Library Bill of Rights*, which states that: "Libraries which make exhibit spaces and meeting rooms available to the public they serve should make such facilities available on an equitable basis, regardless of the beliefs or affiliations of individuals or groups requesting their use."[47]

The following types of activities are considered by the IRS to be "electioneering" and their existence in a library can cause problems with an organization's tax-exempt status:

♦ Publication or distribution of written or printed statements on behalf of, or in opposition to a candidate;

♦ Attempts to influence the selection, nomination, election, or appointment of any individual to any federal, state, or local public office;

♦ Contributions to any political campaign;

♦ Voter education activities in which the organization presents a bias on certain issues;

♦ Payment of salaries or expenses of campaign workers.[48]

In addition to limits on electioneering, a nonprofit agency can also lose tax-exempt status by spending too much money attempting to influence legislation. An attempt to influence legislation is called "grassroots" campaigning. (See below for more information on "grassroots" campaigns.) Since lobbying groups are not tax-exempt under section 501(c)(3), the IRS will revoke an organization's tax-exempt status if it determines that the purpose of the group is lobbying. This prohibition of lobbying includes money spent by libraries and archives that are trying to get more funding from the government. (In order to avoid this problem, libraries and archives should make sure that their lobbying expenditures fall within the limits listed below.)

An example of a grassroots campaign would be urging patrons to write a letter to the legislature asking for more funding for libraries. This is often mistaken as being part of a public relations campaign, but the IRS treats this behavior as an attempt to influence legislation. In other words, it is considered grassroots lobbying.[49] The definition of a grassroots attempt to influence legislation is as follows:

> (A) any attempt to influence any legislation through an attempt to affect the opinions of the general public or any segment thereof, and
> (B) any attempt to influence any legislation through communication with any member or employee of a legislative body, or with any government official or employee who may participate in the formulation of the legislation.[50]

There are some exceptions to the general rule on influencing legislation. These include "making available the results of nonpartisan analysis, study, or research"[51] and "providing of technical advice or assistance (where such advice would otherwise constitute the influencing of legislation) to a governmental body or to a committee or other subdivision thereof in response to a written request by such body or subdivision."[52] The rule limiting grassroots lobbying *does not* apply to advocacy in front of administrative agencies or bodies.[53] This type of appearance would not be considered lobbying.

Also, the officers and staff of a nonprofit association may appear before a legislative body "with respect to a possible decision of such body which might affect the existence of the organization, its powers and duties, tax-exempt status, or the deduction of contributions to the organization."[54] The IRS does not consider this situation to be lobbying.[55]

Although the grassroots lobbying rule does not prevent members of an association from discussing impending legislation, asking members to influence legislation or asking members to get others to influence legislation is considered grassroots lobbying. Under IRS rules, a tax-exempt organization may only spend up to 25 percent of its lobbying expenditures on grassroots lobbying. If the organization spends more than this limit, its tax-exempt status will be jeopardized.[56] Also, the IRS will impose a 5 percent excise tax on the excess lobbying expenditures of an organization, and on any managers who willfully disregard the IRS rule.[57] (For a more detailed discussion of the difference between grassroots lobbying and public relations efforts or marketing campaigns, please refer to the article I co-authored with Robin McGinnis on this topic.)[58]

One difficulty that many nonprofits face is trying to determine how much lobbying is too much. The tax-exempt status will be jeopardized if attempting to influence legislation is a "substantial part" of the organization's activities. In order to provide more guidance, the IRS has adopted a voluntary set of limits. A nonprofit organization can elect to be bound under sections 501(h) and 4911 of the Internal Revenue Code. To make this election, the organization needs to file IRS form 5768 (Election to Make Expenditures to Influence Legislation).[59] Once the nonprofit files form 5768, the provisions of section 501(h) and section 4911 will apply.[60] The IRS regulations for section 501(h) provide much more guidance than the nebulous "substantial part" test. Table 12.1 explains the limits contained in sections 501(h) and 4911(c)(2):[61]

Table 12.1. Limits for 26 U.S.C. 501(h) and 26 U.S.C. 4911(c)(2).

Exempt Purpose Expenditures	Total Nontaxable	Grassroots Nontaxable
Up to $500,000	20%	5%
$500,000 to $1,000,000	$100,000 + 15% of excess over $500,000	$25,000 + 3.75% of excess over $500,000
$1,000,000 to $1,500,000	$175,000 + 10% of excess over $1,000,000	$43,750 + 2.5% of excess over $1,000,000
$1,500,000 to $17,000,000	$225,000 + 5% of excess over $1,500,000	$56,250 + 1.25% of excess over $1,500,000
Over $17,000,000	$1,000,000	$250,000

In my opinion, all libraries should elect to file form 5768. The definition of "substantial part" is not at all clear, and nonprofit associations have gotten into trouble while trying to interpret the meaning of the term "substantial." On the other hand, the IRS regulations in sections 501(h) and 4911 give libraries a good idea of how much is too much.

Another issue nonprofits face involves affiliated organizations such as Friends of the Library groups and library foundations. If a group is considered to be an affiliated organization, then its income from unrelated business will be taxable for the parent organization as well. For example, if the local Friends of the Library group makes money from running a coffee shop, the library may have to pay taxes on this income. This is why it is important for Friends of the Library groups to be truly separate from the library, with a separate board of directors, and with limited direction from the parent library.

If the IRS finds that the group is an affiliated organization, substantial lobbying expenses above the limits in 501(h) and 4911 will be considered to be expenditures of the parent organization. The IRS will consider an affiliated organization as part of the parent group for the purposes of lobbying expenses if:

> (A) The governing instrument of one such organization requires it to be bound by decisions of the other organization on legislative issues, or
>
> (B) The governing board of one such organization includes persons who—
>
> (i) Are specifically designated representatives of another such organization or are members of the governing board, officers, or paid executive staff members of such other organization, and
>
> (ii) By aggregating their votes, have sufficient voting power to cause or prevent action on legislative issues by the first such organization.[62]

In addition to lobbying expenditures and unrelated business taxes, affiliated organizations are sometimes considered by courts to be the same organization for purposes of assigning liability in lawsuits. This is known as "piercing the corporate veil." Courts will pierce the corporate veil if they believe that the two entities are really one, or that the incorporation of the separate entity was done for the purposes of fraud. An example of this type of fraud was the creation of separate business entities by Enron in order to hide the corporation's losses.[63]

In order to avoid being considered to be affiliated organizations, the associations should really be separate. There should be separate articles of incorporation, bylaws, board members, etc. This separation will help to prevent the IRS from ruling that the two organizations are really one.

The IRS grants tax-exempt status, but only for organizations that have an exempt purpose. These organizations must agree not to engage in any electioneering at all, and not to engage in lobbying as a substantial portion of their activities.

Obtaining and maintaining tax-exempt status under Internal Revenue Code section 501(c)(3) is often a prerequisite for obtaining grants from private foundations. Obtaining tax-exempt status is also necessary in order to solicit donations, since a donation to a 501(c)(3) organization may be deducted on the donor's income tax return. Knowing and understanding the IRS rules is essential in order to help maintain tax-exempt status. (And you thought that all librarians had to do was to read books!)

Conclusion

Librarians and archivists have often undertaken the task of forming nonprofit groups. Thus, information professionals need to know how to undertake such a task. The effective governance of a nonprofit organization depends not only on the people who work for the group but also on the quality of the articles of incorporation, the quality of the bylaws, and the quality of the board. An organization should always have a clear mission statement, and this statement should be reviewed every few years to see whether it needs modification.

The board of directors is of great importance. The board members must fulfill their fiduciary duties to the organization. Board members and executive officers should develop and adhere to a clearly expressed policy on conflicts of interest. Finally, the organization should have transparent governance and should meet the standards of the Sarbanes-Oxley Act.

By ensuring that the nonprofit is well governed, the board members, officers, and staff will be taking an important step towards fulfilling the mission of the organization. After all, libraries and archives exist for the purpose of serving the public.

Notes

Chapter 1

1. Alexander Pope, *An Essay on Criticism* 1-15 (1711).

2. 48 C.F.R. § 1 et seq.

3. Sony Corporation of America et al. v. Universal City Studios, Inc., 464 U.S. 417 (1984).

4. A&M Records v. Napster, Inc., 239 F.3d 1004, 2001 U.S. App. LEXIS 5446, 2001 Cal. Daily Op. Service 1255, 2001 D.A.R. 1611, Copy. L. Rep. (CCH) P28200, 57 U.S.P.Q.2d (BNA) 1729 (9th Cir. Cal. 2001); *injunction granted*, A&M Records, Inc. v. Napster, Inc., 2001 U.S. Dist. LEXIS 2186, Copyright Law Reporter (CCH) P28213 (N.D. Cal. Mar. 5, 2001); *stay granted by, in part*, in re Napster, Inc. Copyright Litigation, 191 F. Supp. 2d 1087, 2002 U.S. Dist. LEXIS 2963, Copy. L. Rep. (CCH) P28386, 2002-1 Trade Cases (CCH) P73588, 61 U.S.P.Q.2d (BNA) 1877 (N.D. Cal. 2002); *affirmed by*, A&M Records, Inc. v. Napster, Inc., 284 F.3d 1091, 2002 U.S. App. LEXIS 4752, 2002 D.A.R. 3223, 52 Fed. R. Serv. 3d (Callaghan) 5, 62 U.S.P.Q.2d (BNA) 1221 (9th Cir. Cal. 2002); *Stay granted by, Motion granted by, in part, Motion denied by, in part*, in re Napster, Inc. Copyright Litigation, 2004 U.S. Dist. LEXIS 7236 (N.D. Cal. Feb. 22, 2004).

5. Metro-Goldwyn-Mayer Studios Inc. v. Grokster, Ltd., 162 L. Ed. 2d 781, 125 S. Ct. 2764, 2005 U.S. LEXIS 5212, 18 Fla. L. Weekly Fed. S 547, 33 Media L. Rep. (BNA) 1865, 75 U.S.P.Q.2d (BNA) 1001 (2005), *available at* http://laws.findlaw.com/us/000/04-480.html.

6. *id*. The Grokster and StreamCast cases were joined, and the courts considered these two cases together.

7. 17 U.S.C. § 201(b).

8. Sonny Bono Copyright Term Extension Act of 1998, S. 105-505. Signed into law on October 27, 1998.

9. 17 U.S.C. § 107.

10. 17 U.S.C. § 110(2).

11. Mark Radcliffe, *Patent, Trademark, and Trade Secret Law* § 2 Findlaw Professionals *at* http://profs.lp.findlaw.com/patents/patents_2.html, *excerpted from* Mark Radcliffe, *The Multimedia Law and Business Handbook* (Ladera Press 1999).

12. *id*.

13. Tasini v. New York Times Co., 533 U.S. 483, 150 L. Ed. 2d 500, 121 S. Ct. 2381 (2001). Previous incarnations of the case include: 972 F. Supp. 804, 1997 (this case will be referred to as "Tasini I"); *reconsideration denied*, Tasini

v. New York Times Co., 981 F. Supp. 841, 1997 U.S. Dist. LEXIS 17140 (S.D.N.Y. 1997); *reversed and remanded*, 192 F.3d 356, 1999 (2d Cir. N.Y. 1999), *opinion withdrawn by Court and replaced by* 206 F.3d 161 (this case will be referred to as "Tasini II"), *writ of certiorari granted*, 148 L. Ed. 2d 434, 121 S. Ct. 425. For related proceeding, *see also*, Marx v. Globe Newspaper Co., 2001 Mass. Super. LEXIS 9 (Mass. Super. Ct. Jan. 11, 2001).

14. 114 Stat. 2763A-335, *codified at* 20 U.S.C. §§ 9134(f)(1)(A)(i) and (B)(i) and at 47 U.S.C. §§ 254(h)(6)(B)(i) and (C)(i).

15. American Library Association v. United States, 201 F. Supp. 2d 401 (E.D. Pa. 2002). [Hereinafter "District Court Opinion."]

16. United States v. American Library Association, 539 U.S. 194; 123 S. Ct. 2297; 156 L. Ed. 2d 221; 2003 U.S. LEXIS 4799; 71 U.S.L.W. 4465 (2003), *available at* http://laws.findlaw.com/us/000/02-361.html. [Hereinafter "CIPA Case."]

17. 29 U.S.C. § 201 – 29 U.S.C. § 209.

18. 42 U.S.C. § 12101 et seq.

19. 29 U.S.C. § 2611 et seq.

20. Sarbanes-Oxley Act of 2002, PL 107-204, 116 Stat 745.

21. *A Uniform System of Citation* (17th ed., Harvard Law Review Association 2000). Peter Martin has created an online citation manual based on Bluebook style; *see*, Peter W. Martin, *Introduction to Basic Legal Citation* (Cornell Legal Information Institute 2003), *available at* http://www.law.cornell.edu/citation.

22. Bureau of National Affairs, *U.S. Law Week Product Structure* (last accessed August 28, 2005), *available at* http://www.bna.com/products/lit/uslw.htm.

Chapter 2

1. Some of the material in this chapter was previously used in Bryan M. Carson, *"The Tie That Binds": The Nuts and Bolts of Contract Formation*, 16-2 Against the Grain 75-77 (April 2003), and in Bryan M. Carson, *Consideration and the Statute of Frauds: Necessary Elements in the Formation and Enforcement of Contracts*, 16-3 Against the Grain 72-75 (June 2004).

2. Uniform Commercial Code (as amended 2005), *available at* http://www.law.cornell.edu/uniform/ucc.html.

3. Juan C. Sallichs Pon, *Modernization of Puerto Rico's Commercial Law*, 5 The Bomchil Group Newsletter (1998), *available at* http://www.bomchilgroup.org/puesep98.html.

4. 17A Am. Jur. 2d Contracts § 24. According to Words & Phrases, "A 'contract' is the coming together of two minds on a thing done or to be done." [*Quoting* Charles R. Shepard, Inc, v. Clement Brothers Co., 177 F. Supp. 288, 290 (D.C.N.C.).] Words & Phrases further defines a contract as "a deliberate engagement between competent parties to do or to abstain from doing some

act." 8A Words & Phrases Contract (1960), *quoting* Federal Surety Co. v. Pitts, 29 S.W.2d 1046, 119 Tex. 330 (1930).

5. 17A Am. Jur. 2d Contracts § 24 (2004).

6. *id.* at § 26, *quoting* Baehr v. Penn-O-Tex Oil Corp., 258 Minn. 533, 104 N.W.2d 661 (1960).

7. *id.*

8. Morrow v. De Vitt, 160 S.W.2d 977, 983 (Tex. Civ. App. 1942).

9. Cronin v. National Shawmut Bank, 27 N.E.2d 717, 721, 306 Mass. 302 (1940).

10. 2 Encyclopedia of Business Request for Proposal (2nd ed., Gale Group 2000).

11. 17A Am. Jur. 2d Contracts § 113 (2004), *quoting* Becker v. Colonial Life Ins. Co., 153 App. Div. 382, 138 N.Y.S. 491 (N.Y. App. Div. 1912).

12. Gordon D. Schaber and Claude D. Rohwer, *Contracts in a Nutshell* 75 (3d ed., West Publishing 1990).

13. 8A Words & Phrases Consideration (1951), *quoting* Williams Mfg. Co. v. Prock, 86 F. Supp. 447, 448 (D.C. Tex. 1949).

14. *id.*, *quoting* Smaller War Plants Corp. v. Queen City Lumber Co., 27 So.2d 531, 535, 200 Miss. 627 (1946).

15. Laurence P. Simpson, *Handbook on the Law of Contracts* 87 (West Publishing 1954).

16. Federal Reserve Bank of Minneapolis, *What's a Dollar Worth?* (based on *Cost of Living Index* by Albert Rees), *available at* http://minneapolisfed.org/Research/data/us/calc/hist1800.cfm.

17. Hamer v. Sideway, 124 N.Y. 538, 124 N.Y. (N.Y.S.) 538, 27 N.E. 256, 1891 N.Y. LEXIS 1396, 21 Am. St. Rep. 693, 12 L.R.A. 463 (1891).

18. *id.*, *quoted in* Simpson *at* 89.

19. William L. Clark, Jr., *Handbook On The Law Of Contracts* 149 (West Publishing 1931).

20. Clark *at* 155.

21. Clark *at* 161.

22. 17 C.J.S. 2D contracts § 76 (1963).

23. This price came from a posting on a Web discussion board entitled *Marijuana, Availability/Prices in Your Area*, which I found via a search engine. Posting of Sleeper, (no email) to Somni-Forum, (September 18, 2003), *available at* http://opium.poppies.org/index.php?act=ST&f=8&t=5944&).

24. Charles G. Bakaly, Jr., and Joel M. Grossman, *Modern Law of Employment Contracts: Formation, Operation, and Remedies for Breach* § 3.2. (Law & Business Inc.1983).

25. Rinke-Noonan, Ltd., *Law for Laymen*, (last visited June 12, 2005), *available at* http://www.rnoon.com/lawlaymen/contracts/writing.html.

26. *Act for the Prevention of Frauds and Perjuries*, 29 Car. II, c. 3 (1677). For more information about the history of the Statute of Frauds, *see* Lloyd Rain, *The Statute of Frauds: Its Origins, Its Persistence, and Its Potential Demise*, Purchasing Link (November 2002), *available at*

http://www.naeb.org/Purchasing_Link/Commentaries/Nov2002_LR_Comment
ary.htm.

27. *id.*

28. *id.*

29. Bakaly and Grossman § 5.2.

30. *id.* at § 5.3.

31. Rain.

32. *id.*

33. Jane Mallor, Business Law and the Regulatory Environment 456 (Ir-
win/McGraw-Hill 2001), *available at*
http://www.csun.edu/~bz51361/gateway/statute.frauds.pdf.

34. *Form, Formation and Readjustment of Contract*, Uniform Commercial
Code § 2.2, *available at* http://www.law.cornell.edu/ucc/2/2-201.html

35. "Contracts to which the Government is a party generally are subject to
the same rules of contract law as are contracts between individuals. When the
United States enters into a commercial type of transaction it sheds its cloak of
sovereignty and is treated by the law as a private person in similar circumstances." *Government Contracts: Law Administration Procedure* § 1.20
(Mathew Bender n.d.). *See also*, Cooke v. United States, 91 U.S. 389, 1 Otto
389, 23 L. Ed. 237, 1875 U.S. LEXIS 1381 (1875); Bank of Arizona v. Thomas
Haverty Co., 232 U.S. 106, 58 L. Ed. 526, 34 S. Ct. 235, 1914 U.S. LEXIS
1464 (1914); Maxima Corp. v. United States, 847 F.2d 1549, 1988 U.S. App.
LEXIS 6990, 34 Cont. Cas. Fed. (CCH) P75497, 104 A.L.R. Fed. 629 (Fed.
Cir. 1988); Woodbury v. United States, 192 F. Supp. 924, 1961 U.S. Dist.
LEXIS 5139 (D. Or. 1961).

36. 48 C.F.R. § 1 et seq.

37. 15 U.S.C. § 631 et seq.

38. 41 U.S.C. § 421(c)(1).

39. Steven W. Feldman, *Government Contract Awards: Negotiation and
Sealed Bidding* § 3:03 (Clark Boardman Callaghan n.d.).

40. Jeffrey A. Helewitz, *Basic Contract Law for Paralegals* 288 (3d ed.,
Aspen Law and Business 2000).

41. Helewitz *at* 291.

42. Black's Law Dictionary 494 (5th ed. 1979).

43. E. Allen Farnsworth, *Farnsworth on Contracts* § 2.19 (3d ed., Aspen
Publishers 2004). *See*, Feinberg v. Pfeiffer Co., 322 S.W.2d 163 (Mo. Ct. App.
1959); Chesus v. Watts, 967 S.W.2d 97 (Mo. Ct. App. 1998). For an alternative
holding, *see* Langer v. Superior Steel Corp., 161 A. 571 (Pa. Super. Ct. 1932).

44. Farnsworth § 219. *See*, Roberts-Horsfield v. Gedicks, 118 A. 275 (Ct.
Chancery N.J. 1922).

45. Farnsworth § 219, *quoting* Siegel v. Spear & Co., 138 N.E. 414 (N.Y.
1922).

46. Farnsworth § 219. *See*, Danby v. Osteopathic Hospital Association,
104 A.2d 903 Del. 1954); Jewish Federation of Central New Jersey v. Baron-
dess, 234 N.J. Super. 526, 560 A.2d 1353, (N.J. Super. Ct. 1989); Beatty v.

Western College of Toledo, 177 Ill. 280, 52 N.E. 432, 69 Am. St. Rep. 242, 42 L.R.A. 797 (1898).

47. Farnsworth § 219, *quoting* I. & I. Holding Corp. v. Gainsburg, 276 N.Y. 427, 276 N.Y. (N.Y.S.) 427, 12 N.E.2d 532, 1938 N.Y. LEXIS 1204, 115 A.L.R. 582 (1938).

48. Farnsworth § 219, *quoting* Allegheny College v. National Chautauqua County Bank, 246 N.Y. 369, 159 N.E. 173, 1927 N.Y. LEXIS 886, 57 A.L.R. 980 (1927).

49. Farnsworth § 219, *quoting* Gordon v. Skokie, 21 Ill. 2d 569, 173 N.E.2d 504, 1961 Ill. LEXIS 347 (1961). For cases with the opposite ruling, *see*, Mt. Sinai Hospital, Inc. v. Jordan, 290 So. 2d 484, 1974 Fla. LEXIS 4417 (Fla. 1974); Virginia School of the Arts v. Eichelbaum, 254 Va. 373, 493 S.E.2d 510, 1997 Va. LEXIS 115 (1997).

50. Farnsworth § 2.19. *See*, Richey v. Board of Education, 346 Mich. 156, 77 N.W.2d 361, 1956 Mich. LEXIS 302 (1956); Hamer v. Sidway, 124 N.Y. 538, 124 N.Y. (N.Y.S.) 538, 27 N.E. 256, 1891 N.Y. LEXIS 1396, 21 Am. St. Rep. 693, 12 L.R.A. 463 (1891); Kirksey v. Kirksey, 8 Ala. 131, 1845 Ala. LEXIS 320 (1845).

51. Farnsworth § 219.

52. Restatement (Second) of Contracts § 377 (1987).

53. Howard O. Hunter, *Modern Law of Contracts* § 1:2 (Rev. ed., Warren Gorham Lamont 1993).

54. Farnsworth § 219 p. 174.

55. Samuel Williston, *Treatise on the Law of Contracts* § 7.2 (4th ed., West Group 2001).

56. 27A A. Jur. 2d Equity § 1 (1996).

57. 30A C.J.S. 2d Equity § 2 (1992).

58. *id*.

59. 71 Am. Jur. 2d Specific Performance § 1 (2001), *quoting* Haire v. Patterson, 63 Wash. 2d 282, 386 p.2d 953 (1963).

60. John D. Calamari and Joseph M. Perillo, *The Law of Contracts* (Hornbook) 360 (4th ed., West Group 1998).

61. *id*.

62. *See*, Jane M. Friedman, *Contract Remedies in a Nutshell* § 2.4 *at* 89-90 (West Publishing 1981).

63. *id*.

64. Friedman *at* 93.

65. Williston § 12:1.

66. Williston § 12:1.

67. Missouri Revised Code § 434.100(1) Contracts Against Public Policy.

68. Williston § 12:1.

Chapter 3

1. Portions of this chapter have previously been published by the author in his column in the journal *Against the Grain*; however, this chapter represents more than just a reprinting of the columns. This chapter also contains a great deal of original material that has not previously been published.

2. 6 West's Encyclopedia of American Law Intellectual Property § 183 (1998).

3. 17 U.S.C. § 102.

4. *id.*

5. Mark Radcliffe, *Copyright Law*, Findlaw Professionals § 2, *available at* http://profs.findlaw.com/copyright/copyright_2.html. *Excerpted from* Mark Radcliffe, *The Multimedia Law and Business Handbook* (Ladera Press 1999).

6. Radcliffe *at* § 3, *available at* http://profs.findlaw.com/copyright/copyright_3.html.

7. "'Literary works' are works, other than audiovisual works, expressed in words, numbers, or other verbal or numerical symbols or indicia, regardless of the nature of the material objects, such as books, periodicals, manuscripts, phonorecords, films, tapes, disk, or cards, in which they are embodied." 17 U.S.C. § 101.

8. One condition of using non-copyrighted government materials is that you must include a statement with your copyright notice saying that your copyright excludes government works.

9. 17 U.S.C. § 106.

10. 17 U.S.C. § 101(3).

11. 17 U.S.C. § 103.

12. Dastar Corporation v. 20th Century Fox Film Corporation, 539 U.S. 23; 123 S. Ct. 2041; 156 L. Ed. 2d 18 (2003), *available at* http://www.acm.org/usacm/PDF/Legal/Dastar_v_Twentieth_Century.pdf.

13. Donovan (Donovan P. Leitch), *Roots of Oak*, *on* Open Road (Epic Records 1970). The sheet music was published in Los Angeles by Peer International Corp. in 1970. *Roots of Oak* is registered with Broadcast Music International, BMI work #1269007. Donovan is a registered member of the American Society of Composers and Producers (A.S.C.P.) and Broadcast Music International (B.M.I.).

14. Jack Montgomery is also the collection development coordinator at Western Kentucky University Libraries.

15. Jack G. Montgomery, Jr., *Roots of Oak*, *on* Everywhere I Look (Shadow Dancer Music 2004). For more information about this album, *see* http://www.cdbaby.com/cd/jackmontgomery2. Montgomery is a registered member of A.S.C.P.

16. 17 U.S.C. § 101.

17. *See*, U.S. Copyright Office, Circular 38a: International Copyright Relations of the United States (January 2003), *available at*

http://www.copyright.gov/circs/circ38a.html. *See also*, U.S. Copyright Office, Appendix II: Berne Convention Implementation Act of 1988, *Circular 92: Copyright Law of the United States of America and Related Laws Contained in Title 17 of the United States Code* (last accessed September 11, 2005), *available at* http://www.copyright.gov/title17/92appii.html.

18. Circular 38a.

19. Radcliffe § 7, *available at* http://profs.findlaw.com/copyright/copyright_7.html.

20. Convention Establishing the World Intellectual Property Organization, (signed July 14, 1967; amended September 28, 1979), *available at* http://www.wipo.org/treaties/convention/index.html.

21. For a complete list of copyright treaties to which the United States is a party, *see* Circular 38a.

22. World Intellectual Property Organization, *General Information*, (last visited June 13, 2005), *available at* http://www.wipo.int/about-wipo/en/gib.htm.

23. *id.*

24. Some of the treaties and conventions that WIPO administers include: the Paris Convention for the Protection of Industrial Property; the Berne Convention for the Protection of Literary and Artistic Works; the Rome Convention for the Protection of Performers, Producers of Phonograms and Broadcasting Organizations; the Geneva Convention for the Protection of Producers of Phonograms against Unauthorized Duplication of Their Phonograms; the Nairobi Treaty on the Protection of the Olympic Symbol; the Madrid Agreement for the Repression of False or Deceptive Indications of Source on Goods; the Trademark Law Treaty; the Brussels Convention Relating to the Distribution of Programme-Carrying Signals Transmitted by Satellite; the WIPO Copyright Treaty; the Patent Law Treaty; and the WIPO Performances and Phonograms Treaty. *id.*

25. 17 U.S.C. § 107.

26. 17 U.S.C. § 107.

27. The correct quotation is:
Good name in man and woman, dear my lord,
Is the immediate jewel of their souls:
Who steals my purse steals trash; 'tis something, nothing;
'Twas mine, 'tis his, and has been slave to thousands;
But he that filches from me my good name
Robs me of that which not enriches him
And makes me poor indeed.
–Iago *in* Othello, Act III, scene 3, lines 159-61.

28. 17 U.S.C. § 502.

29. 17 U.S.C. § 503.

30. 17 U.S.C. § 509.

31. 17 U.S.C. § 506.

32. 17 U.S.C. § 504.

33. 17 U.S.C. § 505.

34. Nicholas Read, *Top court rescues harried Potter publisher: Injunction bars leaks of plot after B.C. store sells 14 copies by mistake*, Edmonton (Alberta) Journal *at* A1 (July 12, 2005).

35. Lora Grindlay, *Potter fans return early copies: But then Mac's in Calgary sells top-secret book*, Vancouver Province *at* A2 (July 13, 2005).

36. A&M Records v. Napster, Inc., 239 F.3d 1004, 2001 U.S. App. LEXIS 5446, 2001 Cal. Daily Op. Service 1255, 2001 D.A.R. 1611, Copy. L. Rep. (CCH) P28200, 57 U.S.P.Q.2d (BNA) 1729 (9th Cir. Cal. 2001); *injunction granted*, A&M Records, Inc. v. Napster, Inc., 2001 U.S. Dist. LEXIS 2186, Copy. L. Rep. (CCH) P28213 (N.D. Cal. Mar. 5, 2001); *Stay granted by, in part*, in re Napster, Inc. Copyright Litig., 191 F. Supp. 2d 1087, 2002 U.S. Dist. LEXIS 2963, Copy. L. Rep. (CCH) P28386, 2002-1 Trade Cas. (CCH) P73588, 61 U.S.P.Q.2d (BNA) 1877 (N.D. Cal. 2002); *affirmed by*, A&M Records, Inc. v. Napster, Inc., 284 F.3d 1091, 2002 U.S. App. LEXIS 4752, 2002 Cal. Daily Op. Service 2635, 2002 D.A.R. 3223, 52 Fed. R. Serv. 3d (Callaghan) 5, 62 U.S.P.Q.2d (BNA) 1221 (9th Cir. Cal. 2002); *Stay granted by, Motion granted by, in part, Motion denied by, in part*, in re Napster, Inc. Copyright Litig., 2004 U.S. Dist. LEXIS 7236 (N.D. Cal. Feb. 22, 2004).

37. *id.*

38. *id.*

39. Dan Nystedt, *Dell, Napster Team on Music for Students: Companies are offering discounted hardware and software to lure students away from illegal file sharing*, PC World Online (July 7, 2005), *available at* http://www.pcworld.com/news/article/0,aid,121736,00.asp.

40. 18 U.S.C. § 2319B.

41. *id.*

42. 17 U.S.C. § 504.

43. *id.*

44. Sony Corporation of America et al. v. Universal City Studios, Inc., 464 U.S. 417 (1984).

45. Sony *at* 421.

46. Sony *at* 425, *quoting* Columbia Broadcasting System, Inc. v. Democratic National Committee, 412 U.S. 94, 102 (1973).

47. Sony *at* 424.

48. Sony *at* 439. The Supreme Court referenced several cases. *See*, The Trade-Mark Cases, 100 U.S. 82, 91-92 (1879); *see also* United Drug Co. v. Theodore Rectanus Co., 248 U.S. 90, 97 (1918) (trademark right "has little or no analogy" to copyright or patent); McLean v. Fleming, 96 U.S. 245, 254 (1878); Canal Co. v. Clark, 13 Wall. 311, 322 (1872).

49. Sony *at* 442.

50. Metro-Goldwyn-Mayer Studios, Inc. v. Grokster, Ltd., 162 L. Ed. 2d 781, 125 S. Ct. 2764, 2005 U.S. LEXIS 5212, 18 Fla. L. Weekly Fed. S 547, 33 Media L. Rep. (BNA) 1865, 75 U.S.P.Q.2d (BNA) 1001 (2005), *available at* http://laws.findlaw.com/us/000/04-480.html.

51. Grokster *at* 10. Because the final version of the opinion had not yet been released as of the time of this writing (Summer 2005), I am citing to the LEXIS page numbers.

52. Grokster *at* 17.

53. Grokster *at* 19.

54. Grokster *at* 25-26.

55. Grokster *at* 38, *quoting* Sony ("If vicarious liability is to be imposed on Sony in this case, it must rest on the fact that it has sold equipment with constructive knowledge" of the potential for infringement. Sony *at* 439.")

56. Grokster *at* 38.

57. Grokster *at* 44, *quoting* Rumford Chemical Works v. Hecker, 20 F. Cas. 1342, 1346 (No. 12,133) (CC N. J. 1876) (demonstrations of infringing activity along with "avowals of the [infringing] purpose and use for which it was made" supported liability for patent infringement).

58. Grokster *at* 44.

59. Grokster *at* 46.

60. Grokster *at* 48.

61. Grokster *at* 66 (Breyer, J., Dissenting), *quoting* Sony.

62. Grokster *at* 74-76 (Breyer, J., Dissenting).

63. Grokster *at* 78 (Breyer, J., Dissenting).

64. 17 U.S.C. § 201(b).

65. Work for hire, 17 U.S.C. § 101(2).

66. Community For Creative Non-Violence et al. v. Reid, 490 U.S. 730; 109 S. Ct. 2166; 104 L. Ed. 2d 811 (1989).

67. Reid *at* 739. *See also*, Consumer Product Safety Commission v. GTE Sylvania, Inc., 447 U.S. 102, 108 (1980).

68. Reid *at* 739, *quoting* NLRB v. Amax Coal Co., 453 U.S. 322, 329 (1981); *see also* Perrin v. United States, 444 U.S. 37, 42 (1979).

69. Reid *at* 739-740. *See*, Kelley v. Southern Pacific Co., 419 U.S. 318, 322-323 (1974); Baker v. Texas & Pacific R. Co., 359 U.S. 227, 228 (1959) (per curiam); Robinson v. Baltimore & Ohio R. Co., 237 U.S. 84, 94 (1915). *See also*, NLRB v. Hearst Publications, Inc., 322 U.S. 111, 124-132 (1944); Restatement (Second) of Agency § 228 (1958).

70. Reid *at* 743.

71. Reid *at* 753, *quoting* Holt v. Winpisinger, 258 U.S. App. D. C. 343, 351, 811 F.2d 1532, 1540 (1987).

72. Reid *at* 753, *quoting* Circuit Court opinion *at* 270 U.S. App. D. C. 35 n. 11, 846 F.2d 1494 n. 11.

73. Reid *at* 753, *quoting* 17 U.S.C. § 101 n32.

74. Reid *at* 752-53.

75. District Court opinion, Community For Creative Non-Violence v. Reid, 1991 U.S. Dist. LEXIS 21020, Copy. L. Rep. (CCH) P24384 (D.D.C. Jan. 7, 1991).

76. 17 U.S.C. § 101.

77. House Report No. 94-1476 § 201 (1976).

78. *See* 17 U.S.C. § 201.

79. Work for hire, 17 U.S.C. § 101(2).

80. *id.*

81. 17 U.S.C. § 201(d)(1).

82. Melville B. Nimmer and David Nimmer, *Nimmer on Copyright*, Form 28-1 (Mathew Bender 1993).

83. 17 U.S.C. § 201(d)(2).

84. *Nimmer on Copyright* § 5.03 B(1)(b)(I).

85. *id.*

86. Indiana University Office of Research and University Graduate School, *Intellectual Property Policy* (adopted May 9, 1997), *available at* http://www.indiana.edu/rugs/respol/intprop.html.

87. Western Kentucky University, *Intellectual Property Policy* (adopted January 28, 2000), *available at* http://www.wku.edu/Dept/Support/SponsPrg/grants/ip_997.htm.

88. Northern Kentucky University, *Intellectual Property Policy* (adopted December 20, 1999), *available at* http://www.nku.edu/senate/intellect.pdf.

89. Western Kentucky University, *Intellectual Property Policy.*

90. Western Kentucky University, *Intellectual Property Policy.*

91. I coined this phrase.

92. 17 U.S.C. § 108(a).

93. 17 U.S.C. § 108(b).

94. 17 U.S.C. § 108(c)

95. 37 C.F.R. § 201.39, *available at* http://www.copyright.gov/title37/201/37cfr201.39.pdf.

96. 37 C.F.R. § 201.39, Appendix A, *available at* http://www.copyright.gov/title37/201/37cfr201.39.pdf.

97. 17 U.S.C. § 108(c).

98. 17 U.S.C. § 108(c).

99. 17 U.S.C. § 108(d).

100. 17 U.S.C. § 108(e).

101. 17 U.S.C. § 108(f).

102. 17 U.S.C. § 108(g).

103. 17 U.S.C. § 108(f).

104. 37 C.F.R. § 201.14, *available at* http://www.copyright.gov/title37/201/37cfr201.14.pdf.

105. For a digital facsimile of the Copyright Act of 1790, *see* http://earlyamerica.com/earlyamerica/firsts/copyright/centinel.jpg.

106. John Naughton, Business & Media: Media: *The Networker: Mickey Mouse threatens to block all ideas in future*, The Observer (February 24, 2002).

107. Naughton *at* 8.

108. 17 U.S.C. § 302.

109. Bill Holland, *Congress Extends C'right Term; WIPO Passage Seen*, Billboard *at* 5 (October 17, 1998).

110. Sonny Bono Copyright Term Extension Act of 1998, S. 105-505;

signed into law on October 27, 1998.

111. For more information on the genesis of this case, including its background in the District Court and the Court of Appeals, *see* Bryan M. Carson, *I got you babe! The Sonny Bono Copyright Term Extension Act & Eldred v. Ashcroft*, 14-3 Against the Grain 59 (June 2002).

112. World Intellectual Property Organization, (last visited June 13, 2005) *at* http://www.wipo.org/about-wipo/en/.

113. *Sonny Bono Copyright Term Extension Act*, Pub. L. No. 105-298, 112 Stat. 2827. [Hereinafter "CTEA."]

114. CTEA.

115. Eldred v. Ashcroft, 537 U.S. 186; 123 S. Ct. 769; 154 L. Ed. 2d 683 (2003), *quoting* 141 Cong. Rec. 6553 (1995) (statement of Sen. Feinstein); *see* 144 Cong. Rec. S12377 (daily ed. Oct. 12, 1998) (statement of Sen. Hatch).

116. *See*, Carson.

117. Bill Holland, *Suit Challenges C'right Extension*, Billboard *at* 6 (January 30, 1999).

118. Eldred v. Reno *sub nom* Eldred v. Ashcroft, 74 F. Supp. 2d 1; 1999 U.S. Dist. LEXIS 18862; 53 U.S.P.Q.2d (BNA) 1217; Copy. L. Rep. (CCH) P27, 998 (D.D.C. October 28, 1999), *available at* http://eon.law.harvard.edu/openlaw/eldredvashcroft/opinion.html. The opinion relies heavily on United Video v. F.C.C., 890 F.2d 1173, 1191 (D.C. Cir. 1989) and Harper and Row Publishers, Inc. v. Nation Enterprises, 471 U.S. 539, 556 (1985).

119. Eldred v. Reno, 345 U.S. App. D.C. 89; 239 F.3d 372; 2001 U.S. App. LEXIS 2335; 57 U.S.P.Q.2d (BNA) 1842; Copy. L. Rep. (CCH) P28,219 (D.C. Cir. February 20, 2001 *As Amended*); *Rehearing Denied*, 2001 U.S. App. LEXIS 15628 (July 13, 2001), *available at* http://cyber.law.harvard.edu/cc/dcaopinion.html.

120. Eldred v. Ashcroft, 537 U.S. 186; 123 S. Ct. 769; 154 L. Ed. 2d 683 (2003).

121. *id.* at 205.

122 *id.* at 219, *quoting* Harper & Row, Publishers, Inc. *v.* Nation Enterprises, 471 U.S. 539, 558 (1985).

123. Lolly Gassaway, *When U.S. Works Pass Into the Public Domain*, University of North Carolina Task Force on Intellectual Property, *available at* http://www.unc.edu/~unclng/public-d.htm (updated November 4, 2003).

124. U.S. Constitution, Article 1, Section 8, Clause 8, *available at* http://caselaw.lp.findlaw.com/data/constitution/article01/.

125. Mark Radcliffe, *Patent, Trademark, and Trade Secret Law* § 1 Findlaw Professionals *available at* http://profs.lp.findlaw.com/patents/patents_1.html. *Excerpted from* Mark Radcliffe, *The Multimedia Law and Business Handbook* (Ladera Press 1999).

126. *id.*

127. *id.*

128. *id.*

129. 35 U.S.C. § 101.

130. 35 U.S.C. § 103.

131. Radcliffe *at* § 1.

132. Renae Speck, Patent Law, address at A Primer on Intellectual Property Law (September 23, 2005) (PowerPoint slide handout on file with author).

133. Robert A. Heinlein, *Stranger in a Strange Land* (Putnam 1961).

134. Robert A. Heinlein, *Expanded Universe*, at 516-518 (Ace Books, 1982).

135. *id.*

136. AT&T, *Inventing the Telephone* (2005), *available at* http://www.att.com/history/inventing.html.

137. House Report No. 109-2795 § 102.

138. Statement of Gary Griswold, Past President, American Intellectual Property Law Association, Before the Subcommittee on Courts, the Internet and Intellectual Property, United States House of Representatives, (June 9, 2005), *available at* http://www.aipla.org/Content/ContentGroups/Legislative_Action/109th_Congr ess/Testimony5/HouseStmt_PatentAct2005.pdf. *See* Mark A. Lemley and Colleen V. Chien, *Are the U.S. Patent Priority Rules Really Necessary?*, 54 Hastings Law Journal 1299 (2003). *See also*, Gerald J. Mossinghoff, *Small Entities and the "First to Invent" System: An Empirical Analysis*, Washington Legal Foundation (2005), *available at* http://www.wlf.org/upload/MossinghoffWP.pdf.

Chapter 4

1. Portions of this chapter have previously been published in my column in the journal *Against the Grain*; however, this chapter represents more than just a reprinting of the columns. This chapter also contains a great deal of original material that has not previously been published.

2. 17 U.S.C. § 107.

3. *id.*

4. William F. Patry, *The Fair Use Privilege in Copyright Law* (Washington, D.C.: Bureau of National Affairs, 1985) *at* 361.

5. 17 U.S.C. § 107.

6. American Geophysical Union et al. v. Texaco, Inc., 60 F.3d 913; 1994 U.S. App. LEXIS 40786; 35 U.S.P.Q.2d (BNA) 1513; Copy. L. Rep. (CCH) *at* 27,417; 144 A.L.R. Fed. 745 (2d Cir. 1994).

7. American Geophysical Union et al. v. Texaco, Inc., 802 F. Supp. 1; 1992 U.S. Dist. LEXIS 10540; 23 U.S.P.Q.2d (BNA) 1561; Copy. L. Rep. (CCH) *at* 26,956.

8. *Texaco, Publishers Agree to Settle Copyright Case*, Copyright & fair use (Stanford University Libraries 1995).

9. Texaco *at* 922.

10. Basic Books, Inc. v. Kinko's Graphics Corp., 758 F. Supp. 1522, 1991 U.S. Dist. LEXIS 3804, Copy. L. Rep. (CCH) *at* 26709, 18 U.S.P.Q.2d (BNA) 1437 (S.D.N.Y. 1991).

11. Princeton University Press et al. v. Michigan Document Services, Inc., 99 F.3d 1381; 1996 U.S. App. LEXIS 29132; 1996 F.E.D. App. 0357P (6th Cir.); 40 U.S.P.Q.2d (BNA) 1641; Copy. L. Rep. (CCH) *at* 27,579 (6th Cir. 1996).

12. Feist Publications, Inc. v. Rural Telephone Service Co., Inc., 499 U.S. 340; 111 S. Ct. 1282; 113 L. Ed. 2d 358; 1991 U.S. LEXIS 1856; 59 U.S.L.W. 4251; 18 U.S.P.Q.2d (BNA) 1275; Copy. L. Rep. (CCH) *at* 26,702; 68 Rad. Reg. 2d (P & F) 1513; 18 Media L. Rep. 1889; 121 P.U.R.4th 1; 91 Cal. Daily Op. Service 2217; 91 Daily Journal DAR 3580.

13. Feist *at* 343-344.

14. Feist *at* 344, *quoting* Harper & Row, Publishers, Inc. *v.* Nation Enterprises, 471 U.S. 539, 556 (1985).

15. Feist *at* 344, *quoting* the Brief for Respondent *at* 24.

16. Feist *at* 344-345.

17. Feist *at* 346, *quoting* M. Nimmer & D. Nimmer, Copyright, § 1.08[C][1](1990).

18. Feist *at* 347, *quoting* Patterson & Joyce, Monopolizing the Law: The Scope of Copyright Protection for Law Reports and Statutory Compilations, 36 UCLA L. Rev. 719, 763, n. 155 (1989).

19. Feist *at* 347.

20. Feist *at* 347.

21. Feist *at* 358-361.

22. Feist *at* 363.

23. Basic Books, Inc. v. Kinko's Graphics Corp., 758 F. Supp. 1522, 1991 U.S. Dist. LEXIS 3804, Copy. L. Rep. (CCH) P26709, 18 U.S.P.Q.2d (BNA) 1437 (S.D.N.Y. 1991).

24. Princeton University Press et al. v. Michigan Document Services, Inc., 99 F.3d 1381; 1996 U.S. App. LEXIS 29132; 1996 F.E.D. App. 0357P (6th Cir.); 40 U.S.P.Q.2d (BNA) 1641; Copy. L. Rep. (CCH) *at* 27,579 (6th Cir. 1996).

25. *See*, Michigan Document Services *at* 1389; Kinko's *at* 1534.

26. *See*, Michigan Document Services *at* 1389.

27. Pierre N. Leval, *Toward a Fair Use Standard*, 103 Harvard Law Review 1105, 1122 (1990).

28. Maxtone-Graham v. Burtchaell, 803 F.2d 1253; 1986 U.S. App. LEXIS 32487; 231 U.S.P.Q. (BNA) 534; Copy. L. Rep. (CCH) P26,014; 5 Fed. R. Serv. 3d (Callaghan) 849; 13 Media L. Rep. 1513, *quoting* Sony Corp., Williams & Wilkins Co. v. United States, 203 Ct. Cl. 74, 487 F.2d 1345, 180 U.S.P.Q. (BNA) 49 (1973), aff'd (per curiam), 420 U.S. 376, 43 L. Ed. 2d 264, 95 S. Ct. 1344, 184 U.S.P.Q. (BNA) 705 (1975).

29. Maxtone-Graham, *quoting* Bramwell v. Halcomb, 3 My. & Cr. (Ch.) 736, 738 (1837).

30. Stephana I. Colbert and Oren R. Griffin, *The Impact of "Fair Use" in the Higher Education Community: A Necessary Exception?* 62 Albany Law Review 437, 446-447 (1998).

31. Harper & Row, Publishers, Inc. v. Nation Enterprises, 471 U.S. 539; 105 S. Ct. 2218; 85 L. Ed. 2d 588; 1985 U.S. LEXIS 17; 53 U.S.L.W. 4562; 225 U.S.P.Q. (BNA) 1073; 11 Media L. Rep. 1969 (1985). (Hereinafter Ford Case.)

32. Gerald R. Ford, *A Time to Heal: The Autobiography of Gerald R. Ford* (Harper & Row 1979).

33. *Behind the Nixon Pardon*, 228-13 Nation 353 (April 17, 1979).

34. Ford Case *at* 565, *quoting* Reply Brief for Petitioners 16, n. 8.

35. 557 F.Supp. 1067, 1072.

36. *See,* e.g., Roy Export Co. Establishment v. Columbia Broadcasting System, Inc., 503 F.Supp. 1145 (taking of 55 seconds out of 1 hour and 29-minute film deemed qualitatively substantial).

37. Sheldon v. Metro-Goldwyn Pictures Corp., 81 F.2d 49, 56 (2d Cir. 1936), *cert. denied*, 298 U.S. 669 (1936).

38. Ford Case *at* 564-565.

39. Creedence Clearwater Revival, *Cosmo's Factory* (Fantasy Records 1970).

40. Creedence Clearwater Revival, *Green River* (Fantasy Records 1969).

41. John Fogerty, *Centerfield* (Burbank, CA: Warner Brothers Records, 1985).

42. The company claimed that there was also a similarity with the subject matter (but not the content) of the song "Bad Moon Rising." According to Songfacts.com, portions of the lyrics for "Bad Moon Rising" were inspired by the movie version of *The Devil and Daniel Webster*. Since "Run Through the Jungle" and "The Old Man Down the Road" were about the devil, the company claimed that the influence of *The Devil and Daniel Webster* was pervasive throughout the three songs.

43. Hemingway v. Random House, Inc. 53 Misc.2d 462 (Sup. Ct. N.Y. County, 1967), *affirmed on other grounds*, 23 N.Y.2d 341, 296 N.Y.S.2d 771 (1969).

44. Hemingway *at* 464.

45. Hemingway *at* 470.

46. David L. Lange, *Theory and Practice in Copyright*, Address at Intellectual Property in the Digital Age (University of Wisconsin School of Education/University of Wisconsin Law School, May 8, 2001).

47. Sony Corporation of America et al. v. Universal City Studios, Inc., 464 U.S. 417 (1984).

48. Sony *at* 425, *quoting* Columbia Broadcasting System, Inc. v. Democratic National Committee, 412 U.S. 94, 102 (1973).

49. Hustler Magazine v. Falwell, 485 U.S. 46; 108 S. Ct. 876; 99 L. Ed. 2d 41; 1988 U.S. LEXIS 941; 56 U.S.L.W. 4180; 14 Media L. Rep. 2281 (1988).

50. Luther R. Campbell aka luke skyywalker, et al. v. Acuff-Rose Music,

Inc., 510 U.S. 569; 114 S. Ct. 1164; 127 L. Ed. 2d 500; 1994 U.S. LEXIS 2052; 62 U.S.L.W. 4169; 29 U.S.P.Q.2d (BNA) 1961; Copy. L. Rep. (CCH) P27,222; 22 Media L. Rep. 1353; 94 Cal. Daily Op. Service 1662; 94 Daily Journal DAR 2958; 7 Fla. L. Weekly Fed. S 800 (1994). [Hereinafter "2 Live Crew."]

51. SunTrust Bank v. Houghton Mifflin Company, 268 F.3d 1257; 2001 U.S. App. LEXIS 21690; 60 U.S.P.Q.2d (BNA) 1225; Copy. L. Rep. (CCH) P28,326; 14 Fla. L. Weekly Fed. C 1391. [Hereinafter "The Wind Done Gone."]

52. Flynt *at* 48.

53. Flynt *at* 48.

54. *id.*

55. Flynt *at* 48.

56. For more information on libel, slander, and defamation, *see*, Bryan M. Carson, *Legally Speaking: Libel*, 12-4 Against the Grain 63 (September 2000).

57. Flynt *at* 47.

58. Falwell v. Flynt, 797 F.2d 1270, 1986 U.S. App. LEXIS 27744, 13 Media L. Rep. (BNA) 1145, 21 Fed. R. Evid. Serv. (CBC) 401 (4th Cir. Va. 1986).

59. Chief Justice Rehnquist delivered the opinion of the Court, in which Brennan, Marshall, Blackmun, Stevens, O'Connor, and Scalia joined. Justice White filed an opinion concurring in the judgment, and Justice Kennedy took no part in the consideration or decision of the case.

60. Flynt *at* 50.

61. Flynt *at* 56.

62. 2 Live Crew.

63. 2 Live Crew, *Oh, Pretty Woman*, music and lyrics by Luther R. Campbell [Miami: Luke Records, 1989). Lyrics *available at* http://www.seeklyrics.com/lyrics/2-Live-Crew/Pretty-Woman.html.

64. 2 Live Crew *at* 582, *quoting* 6th Circuit opinion, Acuff-Rose Music, Inc. v. Campbell, 972 F.2d 1429, 1442.

65. 2 Live Crew *at* 583.

66. SunTrust Bank v. Houghton Mifflin Company, 136 F. Supp. 2d 1357, 1386.

67. The Wind Done Gone *at* 1260.

68. The Wind Done Gone *at* 1265.

69. The Wind Done Gone *at* 1268, *quoting* 2 Live Crew *at* 582.

70. The Wind Done Gone *at* 1268-1269.

71. According to the Wind Done Gone opinion:
In the world of GWTW, the white characters comprise a noble aristocracy whose idyllic existence is upset only by the intrusion of Yankee soldiers, and, eventually, by the liberation of the black slaves. Through her characters as well as through direct narration, Mitchell describes how both blacks and whites were purportedly better off in the days of slavery: "The more I see of emancipation the more criminal I think it is. It's just ruined the darkies," says Scarlett

O'Hara. [Margaret Mitchell, Gone with the Wind *at* 639 (Macmillan 1936).]

The Wind Done Gone *at* 1270. [Citations omitted.] For those of us who are more familiar with the movie than the book, the amount of racism portrayed in the novel is absolutely chilling.

72. The Wind Done Gone *at* 1273, *quoting* Elsmere Music, Inc. v. National Broad'g Co., 623 F.2d 252, 253 n. 1 (2d Cir. 1980).

73. The Wind Done Gone *at* 1273, *quoting* Campbell, 510 U.S. *at* 588, 114 S. Ct. *at* 1176 (numeration and emphasis added).

74. The Wind Done Gone *at* 1273-4.

75. Interview by Rosalie Seidler with Thornton Wilder, New York, N.Y. (December 14, 1956), *in* Writers at work: The Paris review interviews (Malcom Crawley ed., Viking Press 4th series 1958) *at* 104 [originally published in the Paris Review].

76. Copyright Basics, U.S. Copyright Office (June 1998), *available at* http://library.lp.findlaw.com/scripts/getfile.pl?FILE=federal/copy/copy000002 &TITLE=Subject&TOPIC=intellectual%20property_copyright_1#hsc.

77. David G. Post and Thomas R. Trempus, *An Introduction to Copyright Law*, Address at Internet Law Update (Pennsylvania Bar Institute April 9, 1986), *available at* http://www.temple.edu/lawschool/dpost/copyrit.htm.

78. Edward Samuels, *The Public Domain in Copyright Law*, 41 Journal of the Copyright Society 137 (1993), *available at* http://www.nyls.edu/samuels/copyright/beyond/articles/public.html. *See also*, Melville B. Nimmer and David Nimmer, *Nimmer on Copyright* § 8C.02. (Mathew Bender 1978).

79. 17 U.S.C. § 103(b)(1). *See also*, Samuels *at* 139.

80. Nimmer *at* § 8C.02. *See also*, Samuels *at* 137.

81. *id.*

82. Stanley v. Columbia Broadcasting System, Inc., 35 Cal.2d 653, 221 P.2d 73 (S. Ct. Cal. 1950).

83. The copyright law protects "original works of authorship fixed in any tangible medium of expression, now known or later developed, from which they can be perceived, reproduced, or otherwise communicated, either directly or with the aid of a machine or device." 17 U.S.C. § 102.

84. Stanley *at* 29.

85. Stanley *at* 30, *quoting* California Civil Code § 980.

86. Stanley *at* 672-673 (Traynor, J., Dissenting).

87. Nimmer *at* § 8C.02.

88. Nimmer *at* § 8C.02.

89. Hemingway v. Random House, Inc. 53 Misc.2d 462 (Sup. Ct. N.Y. County, 1967), *affirmed on other grounds*, 23 N.Y.2d 341, 296 N.Y.S.2d 771 (1969).

90. Hemingway *at* 464.

91. Hemingway *at* 466. The cases cited by the opinion in support of their argument are: Smith v. Little, Brown & Co., 245 F. Supp. 451 (U.S. Dist. Ct., S.D.N.Y., 1966), affd. 360 F.2d 928 (2d Cir., 1966); Fendler v. Morosco, 253

N.Y. 281 (1930); Malkin v. Dubinsky, 25 Misc. 2d 460 (Sup. Ct., N.Y. County, 1960).

92. Hemingway *at* 466-467.

93. Rosemont Enterprises v. Random House, 366 F.2d 303 (2d Cir., 1966).

94. Rosemont *at* 307, *quoted in* Hemingway *at* 467. The Rosemont court also cited Harriss v. Miller, 50 U.S.P.Q. 306, 309 (S.D.N.Y. 1941).

95. 17 U.S.C. § 102.

96. Nimmer *at* § 2.02.

97. *id.*

98. Kenneth D. Crews, *Roadmap for Copyright Compliance, in* Copyright Law and Graduate Research (ProQuest Information and Learning, Dissertation Publishing 2000), *available at*
http://www.umi.com/hp/Support/DServices/copyrght/Part3.html.

99. 17 U.S.C. § 102.

100. Georgia Harper, *Ownership of Lectures: Commercial Notetaking in University Courses*, Crash Course in Copyright (University of Texas System 2001), *available at*
http://www.utsystem.edu/OGC/IntellectualProperty/lectures.htm.

101. Harper.

102. 17 U.S.C. § 303.

103. Crews.

104. Wheaton v. Peters, 33 U.S. (8 Peters) 591 (1834).

105. *See*, Robert W. Clarida, *Publish or Perish: Clock Is Ticking for Unpublished Works*, Legal Language Services (December 2000), *available at* http://www.legallanguage.com/lawarticles/Clarida010.html. *See also*, Nimmer *at* § 2.04 (discussing computer software and digital publications).

106. Clarida.

107. *Copyright Registration for Online Works*, Copyright Office Circular 66 (June 1999), *available at* http://www.loc.gov/copyright/circs/circ66.html.

108. Clarida.

109. *Copyright Office Compendium II: Copyright Office Procedures* § 905.03, U.S. Copyright Office (1984).

110. Salinger v. Random House, 811 F.2d 90 (2d Cir. 1987).

111. Wright v. Warner Books, 748 F. Supp. 105 (S.D.N.Y. 1990).

112. Salinger *at* 92. *See also*, Ian Hamilton, J. D. *Salinger: A Writing Life*, (Random House 1986).

113. Salinger *at* 93.

114. Harper & Row, Publishers, Inc. v. Nation Enterprises, 471 U.S. 539, 564 (1959).

115. Hemingway v. Random House, Inc. 53 Misc.2d 462 (Sup. Ct. N.Y. County, 1967), *affirmed on other grounds*, 23 N.Y.2d 341, 296 N.Y.S.2d 771 (1969). There is a more extensive discussion of this issue in my column in the February 2002 issue of *Against the Grain*.

116. Salinger *at* 94.

117. Salinger *at* 94-95 (*quoting* Nimmer *at* § 5.04).

118. Salinger *at* 94-95 (*quoting* Nimmer *at* § 5.04).

119. Salinger *at* 97.

120. Salinger *at* 100.

121. Wright v. Warner Books, 748 F. Supp. 105 (S.D.N.Y. 1990).

122. Margaret Walker, *Richard Wright: Daemonic Genius; A Portrait of the Man, a Critical Look at His Work* (Warner Books 1988).

123. Wright *at* 107.

124. Wright *at* 109.

125. Wright *at* 110. The judge went on to say that even if the letters were considered unpublished, the use of quotations was allowed by the doctrine of fair use.

126. Wright *at* 110.

127. Wright v. Warner Books, Inc., 953 F.2d 731, 1991 U.S. App. LEXIS 28198, Copy. L. Rep. (CCH) P26830, 19 Media L. Rep. (BNA) 1577, 20 U.S.P.Q.2d (BNA) 1892 (2d Cir. N.Y. 1991) (hereafter "Wright II").

128. Wright II *at* 740.

129. Wright *at* 113.

130. Clarida.

131. Nimmer *at* § 4.10.

132. Certified Engineering, Inc., v. First Fidelity Bank, N.A., 849 F. Supp. 318 (D.N.J. 1994).

133. Nimmer *at* § 4.10, n. 2.1.

134. Copyright Office Compendium II *at* § 905.02.

135. Clarida.

136. Nimmer *at* § 4.04, 4.10.

137. Nimmer *at* § 4.13, *quoting* Intown Enterprises, Inc. v. Barnes, 721 F. Supp. 1263, 1265 (D. Colo. 1992).

138. Crews.

139. Crews.

140. Crews.

141. 17 U.S.C. § 303.

142. 17 U.S.C. § 303.

143. Nimmer *at* § 9.01[b][2].

144. Clarida.

145. Crews.

146. 17 U.S.C. § 303.

147. 17 U.S.C. § 303.

Chapter 5

1. 17 U.S.C. § 107.

2. 17 U.S.C. § 110.

3. 17 U.S.C. § 110(1).

4. 17 U.S.C. § 110(2).

5. 17 U.S.C. § 107.

6. House Report No. 94-1476, U.S. House of Representatives (1976), *available at* http://www.rbs2.com/copyr2.htm.

7. *id.*

8. *id.*

9. *id.*

10. *See*, Georgia Harper, *Copyright in the Classroom, Fair Use: Reserve Room Operations, Print Copies*, University of Texas System Office of the General Counsel (last modified January 30, 2003), *available at* http://www.utsystem.edu/ogc/intellectualproperty/l-respri.htm.

11. Association of American Publishers, *Frequently Asked Questions about E-Reserves* (last updated May 17, 2004), *available at* http://www.publishers.org/about/pdf/E-ReserveFAQ.doc.

12. *id.*

13. National Information Infrastructure Task Force Working Group on Intellectual Property Rights, *Conference on Fair Use* (1994-1996), *available at* http://www.utsystem.edu/ogc/intellectualproperty/confu.htm.

14. Paul R. Pival, *Legal Battle Brews over Texts on Electronic Reserve at U. of California Libraries*, The Distant Librarian, (April 12, 2005), *available at* http://distlib.blogs.com/distlib/2005/04/legal_battle_br.html.

15. Harper.

16. American Library Association, *Fair Use and Electronic Reserves* (March 2004), *available at* http://www.ala.org/ala/washoff/WOissues/copyrightb/fairuseandelectronicreserves/ereservesFU.htm.

17. *id.*

18. For example, Touro International University, the distance education section of Touro College in New York, provides Ph.D. degrees in Business Administration and Health Sciences. The degrees do not require any residency. This program is fully accredited by the Commission on Higher Education of the Middle States Association of Colleges and Schools. *See*, Touro's Website *at* http://www.tourou.edu.

19. For a history of distance education efforts, *see* Bizhan Nasseh, *A Brief History of Distance Education* (1998), *available at* http://www.seniornet.org/edu/art/history.html. *See also*, Gary A. Berg, *Public Policy on Distance Learning in Higher Education: California State and Western Governors Association Initiatives*, 6-11 Education Policy Analysis Archives (June 12, 1998), *available at* http://epaa.asu.edu/epaa/v6n11.html.

20. This provision came from the original language used in the 1976 Act. 17 U.S.C. § 110(2) (amended 2002).

21. *id.*

22. On May 6-9, 2001, I went to Madison, Wisconsin, to attend the conference Intellectual Property in the Digital Age. The conference began two days after the joint agreement was negotiated. Many of the negotiators were participants at this conference, and the agreement was reported at that time.

23. Technology, Education and Copyright Harmonization Act of 2001,

107 S. 487; Pub. L. No. 107-273 § 13301; 116 Stat. 1758 § 13301; *codified at* 17 U.S.C. § 110(2) - § 110(11) (2002).

24. 147 Congressional Record D 688 (2001).

25. 148 Congressional Record D 772 (2002).

26. House Report 107-687 (2002).

27. 148 Congressional Record H 6691 (2002).

28. 17 U.S.C. § 110(2).

29. *id.*

30. 17 U.S.C. § 110(11).

31. *id.*

32. *id.*

33. *id.*

34. 17 U.S.C. § 110(11).

35. *id.*

36. This is a reference to the Digital Millennium Copyright Act, 17 U.S.C. Section 1201 et seq.

37. The DVD zones are as follows:

♦ Zone 1: North America;

♦ Zone 2: Europe, Japan, South Africa, Israel, Lebanon, Mid-East;

♦ Zone 3: Korea;

♦ Zone 4: South America and Australia;

♦ Zone 5: Russia, North-East countries, Africa;

♦ Zone 6: China;

♦ Zone 7: Reserved;

♦ Zone 8: Special international venues (airplanes, ships, etc.).

See, DVD Zones and Map (last accessed September 12, 2005), *available at* http://www.its-digitalmedia.com/dvd_zones_and_map.htm.

38. 17 U.S.C. § 110(2).

39. *id.*

40. One professor at Western Kentucky University has dealt with the issue of performances for her distance education students by having each student join Netflicks (www.netflicks.com/). The students can then rent any video or DVD and it will be sent through the mail.

41. Professor Crews is the Associate Dean of the Faculties for Copyright Management and director of the Copyright Management Center at Indiana University-Purdue University, Indianapolis; he holds a joint appointment in the Indiana University School of Law, Indianapolis and in the IU School of Library and Information Science.

42. Kenneth Crews, *New Copyright Law for Distance Education: The Meaning and Importance of the TEACH Act* (last updated November 10, 2003), *available at* http://www.copyright.iupui.edu/teach_summary.htm).

43. David L. Lange, *Theory and Practice in Copyright*, address at Intellectual Property in the Digital Age (University of Wisconsin School of Educa-

tion/University of Wisconsin Law School, May 8, 2001).

44. MaryBeth Peters, Address at Intellectual Property in the Digital Age (University of Wisconsin School of Education/University of Wisconsin Law School, May 7, 2001).

Chapter 6

1. *See*, United States Patent and Trademark Office (last visited June 16, 2005), *available at* http://www.uspto.gov/.

2. Although the full name is almost never used, OCLC stands for "Online Computer Library Center."

3. *See*, Bryan M. Carson, *Dewey, Dastar, and the OCLC-Library Hotel Dispute: A Question of Trademark or Copyright*, 15-6 Against the Grain 70 (December 2003).

4. Although portions of this chapter have been previously published in my columns in *Against the Grain*, there is also a significant amount of material in this chapter that has not been published elsewhere.

5. Mark Radcliffe, *Patent, Trademark, and Trade Secret Law* § 2 Findlaw Professionals (last accessed July 25, 2005), *available at* http://profs.lp.findlaw.com/patents/patents_2.html. *Excerpted from* Mark Radcliffe, *The Multimedia Law and Business Handbook* (Ladera Press 1999).

6. *id.*

7. *id.*

8. Walter E. Hurst and Fred Woessner, *How to Register a Trademark: Protect Yourself Before You Lose Your Priceless Trademark* § 2 (Seven Arts Press 1983).

9. Radcliffe.

10. Julie Ann Gregory, *Basic Trademark Law: Tips for Selecting and Developing Strong Trademark Rights*, address at the Louisville Bar Association (June 15, 2005) (transcript available at the Louisville Bar Association).

11. *Official Gazette of the Patent and Trademark Office* (last accessed September 25, 2005), *available at* http://www.uspto.gov/web/trademarks/tmog.

12. 60 Stat. 427.

13. 104 P.L. 98, 109 Stat. 985, *codified at* 15 U.S.C. § 1125 et seq.

14. 15 U.S.C. § 1052.

15. Gregory.

16. *id.*

17. *id.*

18. American Heritage Dictionary of the English Language 1316 (New College ed. 1976).

19. Gregory.

20. Needham J. Boddie II, *Types of Trademark Protection, available at* http://www.myersbigel.com/tm_articles/trade_mark1.htm (last modified 1997).

21. *id.* Boddie does point out that "registration on the supplemental regis-

ter does not preclude an applicant from later applying to register on the principal register if the mark has become sufficiently distinctive through use."

22. 15 U.S.C. § 1125.

23. 15 U.S.C. § 1125(c)(1), *available at* http://www4.law.cornell.edu/uscode/15/1125.html.

24. Kenneth DeLeon, *Creating a Protectable and Marketable Trademark*, Registering a Trademark.com (last visited February 28, 2005), *available at* http://www.registeringatrademark.com/protectable-marketable-trademark.shtml.

25. Rodger Braunfeld and Thomas O. Wells, *Intellectual Property Protection*, *available at* http://informatica.uv.es/iiguia/2000/IPI/material/intellectual_prop.pdf.

26. Original Appalachian Artworks, Inc. v. Topps Chewing Gum, 642 F.Supp. 1031 (N.D.Ga.1986).

27. Moseley v. V Secret Catalog, 537 U.S. 418; 123 S. Ct. 1115; 155 L. Ed. 2d 1; 2003 U.S. LEXIS 1945; 71 U.S.L.W. 4126; 65 U.S.P.Q.2d (BNA) 1801 (2003).

28. *id.*

29. *id.* at 423.

30. *id.*

31. *id.*

32. *id.* at 423-424.

33. *id.* at 424.

34. V Secret Catalogue, Inc. v. Moseley, 2000 U.S. Dist. LEXIS 5215, Civ. Action No. 3:98CV-395-S (WD Ky., Feb. 9, 2000).

35. V Secret Catalogue, Inc. v. Moseley, 259 F.3d 464 (6th Cir. 2001).

36. Moseley *at* 433.

37. *id.*

38. Scot A. Duvall, *A Work of Progess, in Progress: The Trademark Dilution Revision Act of 2005*, address at the Louisville Bar Association (June 15, 2005) (transcript available at the Louisville Bar Association).

39. *id.*

40. Moseley *at* 432. *See,* Robert N. Klieger, *Trademark Dilution: The Whittling Away of the Rational Basis for Trademark Protection*, 58 University of Pittsburgh Law Review 789, 812-813, and n. 132 (1997).

41. H.R. 109-683 (2005), introduced February 9, 2005; passed by House April 19, 2005.

42. H.R. 109-683 § 2(C).

43. H.R. 109-683 § 2(2)(B).

44. David L. Lange, *Theory and Practice in Copyright*, Address at Intellectual Property in the Digital Age (University of Wisconsin School of Education/University of Wisconsin Law School, May 8, 2001).

45. Flynt *at* 53, *quoting* Mark Long, *The Political Cartoon: Journalism's Strongest Weapon*, The Quill, 56, 57 (Nov. 1962).

46. Hustler Magazine v. Falwell, 485 U.S. 46, 53-54; 108 S. Ct. 876; 99 L.

Ed. 2d 41; 1988 U.S. LEXIS 941; 56 U.S.L.W. 4180; 14 Media L. Rep. 2281 (1988).

47. H.R. 109-683(3).

48. Duvall.

49. 2 Live Crew *at* 583.

50. Dastar Corporation v. 20th Century Fox Film Corporation, 539 U.S. 23; 123 S. Ct. 2041; 156 L. Ed. 2d 18 (2003), *available at* http://www.acm.org/usacm/PDF/Legal/Dastar_v_Twentieth_Century.pdf.

51. *See*, e.g., O. & W. Thum Co. v. Dickinson, 245 F. 609, 621 (6th Cir. 1917).

52. Dastar *at* note 1. *See*, e.g., Williams v. Curtiss-Wright Corp., 691 F.2d 168, 172 (3d Cir. 1982).

53. Federal Electric Co. v. Flexlume Corp., 33 F.2d 412, 1929 U.S. App. LEXIS 2734, 2 U.S.P.Q. (BNA) 107 (7th Cir. 1929).

54. John T. Cross, *Giving Credit Where Credit Is Due: Revisiting the Doctrine of Reverse Passing Off in Trademark Law*, 72 Wash. L. Rev. 709, 716 (1997).

55. Cross *at* 721.

56. Cross *at* 726.

57. Cross *at* 727.

58. Cross *at* 730.

59. Cross *at* 730.

60. *See*, Big O Tires Website (last visited September 13, 2005), *available at* http://www.bigotires.com. Big O Tires operates in 21 states, including Kentucky, Indiana, Michigan, and every state west of the Mississippi except for Arkansas, Louisiana, Minnesota, and North Dakota.

61. Peter Gunst, *Protect Your Brand, Protect Your Business*, Astrachan Gunst Thomas P.C. (last modified January 25, 2005), *available at* http://www.agtlawyers.com/thefirm/newsitem.php?item=142.

62. *id*. The decision in the Big O case is unpublished and not available.

63. Dastar Corporation v. 20th Century Fox Film Corporation, 539 U.S. 23; 123 S. Ct. 2041; 156 L. Ed. 2d 18 (2003), *available at* http://www.acm.org/usacm/PDF/Legal/Dastar_v_Twentieth_Century.pdf.

64. This information is taken directly from the Supreme Court opinion in Dastar.

65. Dastar *at* 27.

66. *id*.

67. 15 U.S.C. § 1125(a).

68. Twentieth Century Fox Film Corp. v. Entertainment Distributing, 34 Fed. Appx. 312 *at* 316 (9th Cir. 2002).

69. Entertainment Distributing *at* 314. This language from the 9th Circuit was also quoted in the Supreme Court opinion.

70. Dastar *at* 33, *quoting* Sears, Roebuck & Co. v. Stiffel Co., 376 U.S. 225, 230 (1964); *see also*, Kellogg Co. v. National Biscuit Co., 305 U.S. 111, 121.122 (1938).

71. Dastar *at* 33, *quoting* TrafFix Devices, Inc. v. Marketing Displays, Inc., 532 U.S. 23, 29 (2001).

72. Dastar *at* 33, *quoting* Bonito Boats, Inc. v. Thunder Craft Boats, Inc., 489 U.S. 141, 150-151 (1989).

73. Dastar *at* 34.

74. For a different proposition that lends support to this conclusion, *see*, 17 U.S.C. § 202 (distinguishing between a copyrighted work and "any material object in which the work is embodied").

75. Dastar *at* 37, *citing* Eldred v. Ashcroft, 537 U.S. 186, 208 (2003).

76. Jonathan Band and Matt Schruers, *Dastar, Attribution, and Plagiarism*, 33-1 AIPLA Quarterly Journal 2 (Winter 2005).

77. *id.* at 11.

78. This endnote is dedicated to Ronald D. Raitt, Professor Emeritus of Law at the University of Toledo. Professor Raitt was my Civil Procedure professor in law school and has had a very large influence on my career. He is an absolutely amazing teacher and mentor. Professor Raitt became a faculty member in 1966, teaching in the areas of Civil Procedure, Evidence, and Products Liability. Professor Raitt, a graduate of the University of Nebraska, has been a pilot in the United States Air Force, Assistant U.S. Attorney and Minority Counsel, Antitrust and Monopoly Subcommittee of the Judiciary Committee of the United States Senate. Professor Raitt retired in 2004. "You get one pull on the litigation lever" is one of his favorite expressions.

79. The domain name examples in this section are fictional. They are intended only as examples.

80. *Everything you always wanted to know about the Internet—and then some* (last accessed April 25, 2001), *available at* http://www.merinodesign.com/Webdesigntips.htm.

81. *id.*

82. Internet Corporation for Assigned Names and Numbers (ICANN), *ICANN Fact Sheet* (last accessed April 25, 2001), *available at* http://www.icann.org/fact-sheet.htm.

83. *id.*

84. ICANN, *New TLD Program* (last accessed April 25, 2001), *available at* http://www.icann.org/TLDS.

85. *id.*

86. *id.*

87. 113 Stat. 2501, P.L. 106-113 (1999), *available at* http://www.mama-tech.com/antipiracy.html.

88. *id.*

89. ICANN, *Uniform Domain-Name Dispute-Resolution Policy* (August 26, 1999), *available at* http://www.icann.org/udrp/udrp-policy-24oct99.htm. *See also*, ICANN, *Rules for Uniform Domain Name Dispute Resolution Policy* (October 24, 1999), *available at* http://www.icann.org/udrp/udrp-rules-24oct99.htm.

90. Federal Trade Commission, *What's Dot and What's Not: Domain*

Name Registration Scams, FTC Consumer Alert (December 2000), *available at* http://www.ftc.gov/bcp/conline/pubs/alerts/domainalrt.htm.

91. T. R. Halvorson and Reva Basch, *Law of the Super Searchers: The Online Secrets of Top Legal Researchers* (CyberAge Books 2000).

92. T. R. Halvorson, LexNotes, *available at* http://www.lexnotes.com/index.shtml.

93. *id.*

94. T. R. Halvorson, trh@lexnotes.com, posting to law-lib@ucdavis.edu (March 12, 2001).

95. *id.*

96. T. R. Halvorson, *Lex Domains—Partial Listing*, LexNotes (last accessed September 27, 2005), *available at* http://www.lexnotes.com/tm/lexdomains.shtml.

97. Karen Mahnk, karenpdo@gate.net, posting to law-lib@ucdavis.edu (March 13, 2001).

98. Mead Data Central, Inc. v. Toyota Motor Sales, U.S.A., Inc., 875 F.2d 1026 (2nd Cir., 1989).

99. Mead Data Central *at* 1027, *quoting* Edward C. Pinkerton, *Word for Word* at 179 (Verbatum Books 1982).

100. Mead Data Central *at* 1027, *quoting* Oxford Latin Dictionary (Clarendon Press 1982); Charlton Thomas Lewis and Charles Short, *A Latin Dictionary Founded on Andrews' Edition of Freund's Latin Dictionary* (1879, 1980); Charlton Thomas Lewis, *An Elementary Latin Dictionary: With Brief Helps for Latin Readers* (Oxford University Press 1891, 1979).

101. *id.* at 1029, footnote 2.

102. *id. See also*, Ardena L. Walsh, walshal@cooley.edu, posting to law-lib@ucdavis.edu (March 13, 2001).

103. Black's Law Dictionary *at* 920-925 (7th ed. 1999). *See also*, Bryan M. Carson, bryan.carson@wku.edu, posting to law-lib@ucdavis.edu (March 13, 2001).

104. *id.*

105. T. R. Halvorson, LexNotes (last modified December 18, 2004), *available at* http://www.lexnotes.com/.

106. 17 U.S.C. § 106(1).

107. 17 U.S.C. § 106(3).

108. 17 U.S.C. § 106(5).

109. 17 U.S.C. § 106(6).

110. 17 U.S.C. § 101.

111. 17 U.S.C. § 101.

112. A&M Records v. Napster, Inc., 239 F.3d 1004 (9th Circuit, 2001).

113. *See*, 17 U.S.C. § 101.

114. Randel S. Springer, *What Is Framing?* Business Power Law.Com (last accessed August 14, 2005), *available at* http://www.businesspowerlaw.com/13/300?PHPSESSID=e32c0cdce9fe224b2d 6b55463a4a17db.

115. Ticketmaster Corp. v. Tickets.com, Inc., 2003 U.S. Dist. LEXIS 6483; Copy. L. Rep. (CCH) *at* 28,607 (C.D.Cal., 2003).

116. *Spider*, WhatIs.com, *available at* http://whatis.techtarget.com/definition/0,,sid9_gci213035,00.html.

117. Ticketmaster *at* 15. [Since this case is unpublished, I am using the LEXIS page numbers.]

118. Ticketmaster *at* 21, *quoting* Reply Brief *at* 10.

119. Ticketmaster *at* 21-23.

120. Springer.

121. For more information on Trademark, *see* Bryan Carson, *Legally Speaking—Dewey, Dastar, and the OCLC-Library Hotel Dispute: A Question of Trademark or Copyright*, 15-6 Against the Grain 70 (December 2003 / January 2004).

122. Washington Post v. TotalNews Order of Dismissal [unpublished], 97 Civ. 1190 (S.D.N.Y.), *available at* http://legal.Web.aol.com/decisions/dlip/washorde.html.

123. TotalNews.

124. For example, *see* Michael A. Stoker, Comment: *Framed Web Pages: Framing the Derivative Works Doctrine on the World Wide Web*, 67 University of Cincinnati Law Review 1301 (Summer 1999); Springer; Lloyd L. Rich, *Internet Legal Issues: Framing*, The Publishing Law Center, *available at* http://www.publaw.com/framing.html; Ivan Hoffman, *Linking and Crawling Issues* (2003) *available at* http://www.ivanhoffman.com/linking.html.

125. 17 U.S.C. § 1201.

126. Erin Joyce, *Hacker Mag 2600 Drops DMCA Fight*, Internet News.Com (July 3, 2003), *available at* http://www.internetnews.com/bus-news/article.php/1380791.

127. American Jurisprudence 2d *Libel and Slander* § 6.

128. Mitchell v. Random House, Inc., 703 F.Supp. 1250 (S.D.Miss., 1988).

129. Moldea v. New York Times Co., 15 F.3d 1137 (C.A.D.C.,1994).

130. For more information on defamation, *see* Bryan M. Carson, *Legally Speaking: Libel*, 12-4 Against the Grain 79 (September 2000).

131. Nolo Press, *Trade Secret Basics FAQ*, Findlaw.com (accessed July 20, 2004), *available at* http://biz.findlaw.com/intellectual_property/nolo/faq/90781CA8-0ECE-4E38-BF9E29F7A6DA5830.html.

132. *id.*

133. National Conference of Commissioners on Uniform State Laws, *Uniform Trade Secrets Act with 1985 Amendments* (August 2-9, 1985), *available at* http://www.law.upenn.edu/bll/ulc/fnact99/1980s/utsa85.htm.

134. 18 U.S.C. §§ 1831 to 1839. According to Findlaw, "The EEA punishes intentional stealing, copying or receiving of trade secrets 'related to or included in a product that is produced for or placed in interstate commerce.' (18 U.S.C. 1832.) Penalties for violations are severe: Individuals may be fined up

to $500,000 and corporations up to $5 million. A violator may also be sent to prison for up to ten years. If the theft is performed on behalf of a foreign government or agent, the corporate fines can double and jail time may increase to 15 years. (18 U.S.C. 1831.) In addition, the property used and proceeds derived from the theft can be seized and sold by the government. (18 U.S.C. §§ 1831, 1834.)"

135. For the complete text of the advertisement, see *Ethnic Groups: Chinese, TV Acres* (accessed July 20, 2004), *available at* http://www.tvacres.com/ethnic_chinese.htm.

136. Findlaw.

137. PepsiCo, Inc., v. Redmond, 54 F.3d 1262; 1995 U.S. App. LEXIS 10903; 35 U.S.P.Q.2d (BNA) 1010 (7th Circuit, 1995).

138. Ivan Hoffman, *Inevitable Disclosure of Trade Secrets* (accessed July 20, 2004), *available at* http://www.ivanhoffman.com/inevitable.html.

139. Redmond *at* 1268.

140. Redmond *at* 1271.

141. Whyte v. Schlage Lock Co., 101 Cal. App. 4th 1443; 125 Cal. Rptr. 2d 277; 2002 Cal. App. LEXIS 4634 (Cal. App., 2002).

142. Whyte *at* 1462-3.

143. 18 U.S.C. §§ 1831 to 1839.

144. Findlaw. *See*, 18 U.S.C. § 1832.

145. Findlaw. *See*, 18 U.S.C. § 1831.

146. 18 U.S.C. §§ 1831, 1834.

Chapter 7

1. Kenneth L. Port, Charles R. McManis, Terence P. McElwee, and Faye M. Hammersley, *Licensing Intellectual Property in the Digital Age* (Durham, NC: Carolina Academic Press, 1999).

2. Black's Law Dictionary, License, Patents (5th edition, 1979), *quoting* De Forest Radio Telephone & Telegraph Co. v. Radio Corporation of America, 9 F.2d 150, 151 (D. Del. 1925), aff'd 20 F.2d 598 (3d Cir. 1927).

3. Port *at* 287.

4. Western Electric Co., Inc., v. Pacent Reproducer Corporation, 42 F.2d 116, 118 (2d Cir. 1930).

5. Western Electric *at* 118.

6. Western Electric *at* 118.

7. 17 U.S.C. § 106(3).

8. According to House Report No. 94-1476, which was prepared to accompany §106 of the Copyright Act, "Under this provision the copyright owner would have the right to control the first public distribution of an authorized copy or phonorecord of his work, whether by sale, gift, loan, or some rental or lease arrangement. Likewise, any unauthorized public distribution of copies or phonorecords that were unlawfully made would be an infringement. As section

109 makes clear, however, the copyright owner's rights under section 106(3) cease with respect to a particular copy or phonorecord once he has parted with ownership of it."

9. 17 U.S.C. § 109(a).

10. 17 U.S.C. § 109(b)(1)(a).

11. 17 U.S.C. § 109(b)(1)(a).

12. License, Word IQ (last accessed February 26, 2005), *available at* http://www.wordiq.com/definition/Licensing.

13. Lisa Browar, Cathy Henderson, Michael North, and Tara Wenger, Licensing the Use of Special Collections Materials, RBM 3 no2 *at* 124-44 (Fall 2002).

14. Uniform Computer Information Transactions Act (Draft for Approval, July 23-30, 1999), *available at* http://www.law.upenn.edu/bll/ulc/ucita/citam99.htm.

15. Raymond T. Nimmer, *UCITA and the Continuing Evolution of Digital Licensing Law*, 24 Licensing Journal 7 (June 2004).

16. *id.*

17. Cem Kaner, *In My Opinion: Objections to the Proposed Uniform Computer Information Transactions Act*, 4 Cyberspace Lawyer 14 (1999).

18. David Mirchin, *Online Contracts*, Third Annual Internet Law Institute 351, 355 (Practicing Law Institute June 14-15, 1999).

19. Christy Hudgins-Bonafield, *UCC 2B: The New Law of Shrink-Wrap*, Network Computing (April 19, 1999), *available at* http://www.networkcomputing.com/1008/1008f1side5.html.

20. American Library Association, *UCITA History* (last accessed September 16, 2005), *available at* http://www.ala.org/ala/washoff/oitp/emailtutorials/ucitaa/05.htm. Raymond Nimmer, an expert in intellectual property and professor at the University of Houston Law Center, was named Reporter of the UCC Article 2B drafting committee.

21. James W. Fiscus, *American Law Institute Withdraws Sponsorship of UCC Article 2B*, The Bulletin (Summer 1999), *available at* http://www.sfwa.org/news/2b.htm.

22. Letter from Robert L. Oakley, Washington Affairs Representative, American Association of Law Libraries, and Jim Heller, Chair, American Association of Law Libraries Copyright Committee, to Professor Raymond Nimmer, Reporter, UCC Article 2B Drafting Committee (March 27, 1997).

23. Brenda Sandburg, *UCC2B Is Dead—Long Live UCITA: Supporters face a big battle to pass a uniform information licensing law for the Internet*, The Recorder/Cal Law (May 27, 1999), *available at* http://www.lawnewsnet.com/stories/A1807-1999May26.html.

24. Kaner *at* 14.

25. Fiscus.

26. Sandburg.

27. *Electronic Commerce Legislation: Gaining Momentum and Changing*

Direction, ITEC Law Alert (June 1999), *available at* http://www.mbc.com/newsletters/Itec/Itec699.htm.

28. Letter from Duane E. Webster, Executive Director, Association of Research Libraries, to Gene N. Lebrun, President, National Conference of Commissioners on Uniform State Laws (July 12, 1999).

29. Letter from Barbara Simons, President, Association for Computing Machinery, to the National Conference of Commissioners on Uniform State Laws (July 12, 1999), *available at* http://www.acm.org/usacm/copyright/usacm-ucita.html.

30. On July 23, 1999, the Attorney General of Oklahoma wrote a letter of opposition to Gene Lebrun, the president of NCCUSL. The Attorneys General of Connecticut, Idaho, Indiana, Iowa, Kansas, Maryland, Nevada, New Mexico, North Dakota, Pennsylvania, Vermont, Washington, and the Administrator of the Georgia Fair Business Practices Act signed this letter. Letter from W. A. Drew Edmondson, Attorney General of Oklahoma, to Gene Lebrun, President, National Conference of Commissioners on Uniform State Laws (July 23, 1999), *available at* http://www.badsoftware.com/aglet1.htm.

On July 28, 1999, the Attorney General of Oklahoma sent a second letter indicating that the Attorneys General of California, Arizona, Arkansas, Florida, Minnesota, Mississippi, Missouri, New Jersey, Tennessee, West Virginia, and Wisconsin agreed with the principles stated in the July 23, 1999, letter and were united in their opposition to UCITA. Letter from W. A. Drew Edmondson, Attorney General of Oklahoma, to Gene Lebrun, President, National Conference of Commissioners on Uniform State Laws (July 28, 1999), *available at* http://www.badsoftware.com/aglet2.htm.

Eventually several other state Attorneys General joined the opposition camp. In addition to the states that had previously signed letters (Arizona, Arkansas, California, Connecticut, Florida, Georgia, Idaho, Iowa, Minnesota, Mississippi, Missouri, Nevada, New Jersey, New Mexico, Pennsylvania, Tennessee, Vermont, West Virginia, and Wisconsin), several new states and territories have signed their opposition to UCITA. The new entities include Colorado, Delaware, Louisiana, Maine, Massachusetts, Michigan, Montana, New Hampshire, New York, Northern Marianas, Ohio, Oregon, Virgin Islands, and Wyoming. Several states, which had previously signed letters, did not sign the most recent one; these states include Indiana, Kansas, Maryland (which had already passed the statute), North Dakota, and Washington. Letter from the National Association of Attorneys General to Carlyle C. Ring, Commissioner, National Conference of Commissioners on Uniform State Laws (Nov. 13, 2001), *available at* http://www.affect.ucita.com/pdf/Nov132001_Letter_from_AGs_to_Carlyle_Ring.pdf.

31. The delegates voting against the bill represented Alaska, Iowa, Minnesota, Nebraska, North Carolina, and Utah. *Copyright and Intellectual Property News*, Association for Computing Machinery Website (last accessed October 28, 1999), *available at* http://www.acm.org/usacm/copyright.

32. Ed Foster, *What Is UCITA?* Info World Electronic (August 30, 1999),

available at http://archive.infoworld.com/cgi-bin/displayStory.pl?/features /990531ucita1.htm.

33. James Love, james.love@cptech.org, posting to ecom-merce@essential.org (May 28, 1999), *available at* http://lists.essential.org/random-bits/msg00104.html.

34. David A. Rice, drice@law.rwu.edu, posting to cni-copyright@CNI.ORG (June 1, 1999), *available at* http://www.cni.org/Hforums/cni-copyright/1999-02/0424.html.

35. Raymond T. Nimmer, *UCITA and the Continuing Evolution of Digital Licensing Law*, 24 Licensing Journal 7 (June 2004).

36. *id.*

37. Letter from Cem Kaner to the American Law Institute (October 1997), *available at* http://www.badsoftware.com/ali.htm.

38. Cem Kaner, *Why Writers Should Actively Oppose the Uniform Computer Information Transactions Act (UCITA)* (June 19, 1999), *available at* http://www.nwu.org/pic/ucita2.htm.

39. Uniform Computer Information Transactions Act § 103(2)(B) Reporter's Notes (Draft for Approval, July 23-30, 1999). *See also, id.* § 102(12); *id.* § 102(69), *available at* http://www.law.upenn.edu/bll/ulc/ucita/citam99.htm.

40. Bill Gates, *The Road Ahead* (Viking Press 1995).

41. *See*, Jonathan Franklin, *The Perils of Clicking 'I Agree': UCITA and Intellectual Freedom*, 19-1 Alki 10 (March 2003).

42. Why Writers Should Actively Oppose the Uniform Computer Information Transactions Act (UCITA).

43. *id.*

44. Hudgins-Bonafield.

45. Mirchin *at* 357.

46. Sandburg.

47. Debra Gersh Hernandez, *Newspaper, Magazine Associations Oppose Plan to Regulate States' Licensing of Computer Information*, Newspaper Association of America Press Release (August 1999), *available at* http://www.naa.org/about/news/08_ucita.html.

48. Letter from the Working Group on Consumer Protection, American Bar Association Business Law Section, Committee on the Law of Cyberspace, Subcommittee on Electronic Commerce to Gene Lebrun, President, National Conference of Commissioners on Uniform State Laws (June 10, 1999), *available at* http://tao.ca/wind/rre/0713.html.

49. Holly K. Towle, *Drafting and Updating Online Contracts and Website Disclaimers*, Third Annual Internet Law Institute 427, 435 (Practicing Law Institute June 14-15, 1999).

50. Tasini v. New York Times Co., 533 U.S. 483, 150 L. Ed. 2d 500, 121 S. Ct. 2381 (2001). Previous incarnations of the case include: 972 F. Supp. 804, 1997 (this case will be referred to as "Tasini I"); *reconsideration denied*, Tasini v. New York Times Co., 981 F. Supp. 841, 1997 U.S. Dist. LEXIS 17140 (S.D.N.Y. 1997); *reversed and remanded*, 192 F.3d 356, 1999 (2d Cir. N.Y.

1999); *opinion withdrawn by Court and replaced by* 206 F.3d 161 (this case will be referred to as "Tasini II"); *writ of certiorari granted*, 148 L. Ed. 2d 434, 121 S. Ct. 425. For related proceeding, *see also*, Marx v. Globe Newspaper Co., 2001 Mass. Super. LEXIS 9 (Mass. Super. Ct. Jan. 11, 2001).

51. Tasini I *at* 806.

52. Tasini I *at* 806.

53. "At the dawn of a new millennium, the United States is in the midst of unprecedented technological change in which our capacity to produce, transmit, and receive information increases daily. The electronic media . . . have redefined the ways in which consumers acquire this information. As communicative technology grows, conflicts over ownership of creative content are inevitable, giving rise to the need to reevaluate the rules of ownership of intellectual property in the modern environment of electronic publishing." Robert Meitus, Note, *Interpreting the Copyright Act's Section 201(c) Revision Privilege with Respect to Electronic Media*, 52 Federal Communications Law Journal 749, 750 (May 2000). *See also*, Dom F. Atteritano, Note, *The Growing Financial Pie of Online Publication: Tasini's New-Use Analysis Leaves Freelance Authors Less Than Crumbs*, 27 Hofstra Law Review 377 (Winter 1998); Michael Spink, Comment, *Authors Stripped of Their Electronic Rights in Tasini v. New York Times Co.*, 32 John Marshall Law Review 409 (Winter 1999).

54. *See also*, Bryan M. Carson, *Databases, Tasini and the Information Age*, 13-2 Against the Grain 60 (April 2001); Bryan M. Carson, *Copyright, Tasini, and Our New Reality*, 13-5 Against the Grain 75 (November 2001). These two articles go into much greater detail about the *Tasini* case.

55. The copyright law states that "In the case of a work made for hire, the employer or other person for whom the work was prepared is considered the author for purposes of this title, and, unless the parties have expressly agreed otherwise in a written instrument signed by them, owns all of the rights comprised in the copyright." 17 U.S.C. § 201(b).

56. 17 U.S.C. § 103.

57. Tasini I *at* 812.

58. Tasini I *at* 812, *quoting* Melville B. Nimmer and David Nimmer, *Nimmer on Copyright* § 3.02, *at* 3-8 (1996 ed.). *See also*, Michael A. Forhan, Note, *Tasini v. New York Times: The Write Stuff for Copyright Law?* 27 Capital University Law Review 863, 868 (1999); Alice Haemmerli, Commentary, *Tasini v. New York Times Co. Symposium on Electronic Rights in International Perspective*, 22 Columbia-VLA Journal of Law and the Arts 129 (Winter 1998); Dina Marie Pascarelli, Case Note, *Electronic Rights: After Tasini Who Owns That, When? Tasini v. New York Times*, 8 DePaul-LCA Journal of Art and Entertainment Law 45 (Fall 1997).

59. David E. Rigney, *What Constitutes a "Compilation" Subject to Copyright Protection—Modern Cases*, 88 A.L.R. Fed. 151.

60. Rigney, *quoting* Broderbund Software, Inc. v. Unison World, Inc. (1986, N.D. Cal.), 648 F. Supp. 1127, 231; U.S.P.Q. 700.

61. New York Times v. Tasini, 533 U.S. 483; 121 S. Ct. 2381; 150 L. Ed.

2d 500; 2001 U.S. LEXIS 4667; 69 U.S.L.W. 4567; 59 U.S.P.Q.2d (BNA) 1001; 29 Media L. Rep. 1865 (2001). [Hereinafter "Tasini."]

62. *See* 17 U.S.C. § 102(a).

63. Tasini *at* 2383, *quoting* Brief for Petitioner *at* 23.

64. *id*.

65. Tasini *at* 2392.

66. Tasini *at* 2392, *citing* 17 U.S.C. 106(1), (3). Cf. Ryan v. Carl Corp., 23 F.Supp. 2d 1146 (N.D. Cal. 1998) (holding copy shop in violation of 201(c)).

67. Tasini *at* 2383.

68. Tasini *at* 2384. *See also*, Brief for Petitioner *at* 23; Amicus Curiae Brief from Advance Publishers *at* 5; Amici Curiae Brief of Ken Burns, Doris Kearns Goodwin, Richard N. Goodwin, David M. Kennedy, David McCullough, Jack N. Rakove, and Gordon S. Wood in support of Petitioners *at* 11-14; Brief of Amicus Curiae of the National Geographic Society in Support of Petitioners.

69. Tasini *at* 2381, *quoting* Brief for Petitioner *at* 23.

70. *id*.

71. Tasini *at* 2381, *quoting* Amici Curiae Brief of the American Library Association and the Association of Research Libraries in Support of Respondents *at* 3.

72. Tasini *at* 2381, *quoting* Amici Curiae Brief of the American Library Association and the Association of Research Libraries in Support of Respondents *at* 6. *See also*, Amici Curiae Brief of Ellen Schrecker, Stanley N. Katz, David Montgomery, Linda Gordon, Leon F. Litwack, Blanche Wiesen Cook, Pete Daniel, Marilyn B. Young, Alan Trachtenberg, Peter Rachleff, Lawrence S. Wittner, William R. Taylor, and David L. Schalk in Support of Respondents.

73. Brief for Petitioner *at* 23.

74. The Copyright Clearance Center's Website is http://www.copyright.com. To contact the CCC, use the following address: Copyright Clearance Center, 222 Rosewood Drive, Danvers, MA 01923; Phone: 978-750-8400; Fax: 978-646-8600; E-mail: info@copyright.com.

75. Marc Lindsey, *Copyright Law on Campus* at 12 (Washington State University Press, 2003).

76. Carrie Russell, *Complete Copyright: An Everyday Guide for Librarians* at 114 (Office for Information Technology Policy, American Library Association, 2004).

77. ASCAP's Website is at http://www.ascap.com. ASCAP has offices in New York, Los Angeles, London, Nashville, Miami, Chicago, Atlanta, and Hato Rey, Puerto Rico.

78. The BMI Website is at http://www.bmi.com. They have offices in New York, Nashville, Los Angeles, Atlanta, London, Miami, and Hato Rey, Puerto Rico.

79. The SESAC Website is at http://www.sesac.com. Their headquarters are in Nashville, with offices in New York, Santa Monica, and London.

80. The Website for the Harry Fox Agency is at http://www.harryfox.com.

Their office is located at: 711 Third Ave, New York, NY 10017; Telephone: 212-370-5330; Fax: 646-487-6779.

81. The Motion Picture Licensing Corporation Website is at http://www.mplc.com. Their offices are located at 5455 Centinela Avenue, Los Angeles, CA 90066-6970; Telephone: 800-462-8855, 310-822-8855; Fax: 310-822-4440; info@mplc.com.

82. Motion Picture Licensing Corporation Website (last accessed July 27, 2005), *available at* http://www.mplc.com.

83. The Movie Licensing USA Website is at http://www.movlic.com. You may contact them at: Movie Licensing USA, 201 South Jefferson Avenue, St. Louis, MO 63103-2579; Fax: 1-877-876-9873; mail@movlic.com. For K-12 schools, call toll-free 877-321-1300; for public libraries, call toll-free 888-267-2658.

84. Their Website is at http://www.aact.org. You can contact AACT at: 8402 Briarwood Cr., Lago Vista, TX 78645; Telephone: 512-267-0711; Toll-free: 866-687-2228; Fax: 512-267-0712.

85. *id.*

86. Visit their Website at http://www.dramatists.com. You may contact the Dramatists Play Service at: 440 Park Avenue South, New York, NY 10016; Telephone: 212-683-8960; Fax: 212-213-1539.

87. Baker's Website is at http://www.bakersplays.com. Baker's mailing address is: P.O. Box 699222, Quincy, MA 02269-9222; Telephone: 617-745-0805; Fax: 617-745-9891. They also maintain a reading room and store that is open to the public at 1445 Hancock Street, Quincy, MA.

88. Their Website is at http://www.samuelfrench.com. Contact: Samuel French, Inc., 7623 Sunset Blvd., Hollywood, CA 90046-2795; Telephone: 323-876-0570; Fax: 323-876-6822; info@samuelfrench.com.

Chapter 8

1. Paul D. Healey, *In Search of the Delicate Balance: Legal and Ethical Questions in Assisting the Pro Se Patron*, 90 Law Library Journal 129, 131 (1998).

2. In the movie *O Brother Where Art Thou?* (Touchstone Home Video 2000), George Clooney's character (Ulysses Everett McGill) was in prison for practicing law without a license.

3. Yvette Brown, *From the Reference Desk to the Jail House: Unauthorized Practice of Law and Librarians*, 13(4) Legal Reference Services Quarterly 31 (1994).

4. Agran v. Shapiro, 273 P.2d 619 (1954).

5. State *ex rel* Oregon State Bar v. Wright, 280 Ore. 713, 573 P.2d 294.

6. Gardner v. Conway, 234 Minn. 468, 48 N.W.2d 788.

7. Virginia State Bar Committee on the Unauthorized Practice of Law, Opinion No. 127 (February 2, 1989); Virginia Opinion No. 152 (July 2, 1991);

Opinion No. 161 (November 16, 1994), *available at*
http://www.vsb.org/profguides/upl/opinions/index.html. For a good discussion
of these decisions, *see,* Kevin Harwell, *Legal Issues Relating to Patent Searching in Publicly Accessible Libraries,* 25-2 Journal of Government Information
31, 33-35 (1998).

8. Virginia Opinion No. 127.

9. Virginia Opinion No. 127.

10. Virginia Opinion No. 152.

11. Virginia Opinion No. 161.

12. Virginia Opinion No. 161.

13. Virginia Opinion No. 161.

14. Virginia Opinion No. 161.

15. Harwell *at* 35, *citing* Harry U. Moatz, *Ethical Problems for PTDL Librarians: How Far Can You Go?* Address at the Annual Training Conference
for Patent and Trademark Depository Libraries, Arlington, VA, March 19,
1995.

16. *id.*

17. Paul D. Healey, *Chicken Little at the Reference Desk: The Myth of Librarian Liability,* 87 Law Library Journal 515 (1995). Healey has also published an excellent annotated bibliography of articles on the topic of UPL. *See,*
Paul D. Healey, *Pro Se Users, Reference Liability, and the Unauthorized Practice of Law: Twenty-five Selected Readings,* 94 Law Library Journal 133 (Winter 2002).

18. Barbara C. Beattie, *A Guide to Medical Reference in the Public Library,* 27 Public Libraries 172, 173 (Winter 1988).

19. Beattie *at* 173.

20. Reference and User Services Association, *Guidelines for Medical, Legal, and Business Responses* (June 2001), *available at*
http://www.ala.org/ala/rusa/rusaprotools/referenceguide/guidelinesmedical.htm.

21. *id.*

22. RUSA Guidelines § 2.3.5.

23. For example, the Ohio Revised Code states that "[n]o person shall operate a motor vehicle . . . on any street, highway, or property open to the public
for vehicular traffic without being in reasonable control of the vehicle. . . ."
Ohio Revised Code § 4511.202, Operation without Reasonable Control.

24. FDIC v. O'Melveny and Myers, 969 F.2d 744 (9th Cir. 1992).

25. Michael J. Polelle, *Who's on First, and What's a Professional?* 33
University of South Florida Law Review 205, 206 (1999).

26. *See,* Teresa Pritchard and Michelle Quigley, *The Information Special-
ist: A Malpractice Risk Analysis,* 13-3 Online 57 (May 1989); John H. Everett,
*Independent Information Professionals and the Question of Malpractice Liabil-
ity,* 13-3 Online 65 (May 1989); Martha J. Dragich, *Information Malpractice:
Some Thoughts on the Potential Liability of Information Professionals,* 8-3
Information Technology and Libraries 265 (September 1989).

27. Dragich *at* 265. *See also,* Alan Angoff, *Library Malpractice Suit:*

Could It Happen to You? 7 American Libraries 489 (September 1976).

28. Dragich *at* 266.

29. *See*, Gardiner Park Development v. Matherly Land Surveying, 2005 Ky. App. LEXIS 104, 19-20 (April 29, 2005); *review granted by* Matherly Land Surveying v. Gardiner Park Development, 2006 Ky. LEXIS 26 (Ky., Feb. 15, 2006); *consolidated* 2006 Ky. LEXIS 91 (Ky., April 12, 2006). NOTE: this opinion is not final and shall not be cited as authority in any courts of the Commonwealth of Kentucky.

30. Gardiner Park. There is also a body of literature in the field of leadership that deals with the issue of professionalism, most notably in terms of education and social work. *See, e.g.*, Henry Mintzberg, *The Professional Bureaucracy, in* ASHE Reader on Organization and Governance in Higher Education 50 (Marvin Peterson ed., 1986).

31. Polelle *at* 205, *quoting* William J. Goode, *The Semi-Professions and Their Organization*, in The Semi-Professions and Their Organization, 267 (Amitai Etzioni ed., 1969).

32. Polelle *at* 205.

33. Dragich *at* 266, *quoting* Anne Mintz, *Information Practice and Malpractice*, 38 Library Journal 41 (September 15, 1985).

34. Dragich *at* 267.

35. Dragich *at* 267.

36. Polelle *at* 227.

37. Chase Scientific Research, Inc. v. NIA Group, Inc., 96 N.Y.2d 20; 749 N.E.2d 161; 725 N.Y.S.2d 592, 597 (N.Y.App. 2001).

38. Chase Scientific Research *at* 29 (749 N.E.2d 161, 166).

39. *id.*

40. *id.*

41. *id.*

42. For example, *see* KRS 275.015(20).

43. Gardiner Park, *quoting* Jilek v. Berger Electric, Inc., 441 N.W.2d 660, 662 (N.D. 1989).

44. Garden v. Frier, 602 So. 2d 1273, 1275 (Fla. 1992).

45. Gardiner Park.

46. Webster's New World Dictionary, Profession (Second College Edition 1980).

47. Black's Law Dictionary, Profession (5th ed. 1981).

48. Jilek *at* 662-663.

49. 29 U.S.C. § 152(12).

50. Garden.

51. Jilek *at* 663.

52. EWAP v. Osmond, 153 Cal. App.3d 842, 200 Cal. Reporter 674 (1984).

53. EWAP *at* 852, *quoting* William Lloyd Prosser, *Handbook of the Law of Torts* (4th ed., West Publishing 1971) *at* § 113.

54. EWAP *at* 853, *quoting* Restatement (Second) of Torts § 581, Com-

ment e (1965).

55. Brocklesby v. Jeppesen, 767 F.2d 1288 (9th Cir. 1985), cert. den., 474 U.S. 1101 (1986).

56. Dragich *at* 270.

57. 745 ILCS 10/2-210.

58. Vacwell Engineering v. B.D.H. Chemicals Ltd, 1 QB 88 (1971), 3 All ER 1681 (1969), 3 WLR 927 (1969), 7 KIR 286.

59. *id.*

60. *id.*

61. *id.*

62. *id.*

63. "In 1899, another French scientist, named GAUTIER, also in the ANNALES DE CHIMIE ET DE PHYSIQUE, wrote [about a violent explosion]." *id.* The other works that the Court is discussing are (respectively): Joseph William Mellor, *A comprehensive treatise on inorganic and theoretical chemistry*, (Longmans, Green and Co. 1924); Leopold Gmelin, *Gmelin Handbuch der anorganischen Chemie* (Springer-Verlag 1926); and Jocelyn Field Thorpe, Martha Annie Whiteley, and Sir T. E. Thorpe, *Dictionary of Applied Chemistry* (Longmans, Green 1937).

64. *id.*

65. Norbert Adolph Lange, *Handbook of Chemistry*, Annual (McGraw-Hill Book Co., 1937-1961). This resource is now: Norbert Adolph Lange and J. G. Speight, *Lange's Handbook of Chemistry* (16th ed., McGraw-Hill 2005).

66. William Reed Veazey and Charles David Hodgman, *Handbook of Chemistry and Physics*, Annual (Chemical Rubber Publishing Co. 1913-1977). This work is now: *CRC Handbook of Chemistry and Physics*, Annual (CRC Press, 1978 –).

67. *The Merck Index: An Encyclopedia for the Chemist, Pharmacist, Physician, and Allied Professions* (Merck & Co. 1952). This resource is now: *The Merck Index: An Encyclopedia of Chemicals, Drugs, and Biologicals* (Merck 2001).

68. N. Irving Sax, *Dangerous Properties of Industrial Materials* (2d ed., Reinhold 1963). This work is now: Richard J. Lewis, Sr., and N. Irving Sax, *Sax's Dangerous Properties of Industrial Materials* (11th ed., Wiley-Interscience 2004).

69. On June 28, 2006, I used *Knovel Library* to look up boron tribromide in the most recent e-book editions of *Lange's Handbook of Chemistry*, *Sax's Dangerous Properties of Industrial Materials*, *The CRC Handbook of Chemistry and Physics*, and *The Merck Index: An Encyclopedia of Chemicals, Drugs, and Biologicals*. Each of these sources currently has information on the vigorous reaction of boron tribromide with water, so they have all fixed the error that led to the *Vacwell* case.

70. *id.*

71. Reference and User Services Association, *Guidelines for Medical, Legal, and Business Responses* (June 2001), *available at*

http://www.ala.org/ala/rusa/rusaprotools/referenceguide/guidelinesmedical.htm.

72. RUSA guidelines are available full text at
http://www.ala.org/ala/rusa/rusaprotools/referenceguide/referenceguidelines
.htm.

73. Association of Specialized and Cooperative Library Agencies, *Guidelines for Library and Information Services for the American Deaf Community* (1995). The guidelines are not available online, but may be ordered for $9 from the ASCLA.

74. Association of Independent Information Professionals, *Code of Ethical Business Practices* (as amended April 20, 2002), *available at* http://www.aiip.org/AboutAIIP/aiipethics.html.

75. Phil Sykes, *Liability for Information Provision: Spectre or Reality?* 43-5 ASLIB Proceedings 189, 192 (May 1991).

Chapter 9

1. *Uniting and Strengthening America by Providing Appropriate Tools Required to Intercept and Obstruct Terrorism (USA PATRIOT) Act of 2001,* Public Law Number 107-56 (October 26, 2001), *available at* http://www.ins.gov/graphics/lawsregs/PATRIOT.pdf.

2. Herbert N. Foerstel, *Surveillance in the Stacks* at 11 (Greenwood 1991), *quoting* Robert D. McFadden, *FBI in New York Asks Librarians' Aid in Reporting on Spies,* New York Times *at* A1 (September 18, 1987).

3. Foerstel *at* 22.

4. McFadden.

5. Foerstel *at* 59, quoting *Nightline with Ted Koppel* (ABC Television, July 13, 1988).

6. U.S. Constitution, 4th Amendment.

7. *See,* Gail Armist, Note, *Freitas After Villegas: Are "Sneak and Peek" Search Warrants Clandestine Fishing Expeditions?* 26 San Diego Law Review 933 (1989).

8. United States v. Jeffers, 432 U.S. 48, 51; 72 S.Ct. 93; 96 L.Ed. 59 (1951).

9. Johnson v. United States, 333 U.S. 10; 68 S.Ct. 367; 92 L.Ed. 436 (1948).

10. Johnson *at* 13-14.

11. Johnson *at* 13-14.

12. Wayne R. LaFave and Jerold H. Israel, *Criminal Procedure* (Hornbook Series) *at* 110 (West Publishing Company 1985).

13. Dumbra v. United States, 268 U.S. 435, 441 (1925).

14. U.S. Constitution, Fourth Amendment.

15. Marron v. United States, 275 U.S. 192, 196; 48 S.Ct. 74; 72 L.Ed. 231 (1927).

16. U.S. Constitution, Fourteenth Amendment, § 1.

17. United States. v. Sokolow, 490 U.S. 1, 7 (1989).

18. Florida v. Royer, 460 U.S. 491, 500 (1983).

19. Royer *at* 500.

20. Lewis and Associates, *Shoplifting or Embezzlement* (last accessed October 1, 2005), *available at*
http://www.lewisatlaw.com/html/criminallaw/shoplifting.html.

21. Hewlett-Woodmere Public Library v. Phyllis Rothman, 108 Misc. 2d 715; 438 N.Y.S.2d 730; 1981 N.Y. Misc. LEXIS 2278 (D.C.N.Y., Second District, Nassau County, May 1, 1981).

22. Hewlett-Woodmere *at* 718. The court in Hewlett-Woodmere is relying on Monell v. New York City Dept. of Social Service, 436 U.S. 658; 98 S. Ct. 2018; 56 L. Ed. 2d 611 (1978).

23. Although most states have fairly straightforward library privacy statutes, a few states put the laws in unusual places. For example, the Georgia and New York library privacy laws are part of these states' evidence codes, and the library privacy laws in Hawaii and Kentucky come from binding Attorney General opinions. For more information, *see* Bryan M. Carson, *Surveying Privacy: Library Privacy Laws in the Southeastern United States*, 49 Southeastern Librarian 19 (Jan. 2002).

24. Secretary's Advisory Committee on Automated Personal Data Systems, U.S. Department of Health, Education, and Welfare, *Records, Computers, and the Rights of Citizens: Report of the Secretary's Advisory Committee on Automated Personal Data Systems* 40-41 (Government Publications Office 1973).

25. Code of Ethics of the American Library Association.

26. I.C.A.R. 32.

27. 9 Idaho Statutes § 9-340E.

28. Tennessee Code Annotated § 10-8-101(2).

29. Tennessee Code Annotated § 10-8-101(1).

30. South Carolina Code Annotated § 60-4-10.

31. 75 Illinois Compiled Statutes § 70/1(C)(1).

32. Nevada Revised Statutes § 239.013 (2004).

33. Georgia Code Annotated § 24-9-46.

34. Virginia Code Annotated § 2.1-342.01.

35. Louisiana Revised Statutes § 44:13(a).

36. Louisiana Revised Statutes § 44:13(b).

37. Colorado Revised Statutes § 24-90-119.

38. Iowa Code § 22.7(a)(13).

39. Rhode Island General Laws § 11-18-32(a).

40. Arkansas Code Annotated § 13-2-701(b).

41. 20 U.S.C. § 1232g.

42. Arizona Revised Statutes § 41-1354(b)(1) – § 41-1354(b)(3).

43. Tennessee Code Annotated § 10-8-102(b).

44. Arkansas Code Annotated § 13-2-703(b).

45. Alaska Stat. § 40.25.140.

46. Ohio Revised Code § 149.432(3)(b)(1).

47. Minn. Stat. § 13.40.

48. D.C. Code Annotated § 39-108.

49. D.C. Code Annotated § 39.108.

50. D.C. Code Annotated § 39.108.

51. The Idaho statute is placed with the state Open Records Act, which is contained within the evidence code. *See,* 9 Idaho Statutes § 9-340E.

52. Vincent DiCarlo, *Summary of the Rules of Evidence: The Essential Tools for Survival in the Courtroom,* Findlaw for Legal Professionals (April 26, 2001), *available at* http://profs.lp.findlaw.com/litigation/evidence13.html.

53. The marital communications privilege belongs to both spouses jointly, which means that both parties have to consent in order for the witness to testify. The spousal privilege and the marital privilege do not apply in situations where one spouse is suing the other, or where one spouse is charged with a crime against the other spouse.

54. The list of privileges is based on DiCarlo. His list contained a number of other privileges available in California that are not widely recognized; I have only included those privileges which are generally recognized. *See,* http://profs.lp.findlaw.com/litigation/evidence13.html.

55. Cal. Const., Art. I § 2(b).

56. Georgia Code Annotated § 24-9-46.

57. 1981 Kentucky Attorney General Opinion 2-718, OAG 81-159, *quoting* KRS § 61.878(1)(a). April 21, 1981.

58. 1981 Kentucky Attorney General Opinion 81-159. April 21, 1981.

59. 1982 Kentucky Attorney General Opinion 2-164, OAG 82-149. March 12, 1982.

60. *id.*

61. OIP Opinion Letter No. 90-30 (October 23, 1990), Department of the Attorney General, Office of Information Practices, State of Hawaii. (Hereafter Hawaii AG.)

62. State v. Tanaka, 67 Haw. 658, 701 P.2d 1274 (1985).

63. Hawaii AG, *quoting* 41 Op. Att'y. Gen. Or. 435 (1981).

64. Martin v. City of Struthers, 318 U.S. 141, 143 (1943).

65. Talley v. California, 362 U.S. 60 (1960).

66. Gibson v. Florida Legislative Investigation Committee, 372 U.S. 539 (1963); Bates v. City of Little Rock, 361 U.S. 516 (1960); NAACP v. Alabama, 357 U.S. 449 (1958).

67. Thomas v. Collins, 323 U.S. 516 (1945).

68. Griswold v. Connecticut, 381 U.S. 479 (1965).

69. Lamont v. Postmaster General, 381 U.S. 301 (1965).

70. DeGregory v. Attorney General of New Hampshire, 383 U.S. 825 (1966).

71. Sweenzy v. New Hampshire, 354 U.S. 234 (1957).

72. Hawaii AG opinion, *quoting* Stanley v. Georgia, 394 U.S. 557 (1969). This list comes from the Texas AG opinion that was quoted by the Hawaii AG.

See, Att'y. Gen. Tex. Open Records Decision No. 100 (July 10, 1975).

73. Hawaii AG Opinion.

74. Hawaii AG, *quoting* Haw. Rev. Stat. 92F-3 (Supp. 1989).

75. OIP Opinion Letter No. 93-21 (1993), Department of the Attorney General, Office of Information Practices, State of Hawaii, *available at* http://www.state.hi.us/oip/opinionletters/opinion%2093-21.PDF.

76. Uniting and Strengthening America by Providing Appropriate Tools Required to Intercept and Obstruct Terrorism (USA PATRIOT) Act of 2001, P.L. 107-56, 115 Stat. 272 (October 26, 2001), *available at* http://www.epic.org/privacy/terrorism/hr3162.html. (Hereinafter "PATRIOT Act.")

77. For example, *see*, Michael J. Woods, *Counterintelligence and Access to Transactional Records: A Practical History of USA PATRIOT Act Section 215*, 1 Journal of National Security Law & Policy 37 (2005); Grant T. Harris, *The CIA Mandate and the War on Terror*, 23 Yale Law & Public Policy Review 529 (Spring 2005).

78. *See*, Thomas P. Ludwig, *The Erosion of Online Privacy Rights in the Recent Tide of Legislaton*, 8 Computer Law Review and Technology Journal 131 (2003).

79. Susan Nevelow Mart, *Protecting the Lady from Toledo: Post-USA Patriot Act Electronic Surveillance at the Library*, 96 Law Library Journal 449, 451 (Summer 2004).

80. Foreign Intelligence Surveillance Act of 1978, Pub.L.No. 95-511, 92 Stat. 1783, *codified at* (as amended) 50 U.S.C. §§ 1801-1811, 1821-1829, 1841-1846, 1861-1862.

81. David S. Jonas, *The Foreign Intelligence Surveillance Act through the Lens of the 9/11 Commission Report: The Wisdom of the Patriot Act Amendments and the Decision of the Foreign Intelligence Surveillance Court of Review*, 27 North Carolina Central Law Journal 95, 96 (2005).

82. *id.* at 97.

83. PATRIOT Act § 218.

84. Jonas *at* 97.

85. PATRIOT Act §§ 206, 214, 216, 218.

86. Shelley Murphy, Wiretap Tapes Portray Fears of Mob Rivals, Boston Globe B11 (December 5, 2003), *available at* http://www.thelaborers.net/lexisnexis/articles/wiretap_tapes_portray_fears_of.htm.

87. PATRIOT Act § 216.

88. *See*, Bob Barr, Testimony on the USA PATRIOT Act before the Senate Select Committee on Foreign Intelligence (April 19, 2005), *available at* http://www.checksbalances.org/barr%20PA%20testimony.pdf. (Hereinafter "Barr Testimony.")

89. PATRIOT Act § 216.

90. Barr Testimony.

91. PATRIOT Act § 215(a)(1).

92. PATRIOT Act § 215(c)(1). *See*, Bob Barr, *The USA PATRIOT Act and Progeny Threaten the Very Foundation of Freedom*, 2 Georgetown Journal of Law and Public Policy 385, 391 (Summer 2004).

93. *id.*

94. U.S. Constitution, Fourth Amendment, *available at* http://caselaw.lp.findlaw.com/data/constitution/amendments.html.

95. Doe v. Ashcroft, 334 F.Supp.2d 471 (S.D.N.Y. 2004). The court in the *Doe* case was not considering a challenge against this section; however, the judge did suggest that he thought this provision was unconstitutional.

96. Barr Testimony.

97. Barr Testimony.

98. *id.*

99. PATRIOT Act § 505(a)(1).

100. PATRIOT Act § 505(a)(2)(B)(2).

101. Doe *at* 494-495. *See*, U.S. Const. Amend. IV; United States v. Streifel, 665 F.2d 414 (2d Cir. 1981). *See also*, United States v. Morton Salt Co., 338 U.S. 632, 651-52, 94 L. Ed. 401, 70 S. Ct. 357, 46 F.T.C. 1436 (1950).

102. Doe *at* 495, *citing* United States v. Bailey (*in re* Subpoena Duces Tecum), 228 F.3d 341, 348 (4th Cir. 2000).

103. Doe *at* 506.

104. PATRIOT Act § 215(d).

105. *See*, Brian A. Freeman, *Trends in First Amendment Jurisprudence: Expiating the Sins of Yoder and Smith: Toward a Unified Theory of First Amendment Exemptions from Neutral Laws of General Applicability*, 66 Missouri Law Review 9 (Winter 2001). *See also*, Edward C. Walterscheid, *Musings on the Copyright Power: A Critique of Eldred v. Ashcroft*, 14 Albany Law Journal of Science & Technology 309 (2004).

106. *See*, Robert H. Whorf, *The Dangerous Intersection at "Prior Restraint" and "Time, Place, Manner": A Comment on Thomas v. Chicago Park District*, 3 Barry Law Review 1 (Fall 2002).

107. *See* R.A.V. v. City of St. Paul, 505 U.S. 377, 120 L. Ed. 2d 305, 112 S. Ct. 2538 (1992).

108. Doe *at* 511, *citing* United States v. Playboy Entertainment Group, Inc., 529 U.S. 803, 813, 146 L. Ed. 2d 865, 120 S. Ct. 1878 (2000) (applying strict scrutiny to a content-based restriction); *see also* R.A.V. v. City of St. Paul *at* 382 ("Content-based regulations are presumptively invalid."); Bantam Books, 372 U.S. 58, 70 (holding that prior restraints on speech bear a "heavy presumption" against constitutionality).

109. Doe *at* 511, *citing* Reno v. ACLU, 521 U.S. 844, 874, 138 L. Ed. 2d 874, 117 S. Ct. 2329 (1997).

110. Doe *at* 511, *citing* Turner Broad. Sys., Inc. v. FCC, 520 U.S. 180, 189, 137 L. Ed. 2d 369, 117 S. Ct. 1174 (1997).

111. Doe *at* 511.

112. Doe *at* 514.

113. Doe *at* 519.

114. Posting of Don Wood, dwood@ala.org, member-forum@ala.org (October 26, 2001), *available at* http://www.ala.org/alaorg/oif/alertusaPATRIOTact.html.

115. Wood e-mail. You may contact the ALA Office of Intellectual Freedom at 312-280-4222 or 800-545-2433, ext. 4222. Their Fax number is 312-280-4227.

116. Dan Eggen, *Library Challenges FBI Request: Patriot Act Prohibits Details of Lawsuit from Being Released*, Washington Post A11 (August 26, 2005), *available at* http://www.washingtonpost.com/wp-dyn/content/article/2005/08/25/AR2005082501696.html?nav=rss_politics.

117. National Security Letter from Michael J. Wolfe, Special Agent in Charge, FBI New Haven Division, to Kenneth Sutton, Systems and Telecommunications Manager, Library Connection, Inc. (Federal Bureau of Investigation May 19, 2005), *available at* http://www.aclu.org/images/nationalsecurityletters/asset_upload_file924_25995.pdf.

118. Bryan M. Carson, *John Doe and the PATRIOT Act*, 18-4 Against the Grain 72 (September 2006).

119. USA PATRIOT Act Improvement and Reauthorization Act of 2005 (H.R. 3199).

120. *See*, A.S., *Congress Extends PATRIOT Act Five Weeks*, 37-2 American Libraries 9 (February 2006); *Congress Likely to Extend PATRIOT Act by Five Weeks*, CongressDaily at 12 (February 1, 2006).

121. The Senators voting no on the bill were Daniel Akaka (D-HI), Jeff Bingaman (D-NM), Robert Byrd (D-WV), Russell Feingold (D-WI), Tom Harkin (D-IA), Jim Jeffords (I-VT), Patrick Leahy (D-VT), Carl Levin (D-MI), Patty Murray (D-WA), and Ron Wyden (D-OR). Senator Daniel Inouye (D-Hawaii) did not vote. *Agreement to Conference Report, USA PATRIOT Act Improvement and Reauthorization Act of 2005 (H.R. 3199)*, 109th Congress, 2nd Session, 2006 Senate Vote No. 29 (Congressional Information Service, LEXIS, March 2, 2006).

122. *House Renews USA PATRIOT Act in a Cliffhanger Vote*, Chicago Tribune (March 8, 2006); *available at* http://www.chicagotribune.com/news/nationworld/chi-0603080183mar08,1,6115495.story?coll=chi-newsnationworld-hed. The renewal was supported by 214 Republicans and 66 Democrats and opposed by 13 Republicans, 124 Democrats, and one independent. *See*, Laurie Kellman, *Revised Patriot Act Wins Narrow Approval in House, Many Still Opposed Despite Concessions*, San Jose Mercury News (March 8, 2006); *available at* http://www.mercurynews.com/mld/mercurynews/news/politics/14045829.htm.

123. Press Release, U.S. Department of Justice, *Fact Sheet: USA PATRIOT Act Improvement and Reauthorization Act of 2005* (March 2, 2006); *available at* http://releases.usnewswire.com/GetRelease.asp?id=61784.

124. H.R. 3199 § 106(a)(3), 109th Congress (2006) (enacted).

125. H.R. 3199 § 3511(b)(2).

126. H.R. 3199 §§ 106(d)(1)(A) and 106(d)(2)(C).

127. H.R. 3199 § 106(d)(1)(B).

128. H.R. 3199 § 106(d)(2)(C).

129. Kellman.

130. H.R. 3199 § 118(d). *See also*, H.R. 3199 § 119(g), pertaining to auditing reports to Congress. This section uses the same definition for National Security Letters.

131. This portion of the chapter was previously published as Bryan M. Carson, *Tarasoff, Patron Confidentiality, and Duty to Society: An Ethical Quandary*, 16-3 Against the Grain 76 (June 2004).

132. Richard Rubin, Book Review: *Ethics and Librarianship, by Robert Hauptman*, 29-4 Journal of Academic Librarianship 268 (July 2003).

133. Robert Hauptman, *Professionalism or Culpability? An Experiment in Ethics*, 50 Wilson Library Bulletin 626 (April 1976).

134. American Library Association, *Code of Ethics of the American Library Association* (Adopted June 28, 1995); American Library Association, *Library Bill of Rights* (Adopted June 18, 1948; as amended February 2, 1961 and January 23, 1980); American Library Association/Association of American Publishers, *Freedom to Read Statement* (Adopted June 25, 1953, by the ALA Council and the AAP Freedom to Read Committee, as amended June 30, 2004). These materials are available on the American Library Association web page at http://www.ala.org/Template.cfm?Section=censorship&template=/ContentManagement/ContentDisplay.cfm&ContentID=100774.

135. Yanqing Li, *Hate Speech, Censorship, and Librarians' Dilemma*, 22-1/2 Current Studies in Librarianship 4 (Spring/Fall 1998).

136. Robert G. Wengert, *Some Ethical Aspects of Being an Information Professional*, 49-3 Library Trends 486 (Winter 2001).

137. *In re* Estate of Julius Freeman, 355 N.Y.S.2d 336 (1974), *quoted in* Randy Diamond and Martha Dragich, *Professionalism in Librarianship: Shifting the Focus from Malpractice to Good Practice*, 49-3 Library Trends 395 (Winter 2001).

138. Wengert.

139. Richard E. Rubin, *Ethical Aspects of Reference Service, in* Richard E. Bopp and Linda C. Smith, *Reference and Information Services: An Introduction* (Englewood, CO: Libraries Unlimited, 2001).

140. *id.*

141. Derek Humphry, *Final Exit: The Practicalities of Self-Deliverance and Assisted Suicide for the Dying* (Hemlock Society 1991).

142. Rubin (Bopp & Smith).

143. Leslie Harris & Associates, *Children and Privacy in School Libraries* (American Library Association Office for Information Technology Policy 2002), *available at* http://www.fontanalib.org/Children%20and%20Privacy%20in%20School%20

Libraries.htm.

144. 32 Words and Phrases 627 *Person In Loco Parentis.*

145. *See,* Kevin P. Dwyer, David Osher, and C. Warger, *Early Warning, Timely Responses: A Guide to Safe Schools* (U.S. Department of Education/American Institutes for Research/National Association of School Psychologists 1998); Judy Blankenship, *Heeding the Signs: Without Help Troubled Kids Can Explode in Rage,* 4-3 Northwest Education 40 (Spring 1999); Ed-Source, Inc., *Keeping Schools and Students Safe,* EdFact Resource Guide (1999); Kevin P. Dwyer, David Osher, and Catherine C. Hoffman, *Creating Responsive Schools: Contextualizing Early Warning, Timely Response,* 66-3 Exceptional Children 347 (Spring 2000); Kevin P. Dwyer and David Osher, *Safeguarding Our Children: An Action Guide, Implementing Early Warning, Timely Response* (U.S. Department of Education/American Institutes for Research/Center for Effective Collaboration and Practice/National Association of School Psychologists 2000). Most of these documents are available from ERIC.

146. 9 Louisiana Revised Statutes § 2800.2 (Supp. 1988), *available at* http://www.lsbep.org/duty_to_warn.htm.

147. Tarasoff v. Regents of the University of California, 17 Cal.3d 425, 551 P.2d 334 (Cal. 1976), *available at* http://login.findlaw.com/scripts/callaw?dest=ca/cal3d/17/425.html.

148. Tarasoff, *quoting* J. G. Fleming and B. Maximov, *The Patient or His Victim: The Therapist's Dilemma,* 62 Cal.L.Rev. 1025, 1067 (1974).

149. Although cases from Canada are not binding in the United States, lawyers often cite cases from Canada, Britain, Australia, and other common law countries in an effort to persuade U.S. courts to rule in a similar way.

150. Smith v. Jones, 1 S.C.R. 455 (Supreme Court of Canada, 1999).

151. Smith v. Jones.

152. William S. Clark, *Duty to Warn and Confidentiality* (Harper Grey Easton Litigation 2002), *available at* http://www.hgelaw.com/publications/pdfs/Duty_to_Warn.pdf.

153. Smith v. Jones.

Chapter 10

1. Most of this chapter was previously published as Bryan M. Carson, *"To Filter or Not to Filter: That Is the Question": A Brief Discussion of Internet Use Policies,* 15-4 Against the Grain 86 (September 2003).

2. 114 Stat. 2763A-335, *codified at* 20 U.S.C. §§ 9134(f)(1)(A)(i) and (B)(i) and at 47 U.S.C. §§ 254(h)(6)(B)(i) and (C)(i).

3. United States v. American Library Association, 539 U.S. 194; 123 S. Ct. 2297; 156 L. Ed. 2d 221; 2003 U.S. LEXIS 4799; 71 U.S.L.W. 4465 (2003), *available at* http://laws.findlaw.com/us/000/02-361.html. (Hereinafter "CIPA Case.")

4. CIPA Case.

5. Since the legal definition of a "minor" is a person under the legal age of 18, this provision applies to young adults, even though most of the discussion uses the term "children."

6. 20 U.S.C. §§ 9134(f)(1)(A)(i) and (B)(i).

7. 47 U.S.C. §§ 254(h)(6)(B)(i) and (C)(i).

8. American Library Association v. United States, 201 F. Supp. 2d 401 (E.D. Pa. 2002). (Hereinafter "District Court Opinion.)

9. District Court Opinion at 453.

10. id.

11. District Court Opinion at 408.

12. "According to the plaintiffs, these content-based restrictions are subject to strict scrutiny under public forum doctrine, see Rosenberger v. Rector & Visitors of Univ. of Va., 515 U.S. 819, 837, 132 L. Ed. 2d 700, 115 S. Ct. 2510 (1995), and are therefore permissible only if they are narrowly tailored to further a compelling state interest and no less restrictive alternatives would further that interest, see Reno v. ACLU, 521 U.S. 844, 874, 138 L. Ed. 2d 874, 117 S. Ct. 2329 (1997)." District Court Opinion at 407.

13. District Court Opinion at 409.

14. CIPA Case.

15. See, Adam S. Hochschild, Note, *The Modern Problem of Supreme Court Plurality Decisions: Interpretation in Historical Perspective*, 4 Washington University Journal of Law & Policy 261, 271 (2000).

16. David C. Bratz, Comment, *Stare Decisis in Lower Courts: Predicting the Demise of Supreme Court Precedent*, 60 Washington University Law Review 87, 99 (1984).

17. Marks v. United States, 430 U.S. 188 (1977).

18. Marks at 193.

19. For more information on plurality decisions, see John F. Davis & William L. Reynolds, *Juridical Cripples: Plurality Opinions in the Supreme Court*, 1974 Duke Law Journal 59; Ken Kimura, *A Legitimacy Model for the Interpretation of Plurality Decisions*, 77 Cornell Law Review 1593 (1992); Burt Neuborne, *The Binding Quality of Supreme Court Precedent*, 61 Tulane Law Review 991 (1987); Laura Krugman Ray, *The Justices Write Separately: Uses of the Concurrence by the Rehnquist Court*, 23 U.C. Davis Law Review 777 (1990); Igor Kirman, Note, *Standing Apart to Be a Part: The Precedential Value of Supreme Court Concurring Opinions*, 95 Columbia Law Review 2083 (1995); Linda Novak, Note, *The Precedential Value of Supreme Court Plurality Decisions*, 80 Columbia Law Review 756 (1980); William G. Peterson, Note, *Splintered Decisions, Implicit Reversal and Lower Federal Courts: Planned Parenthood v. Casey*, 1992 Brigham Young University Law Review 289 (1992); Note, *Plurality Decisions and Judicial Decisionmaking*, 94 Harvard Law Review 1127 (1981); Comment, *Supreme Court No-Clear-Majority Decisions: A Study in Stare Decisis,* 24 University of Chicago Law Review 99 (1956); Mark Alan Thurmon, Note, *When the Court Divides: Reconsidering the Precedential Value of Supreme Court Plurality Decisions*, 42 Duke Law Jour-

nal 419 (1992).

20. Chief Justice Rehnquist is relying on National Endowment for Arts v. Finley, 524 U.S. 569 (1998).

21. National Endowment for Arts v. Finley.

22. CIPA Case *at* 205 (Opinion of Chief Justice Rehnquist).

23. *id.*

24. *id.*

25. *id.*

26. Posting of Keith Michael Fiels, kfiels@ala.org, to rusaaccess@ala.org, (July 16, 2003), *available at* http://www.rpls.ws/Links/CIPA2.htm.

27. 20 U.S.C. § 9134(f)(3); 47 U.S.C. § 254(h)(6)(D). The E-rate allows disabling "during use by an adult." 47 U.S.C. § 254(h)(6)(D). Under the guidelines of the LSTA grant, any person is permitted to request that the filter be disabled. 20 U.S.C. § 9134(f)(3).

28. CIPA Case *at* 209 (Opinion of Chief Justice Rehnquist).

29. CIPA Case *at* 211-212.

30. CIPA Case *at* 216 (Breyer, J., Concurring).

31. *id.* at 219.

32. Justice Breyer is relying on *in re* Federal-State Joint Board on Universal Service: Children's Internet Protection Act, 16 FCC Record 8182, 8183, § 2, 8204 and § 53 (2001). This report leaves determinations regarding the appropriateness of compliant Internet safety policies and their disabling to local communities.

33. CIPA Case *at* 219-220 (Breyer, J., Concurring).

34. CIPA Case *at* 214-215 (Kennedy, J., Concurring).

35. This argument is used in Justice Stevens' dissenting opinion *at* 226.

36. District Court Opinion *at* 457.

37. District Court Opinion *at* 466.

38. CIPA Case *at* 226 (Stevens, J., Dissenting).

39. *id.* at 226-227.

40. *id.* at 232.

41. CIPA Case *at* 236-237 (Souter, J., Dissenting).

42. CIPA Case *at* 240-243 (Souter, J., Dissenting).

43. 47 U.S.C. § 254(h)(6)(D).

44. 20 U.S.C. § 9134(f)(3).

45. Hewlett-Woodmere Public Library v. Phyllis Rothman, 108 Misc. 2d 715; 438 N.Y.S.2d 730; 1981 N.Y. Misc. LEXIS 2278 (D.C.N.Y., Second District, Nassau County, May 1, 1981).

Chapter 11

1. Steven R. Lainoff, Stephen Bates, and Chris Bowers, *Attributing the Activities of Corporate Agents under U.S. Tax Law: A Fresh Look from an Old Perspective*, 38 Georgia Law Review 143, 145-46 (Fall 2003), *quoting* Re-

statement (Second) of Agency § 1(1) (1958) (hereinafter "Restatement").

2. Donald C. Langevoort, *Agency Law Inside the Corporation: Problems of Candor and Knowledge*, 71 University of Cincinnati Law Review 1187, 1188 (Summer 2003).

3. Lainoff *at* 146, *quoting* Esmond Mills v. Commissioner, 132 F.2d 753, 755 (1st Cir. 1943), *affirming and quoting* Board of Tax Appeals Memorandum Decision (CCH) Dec. 12,559-B (June 11, 1942).

4. Restatement § 7 comment.

5. Restatement § 267.

6. Restatement § 8 comment B. *See also*, Nancy R. Furnari, Comment, *Are Traditional Agency Principles Effective for Internet Transactions, Given the Lack of Personal Interaction?* 63 Albany Law Review 537 (1999).

7. Furnari *at* 546-548.

8. *id.*

9. Alan R. Seher and Marc S. Weissman, *Common Law Agency & Its Application to the Real Estate Profession*, International Real Estate Digest, *available at* http://www.ired.com/buymyself/agency/970312.htm.

10. Seher and Weissman.

11. Restatement *at* § 14 comment.

12. Studebaker v. Nettie's Flower Garden, Inc., 842 S.W.2d 227, 229 (Mo. App. 1992).

13. American Bar Association, *The American Bar Association Guide to Workplace Law* at 4-5 (Three Rivers Press 1997).

14. Restatement *at* § 220.

15. John Leidecke, *Employment-at-Will, in* A Guide to Rhode Island Employment Law (2d ed., Institute for Labor Studies and Research 2004), *available at* http://www.rilaborinstitute.org/employment_guide_2001/chapter_1.html.

16. *id.*

17. Act for the Prevention of Frauds and Perjuries, 29 Car. II, c. 3 (1677). *See also*, Charles G. Bakaly, Jr., and Joel M. Grossman, *Modern Law of Employment Contracts: Formation, Operation, and Remedies for Breach* § 3.2. (Law & Business Inc. 1983).

18. Bakaly and Grossman *at* § 5.3.

19. For an example of an academic personnel manual, *see*, Mississippi Gulf Coast Community College, *MGCCC Administrative Handbook* (revised November 2004), *available at* http://www.mgccc.edu/AH/ah.cgi.

20. Kurt H. Decker and H. Thomas Felix II, *Drafting and Revising Employment Handbooks* § 2.3 (John Wiley & Sons 1991), *citing* Woolley v. Hoffmann-LaRoche, Inc., 99 N.J. 284, 491 A.2d 1257 (1985).

21. For example, *see*, Elton S. Karrmann Library, *Karrmann Library Personnel Manual* (University of Wisconsin-Platteville June 1998), *available at* http://www.uwplatt.edu/library/admin/personnel.html.

22. Western Kentucky University, *Faculty Handbook* (16th ed. 2004), *available at*

http://www.wku.edu/Dept/Support/AcadAffairs/handbook/handbook.pdf.

23. Western Kentucky University Department of Library Public Service, *WKU DLPS Promotion Guidelines* (1992), *available at* http://www.wku.edu/Library/dlps/pdf/wkudlpspromotionguidelines.pdf.

24. Jeff Gordon, *Schembechler Loses Another One—His Job*, St. Louis Post-Dispatch *at* 7D (August 5, 1992).

25. *Conflicts and Rivalries*, Crain's Detroit Business *at* E-22 (Spring 2005), *available at* http://www.crainsdetroit.com/static/911.pdf.

26. Decker and Felix *at* § 2.3.

27. *See*, Francis L. Van Dusen, Jr., *Mid-Employment Covenant Not to Compete Held Unenforceable When Signed by At-Will Employee*, Miller Nash LLP (November 2004), *available at* http://www.millernash.com/showarticles.asp?Show=398.

28. National Labor Relations Board, *The NLRB and You: Representation Cases* (1997), *available at* http://www.nlrb.gov/nlrb/shared_files/brochures/engrep.asp.

29. *id.*

30. 29 U.S.C. §§ 151-169.

31. The FLSA is contained in 29 U.S.C. § 201 – 29 U.S.C. § 209.

32. However, employees under age 20 in their first 90 consecutive calendar days of employment may be paid $4.25/hr; this wage has to rise to $5.15/hr on the 91st calendar day of employment, or on the employee's 20th birthday, whichever occurs first. U.S. Department of Labor Wage and Hour Division, Fact Sheet #29: Fair Labor Standards Act Amendments of 1996 (1996), *available at* http://www.dol.gov/esa/regs/compliance/whd/whdfs29.htm. (This figure is still current as of October 2005.)

33. U.S. Department of Labor, *Professional Employees*, Elaws: FLSA Overtime Security Advisor, *available at* http://www.dol.gov/elaws/esa/flsa/overtime/p1.htm. This figure was current as of the time of writing (October 2005).

34. 29 U.S.C. § 213(a)(1).

35. *id.*

36. U.S. Department of Labor Wage and Hour Division, *Professional Employees*, Fair Pay Fact Sheets by Exemption, *available at* http://www.dol.gov/esa/regs/compliance/whd/fairpay/fs17d_professional.htm.

37. U.S. Department of Labor, *Occupational Index*, Elaws: FLSA Overtime Security Advisor, *available at* http://www.dol.gov/elaws/esa/flsa/overtime/jobs.htm.

38. 29 C.F.R. § 541.

39. *Professional Employees.*

40. U.S. Department of Labor Wage and Hour Division, Fact Sheet #23: *Overtime Pay Requirements of the FLSA* (last accessed August 21, 2005), *available at* http://www.dol.gov/esa/regs/compliance/whd/whdfs23.htm.

41. *id.*

42. State Bar of Nevada, 2002 Young Lawyers Section Compensation

Survey (2002), *available at*
http://www.nvbar.org/News_and_other_information/News%20and%20
Other%20Information_2002_comp_Surv.htm.

43. In the Nevada survey, the 2001 average salary was $72,521 for young lawyers. Applying the rule of thumb that each billable hour includes two hours that are not billable, this means that the average lawyer works 3,762 hours a year. Dividing the average salary by this average number of hours shows that the average young lawyer in Nevada makes around $19.28 per hour. Next time you are disappointed by the low salaries that librarians and archivists make compared to lawyers, remember that we are working far fewer hours than they work.

44. U.S. Department of Labor, *Exemptions from Child Labor Rules in Non-Agriculture*, Elaws—FLSA—Child Labor Rules, *available at* http://www.dol.gov/elaws/esa/flsa/cl/exemptions.asp.

45. U.S. Department of Labor, *Under 16 Child Labor Rules*, Elaws— FLSA—Child Labor Rules, *available at* http://www.dol.gov/elaws/esa/flsa/cl/y16.asp.

46. *id.*

47. *id.*

48. *id.*

49. Title VII of the Civil Rights Act of 1963 (as amended), Pub. L. 88-352, *codified at* 42 U.S.C. § 2000(e) et seq.

50. *id.*

51. U.S. Department of Education Office of Civil Rights, *Know Your Rights* (last accessed August 21, 2005), *available at* http://www.ed.gov/about/offices/list/ocr/know.html.

52. Western Kentucky University, *Ranking Guidelines* (on file with author).

53. Elizabeth R. Ison, *Drug Testing Can Be Critically Important for Employers*, HR California, California Chamber of Commerce (July 2005), *available at* http://www.hrcalifornia.com/cid.cfm?web=346&cid=llu_topstory.

54. *id.*

55. Sue M. Bendavid-Arbiv, *Employment Law: Employers Must Enforce Drug-Testing Policies in a Way That Minimizes Exposure To Tort Claims*, Findlaw.com (reprinted from the Los Angeles Daily Journal, April 2001), *available at* http://library.findlaw.com/2001/Dec/19/130860.html.

56. *id.*

57. *id.*

58. *id.*

59. *id.*

60. *See*, Sandy Smith, *What Every Employer Should Know about Drug Testing in the Workplace*, Occupational Hazards (August 25, 2004), *available at* http://www.occupationalhazards.com/safety_zones/53/article.php?id=12257.

61. Bendavid-Arbiv. *See also*, Smith.

62. The U.S. Equal Employment Opportunity Commission, *Discrimina-*

tory Practices (September 2, 2004), *available at*
http://www.eeoc.gov/abouteeo/overview_practices.html.

63. 42 U.S.C. § 2000e et seq.

64. 42 U.S.C. § 2000e(k).

65. 42 U.S.C. § 12101 et seq.

66. 29 U.S.C. § 621 et seq.

67. *See,* Kelly M. Moore, Case Comment: *Pretext Instructions in Employment Discrimination Cases: Inferring a New Disadvantage for Plaintiffs: Conroy v. Abraham Chevrolet-Tampa, Inc.,* 375 F.3d 1228 (11th Cir. 2004), 57 Florida Law Review 411 (April 2005).

68. *Discriminatory Practices.*

69. Title VII of the Civil Rights Act of 1963 (as amended), Pub. L. 88-352, *codified at* 42 U.S.C. § 2000(e) and following sections.

70. Oshkosh Public Library, *Sexual Harassment Policy* (February 26, 1998), *available at*
http://www.oshkoshpubliclibrary.org/Library_Board/Contracts_Policies/Sexual_Harassment_Policy.html.

71. 29 C.F.R. § 1604.11(a) (2001).

72. Henry L. Chambers, Jr., *(Un)Welcome Conduct and the Sexually Hostile Environment,* 53 Alabama Law Review 733, 743 (Spring 2002).

73. Harris v. Forklift Systems, Inc., 510 U.S. 17 (1993).

74. Chambers *at* 742-743.

75. Harris.

76. Christy M. Hanley, Comment and Casenote, *A "Constructive" Compromise: Using the Quid Pro Quo and Hostile Work Environment Classifications to Adjudicate Constructive Discharge Sexual Harassment Cases,* 73 University of Cincinnati Law Review 259, 260 (Fall 2004), *quoting* Pennsylvania State Police v. Suders, 124 S. Ct. 2342, 2351 (2004).

77. *See* Burns v. McGregor, 955 F.2d 559, 564 (8th Cir. 1992).

78. Kevin Diaz, *Odd alliances, new foes in Minneapolis porn case: The fight of 12 library workers to rid the library of sexually graphic Web sites is at the forefront of a nationwide debate* [Minneapolis] Star Tribune (June 5, 2001).

79. *Library Employees Break the Silence on Sexual Harassment,* Posting of David Burt, to publib@webjunction.org (February 12, 2000), *available at* http://lists.webjunction.org/wjlists/publib/2000-February/047474.html.

80. 114 Stat. 2763A-335, *codified at* 20 U.S.C. §§ 9134(f)(1)(A)(i) and (B)(i) and at 47 U.S.C. §§ 254(h)(6)(B)(i) and (C)(i).

81. Toni Bowers and Brian Hook, *Hostile Work Environment: A Manager's Legal Liability,* Builder.com (October 22, 2002), *available at* http://builder.com.com/5100-6404-5035282.html.

82. U.S. Equal Employment Opportunity Commission, *Federal Laws Prohibiting Job Discrimination: Questions and Answers* (last modified May 24, 2002), *available at* http://www.eeoc.gov/facts/qanda.htm.

83. *Discriminatory Practices.*

84. *Understanding the Americans with Disabilities Act,* Allbusiness.com,

available at http://www.allbusiness.com/articles/EmploymentHR/1316-33-1774.html.

85. *id.*

86. *id.*

87. *See,* Ison; Bendavid-Arbiv.

88. *Understanding the Americans with Disabilities Act.*

89. *id.*

90. *Discriminatory Practices.*

91. *id.*

92. Section 508 of the Rehabilitation Act of 1973 (as amended), *codified at* 29 U.S.C. § 794(d).

93. *Employer Must Engage in Interactive Approach to Avoid ADA Liability,* 13-3/4 Library Personnel News 3 (Fall/Winter 2000).

94. 29 U.S.C. § 2611 et seq.

95. 29 C.F.R. § 825.104.

96. U.S. Department of Labor Wage and Hour Division, *Compliance Assistance: Family and Medical Leave Act (FMLA)*, Elaws, *available at* http://www.dol.gov/esa/whd/fmla/.

Chapter 12

1. Lester M. Salamon, *America's Nonprofit Sector: A Primer* (abridged online 2d ed., Foundation Center 1999), *available at* http://fdncenter.org/learn/bookshelf/salamon/summary.html.

2. 26 U.S.C. § 501(c)(3).

3. Black's Law Dictionary 591 (5th ed. 1979).

4. Foundation Center, *What Is the Difference Between a Private Foundation and a Public Charity?* (2005), *available at* http://fdncenter.org/learn/faqs/html/pfandpc.html.

5. *id.*

6. Minnesota Council of Nonprofits, *How to Start a Nonprofit: Basics* (last accessed July 27, 2005), *available at* http://www.mncn.org/info/basic_start.htm.

7. You may also wish to see the Website for the International Center for Not-for-Profit Law, *available at* http://www.icnl.org.

8. *See,* Chris McDonald, *Creating a Code of Ethics for Your Organization* (last accessed August 27, 2005), *available at* http://www.ethicsweb.ca/codes/. *See also,* Nonprofit Financial Center, *What Goes in a Conflict-of-Interest Policy?* (revised July 2, 2005), *available at* http://www.nonprofits.org/npofaq/16/59.html.

9. Carter McNamara, *Guidelines to Form an Advisory Group*, MAP for Nonprofits (1999), *available at* http://www.mapnp.org/library/boards/advisory.htm.

10. Craig White and Paul Castelloe, *Ten Steps in Forming a 501(c)(3)*

Nonprofit Organization, Center for Participatory Change (2000), *available at* http://www.cpcwnc.org/Toolbox/form501c3.html.

11. Salamon.

12. The New York Public Library (Astor, Lenox, and Tilden Foundations), *Mission Statement* (as revised October 15, 2001), *available at* http://www.nypl.org/pr/mission.cfm.

13. For more information, *see* the IRS Website *at* http://www.irs.gov/businesses/small/article/0,,id=98350,00.html.

14. Greater Cincinnati Library Association, *Articles of Incorporation* (as revised September 11, 1998), *available at* http://www.gclc-lib.org/members/articles.html.

15. *See*, Hurwit & Associates, *Nonprofit Law Resource Library* (2004), *available at* http://www.hurwitassociates.com/l_qa_nonprofitgovernance_bylaws.html.

16. California Secretary of State's Office, *Sample Articles of Incorporation* (March 2005), *available at* http://www.ss.ca.gov/business/corp/pdf/articles/corp_artsnp.pdf.

17. Avalon (PA) Public Library, *Bylaws* (May 16, 2003), *available at* http://www.einetwork.net/ein/avalon/Bylaws.html.

18. Minnesota Council of Nonprofits.

19. Greater Cincinnati Library Association, *Bylaws* (as revised September 11, 1998), *available at* http://www.gclc.org/members/bylaws.html.

20. Attorney General of Minnesota, *Fiduciary Duties of Directors of Charitable Organizations* (last accessed August 27, 2005), *available at* http://www.ag.state.mn.us/charities/charDuties.html.

21. *id.*

22. Thompson & Thompson, P.C., *The Key to Nonprofit Organization Governance* (last accessed August 27, 2005), *available at* http://www.t-tlaw.com/np-02a.htm.

23. *id.*

24. Cater McNamara, *Free Complete Toolkit for Boards*, MAP for Non-profits (1999), *available at* http://www.mapnp.org/library/boards/boards.htm.

25. *id.*

26. BoardSource.org, *Board Essentials* (2002), *available at* http://www.boardsource.org/FullAnswer.asp?ID=97.

27. *Board Essentials.*

28. *Free Complete Toolkit for Boards.*

29. Thompson & Thompson.

30. BoardSource.org, *Nonprofit Essentials* (2002), *available at* http://www.boardsource.org/FullAnswer.asp?ID=89.

31. Thompson & Thompson.

32. Nonprofits.org, *The Nonprofit FAQ* (January 30, 2005), *available at* http://www.nonprofits.org/npofaq/03/16.html.

33. *id.*

34. *id.*

35. *id.*

36. *id.*

37. Sarbanes-Oxley Act of 2002, PL 107-204, 116 Stat. 745.

38. Richard Larkin, *Sarbanes-Oxley and Nonprofits*, 3 BDO Seidman Nonprofit Alert (April 2003), *available at* http://www.bdo.com/about/publications/industry/np_apr_03/article1.asp. For a checklist of actions to take under the Sarbanes-Oxley Act, *see*, Independent Sector, *Sarbanes-Oxley and Implications for Nonprofits* (2004), *available at* http://www.independentsector.org/issues/accountability/checklist.html.

39. Jennifer Reingold, *The Women of Enron: The Best Revenge*, 74 Fast Company 77 (September 2003), *available at* http://www.fastcompany.com/magazine/74/enron_watkins.html.

40. When asked during a press conference whether he trusted Mikhail Gorbachev, President Reagan responded: "Huh? Do I trust him? Well, he's a personable gentleman, but I cited to him a Russian proverb—I'm not a linguist, but I at least learned that much Russian—and I said to him, 'Doveryai, no proveryai.' It means, 'Trust, but verify.'" Press Conference of President Ronald Reagan (June 12, 1987), *printed in* Associated Press, *The President in Venice: Economics, Contra Aid and the Gulf*, New York Times (June 12, 1987) *at* A12.

41. Larkin.

42. 26 U.S.C. § 509.

43. IRS form 1023, *Application for Recognition of Exemption Under Section 501(c)(3) of the Internal Revenue Code* (as revised October 2004), *available at* http://www.irs.gov/pub/irs-pdf/f1023.pdf. Instructions for this form are *available at* http://www.irs.gov/pub/irs-pdf/i1023.pdf.

44. The IRS usually computes this date from when the envelope containing form 1023 was postmarked. *See*, Internal Revenue Service, Instructions for Form 1023 (as revised October 2004), *available at* http://www.irs.gov/pub/irs-pdf/i1023.pdf.

45. The guidelines for tax-exempt status are found at 26 U.S.C. § 501(c)(3).

46. 26 U.S.C. § 501(c)(3).

47. American Library Association, *Library Bill of Rights* (as amended January 23, 1980), *available at* http://www.ala.org/ala/oif/statementspols/statementsif/librarybillrights.htm. The provisions on meeting rooms are found in section VI.

48. Rhonda G. Migdail, *Lobbying and Political Activities—What Every Nonprofit Should Know*, 33-3 Nonprofit World 21 (May-June 1985).

49. 26 U.S.C. § 4911(c)(2).

50. 26 U.S.C. § 4911(d)(1).

51. 26 U.S.C. § 4911(d)(2)(A).

52. 26 U.S.C. § 4911(d)(2)(B).

53. *See*, Judith E. Kindell and John Francis Reilly, *Lobbying Issues* 271 (1997), *available at* http://www.irs.gov/pub/irs-tege/eotopicp97.pdf.

54. 26 U.S.C. § 4911 (d)(2) (C).

55. *id.*

56. David J. Guy, *Library Advocacy: Legal Limits on Lobbying*, Friends & Foundations of California Libraries (last accessed August 27, 2005), *available at* http://www.friendcalib.org/newsstand/f2guy1.htm.

57. *See*, Kindell and Reilly *at* 267.

58. Bryan M. Carson and Robin McGinnis, *Legally Speaking—The Other "L" Word: A Primer for Creating Library Lobbying and Marketing Campaigns While Staying Within the Law*, 16-2 Against the Grain 60 (April 2004).

59. Form 5768 is *available at* http://www.irs.gov/pub/irs-pdf/f5768.pdf.

60. 26 U.S.C. § 504(h) and 26 U.S.C. § 4911.

61. *See*, Kindell and Reilly *at* 289.

62. 26 U.S.C. § 4911(f)(2).

63. For an excellent discussion of Enron's separate business entities and the doctrine of piercing the corporate veil, *see*, Robert B. Thompson, *Corporate Governance After Enron: The First Year*, 40 Houston Law Review 99 (Spring 2003).

Index

© (copyright symbol), 44
® (registration mark), 125
§ (section symbol), 14
2 Live Crew case, 92
2600 Magazine, 148
501(c)(3) status. *See* tax-exempt status

A Uniform System of Citation, 10
AALL (American Association of
  Law Libraries), 164
AAP (Association of American
  Publishers), 110–111, 235
ABA (American Bar Association),
  168
abbreviations in legal citations,
  10–18
Abrons Foundation, 300
abstract ideas, 96–97
academic work, copyrights, 65–67
acceptance of contracts, 23–25
accounting practices, nonprofit
  organizations, 312–314
accredited institutions, definition of,
  116
accuracy of materials and ethics, 187
actual damages for copyright
  infringement, 52–53
ADA (Americans with Disabilities
  Act), 287, 292–295
administrative orders under
  PATRIOT Act, 226, 227
advisory groups, 302–303
affiliated organizations, 318–319
Age Discrimination in Employment
  Act, 287

agency relationship, employment and
  workplace law, 261–265
ALA. *See* American Library
  Association
ALI (American Law Institute),
  164–165
ALR (American Law Reports), 12
American Association of Law
  Libraries, 164
American Bar Association (ABA),
  168
American Intellectual Property Law
  Association, 132
American Law Institute (ALI),
  164–165
American Law Reports (ALR), 12
American Library Association
  (ALA):
    code of ethics, 186–188, 197,
      209, 234–236
    electronic libraries, 172
    fair use, 54–55, 90, 111–112;
      electronic reserves, 111–112;
      parodies, 90; video cassette
      recordings, 54–55
    hostile work environment, 291
    information malpractice, 197
    Internet use policies, 247–248,
      255–256
    PATRIOT Act, interpretation,
      230, 231
American Psychological Association
  (APA), legal citations, 10
Americans with Disabilities Act
  (ADA), 287, 292–295

trade secrets, 155, 156
privacy of patron information and
library records, 7–8, 155–156,
201–246
Attorney General opinions in
Kentucky and Hawaii, 219–221
computer monitoring, 223–225
disclosure that search has been
performed, 227–231
due process, 207–209
ethics, 233–241
evidence code of Georgia and
New York, 214–217
FBI Library Awareness
Program, 202–203
law enforcement visits, 230–231
national security letters, 222,
226–227, 232–233
nondisclosure, 227–230
particularity, 205–207
pen register, 223–224
privileged communications,
215–217
probable cause, 204–205
search and seizure. *See* search
warrants
state privacy laws, 209–221,
242–246
Attorney General opinions,
217–221; for children, 213;
information not protected,
212–214; information
protected, 211–212;
libraries covered,
210; privileged
communications, 215–217;
table of states with details
regarding their privacy
laws, 242–246
subpoenas, 204
suicidal patrons, 236–237
types of information covered,
211–214
types of libraries covered, 210
violence, threats of, 238–240
wiretaps, 223, 224–225, 232

See also Foreign Intelligence
Surveillance Act; PATRIOT
Act
private foundations. *See* nonprofit
organizations
privileged communications, 215–217
under evidence code of Georgia
and New York, 214–217
See also confidentiality
pro se library users, 179–180, 182
probable cause, search warrants, 204,
205
professional employees, 189–194,
277
promise, 27, 35–36
promisees and promisors, 26, 36
promissory estoppel, 34–36
"protect it or lose it," trademarks,
129
provisional patent applications,
73–74
public charities, 300–301
public domain, works entering, 72
public policy, agreements against,
41–42
punitive damages for breach of
contract, 32

qualifications for employment, 280
quantum meruit, 39–40
quantum valebant, 39–40
quasi-contracts, 39–40
quid pro quo harassment, 289

Railway Labor Act, 275
Raitt, Ronald, 138, 157
Randall, Alice, 92–93
rational basis test, 228
Reagan, President Ronald, 313
reasonable accommodations,
292–294
reasonable effort to maintain trade
secrets, 152–153
records. *See* library records
Redmond case, 153–154

About the Author

Bryan M. Carson is an associate professor and Coordinator of Reference & Instructional Services at Western Kentucky University Libraries. He received his B.A. degree in economics from Adrian College, J.D. degree from the University of Toledo, and M.I.L.S. degree from the University of Michigan. He is currently working on a doctorate in higher education leadership and policy at Vanderbilt University's Peabody College for Teachers.

Bryan is a member of the Kentucky and Ohio bars. He has written extensively about intellectual property, access to information, and legal issues relating to libraries, and has spoken at numerous state and regional conferences. He writes a popular column, "Legally Speaking," for the journal *Against the Grain*. Bryan has also taught classes for the Library Media Education (school media) master's degree program at Western Kentucky University.

Bryan is a member of the Kentucky Bar Association, the Louisville Bar Association, the Warren County Bar Association, the American Library Association, the Reference & User Services Association (co-chair, Access to Information Committee), the Library Administration & Management Association (former chair, Public Relations & Marketing Section Governmental Advocacy Skills Committee; member, Education & Training Committee), the Kentucky Library Association (former chair, Library Instruction Roundtable), the Kentucky SOLINET Users Group (former chair), and the American Intellectual Property Association.